Preaching and Narrative in *Piers Plowman*

Preaching and Narrative in *Piers Plowman*

ALASTAIR BENNETT

OXFORD
UNIVERSITY PRESS

Great Clarendon Street, Oxford, OX2 6DP,
United Kingdom

Oxford University Press is a department of the University of Oxford.
It furthers the University's objective of excellence in research, scholarship,
and education by publishing worldwide. Oxford is a registered trade mark of
Oxford University Press in the UK and in certain other countries

© Alastair Bennett 2023

The moral rights of the author have been asserted

All rights reserved. No part of this publication may be reproduced, stored in
a retrieval system, or transmitted, in any form or by any means, without the
prior permission in writing of Oxford University Press, or as expressly permitted
by law, by licence or under terms agreed with the appropriate reprographics
rights organization. Enquiries concerning reproduction outside the scope of the
above should be sent to the Rights Department, Oxford University Press, at the
address above

You must not circulate this work in any other form
and you must impose this same condition on any acquirer

Published in the United States of America by Oxford University Press
198 Madison Avenue, New York, NY 10016, United States of America

British Library Cataloguing in Publication Data
Data available

Library of Congress Control Number: 2023935841

ISBN 978–0–19–288626–2

DOI: 10.1093/oso/9780192886262.001.0001

Printed and bound in the UK by
Clays Ltd, Elcograf S.p.A.

Links to third party websites are provided by Oxford in good faith and
for information only. Oxford disclaims any responsibility for the materials
contained in any third party website referenced in this work.

OXFORD STUDIES IN MEDIEVAL
LITERATURE AND CULTURE

General Editors
Ardis Butterfield and Christopher Cannon

The monograph series Oxford Studies in Medieval Literature and Culture showcases the plurilingual and multicultural quality of medieval literature and actively seeks to promote research that not only focuses on the array of subjects medievalists now pursue – in literature, theology, and philosophy, in social, political, jurisprudential, and intellectual history, the history of art, and the history of science – but also that combines these subjects productively. It offers innovative studies on topics that may include, but are not limited to, manuscript and book history; languages and literatures of the global Middle Ages; race and the post-colonial; the digital humanities, media and performance; music; medicine; the history of affect and the emotions; the literature and practices of devotion; the theory and history of gender and sexuality, ecocriticism, and the environment; theories of aesthetics; medievalism.

To my parents

Acknowledgements

The idea for this book emerged from the doctoral thesis I prepared at the University of Cambridge. I am very grateful to Nicolette Zeeman, who supervised that project, and to Wendy Scase and Barry Windeatt who examined it and suggested how I might develop it for future publication. Some years later, Nicky read a full draft of this book and sent me an invaluable response that helped me see what its final form should look like. Three anonymous readers for Oxford University Press offered detailed and perceptive reports on the typescript that challenged me to refine and extend the argument. Katharine Breen and Ruth Livesey read individual chapters while I was at work on them and made excellent suggestions for how to improve them, and Ardis Butterfield read the whole text in its nearly-final form, and offered valuable guidance on the very last revisions.

For conversation and correspondence about this project, about *Piers Plowman*, and about medieval sermons, I am grateful to Cristina Cervone, Rita Copeland, Rebecca Davis, Curtis Gruenler, Michael Johnston, Veronica O'Mara, Mary Raschko, Ellen Rentz, Arvind Thomas, Lawrence Warner, Sarah Wood, and Siegfried Wenzel, among many others. My thanks to Veronica for loaning me her microfilm of Trinity College, Dublin, MS 241, and to Priscilla Barnum, who shared her unpublished transcript of the Longleat sermons with me. Thank you to Isabel Davis, who invited me to speak about this project at the Birkbeck Medieval Seminar and Nicholas Perkins, who invited me to speak about it at the Oxford University English Faculty Medieval Studies Seminar. The audiences at these events, and at the many conferences where I have presented papers on the research for this book, offered questions and insights that helped me to shape the arguments presented here. Since 2017, it has been a privilege to edit the *Yearbook of Langland Studies* with Katy Breen and Eric Weiskott; I have learned a lot about *Piers Plowman* from them and from reading the excellent work of our contributors. While I was finishing this book, I took part in the online *Piers Plowman* reading group organized by Emily Steiner, which was a great opportunity to discuss the poem with new and experienced readers at a time when we were otherwise isolated from each other by Covid; my thanks to Emily, to the group leaders, and to the other participants. Thank you to my excellent colleagues at Royal Holloway, Catherine Nall and Jennifer Neville, and to colleagues at the other London colleges, all of whom make London a good place to be a medievalist. I continue to learn from the insights of my undergraduate and graduate students at Royal Holloway as they come to medieval literature with fresh eyes and new questions.

I am very grateful to my family and friends for their love and support and good company while I have been at work on this project. Most of all, I am grateful to my wife, Emily Weal, for her patience, encouragement, and love; she made it possible for me to write this book, and also helped me keep it in perspective (most of the time). Our little boy Charlie was born not long after I submitted the final manuscript for this book, and has filled the last few months with his own infectious delight in the world around him. This book is dedicated to my parents, Nigel and Morag Bennett, with love and heartfelt thanks.

Contents

List of Figures   xiii
List of Abbreviations   xv

    Introduction: Preaching and Narrative in *Piers Plowman*   1

1. Preaching on the Coronation: The Prologue and the Sermon of Conscience   34

2. Preaching on the Half-Acre: Fear, Hope, and Narrative in the Second Vision   74

3. Preachers and Minstrels: Study's Complaint and the Feast of Conscience   111

4. Preaching on the Lifetime: Sermons and the 'Self-Constant' Subject in *Piers Plowman*   150

5. Histories of the Self, the World, and the Sermon: Anima and the Tree of Charity   189

    Coda: Atonement and Emplotment at the Harrowing of Hell   222

Works Cited   233
Index   255

List of Figures

1.1	The final page of Henry Harclay's sermon for the feast of Thomas Becket, London, Lambeth Palace, MS 61, fol. 147v. Image courtesy of Lambeth Palace Library.	54
1.1a	Detail showing annotations by Thomas Gascoigne, the poem 'Laus tua, non tua fraus' and the verses '*Sum Rex, sum Princeps*', London, Lambeth Palace, MS 61, fol. 147v. Image courtesy of Lambeth Palace Library.	60
2.1	Archbishop Arundel preaching from a pulpit with a cross bearer standing to his left, from Jean Creton's *Histoire rimée de Richard II* (*La Prinse et mort du roy Richart*). London, British Library, Harley MS 1319, fol. 12r. Courtesy of the British Library.	94
3.1	St Paul preaching, from the Breviary of John the Fearless and Margaret of Bavaria, London, British Library, Additional MS 35311, fol. 238v. Courtesy of the British Library.	122
4.1	Baptism of an infant in a font, from a fifteenth-century English pontifical, London, British Library, Lansdowne MS 451, fol. 224v. Courtesy of the British Library.	154
5.1	A passage from *Piers Plowman* C.16 with the marginal annotation that identifies a 'distinctio caritatis'. London, Senate House Library, MS SL V 17, fol. 69r. © Senate House Library.	190
5.2	The formal division of the *thema*, marked as 'radix sermonis', from a sermon in Oxford, Bodleian Library, MS Bodley 649, fol. 2v. Image courtesy of The Bodleian Libraries, University of Oxford.	196

List of Abbreviations

CCCM	Corpus Christianorum, Continuatio Mediaevalis
CCSL	Corpus Christianorum, Series Latina
CSEL	Corpus Scriptorum Ecclesiasticorum Latinorum
DMLBS	*Dictionary of Medieval Latin from British Sources*
EETS, os	Early English Text Society, original series
EETS, ss	Early English Text Society, supplementary series
LCL	Loeb Classical Library
MED	*Middle English Dictionary*
ODNB	*Oxford Dictionary of National Biography*
OED	*Oxford English Dictionary*
PL	*Patrologiae cursus completus, series latina*
WSA	Works of Saint Augustine, a Translation for the 21st Century
YLS	*Yearbook of Langland Studies*

Introduction

Preaching and Narrative in *Piers Plowman*

William Langland's *Piers Plowman* was written, revised, copied, and read during what Siegfried Wenzel has called a 'golden age' of preaching in late medieval England.[1] The poem describes a world where preaching was a vital part of public, intellectual, and parochial life, and it develops a sophisticated account of the way that sermons engaged and instructed their listeners, illuminating their lived experience and directing their spiritual efforts. Over the course of his allegorical visions, the poem's dreamer-narrator Will encounters representatives of the many different groups who were authorized and obligated to preach in late medieval England: bishops and parish priests, the friars and the secular clergy, as well as individuals whose authority to preach was dubious and contested—charismatic 'lollers' and a corrupt pardoner. The personifications who appear in his dreams often preach to him, too, or offer him sermon-like discourses of instruction and exhortation. While some of these speeches are briefly summarized, others occupy hundreds of lines of verse, with the result that large parts of *Piers Plowman* seem to speak in a preacher's voice. Langland's poem considers the effects that sermons create, both in the immediate moment of their performance and later, as they provide a framework for their listeners to understand their experiences. The most compelling sermons in *Piers Plowman* disclose new ethical imperatives in the complex circumstances of contemporary life and motivate new forms of social and spiritual action that unfold over many of the passūs, or 'steps', that comprise the poem. Langland's examples of corrupt, self-interested preaching, meanwhile, create damaging forms of confusion and spiritual inertia, with long-lasting consequences for the people who hear them.

Langland's central insight into preaching, as I will argue in this book, is that sermons achieved these transformative effects through their characteristic use of narrative. Langland's preachers speak to audiences who are absorbed in the preoccupations of their present moment, experiencing life as a simple succession of uninterpreted events, and provoke them to new action by locating that present

---

[1] Siegfried Wenzel, *Latin Sermon Collections from Later Medieval England: Orthodox Preaching in the Age of Wyclif* (Cambridge: University of Cambridge Press, 2005), xv, referring to the period *c.*1350–*c.*1450. This, as Wenzel notes, is also the period covered by G. R. Owst in *Preaching in Medieval England: An Introduction to Sermon Manuscripts of the Period, c.1350–1450* (Cambridge: Cambridge University Press, 1926).

moment in a larger, interpreted story. A preacher's account of contemporary history reveals the urgent need for social reform; the story of an individual life explains the need for penance and good works; the grand narrative of Christian eschatology explains the origins of sin and the possibilities for atonement. Narratives like these are both galvanizing and enabling for sermon audiences. In some cases, they produce an effect that seems close to *metanoia*, a profound transformation in the listener's way of life. More commonly, however, they clarify the choices that listeners face and serve to refocus their spiritual efforts in the midst of their ordinary experience. As Holy Church explains to Will in the first passus of the poem, sermon narratives encourage people to 'do þe bettre' (B.1.34), a phrase that is echoed by Reason in his sermon to the king and the *commune* in passus 5 (B.5.17), and reformulated by the end of the second vision as the injunction to 'Do wel and haue wel' (B.7.112).[2] Langland, I argue, is interested in the creative, interpretative activity that takes place when preachers reconfigure lived experience in this way, in the discursive resources these acts of narrative interpretation provide for listeners to understand themselves and their social and spiritual relationships in the present time, and in the models they provide for other forms of writing, including his own.

In this book, I employ a critical vocabulary derived from the work of Paul Ricoeur to describe the process by which narratives are made and the way that narrative mediates lived experience. For Ricoeur, the composition of narratives involves the configuration of real or imaginary events into a tensive, provisional unity, organized not by the logic of simple temporal succession, but according to some other pattern of significance that the narrator discerns and seeks to express. This act of configuration, which Ricoeur, translating Aristotle's *muthos*, describes as 'emplotment', is an active, ongoing process that shapes and transforms the way that readers and listeners understand their subjective experiences. It also has wide-ranging implications for ethical, social life: through the discursive mediation of narrative, Ricoeur contends, it becomes possible to think about action in the present moment in relation to an interpreted past and a projected future. I will argue that Ricoeur's account of narrative can illuminate Langland's conception of preaching as a discourse that seeks not only to interpret but also to reshape direct experience. Langland's preachers are engaged in the ongoing labour of emplotment, configuring meaningful narratives from the disparate events of their

---

[2] William Langland, *Piers Plowman: A Parallel-Text Edition of the A, B, C, and Z Versions*, ed. A. V. C. Schmidt, 2nd edn, 2 vols (Kalamazoo, MI: Medieval Institute Publications, 2011). All quotations from the poem are from this edition, and citations are given by version, passus, and line number. Unless otherwise noted, translations of the Latin lines in the poem are from *The Vision of Piers Plowman: A Critical Edition of the B-Text Based on Trinity College Cambridge MS B.15.17*, ed. Schmidt, 2nd edn (London: J. M. Dent, 1995), *Piers Plowman: The A Version*, ed. Míċeál F. Vaughan (Baltimore: Johns Hopkins University Press, 2011), and *Piers Plowman: A New Annotated Edition of the C Text*, ed. Derek Pearsall (Exeter: Exeter University Press, 2008); glosses on the Middle English are also adapted from these editions.

listeners' experiences, disclosing new structures to understand the present time, and establishing the imperatives and opportunities for social and spiritual endeavour. For Langland, as for Ricoeur, the articulation of narrative constitutes an intervention in social life, one that gives rise to new forms of understanding and action.

Langland's presentation of preaching, with its particular focus on the role of narrative, reflects a nuanced, critical understanding, perhaps a practitioner's understanding, of the way that real medieval sermons engaged their audiences. As Wenzel observes in an overview of late medieval preaching *ad populum*, sermons commonly 'set their message in a narrative frame of *Heilsgeschichte*, the history of salvation', a story that began with the creation of the world and the fall of Adam and Eve, turned on the incarnation and crucifixion of Christ, and concluded with the last judgement.[3] The story of salvation encompassed all the other stories a preacher might tell, whether biblical, hagiographical, or historical, and conferred an ultimate significance on them. It also explained the choices facing Christians in the present time, as Christ's atonement on the cross established a New Covenant with human beings, holding out the possibility of salvation as an incentive to turn from sin and do good works. Alan Fletcher writes that popular preaching sought to establish its listeners in an interpreted present, to 'settle...audiences in a position from which they could recognize...how the landscape of their lives was in fact a morally charged landscape, one in which the routes that they took would finally lead to different eternal consequences'.[4] The story of salvation history is 'ever present' in the surviving corpus of sermon texts, as Wenzel argues, and it finds expression in many different aspects of their persuasive, exhortatory rhetoric and their exegetical form.[5] In the chapters that follow, I will read *Piers Plowman* alongside surviving sermon texts, and accounts of preaching in performance, that reveal the dynamic, creative forms this narrative could take, and that describe its effects on contemporary audiences.

The narrative that Wenzel describes is distinct from the short, embedded stories that occupied their own discrete space in some medieval sermons, biblical parables and non-scriptural *exempla*, although it often provided a context to understand them.[6] Both parables and *exempla* can be understood as narrative genres in their own right, and both were adapted and reimagined in other contexts besides the sermon. Biblical parables were recast in a range of devotional and

---

[3] Wenzel, *Latin Sermon Collections*, 245.
[4] Alan J. Fletcher, *Late Medieval Popular Preaching in Britain and Ireland: Texts, Studies, and Interpretations* (Turnhout: Brepols, 2009), 307.
[5] Wenzel, *Latin Sermon Collections*, 245.
[6] *Exempla* were widely anthologized as resources for preachers, and their inclusion in sermons was theorized in the *artes praedicandi* and debated by practitioners. See H. Leith Spencer, *English Preaching in the Late Middle Ages* (Oxford: Clarendon, 1993), 78–82.

literary texts, as Mary Raschko has shown.[7] Illustrative *exempla* were a mainstay of the secular 'mirrors for princes' tradition, a tradition that overlapped with preaching and pastoralia in complex ways, as Rita Copeland has recently demonstrated.[8] Scholarship on parables and *exempla* has emphasized their dynamic, experimental qualities, the opportunities they provided for different communities of readers to think through ethical questions.[9] Langland himself was engaged with these qualities, rethinking biblical parables as part of the allegorical action of his poem, and invoking *exempla* in its pastoral dialogues and debates.[10] In his preaching scenes, however, Langland attends to the narrative logic of the sermon as a whole, rather than to narrative as one of its constituent parts. The work of emplotment that sermons perform, and that constitutes their discursive intervention in the social world, arises from their particular combination of argument, exegesis, and exhortation, as opposed to the citation of other narrative sources.

Piers Plowman draws on multiple traditions of medieval personification allegory, where ideas of personhood, embodiment, and volition could be configured or distributed in a wide range of abstract and seemingly counterintuitive ways.[11] Yet, the poem's personifications are also embroiled in the material realities of its contemporary social world, and the allegorical action brings them into frequent contact with 'realistic representatives of everyday fourteenth-century society', as Jill Mann observes.[12] Preaching scenes in the poem often take place at the meeting point between these different representational modes: sermons are voiced by personifications, but heard by representatives of the late medieval *commune* in various recognizable social contexts. Nicolette Zeeman has recently shown that Langland's personification allegory draws on the longstanding use of prosopopoeia in the literature of educational instruction and philosophical inquiry; in its pastoral dialogues, in particular, *Piers Plowman* is engaged with a rich tradition of writing and

---

[7] Mary Raschko, *The Politics of Middle English Parables: Fiction, Theology, and Social Practice* (Manchester: Manchester University Press, 2019).

[8] Rita Copeland, 'The Porous Genres of Persuasion: A London Preacher and a Royal Advisor in the Fifteenth Century', 210–23 in *'Of latine and of othire lare': Essays in Honour of David R. Carlson*, ed. Richard Firth Green and R. F. Yeager (Toronto: Pontifical Institute of Mediaeval Studies, 2022). On 'the sermon exemplum' in relation to 'the public exemplum' in medieval culture, see also Larry Scanlon, *Narrative, Authority, and Power: The Medieval Exemplum and the Chaucerian Tradition* (Cambridge: Cambridge University Press, 1994), 55–134.

[9] See, for example, Mark Miller, 'Displaced Souls, Idle Talk, Spectacular Scenes: *Handlyng Synne* and the Perspective of Agency', *Speculum* 71 (1996): 606–32; J. Allan Mitchell, *Ethics and Exemplary Narrative in Chaucer and Gower* (Cambridge: Brewer, 2004); and Elizabeth Allen, *False Fables and Exemplary Truth in Later Middle English Literature* (New York: Palgrave Macmillan, 2005).

[10] For a discussion of Langland's treatment of the parable of the Good Samaritan, see Raschko, *Middle English Parables*, 142–76.

[11] On *Piers Plowman* in relation to the larger tradition of personification allegory, see Jason Crawford, *Allegory and Enchantment: An Early Modern Poetics* (Oxford: Oxford University Press, 2017); Julie Orlemanski, 'Langland's Poetics of Animation: Body, Soul, Personification', *YLS* 33 (2019): 159–83; Katharine Breen, *Machines of the Mind: Personification in Medieval Literature* (Chicago: University of Chicago Press, 2021).

[12] Jill Mann, 'Allegory and *Piers Plowman*', 65–82 in *The Cambridge Companion to Piers Plowman*, ed. Andrew Cole and Andrew Galloway (Cambridge: Cambridge University Press, 2014), 65.

thinking about instructive speech and its effects on the student.[13] I will argue that the poem's preaching scenes take place in a related context: drawing on the *artes* and on his own experience of preaching practice, Langland dramatizes the strategies by which preachers engaged their audiences, and considers the psychological complexity of listeners' responses. Staging sermons as part of the allegorical narrative, *Piers Plowman* is also able to register the long-term effects of preaching on both individuals and communities: preaching initiates forms of individual and collective action that extend over several passūs, and on several occasions the dreamer recalls sermons he has previously heard as he looks to explain his present circumstances.

At its most effective, preaching in *Piers Plowman* presents its listeners with narratives that are coherent, unified, and integrated, configuring disparate elements into a cohesive, interpreted whole. These narratives stand in contrast to the fragmentary and discontinuous qualities that so often characterize the dreamer's experience, and which have been theorized extensively by readers of the poem. In her foundational study of the poem's 'episodic form', Anne Middleton described *Piers Plowman* as a series of 'argumentative encounter[s]', each of which follows the same 'basic pattern': an exchange between two or more characters becomes 'charged with opposition' to the point where it breaks off, producing 'a rupture or abrupt shift of ground'.[14] These combative but inconclusive episodes are so 'deeply characteristic' of Langland's compositional practice, Middleton argues, that they might be understood as his 'poetic signature'.[15] Other critics have explored the generative potential of the ruptures that Middleton identifies. D. Vance Smith argues that Langland reflects on the 'problem of beginning' as he resumes his poem after each new interruption, exploring the different models for beginning a text and the new kinds of initiative that a text might produce in the world.[16] Zeeman associates the poem's shifts and ruptures with a reiterative pattern of rebuke and denial, where knowledge and understanding are withheld from the dreamer and from readers of the text. For Zeeman, these moments of deprivation create intense, open-ended forms of desire, which the poem then sublimates towards spiritual ends.[17] Part of my argument in this book is that the sermons in the poem promise to recuperate these fragmentary, inconclusive experiences, by configuring them into a narrative: preaching offers the dreamer a set of resources to conceptualize his life, and his visions, as an interpreted whole.

[13] Nicolette Zeeman, *The Arts of Disruption: Allegory and Piers Plowman* (Oxford: Oxford University Press, 2020), 19–33.
[14] Anne Middleton, 'Narration and the Invention of Experience: Episodic Form in *Piers Plowman*', 91–122 in *The Wisdom of Poetry: Essays in Early English Literature in Honor of Morton W. Bloomfield*, ed. Larry D. Benson and Siegfried Wenzel (Kalamazoo, MI: Medieval Institute Publications, 1982), 92, 96–7.
[15] Middleton, 'Narration and the Invention of Experience', 119.
[16] D. Vance Smith, *The Book of the Incipit: Beginnings in the Fourteenth Century* (Minneapolis: University of Minnesota Press, 2001), 4. Smith positions his project in relation to Middleton's work on pp. 17–18. Smith considers the sermon *thema* as a model for beginning in *Piers Plowman* at 70–74, 82–112.
[17] Zeeman, *Piers Plowman and the Medieval Discourse of Desire* (Cambridge: Cambridge University Press, 2006), 1–19. Zeeman responds to Middleton at 12–13.

Langland's attention to the role of emplotment in contemporary preaching reflects the larger importance of narrative in his own poetic project. As Zeeman has argued, 'narrative figuration constitutes one of the central means by which Langland thinks' in *Piers Plowman*.[18]

Sermons stand at an intersection between two large categories of knowledge that are often distinguished and sometimes opposed in *Piers Plowman*: revealed knowledge, derived from the study of sacred texts, often named as 'clergie' in the poem, and knowledge that arises intuitively or experientially from life, described, from the first passus on, as 'kynde knowynge' (B.1.138).[19] When preachers perform the work of emplotment, they place these forms of knowledge in dialogue, interpreting 'kynde' experience using discursive resources drawn from 'clergie', and reaffirming 'clergie' using evidence drawn from 'kynde'. Langland often refers to the different ways in which a preacher might 'preue' his sermon: the alliterative collocation 'prechen' and 'preuen' recurs in many scenes where characters listen to sermons, or debate the effects of good and bad preaching.[20] In some contexts, 'preueing' a sermon involves the citation of confirmatory authorities, a procedure known as *confirmatio* in the *artes*.[21] In others, however, it describes the way that direct experience might challenge or affirm a preacher's discursive claims. Langland uses the collocation 'prechen' and 'preuen' to explain how a preacher's way of life might confirm or undermine the message of his preaching, fulfilling the longstanding imperative to teach by word and example, *docere verbo et exemplo*, or falling short of it.[22] As Anima declares in the fifth vision, 'to prechen

---

[18] Zeeman, *Discourse of Desire*, 25.

[19] There is an extensive bibliography on Langland's concept of 'kynde'. Important studies include Mary Clemente Davlin, ''Kynde Knowyng' as a Major Theme in *Piers Plowman* B', *Review of English Studies* 22 (1971): 1–19; Hugh White, *Nature and Salvation in Piers Plowman* (Cambridge: Brewer, 1988); Zeeman, 'The Condition of *Kynde*', 1–30 in *Medieval Literature and Historical Inquiry: Essays in Honor of Derek Pearsall*, ed. David Aers (Cambridge: Brewer, 2000); Zeeman, *Discourse of Desire*; and Rebecca Davis, *Piers Plowman and the Books of Nature* (Oxford: Oxford University Press, 2016). Many of these studies consider 'clergie' in opposition to 'kynde'. On 'clergie' in *Piers Plowman*, see also Fiona Somerset, *Clerical Discourse and Lay Audience in Late Medieval England* (Cambridge: Cambridge University Press, 1998), 22–61.

[20] Joseph Wittig, *Piers Plowman: Concordance* (London: Athlone, 2001), s.v.v. 'prechen' and 'preuen'.

[21] In earlier *artes*, *confirmatio* could describe any part of a sermon where a preacher evoked authorities or examples to support his case, but by the fourteenth century, *confirmatio* described a distinct stage in the sermon when, after dividing his *thema*, the preacher would cite authorities to corroborate each of the resulting parts. These authorities would ideally repeat the key word from each part of the division, establishing verbal correspondences (*concordancia*) that reinforce the logical connections. See Wenzel, *Medieval Artes Praedicandi: A Synthesis of Scholastic Sermon Structure* (Toronto: University of Toronto Press, 2015), 75–8. The concatenation of mutually reinforcing proof texts receives a satirical treatment in the final passus of *Piers Plowman*, when the friars 'preche men of Plato, and preue it by Seneca' (B.20.275).

[22] On the history of this imperative, see Caroline Walker Bynum, 'The Spirituality of Regular Canons in the Twelfth Century: A New Approach', *Medievalia et Humanistica*, new series 4 (1973): 3–24; *Docere Verbo et Exemplo: An Aspect of Twelfth-century Spirituality* (Missoula, MT: Scholars Press, 1979); and *Jesus as Mother: Studies in the Spirituality of the High Middle Ages* (Berkeley: University of California Press, 1982), 22–58.

and preuen it noȝt—ypocrisie [hypocrisy] it semeþ!' (B.15.110). Langland also uses this collocation to describe the way that natural examples might reaffirm a preacher's argument, as when Reason 'preue[s]' that recent storms and pestilences are punishments for sin (B.5.13). In contexts like this, I will argue, the language of 'preching' and 'preueing' draws attention to the way that sermons engage with lived experience, configuring real events into narratives, whose claims can be tested, challenged, or reaffirmed through direct observation.

The poem's critical engagement with preaching is an integral part of its commentary on contemporary social and spiritual life, its investigation into the available discourses of instruction and the institutions and individuals who articulate them. Yet the preaching scenes in *Piers Plowman* are also often a site of self-theorization, where Langland considers his literary debts to sermons, and imagines forms of poetry that might extend, subvert, and transcend the practice of contemporary preachers. When Ymaginatif confronts the dreamer about the time he spends composing poetry near the end of the third vision, he challenges him to distinguish his own work from the work that preachers already do: 'for þere are bokes ynowe [enough] / To telle men what Dowel is, and Dobet and Dobest boþe,/ and prechours to preue what it is, of many a peire freres [pair of friars]' (B.12.17–19). In his hesitant, qualified answer, Will suggests that other people's preaching is insufficient to locate the imperatives to do well, and establishes a rationale to continue the labour of emplotment in 'makynge' of his own (B.12.16). Here and elsewhere, I will argue, Langland acknowledges the affinities between preaching and *Piers Plowman*, while also insisting on the distinctiveness of his own poem.

The remainder of this Introduction is divided into three parts. In the first, I position my own project in relation to the existing scholarship on *Piers Plowman* and late medieval preaching, scholarship that has produced some enduring and influential models for reading the poem. Readers have found many analogues for Langland's images and ideas in the surviving corpus of sermon texts and in the compendia that preachers used to compose them, and have looked to the exegetical structures of preaching as an influence on the poem's amorphous and digressive form. Next, I consider the speech of Holy Church from passus 1 as an early and richly elaborated example of preaching in *Piers Plowman*, and one that demonstrates the central role of narrative in sermons as Langland understood it. Here, as I will show, Holy Church reinterprets the dreamer's vision of the contemporary world, where people experience time as a simple succession of events, and invites him to understand his present moment in time as part of a larger narrative. By locating the present time in salvation history, moreover, she discloses new imperatives to 'do wel' and to seek truth. Finally, I offer an introduction to Ricoeur's theory of narrative, which informs my discussion of *Piers Plowman* and medieval preaching through this book. Ricoeur's work, I will argue, serves to illuminate the transformative effects that narrative could produce, both for medieval preachers and for Langland.

Literature and Pulpit

The modern study of medieval English preaching and the study of Langland's relationship to sermon literature begin in the same place, with the pioneering work of G. R. Owst.[23] In an article first published in 1925, Owst identified the angel in the poem's Prologue as an allegorical representation of Thomas Brinton, bishop of Rochester, preaching at the convocation of clergy before the Good Parliament of 1376. With this prominent portrait of an outspoken preacher, he argued, Langland declared his admiration for the 'social message' of the English pulpit and his intention to echo it in his own poem.[24] Owst would return to this claim in two substantial volumes that laid the foundations for the modern study of medieval sermons: *Preaching in Medieval England* (1926), which provided an overview of the theory and practice of preaching from c.1350 to c.1450, and *Literature and Pulpit* (1933), which catalogued correspondences between preaching and poetry in this period.[25] In *Literature and Pulpit*, Owst argued that medieval English preachers had developed a distinctive form of 'realism' and a strident 'social gospel' that contemporary poets sought to emulate and reaffirm, and none so enthusiastically or comprehensively as Langland. *Literature and Pulpit* concludes with a revised version of Owst's 1925 article, where he uses Langland's portrait of Brinton to prove this point once more.

Owst's most famous and frequently quoted statement about *Piers Plowman* first appears as '[a] word...in passing' in *Preaching in Medieval England*, where he writes that Langland's poem 'represents nothing more nor less than the quintessence of English medieval preaching gathered up into a single metrical piece of unusual charm and vivacity'.[26] Derek Pearsall has called this Owst's 'most startling pronouncement', and writes that 'no medieval scholar...ever forgets or recovers from [its] impact'.[27] Andrew Cole has described it as 'an earworm munching through the collective pages of Langland criticism', analogous to Morton Bloomfield's famous claim that reading *Piers Plowman* 'is like reading

---

[23] For a recent assessment of Owst and his legacy, see Pearsall, 'G. R. Owst and the Politics of Sermon Studies', 11–30 in *Preaching the Word in Manuscript and Print in Late Medieval England: Essays in Honour of Susan Powell*, ed. Martha W. Driver and Veronica O'Mara (Turnhout: Brepols, 2013). For an overview of scholarship on preaching and *Piers Plowman* in the twentieth century, see Wenzel, 'Medieval Sermons', 155–72 in *A Companion to Piers Plowman*, ed. John A. Alford (Berkeley: University of California Press, 1988), 156–61.

[24] G. R. Owst, 'The "Angel" and the "Goliardeys" of Langland's Prologue', *Modern Language Review* 20 (1925): 270–9.

[25] Wenzel considers the remarkable achievement of these volumes, and their role in enabling the study of English sermons in the twentieth century, in *Latin Sermon Collections*, xi–xiii.

[26] Owst, *Preaching in Medieval England*, 295. Owst restates this earlier claim in the first edition of *Literature and Pulpit*, quoting himself at 549, but tempers it in the second edition, saying instead that 'we may surely claim that the medieval pulpit helped to fashion much of the poet's fundamental thinking'.

[27] Pearsall, 'G. R. Owst', 12.

a commentary on an unknown text'.[28] Owst's characterization of Langland's poem is unquestionably an overstatement, a distillation of his most hyperbolic claims about medieval poetry and its debts to sermons.[29] More recent criticism has tended to identify the sermon as one of the many genres this poem inhabits and interrogates.[30] Yet, Langland scholars continue to quote this account of *Piers Plowman* as a kind of shorthand that suggests the special interest of preaching both as a subject for Langland's poem and as an influence on his poetry. Owst suggests that the lively culture of English preaching supplied the base metals for whatever alchemy Langland was engaged in, and that his poem might reveal new things about that culture by presenting it in its transmuted form.

Scholarship from the later part of the twentieth century has produced a much more systematic and comprehensive account of the corpus of surviving sermon texts than was available to Owst, and has reconstructed a detailed, if necessarily incomplete, picture of the preaching culture that Langland represents and critiques in *Piers Plowman*. Wenzel has described some thirty-seven collections of Latin sermons made in England between *c.*1350 and *c.*1450, some of which are preserved in multiple manuscript copies.[31] These, in turn, overlap with a list of thirteen manuscripts that contain macaronic sermons in a mixture of Latin and English.[32] The vernacular corpus has also received detailed attention. H. Leith Spencer's *English Preaching in the Late Middle Ages* offers a wide-ranging study of the major Middle English collections from this period, along with some detailed discussion of their complex interrelationships and a compelling account of late medieval English preaching culture, its preoccupations and controversies.[33] The monumental four-volume *Repertorium of Middle English Prose Sermons* by Veronica O'Mara and Suzanne Paul, meanwhile, catalogues over a thousand individual English sermon texts in 162 manuscripts, providing a detailed, descriptive account of the entire surviving vernacular prose corpus as we know it.[34]

---

[28] Andrew Cole, 'Commentaries on Unknown Texts: On Morton Bloomfield and Friedrich Nietzsche', *YLS* 25 (2011): 27. Bloomfield makes this observation in *Piers Plowman as a Fourteenth-Century Apocalypse* (New Brunswick: Rutgers University Press, 1962), 32.

[29] In one extraordinary sequence of footnotes, each beginning with an anaphoric flourish, Owst proposes that Langland's entire knowledge of patristic authorities, of French and Latin, and of legal and commercial practice derived exclusively from sermons and from no other source: *Preaching in Medieval England*, 295–6.

[30] See, for example, Steven Justice, 'The Genres of *Piers Plowman*', *Viator* 19 (1988): 291–306; James Simpson, *Piers Plowman: An Introduction*, 2nd edn (Exeter: Exeter University Press, 2007), 23–4; *Piers Plowman: A New Annotated Edition of the C Text*, ed. Pearsall (Exeter: Exeter University Press, 2008), 12.

[31] Wenzel, *Latin Sermon Collections*.

[32] Wenzel, *Macaronic Sermons: Bilingualism and Preaching in Late-Medieval England* (Ann Arbor: University of Michican Press, 1994), 31–64, 133–211.

[33] Spencer, *English Preaching*. See esp. 269–320 for an introduction to the Middle English collections.

[34] Veronica O'Mara and Suzanne Paul, *A Repertorium of Middle English Prose Sermons*, 4 vols (Turnhout: Brepols, 2007).

Studies like these have shown that books of sermons were compiled for many different purposes. Some collections preserve the work of eminent and prestigious preachers: Thomas Brinton, whose presence Owst discerned in Langland's Prologue, left a book of his own sermons ('librum sermonum meorum') to his cathedral library when he died in 1389, while Robert Rypon's sermons from c.1400–c.1410 were copied into a luxurious manuscript for Durham Cathedral library during his tenure as the subprior there.[35] Other collections, like the *Festial*, composed in the 1380s by the Augustinian canon John Mirk, were intended as a resource for parish priests to use and adapt in their own preaching. In the prologue, Mirk explains that he intended this text as a homiliary for 'mene clerkus' who were obliged to 'teche hore pareschonus [their parishioners]', but who struggled to compose their own sermons for 'defaute of bokus [lack of books] and sympulnys of letture'.[36] Many more, like the two large compilations made at the Benedictine priory at Worcester, or the book of English and Latin sermons now preserved in British Library, Royal MS 18 B XXIII, were miscellaneous collections, assembled by several scribes, sometimes over long periods of time.[37] Texts like these have a complex relationship to sermons that were actually preached: many presumably derive from preachers' notes and listeners' records, and all were available as models for preachers to use as they wrote new sermons of their own.

Inspired in part by Owst, and enabled by these more recent studies of medieval preaching, many scholars have identified new parallels for Langland's images and ideas in sermon literature. Some have drawn further comparisons between Langland's work and the sermons of Thomas Brinton.[38] Others have looked to the wider corpus of sermon material: Wenzel, for example, compares the treatment of Hophni and Phinehas in the C-text Prologue to sermons that read this story in a similar way, as a warning against the neglect of pastoral duties.[39] John Bromyard's *Summa praedicantium*, an eclectic anthology composed in the 1320s

---

[35] *The Sermons of Thomas Brinton, Bishop of Rochester (1373–1389)*, ed. Mary Aquinas Devlin, OP, 2 vols, Camden Third Series 85-6 (London: Royal Historical Society, 1954); Robert Rypon, *Selected Sermons*, ed. and trans. Holly Johnson, 1 of 2 vols (Leuven: Peeters, 2019). I cite the bequest in Brinton's will from Devlin's introduction, 1: xviii, n. 4. On Brinton, see also Wenzel, *Latin Sermons Collections*, 45–9, and on Rypon, see Wenzel, ibid., 66–73.

[36] John Mirk, *Festial*, ed. Susan Powell, 2 vols, EETS, os 334-5 (Oxford: Oxford University Press, 2009–11), 1: 3. On the date of the text, see Powell, 'A New Dating of John Mirk's *Festial*', *Notes and Queries*, ns 29 (1982): 487–9, and Fletcher, 'John Mirk and the Lollards', *Medium Ævum* 56 (1987): 218.

[37] On the two Worcester collections, now Worcester Cathedral Library MSS F.126 and F.10, see Wenzel, *Latin Sermon Collections*, 146–58. The second of these manuscripts contains three vernacular texts alongside the Latin material. See *Three Middle English Sermons from the Worcester Chapter Manuscript F.10*, ed. D. M. Grisdale (Kendal: Wilson, 1939). The English sermons from British Library, Royal MS 18 B XXIII have been edited as *Middle English Sermons*, ed. Woodburn O. Ross, EETS, os 209 (London: Oxford University Press, 1940).

[38] Melvin Gallemore, 'The Sermons of Thomas Brinton and the B Text of *Piers the Plowman*' (PhD thesis, University of Washington, 1966), focussing on B.11-20; see also *C Text*, ed. Pearsall, 115, 243, 245, 292.

[39] Wenzel, 'Eli and His Sons', *YLS* 13 (1999): 137–52.

and 30s and used as a resource by many late medieval preachers, has emerged as a particularly important intertext for parts of *Piers Plowman*.[40] Gillian Rudd, for example, has identified an analogue in Bromyard's *Summa* for Langland's comparison between sinful preachers who are condemned on judgement day and the labourers who built the ark but were drowned in the flood (B.10.396–401).[41] John Alford argued that some of the poem's Latin lines might derive from Bromyard, pointing to examples where Langland's Latin preserves variants that are also found in the *Summa*, and where the thematic organization of quotations in the *Summa* informs the way Langland deploys them.[42] Zeeman turns repeatedly to Bromyard for definitions and distinctions that illuminate Langland's thought on the faculties of apprehension and the sources of knowledge.[43] If scholarship on *Piers Plowman* has moved well beyond Owst's conception of the poem as a vibrant, metrical gathering-up of pre-existing sermon material, then, studies like this reaffirm that Langland had a detailed knowledge of the texts and resources that preachers employed.

Since the mid-twentieth century, scholars have also considered the exegetical form of the *sermo modernus* or 'scholastic sermon' as a potential influence on Langland's poetic practice. Many preachers in the thirteenth and fourteenth centuries composed their sermons by isolating a short quotation from scripture, introducing it as their *thema*, and then developing a series of exegetical *distinctiones* from it, a departure from earlier practice where preachers would discuss the whole Gospel pericope for a given occasion following the example of the patristic homilists. This technique, theorized and codified in the *artes praedicandi*, was sometimes called the 'modum modernum [modern method]' of preaching, and distinguished from the 'antiquus modus [ancient method]' of the fathers.[44] In the early 1960s, both Elizabeth Salter and A. C. Spearing suggested that *Piers Plowman*

---

[40] For an overview of the materials that Bromyard included in his *Summa*, see Keith Walls, *John Bromyard on Church and State: The Summa Predicantium and Early Fourteenth-Century England* (Market Weighton: Clayton-Thorpe, 2007), 45–139. For a recent reassessment of the date of Bromyard's *Summa*, see Alexander William Holland, 'John Bromyard's *Summa Praedicantium*: An Exploration of Late-Medieval Falsity Through a Fourteenth-Century Preaching Handbook' (PhD thesis, University of Kent, 2018), 118–23. On the uses of the *Summa* in surviving sermons, see Christina von Nolcken, 'Some Alphabetical Compendia and How Preachers Used Them in Fourteenth-Century England', *Viator* 12 (1981): 271–88; Wenzel, *Latin Sermon Collections*, 322–7; Holland, 'John Bromyard's *Summa Praedicantium*', 147–56.

[41] Gillian Rudd, 'The state of the Ark: A Metaphor in Bromyard and *Piers Plowman* B.X.396–401', *Notes and Queries*, n.s. 37 (1990): 6–10.

[42] Alford, 'The Role of the Quotations in *Piers Plowman*', *Speculum* 52, no. 1 (1977): 99; Alford, *Piers Plowman: A Guide to the Quotations*, Medieval and Renaissance Texts and Studies, 77 (Binghamton, NY: Medieval and Renaissance Texts and Studies, 1992), e.g. 33, 36, 73, 91. Lawrence Warner has recently identified another example of this phenomenon, noting that Langland's distinctive version of the dictum *pacientes vincunt* is also found in Bromyard; *The Myth of 'Piers Plowman': Constructing a Medieval Literary Archive* (Cambridge: Cambridge University Press, 2014), 65–6.

[43] Zeeman, *Discourse of Desire*, 29 and *passim*.

[44] The modern and antique methods are distinguished in Thomas Waleys, 'De modo componendi sermones', 328–423 in *Artes Praedicandi: Contribution à l'histoire de la rhétorique au moyen âge*, ed.

might be organized like a scholastic sermon, not only at the level of individual passages but also in terms of its overall design.[45] Salter wrote that Langland would recognize the 'fitting beauty' of a discourse that employed poetic techniques for exegetical ends in this way.[46] In the 1970s, Alford argued that Langland composed his poem like a preacher elaborating *distinctiones* from a *thema*, extending the allegorical action through a commentary on a series of interrelated Latin texts.[47] These readers were responding to Bloomfield's account of *Piers Plowman* as a commentary as well as to Owst's account of it as a sermon: the discursive and aesthetic coherence of the poem, they argued, could be seen in its creative treatment of scriptural texts.

Readers have seen both risks and opportunities in comparing Langland's methods of composition with homiletic exegesis. David Aers, writing in 1975, sought to differentiate Langland's searching, exploratory allegory from the exegetical procedures he found in contemporary sermons, which he characterized as mechanical and monotonous.[48] Aers drew this distinction in part to explain why, in his view, the 'exegetical criticism' pioneered by D. W. Robertson Jr could provide only a reductive account of the poem, but he also presented his argument as a direct riposte to Owst, who had mischaracterized *Piers Plowman* as a 'derivative' from the homiletic tradition.[49] More recently, however, scholars have argued that Langland used exegetical forms familiar from sermons to encourage creative, participatory engagement with his own poem: Ryan McDermott construes Langland's compositional practice as a form of tropological invention, where dream vision creates new opportunities for 'truly participatory exegesis', while Curtis Gruenler argues that the poem invites its readers to engage with enigmatic texts as a stimulus to 'participatory play'.[50]

Thomas Marie Charland (Paris: De Vrin, 1936), 344, 345. On these different forms of preaching, see Spencer, *English Preaching*, 228–68, and Wenzel, *Latin Sermon Collections*, 11–14. For an extended account of the 'modern' form, drawn from a wide range of medieval *artes*, see Wenzel, *Medieval Artes Praedicandi*. On the history and development of the *artes*, see Margaret Jennings, '"Non ex virgine": The Rise of the Thematic Sermon Manual', *Collegium Medievale* 1–2 (1992): 27–44; Phyllis B. Roberts, 'The *Artes praedicandi* and the Medieval Sermon', 41–62 in *Preacher, Sermon and Audience in the Middle Ages*, ed. Carolyn Muessig (Leiden: Brill, 2002); Wenzel, 'The Arts of Preaching', 84–96 in *The Cambridge History of Literary Criticism, vol. 2: The Middle Ages*, ed. Alastair Minnis and Ian Johnson (Cambridge: Cambridge University Press, 2005).

[45] Elizabeth Salter, *Piers Plowman: An Introduction* (Oxford: Blackwell, 1962, 2nd edn 1969), esp. 27–57; A. C. Spearing, 'The Art of Preaching and *Piers Plowman*', 107–34 in *Criticism and Medieval Poetry* (London: Arnold, 1964, 2nd edn 1972).

[46] Salter, *Introduction*, 30. Both Salter and Spearing describe Owst's view of the poem as the 'quintessence' of English preaching as revealing but ultimately reductive; see Salter, *Introduction*, 6 n.3, 53 n. 6; Spearing, 'Art of Preaching', 110, 118.

[47] Alford, 'The Role of the Quotations', 99.

[48] David Aers, *Piers Plowman and Christian Allegory* (London: Arnold, 1975). See 33–51 for Aers' characterization of homiletic exegesis.

[49] Aers, *Christian Allegory*, 120.

[50] Ryan McDermott, *Tropologies: Ethics and Invention in England, c.1350–1600* (Notre Dame: University of Notre Dame Press, 2016), 189; Curtis A. Gruenler, *Piers Plowman and the Poetics of Enigma: Riddles, Rhetoric, and Theology* (Notre Dame: University of Notre Dame Press, 2017), *passim* (quotation at 87).

Ralph Hanna, in a recent book that seeks to rehabilitate 'commentative' practices of reading and composition from their association with Robertson's 'exegetical criticism', argues that Langland made innovative use of techniques that were taught in the Latin classroom and then put into practice in the pulpit. For Hanna, *Piers Plowman* unfolds not only as a commentary on scriptural texts but also, increasingly, on its own earlier episodes and versions, so that the techniques of preaching animate the poet's practice of revision.[51] Fletcher, too, argues that the poet's broad acceptance of the 'provisionality' of his text, and his willingness to adapt and revise it, reveals a preacherly attitude to literary composition.[52] In all these readings, exegetical techniques that were tried and tested in the pulpit offer an important model for Langland's distinctive poetic practice.

Scholarly attention to the work of John Wyclif and his followers has flourished in the period since Owst was at work, and many readers of *Piers Plowman* have considered the poem's affinities with radical and heterodox preaching. The Wycliffite movement produced a large corpus of preaching material, designed for a wide (or at least more than clerical) audience, much of it recorded or originally preached in English. After his retirement to Lutterworth in 1381, either John Wyclif or his followers compiled the *Sermones Quadraginta*, a collection of his sermons from the late 1370s, organized for liturgical use.[53] Later in the 1380s, a group of Wycliffite preachers composed the *English Wycliffite Sermons*, a comprehensive programme of preaching for the liturgical year, comprising sermons on the Sunday Gospels, the Gospels for ferial days and the Sunday epistles and sermons for the propers and commons of saints, along with the polemical tracts *Vae octuplex* and 'Of mynystris in þe chirche'. This massive cycle survives in whole or in part in thirty-one manuscripts (a further five preserve individual sermons, or the two polemical tracts together), and it formed the basis for a number of derivative collections.[54] Other controversial sermons achieved wide circulation, too. In 1388, Thomas Wimbledon delivered a sermon at St Paul's Cross in London where he forecast that the world would end in 1400, a form of

---

[51] Ralph Hanna, *Patient Reading/Reading Patience: Oxford Essays on Medieval English Literature* (Liverpool: Liverpool University Press, 2017). On 'commentative' reading and writing, as distinct from Robertsoninan 'exegetical criticism' see 81–5. Elsewhere, Hanna writes that, 'if one moves outside the grammar school, the most usual place to find commentative thought on display is another oral venue— the pulpit' (39). For Langland's 'fundamentally commentative imagination', see 297.

[52] Fletcher, 'The Essential (Ephemeral) William Langland', *YLS* 15 (2002): 75.

[53] On the compilation and transmission of Wyclif's *Sermones Quadraginta*, see William Mallard, 'Dating the *Sermones Quadraginta* of John Wyclif', *Medievalia et Humanistica* 17 (1966): 86–105; Hudson, 'Aspects of the "Publication" of Wyclif's Latin Sermons', 121–9 in *Late Medieval Religious Texts and their Transmission: Essays in Honour of A. I. Doyle*, ed. A. J. Minnis (Cambridge: Brewer, 1994); Wenzel, 'A New Version of Wyclif's *Sermones Quadraginta*', *Journal of Theological Studies* 49, no. 1 (1998): 155–61.

[54] *English Wycliffite Sermons*, ed. Anne Hudson and Pamela Gradon, 5 vols (Oxford: Clarendon, 1983–96). Hudson and Gradon consider the relationship between this cycle and Wyclif's Latin sermons in 3: xcvix–cxlviii, and describe the various collections that derive material from it in 1: 99–106.

calculation that had recently been condemned in academic contexts; this sermon survives in Latin in four manuscripts, and in English in seventeen.[55] Readers of *Piers Plowman* have been careful to differentiate the poem's positions from those expressed in controversial sermons: Fletcher, who compares Langland's views on preaching with those expressed in Wycliffite texts, describes their 'rapprochement' rather than their 'necessary identity', for example.[56] Yet, sermons like this demonstrate that the discourse of preaching was not straightforwardly identified with the institutional authority of the church for Langland or his readers. *Piers Plowman* emerges from a historical moment when sermons might serve as a vehicle for outspoken complaint and heterodox thought.

Discussions of Langland's debts to sermons often consider the possibility that Langland was himself a cleric, familiar with the techniques of preaching and with easy access to the texts and resources a preacher might use.[57] Recent archival work on Langland's historical identity offers some support for these suppositions. Several scholars have recently returned to the suggestion that 'Willielmi de Langlond', named in a memorandum in Trinity College Dublin, MS 212 as the author of the book 'qui vocatur Perys Ploughman' and as the son of Eustace de Rokele, a tenant of the Despensers in Oxfordshire, may have been the same William Rokele who received his first tonsure from the bishop of Worcester in 1338/9, and who later served as the parson of Easthorpe in Essex, then of Redgrave in Suffolk.[58] Robert Adams has traced the different branches of William Rokele's family and their links to other powerful magnates, revealing that William himself enjoyed the protection of the Beauchamps of Warwickshire.[59] Michael Johnston has added more detail to the record of William's clerical career, showing that he assumed his Redgrave benefice in 1354–55, while retaining his benefice at Easthorpe until at least 1356, and considering the possibility that Rokele

---

[55] *Wimbledon's Sermon 'Redde rationem villicationis tue': A Middle English Sermon of the Fourteenth Century*, ed. Ione Kemp Knight (Pittsburgh, PA: Duquesne University Press, 1967). On the delivery and reception of Wimbledon's sermon, see O'Mara, 'Thinking Afresh about Thomas Wimbledon's Paul's Cross Sermon of c.1387', *Leeds Studies in English*, ns. 41 (2010): 155–71. On the controversial status of apocalyptic calculations like this, see Kathryn Kerby-Fulton, *Books Under Suspicion: Censorship and Tolerance of Revelatory Writing in Late Medieval England* (Notre Dame: University of Notre Dame Press, 2006), 42.

[56] Fletcher, *Preaching, Politics and Poetry in Late-Medieval England* (Dublin: Four Courts Press, 1998), 208.

[57] Alford, 'The Role of the Quotations', 99, describes the poet 'eking out his poem slowly, even tediously, while poring over a variety of commentaries and preachers' aids'. See also Middleton, 'The Audience and Public of *Piers Plowman*', 101–23 in *Middle English Alliterative Poetry and its Literary Background*, ed. David Lawton (Cambridge: Brewer, 1982), 110–11.

[58] For the text of the memorandum, see Trinity College Dublin, MS 212, fol. 89v. George Kane offered a preliminary summary of the archival evidence linking William Langland to William Rokele in his entry on Langland for the *ODNB*, drawing on earlier discoveries by Lister Matheson and Oscar Cargill. Kane, 'Langland, William (c.1325–c.1390)', *ODNB*, <https://doi.org/10.1093/ref:odnb/16021>

[59] Robert Adams, *Langland and the Rokele Family: The Gentry Background to 'Piers Plowman'* (Dublin: Four Courts, 2013); see also Adams, 'The Rokeles: An Index for a "Langland" Family History', 85–96 in *Cambridge Companion to 'Piers Plowman'*, ed. Cole and Galloway.

encountered the radical preacher John Ball, who was resident in Colchester while he was parson of Easthorpe.[60] Andrew Galloway, meanwhile, has noted the Rokeles' connections to the court of Queen Isabella at Castle Rising, and shown that William himself exploited his clerical position to facilitate land transactions on behalf of his family.[61] One implication of this research is that the poem's author spent part of his career as a parish priest, with obligations to 'Prechen and praye' for his 'parisshens' (B.Prol.89–90) even if, as Johnston has shown, he was not always present in the parishes where he had the cure of souls.[62]

The poem's early readers certainly included clerics who were authorized to preach.[63] Walter de Brugge, who bequeathed 'unum librum vocatum Pers plewman' to John Wormynton in 1396, was a canon and priest of York; his library included works on canon law, a glossed Psalter, a portiforium, and a Latin dictionary, as well as the gospel harmony *Unum ex quatuor*, all useful materials for preaching.[64] William Palmere, who left a copy of *Piers Plowman* to Agnes Eggesfeld, was rector of St Alphege, Cripplegate, from 1397–1400, while John Wyndill, rector of Arncliffe in Yorkshire from 1394 to 1431, left his copy of the poem to John Kendall, who is named in a later will as the vicar of Grimston in Norfolk.[65] Manuscripts of *Piers Plowman* were also available to friars and monks. One copy of the A text, now Oxford, Bodleian Library, MS Rawlinson Poetry 137,

---

[60] Michael Johnston, 'William Langland and John Ball', *YLS* 30 (2016): 29–74; and Johnston, 'The Clerical Career of William Rokele', *YLS* 33 (2019): 111–25.

[61] Galloway, 'Madame Meed: *Fauvel*, Isabella, and the French Circumstances of *Piers Plowman*', *YLS* 30 (2016): 227–52; Galloway, 'Parallel Lives: William Rokele and the Satirical Literacies of *Piers Plowman*', *Studies in the Age of Chaucer* 40 (2018): 43–111. Alongside these recent studies of William Rokele, Michael Bennett has noted another possible record of Langland in the documentary archive, pointing to an indictment of July 1385, where a 'Willelmum *vocaus* Longwyll' is listed alongside eleven others, charged with aiding and abetting the murder of Sir John Holland: Bennett, 'William Called Long Will', *YLS* 36 (2012): 1–25; Galloway presents new documentary evidence about William 'Longwyll', and considers the possibility that 'Longwyll' and Rokele might be the same person, in 'Long Will and the Scandal of 1385', *YLS* 36 (2022): 45–76.

[62] Scholars engaged in this research have emphasized its provisional quality, since the identification of Langland with Rokele remains an unproven hypothesis. See Galloway, 'Parallel Lives', 44–5. For a cautious response to the Rokele archive, see Kerby-Fulton, *The Clerical Proletariat and the Resurgence of Medieval English Poetry* (Philadelphia: University of Pennsylvania Press, 2021), 78 and note 4.

[63] For a useful overview of the poem's earliest readers and owners, see Simon Horobin, 'Manuscripts and Readers of *Piers Plowman*', 179–97 in *Cambridge Companion to Piers Plowman*, ed. Cole and Galloway, 241–3. See also Middleton, 'Audience and Public', 103–4; Hanna, *William Langland* (Aldershot: Variorum, 1993), 34–6; and Kerby Fulton, 'Langland and the Bibliographic Ego', 67–143 in *Written Work: Langland, Labor, and Authorship*, ed. Justice and Kerby-Fulton (Philadelphia: University of Pennsylvania Press, 1997), 114–18.

[64] Rees Davies, 'The Life, Travels, and Library of an Early Reader of *Piers Plowman*', *YLS* 13 (1999): 49–64; Arvind Thomas, *Piers Plowman and the Reinvention of Church Law in the Late Middle Ages* (Toronto: University of Toronto Press, 2019), 3–5. Walter de Brugge's will is reproduced in *Testamenta Eboracensia: A Selection of Wills from the Registry of York (1300–1551)*, ed. James Raine Sr, James Raine Jr, and John Clay, 6 vols (London: Nichols & Son, 1836–1902), 1: 207–10 (quotation at 209). For an argument that Trinity College Dublin, MS 212 was Brugge's manuscript of *Piers*, see E. St John Brooks, 'The *Piers Plowman* Manuscripts in Trinity College, Dublin', *The Library*, 5th ser., 6 (1951): 151–3.

[65] Robert A. Wood, 'A Fourteenth-Century Owner of *Piers Plowman*', *Medium Ævum* 74 (2005): 248–69.

was the property of the Franciscan Convent in Canterbury by 1500.[66] Another copy of A, now Dublin, Trinity College, MS 213, was probably held at the Benedictine Priory of Durham Cathedral where Robert Rypon had served as prior, and where his sermons were also preserved.[67] *Piers* also found readers among the Benedictines. Parts of Oxford, Bodleian Library, MS Bodley 851, which contains the Z text of the poem, belonged to the Benedictine monk and controversialist John Wells; Kathryn Kerby-Fulton has shown that this manuscript circulated among his students and followers as they moved between Ramsey Abbey and their common house at Gloucester College, Oxford, where their course of study was designed to prepare them for preaching.[68] The Benedictine Hugh Legat, whose sermons survive in both Latin and English, was also a student at Gloucester College and, as Fletcher has argued, apparently a reader of *Piers*.[69] Middleton proposed that some early readers understood the poem as a compendium of didactic material, a kind of pastoral *summa*, leaving open the possibility that they adapted parts of it for use in their sermons.[70] Christine Schott points to annotations in some B-text manuscripts that might reveal readers consulting the poem as a kind of compendium or 'preachers' handbook', although Sarah Wood has recently questioned whether this approach to the poem was widespread among early readers.[71] Lawrence Warner, meanwhile, has shown that the sixteenth-century Benedictine John Brynstan cited *Piers* in his preaching in the way that Middleton and Schott imagine.[72] For these clerical readers, the poem also offered a poetic description of preaching in practice, an account of its immediate and long-term effects on different audiences, that went well beyond the theories of form and composition that were set out in the *artes praedicandi*.

---

[66] Horobin, 'The Scribe of Rawlinson Poetry 137 and the Copying and Circulation of *Piers Plowman*', YLS 19 (2005): 3–26.

[67] On Dublin, Trinity College, MS 213, see *The Wars of Alexander*, ed. Hoyt N. Duggan and Thorlac Turville-Petre, EETS, ss 10 (Oxford: Oxford University Press, 1989), x–xii.

[68] Kerby-Fulton, 'Confronting the Scribe–Poet Binary: The Z-Text, Writing Office Redaction, and the Oxford Reading Circles', 489–515 in *New Directions in Medieval Manuscript Studies and Reading Practices: Essays in Honor of Derek Pearsall*, ed. Kathryn Kerby-Fulton, John Thompson, and Sarah Baechle (Notre Dame: University of Notre Dame Press, 2014). On the establishment of common houses for monks at Oxford, see Wenzel, *Latin Sermon Collections*, 278–9; Wenzel notes that '[t]heir university study was explicitly oriented to the work of preaching' (278).

[69] Fletcher, '*Piers Plowman* and the Benedictines', 43–62 in *Chaucer in Context: A Golden Age of English Poetry*, ed. Gerald Morgan (Oxford: Peter Lang, 2012). Hugh is identified as the author of the first Middle English sermon in Worcester Cathedral Library, MS F.10; see *Three Middle English Sermons*, ed. Grisdale, xi–xiii, and 1–21; Fletcher (*Late Medieval Popular Preaching*, 33–66) demonstrates that Hugh was also the author of the macaronic sermons in Oxford, Bodleian Library, MS Bodley 649, which have been edited by Patrick J. Horner, as *A Macaronic Sermon Collection from Late Medieval England: Oxford, MS Bodley 649*, Studies and Texts 153 (Toronto: Pontifical Institute of Mediaeval Studies, 2006).

[70] Middleton, 'Audience and Public', 109.

[71] Christine Schott, 'The Intimate Reader at Work: Medieval Annotators of *Piers Plowman* B', YLS 26 (2012): 180–1. Sarah Wood, *Piers Plowman and its Manuscript Tradition* (Woodbridge: York Medieval Press, 2022), 4–5.

[72] Warner, *Myth of 'Piers Plowman'*, 75–8.

My debts to this earlier scholarship on late medieval preaching and its relationship to *Piers Plowman* will be clear throughout this book. In the chapters that follow, I read numerous passages from *Piers* alongside analogues in sermon texts and in the ancillary resources that preachers used, and I draw on the *artes* in discussions of Langland's exegetical method and of his poetic form. My analysis takes Langland's own knowledge of preaching, and the interest that preaching held for at least some of his readers, to be well established. The turn to narrative in this book, however, is intended in part to reframe the kinds of questions we might ask about Langland's relationship to sermons. Langland displays a detailed knowledge of the forms and techniques at a preacher's disposal and employs them creatively in the production of his own poetry, but, as I will argue in what follows, he also develops a richly elaborated and highly consequential theory of the way that sermons intervene in social life, reconfiguring their listeners' understanding of the present time as part of a larger, interpreted story. Langland offers a revealing account of the way that late medieval listeners and practitioners thought about sermons in performance, one that goes far beyond the concerns of contemporary *artes*, with their focus on the principles of composition. As *Piers Plowman* unfolds, moreover, it shows how the narrative understanding cultivated in sermons could be deployed in new contexts, including the process of its own composition.

Holy Church and the Story of Salvation

The dreamer's encounter with Holy Church in the Prologue to *Piers Plowman* is the poem's first extended preaching scene, and it demonstrates Langland's conception of the narrative logic that sermons express. Will has already seen several preachers at work as he looks out over the 'fair feeld ful of folk' in the Prologue (B.Prol.17), including a corrupt pardoner and representatives of the four orders of friars, but when Holy Church appears in passus 1 and begins to explain his vision to him, he becomes the audience for a sermon himself for the first time in the poem. Galloway argues that preaching is the natural mode of expression for Holy Church. She represents 'Christian doctrine as stored, expounded, and conveyed through apostolic tradition with complete authority', and, as such, she embodies '"holy" writ... as it extends into sermons permeating and guiding every aspect of life'.[73] As Wenzel has demonstrated, moreover, her speech divides into discrete but interrelated sections that recall the exegetical *distinctiones* of a scholastic sermon, and her argument recalls the movement through '*thema*, definition, development, illustration and example, confirming quotations, and recapitulation'

---

[73] Galloway, *The Penn Commentary on Piers Plowman, vol. 1: C Prologue–Passus 4; B Prologue–Passus 4; A Prologue-Passus 4* (Philadelphia: Pennsylvania University Press, 2006), 148, 152.

that was prescribed and elaborated in the *artes*.[74] This encounter with Holy Church also includes elements of pastoral dialogue, as Will interjects with questions and Holy Church rebukes him; these exchanges point to a longstanding relationship between Holy Church and the dreamer which I will consider in Chapter 4. Here, however, I want to focus on the way this sermon provides a new narrative context for the dreamer's direct experience of life on the field, locating his present moment in a story that emerges from a combination of scriptural exegesis and social commentary, and that provides new focus and direction for his spiritual life.

In the Prologue, Will's vision begins as a sweeping and inclusive allegory of social life in the present day where the different estates pursue their occupations on a field, bounded by a tower on a hill on one side and a dungeon in a valley on the other. In passus 1, Holy Church recasts this vision of the contemporary world by locating it in the context of a larger story, explaining how Truth, who lives in the tower, and Wrong, who lives in the dungeon, have exerted their influence on the field in between. When he saw the field in the Prologue, the dreamer was already able to recognize different forms of temporal change. Commenting on the different estates, for example, he noted the seasonal work of agricultural labourers and remarked on the 'mountynge' discord between the friars and the secular clergy (B.Prol.67). Positioned 'into þe eest an hei3 [high] to þe sonne', the tower of Truth casts a shadow across the field like the gnomen of a sundial, marking the passage of hours and days (B.Prol.13). When Holy Church explains the scene, however, she provides a new, narrative framework to understand these temporal changes, locating them in the larger story of the creation, Fall, and atonement, that is, in the 'ever present' narrative frame of late medieval preaching *ad populum*. The meaning of life on the field, which is partially perceptible in the simple succession of events, emerges in a new and more clearly intelligible way when these events are construed as part of this larger plot. The story that Holy Church has to tell will change the way the dreamer thinks about the ultimate purpose of 'werchynge and wandrynge [working and wandering]' on the field (B.Prol.19); while his first questions concern the 'moneie' and 'tresour' that motivate economic labour (B.1.44–5), his later questions concern his own salvation, as the final reward for his choices and actions: 'Teche me [direct me] to no tresor, but tel me þis ilke [this very thing]—/ How I may saue my soule, þat seint art yholden [you who are held to be holy]' (B.1.83–4).

The sermon of Holy Church is organized around the exegesis of texts. It divides into two main parts that recall the protheme and the main divisions of a sermon constructed according to the *modum modernum*, and each of these parts elaborates on a short, axiomatic statement, which resemble the *antetheme* and the

---

[74] Wenzel, 'Medieval Sermons', 165–7 (quotation at 166).

thema. In the opening part, Holy Church explains that Truth supplies the essential resources that people need to survive. She urges moderation in the use of these gifts in the words of her first axiom: 'Mesure [moderation] is medicine, þou3 þow muchel yerne [although you yearn for a lot]' (B.1.35).[75] In the main divisions, she argues that people should speak truly and be true to their word, and that Truth encourages love above all other virtues. She introduces this part with a second axiom, which she repeats at the midpoint and again at the end: 'Whan alle tresors arn tried [tested]... treuþe is þe beste' (B.1.85, and cf. B.1.135, B.1.207).[76] Holy Church cites a wide range of authorities as she expounds these texts, 'preueing' her claims about moderation and truth using exegetical strategies familiar from the pulpit.[77] After the first statement of the axiom 'treuþe is þe beste', for example, she cites 1 John 4:8, 'Deus caritas [God is love]', much as a preacher might cite a verse from scripture to confirm a new division of his *thema*: '"Whan alle tresors arn tried", quod she, "treuþe is þe beste./ I do it on [adduce the text] *Deus caritas* to deme [prove] þe soþe"' (B.1.85-6).[78] As Mary Clemente Davlin observed, 'truth' and 'love' are at times interchangeable in John's first Epistle: God's truth, for John, is not abstract but instantiated, and is found in the experience of God's love.[79] Adducing this text as a confirmatory authority, then, Holy Church affirms a correspondence between 'treuþe' and *caritas* that John articulates himself. 'Preuing' her *thema* with reference to John, Holy Church reveals one way in which 'treuþe' can be 'tried', through the concatenation of authorities in an exegetical discourse.

This sermon also shows how a discourse organized on exegetical principles can express a narrative logic, however. Holy Church tells stories from the Bible to illustrate and extend her readings of the axioms on moderation and truth, much as contemporary preachers did when expounding scripture. She also locates these individual stories in the larger framework of salvation history, a narrative that is organized around, and that gives expression to, her essential claims. In the

---

[75] On the sources of this axiom and its links to philosophical and pastoral writing on moderation, see *C Text*, ed. Pearsall, 57, and Galloway, *Penn Commentary*, 1: 165-7.

[76] Alford locates another use of this axiom in the Middle English *Secreta Secretorum*: 'More Unidentified Quotations in *Piers Plowman*', *Modern Philology* 81, no. 3 (1984): 278, and see *C Text*, ed. Pearsall, 60. Wenzel, 'Medieval Sermons', 167, compares the second part of Holy Church's speech to the *introductio thematis* of a sermon on Mark 12:30 from the Middle English collection in British Library, Royal MS 18 B XXIII (*Middle English Sermons*, ed. Ross, 198-206). Here too, the preacher repeats his *thema* at the midpoint and again at the end, dividing the argument into two distinct but logically connected halves.

[77] Galloway (*Penn Commentary*, 1: 183) describes this part of the speech as a set of sermon-like *distinctiones* on the axiom.

[78] Galloway (*Penn Commentary*, 1: 185) writes that 'The phrase "do it on" (or "upon") functions in PP as a technical idiom for invoking as support for an argument an example or text, corresponding to *adducere* in Latin sermons.'

[79] Davlin, '*Piers Plowman* and the Gospel and First Epistle of John', *YLS* 10 (1996): 118. Galloway, who notes a series of allusions to 1 John in this sermon, argues that the link between truth and love becomes central to its argument; Galloway, *Penn Commentary*, 1: 153, 159; for other references to 1 John, see Galloway, *Penn Commentary*, 1: 170-71, 174, 175, 185, 186, 203, 212, 213.

protheme on 'Mesure is medicine', Holy Church explains the contemporary world as a product of the creation and of the Fall. Early in her sermon, she explains that Truth is another name for God the creator, the 'fader [father] of feiþ' who 'formed yow alle' (B.1.14). Truth creates the body with its powers of apprehension, and supplies the resources it needs to survive; these, however, must be used in 'mesurable manere' (B.1.19), a point that Holy Church will illustrate with the story of Lot, who drank to excess and committed incest with his daughters. Wrong, meanwhile, is the 'Fader of falshede' (B.1.64), the devil who encouraged Adam and Eve to sin, and who incited the murder of Abel and the betrayal of Christ. He continues to tempt and deceive people in the present day, where 'þe fend and þi flessh folwen togidere [join in pursuit]' (B.1.40), but it is possible to resist him through moderation: 'Mesure is medicine, þou3 þow muchel yerne' (B.1.35). The people who labour on the field inhabit a world that has been shaped by the initial actions of Truth and Wrong and by their ongoing interventions in biblical and contemporary history. They must consider the best way to use the resources that Truth has created for them, and to resist the tricks and temptations of Wrong, at their own particular moment in this unfolding story.

In the main part of her sermon, Holy Church expounds her *thema*, 'Whan alle tresors arn tried... treuþe is þe beste' (B.1.85). As she instantiates this claim in successive divisions on faithful speech and loving action, she also elaborates on her narrative of salvation history, introducing new stories from the Bible and from contemporary life. In the first of these divisions, Holy Church considers the knight's oath as an exemplary instance of faithful speech, and recalls the stories of King David who 'in hise dayes dubbed kny3tes' (B.1.98), and Christ, the 'kyngene kyng [king of kings]', who 'kny3ted' the orders of angels (B.1.105); she then turns to the story of Lucifer, who broke his oath and was cast out of heaven 'Into a deep derk helle' (B.1.115). The choice and arrangement of these stories is determined in part by the exegetical logic of this part of the sermon: Holy Church defines faithful speech, illustrates it in a comparative and superlative degree, then confirms her definition with a negative example. Yet, each one also serves to enrich the narrative she sketched out in the protheme: the creative activity of Truth finds new expression in the investiture of knights, while the treachery of Lucifer, who now inhabits the dungeon in the valley, is part of the story of Wrong. In the second division, Holy Church introduces the incarnation and atonement of Christ as the pre-eminent expression of love, and gestures to several other 'ensamples' from Christ's life and ministry that affirm this reading (B.1.172). Here, she describes the atonement as the central turning point in salvation history, a new creative action by 'þe Fader þat formed vs alle' (B.1.166) and provides his people with the things they need to live well. Here, as in the protheme, Holy Church presents a narrative that creates new ethical imperatives for the dreamer, and for the people who work on the field; in order to save his soul, Will must learn to be 'trewe of his tonge' (B.1.88), and must show love and charity to his neighbours.

This second division contains a compelling image for the narrative shape of salvation history, conceptualized as an interpreted whole. Holy Church imagines love as a 'plante of pees [peace]', which spills out of heaven to take root in the earth, then sends up new shoots that pierce the walls of heaven:

And also þe plante of pees, moost precious of vertues:	
For heuene my3te nat holden it, so was it heuy of hymselue,	
Til it hadde of þe erþe eten his fille.	*eaten*
And whan it hadde of þis fold flessh and blood taken,	*earth*
Was neuere leef vpon lynde lighter þerafter,	*leaf; linden tree*
And portatif and persaunt as þe point of a nedle,	*portable; piercing*
That my3te noon armure it lette ne none hei3e walles.	*armour; stop*
(B.1.152–8)	

The growth of the plant recalls the agricultural patterns of sowing, cultivation, and harvest, that the dreamer observed in the Prologue, where he first perceived the passage of time as a regular cycle of seasons. In the sermon of Holy Church, however, the life of the plant figures salvation history as a single, cohesive narrative: God's love, which has grown heavy since the creation, reaches down to earth at the incarnation of Christ, and then springs up into heaven again after the atonement, creating a precedent for human beings who might themselves pierce heaven with their prayers and enter through its 'hei3e walles' after death.

Langland's plant of peace is itself an exegetical response to a scriptural text as Adams has shown: the image contains an allusion to Ezekiel 34:29, where God declares that he will raise up a 'germen nominatum [bud of renown]' for his people; in the earlier, Septuagint version of this verse, quoted by patristic authors, the 'germen nominatum' is a 'planta pacis', or plant of peace.[80] As Holy Church develops this image, however, it comes to serve as a figure for the narrative of eschatological history itself, a complex process of evolution and change construed as a single story. Cristina Maria Cervone has linked the 'plante of pees' to the patristic topos of the 'leaps of love', invoked in preachers' manuals like the *Fasciculus morum*, which also speaks about salvation history as a continuous series of actions, configured into a narrative whole.[81] Hanna identifies another

---

[80] Adams, 'Editing and the Limitations of *Durior Lectio*', *YLS* 5 (1991): 12–13. See also Galloway, *Penn Commentary*, 1: 206–7.

[81] Cristina Maria Cervone, 'Langland and the Truelove Tradition', *YLS* 22 (2008): 27–55; Cervone, *Poetics of the Incarnation: Middle English Writing and the Leap of Love* (Philadelphia: University of Pennsylvania Press, 2012), 115–17. Cervone notes that, in Middle English, where the verb 'springen' might refer to the action of leaping or to the germination of a plant, the leaps topos was often figured in terms of arboreal growth.

parallel in a sermon by John Waldeby, where God's love, which spills out of heaven at the incarnation, is weighed against Adam's sin on the cross, 'tanquam in equilibria [as if on a balance beam]', and proves to be heavier, raising human souls out of hell and lifting them into heaven, imagining salvation history as a single movement.[82] These are figures that seek to capture the dynamism of salvation history as a single, interpreted whole. The growth and germination of the plant also represent God's insatiable desire for human souls. As John Burrow writes, its slow, biological, development figures the way this desire unfolds and comes to fruition in history, in 'plenitudo temporis [the fullness of time]'.[83] As a figure for the incarnation, atonement, and ascension of Christ, the 'plante of pees' insists that love itself is fully historical: it is enacted in time and revealed in narrative.

The narrative that Holy Church articulates in her sermon provides the dreamer with a new perception of his place in history, and reconfigures his understanding of the choices that confront him in the present moment. The landscape he observed in the Prologue now contains a record of God's creative activity, and of his ongoing interventions in human life. It also maps out the possible fate of each human soul, a point made most explicitly in the C text:

And alle þat worchen þat wikked is, wenden thei sholle	*do what is evil, go, shall*
Aftur here deth day and dwelle ther Wrong is;	*their, where*
And alle þat han wel ywrouhte, wende þey sholle	*have done well*
Estward til heuene, euere to abyde	*to*
There Treuthe is, þe trone that Trinite ynne sitteth.	*throne*
	(C.1.129–33)

Where in the Prologue, the dreamer saw the relationship between the tower, the field, and the dungeon primarily in spatial terms, he now imagines movements eastward and westward that unfold over the course of a human life, understood in the context of a narrated history. The sermon of Holy Church produces a transformation of the dreamer's understanding: not a moment of *metanoia*, necessarily, but a new perception of the opportunities and obligations that confront him in the interpreted present. In her first words to the dreamer, Holy Church remarks that most people on the field are preoccupied with 'worship in þis world', and give no thought to the life to come: 'Of ooþer heuene þan here holde

---

[82] Hanna, '"Put the Load Right on Me": Langland on The Incarnation (With Apologies to the Band)', *Notes and Queries* 66, no. 2 (2019): 197–201. Hanna cites and translates this passage from Oxford, Bodleian Library, MS Laud misc. 296, fol. 4v, at 199, and in n. 6.

[83] John A. Burrow, 'God and the Fullness of Time in *Piers Plowman*', *Medium Ævum* 79 (2010): 300–5.

þei no tale' (B.1.8–9); the story she unfolds for him, however, encourages him to evaluate his daily activities with reference to his own salvation. If the dreamer's original interest in 'tresor' reflected the distracted concerns of an uninterpreted life, his new desire for 'treuþe', which Holy Church describes as the 'beste' treasure, emerges as his own, direct experience is reconfigured by narrative.[84]

In this important early scene in the poem, then, Holy Church offers an extended demonstration of the transformative effects that preaching can achieve, reconfiguring the dreamer's perception of his present moment by locating it in the context of an interpreted, narrative history. In doing so, she sets a precedent that many of the poem's preachers will go on to follow. The sermon of Holy Church shows how the narrative of *Heilsgeschichte*, the 'core message' of preaching *ad populum* in Wenzel's account, could emerge from the concatenation and exegesis of texts and authorities, and how the articulation of this narrative could alter a listener's perception of the world. Before he hears this sermon, the dreamer is absorbed in the sights and experiences of his present moment, just as the people on the field were preoccupied with their immediate concerns. After it, however, he understands his present time as part of an interpreted history, and perceives his capacities and obligations to act in a new way. After she tells the story of Lot, Holy Church speaks her first axiom—the protheme to her sermon—'Mesure is medicine', and notes that this exemplary story should encourage the dreamer 'do þe bettre' (B.1.34). Here, she introduces an injunction that will recur in Reason's sermon in the second vision, and will echo through the rest of the poem reformulated in the Do-wel triad, a call to good action that will continue to require new acts of narrative interpretation.

Time and Narrative

The account of narrative in this book draws on the work of Paul Ricoeur, and especially on his three-volume study *Temps et Récit*, published in English as *Time and Narrative*. Here, Ricoeur approaches narrative as a 'mediating construction' that structures, and ultimately constitutes, the human relationship to time. For Ricoeur, 'time becomes human to the extent that it is articulated through a narrative mode, and narrative attains its full meaning when it becomes a condition of temporal experience'.[85] Ricoeur's account of

---

[84] James Simpson notes the paradox that 'Holy Church devalues earthly treasure, and at the same time adopts the term "tresor" to describe spiritual realities', an example of the way that Langland recuperates the language of economics as a metaphor for spiritual reward. See Simpson, 'Spirituality and Economics in Passus 1–7 of the B Text', *YLS* 1 (1987): 83–103; and also Simpson, 'The Transformation of Meaning: A Figure of Thought in *Piers Plowman*', *Review of English Studies*, ns 37, no. 146 (1986), 161–83.

[85] Paul Ricoeur, *Time and Narrative*, trans. Kathleen McLaughlin and David Pellauer, 3 vols (Chicago: University of Chicago Press, 1990), 1: 52. For an illuminating introduction to this complex

narrative is rooted in twentieth-century hermeneutic phenomenology, where self-understanding emerges indirectly through the interpretation of symbols and texts.[86] Ancient and patristic authors also exert a powerful influence on his thought, however. Ricoeur's investigation of the subjective experience of time begins with a reading of Augustine's *Confessions,* and his account of time in the physical universe draws on Aristotle's *Physics,* texts that framed the medieval discussion of temporality. Still more importantly, Ricoeur understands the composition and interpretation of narratives to be transformative activities that shape and inform people's perceptions of themselves as subjects, of their capabilities and responsibilities as social actors, and of their place in the larger span of human history. For this reason above all, I think, his work provides a theoretical framework that illuminates what medieval preachers did with narrative, and that helps to explain why sermon narratives should be such an important concern for Langland in *Piers Plowman.*

Time and Narrative begins with the well-known passage from Augustine's *Confessions,* book 11, where Augustine asks whether time can be said to exist in the world, given that the past is no longer, the future is not yet, and the present is characterized by its movement into the past. He concludes that time exists exclusively in the soul, which remembers the past, attends to the present, and anticipates the future. While God perceives all time as a unity, Augustine says, the human soul is painfully distended, stretched out in three directions to perceive time as it passes. At a key moment in this argument, Augustine shows how the lived experience of time might be mediated by an encounter with texts. He observes that when he recites a psalm his attention is focussed on the words he is speaking, but he also remembers the part he has spoken already, and anticipates the part he has yet to speak. Although his soul is stretched out in different directions, he is able to perceive the psalm as a unity, and the unity of the psalm lends coherence to his experience of time. Augustine imagines that a life story, or even a universal history, might present similar patterns of coherence to the perceiving soul: what is true of the psalm, he says, is also true of an individual life, and of human history as a whole: 'hoc in tota uita hominis, cuius partes sunt omnes actiones hominis, hoc in toto saeculo filiorum hominum, cuius partes sunt omnes uitae hominum [The same thing happens in the entirety of a person's life, of which all his actions are parts; and the same in the entire sweep of human

---

study, see William C. Dowling, *Ricoeur on Time and Narrative: An Introduction to Temps et Récit* (Notre Dame, IN: University of Notre Dame Press, 2011). Ricoeur also wrote several articles that summarized or anticipated aspects of his argument in *Time and Narrative,* including Ricoeur, 'Narrative Time', 165–86 in *On Narrative,* ed. W. J. T. Michell (Chicago: University of Chicago Press, 1981), and Ricoeur, 'Narrated Time', 338–54 in *A Ricoeur Reader: Reflection and Imagination,* ed. Mario J. Valdés (New York: Harvester Wheatsheaf, 1991).

[86] For an introduction to this tradition, see Günter Figal, 'Hermeneutical Phenomenology', 525–42, in *The Oxford Handbook of Contemporary Phenomenology,* ed. Dan Zahavi (Oxford: Oxford University Press, 2012).

history, the parts of which are individual human lives].'[87] This is a crucial realization for Ricoeur, who argues that '[t]he entire province of narrative is laid out here in its potentiality'.[88]

Ricoeur develops Augustine's insight through a reading of Aristotle's *Poetics*. Here, he focusses on Aristotle's account of *muthos*, or 'emplotment', which he describes as an active process of selection and arrangement: the poet identifies the most important actions and episodes that unfold across a period of time, and then configures them into a unified whole. For Aristotle, Ricoeur observes, the ability to 'grasp [events] together' as a *holos* arises from a kind of 'practical wisdom' (*phronesis*) that allows the poet and his audience to recognize the intelligible in the accidental, and to extrapolate universals from particulars.[89] Ricoeur notes that the logic that governs a poetic plot does not arise from temporal sequence (indeed, Aristotle's theory of emplotment in the *Poetics* makes no reference to his theory of time in the *Physics*). Instead, the plot coheres around some other, atemporal logic, the 'single thought' that the narrative conveys, what medieval readers might call its *res* or its 'gist'.[90] Ricoeur proposes Aristotle's theory of emplotment as an 'opposite reply' to Augustine's account of the distended soul.[91] For Augustine, he says, the experience of time is characterized by 'concordant discordance', as the soul, in its singular intention to perceive time, is pulled in three directions, comprehending past, present, and future. Aristotle, conversely, shows that *muthos* produces a kind of 'discordant concordance' as it identifies the logic that connects disparate events and episodes, 'grasping [them] together' as part of a whole. The activity of composing and interpreting narratives allows the perceiving subject to comprehend temporal experience in new ways, with implications for personal identity, social life, and ethical action.

Ricoeur seeks to refine Aristotle's account of emplotment by arguing that it follows an 'arc of operations' as it reconfigures the lived experience of time. As Ricoeur imagines it, emplotment moves from *mimesis*[1], where listeners recognize 'structures that call for narration' prefigured in their ordinary experience, through *mimesis*[2], where narrative discourse configures disparate events into unified plots, to *mimesis*[3], where the discursive resources of narrative reconfigure a listener's perception of time.[92] Emplotment draws on the practical wisdom that allows us to make inferences about agency and causality in everyday life, Ricoeur argues, while the hermeneutics of narrative extend beyond the texts we read into the world where we read them, providing new ways to understand the time in which

---

[87] Augustine, *Confessionum libri XII*, ed. Martin Skutella, rev. Luca Verheijen, CCSL 27 (Turnhout: Brepols, 1981), 292, (11.xxviii.38); translation from Augustine, *The Confessions*, trans. Maria Boulding, WSA, 1.1 (Hyde Park, NY: New City Press, 1997), 309.
[88] Ricoeur, *Time and Narrative*, 1: 22.   [89] Ricoeur, *Time and Narrative*, 1: 41.
[90] Ricoeur, *Time and Narrative*, 1: 67. For medieval accounts of the *res* or 'gist' of a text, see Mary Carruthers, *The Craft of Thought: Meditation, Rhetoric, and the Making of Images, 400–1200* (Cambridge: Cambridge University Press, 2000), 29–40.
[91] Ricoeur, *Time and Narrative*, 1: 31.   [92] Ricoeur, *Time and Narrative*, 1: 53.

we live.[93] Ricoeur describes *mimesis*³ as 'the intersection of the world of the text and that of the listener or reader'. This moment produces a 'fusion of horizons', a term Ricoeur borrows from Hans-Georg Gadamer, as the narrative text generates new possibilities for understanding, imagination, and speculative thought in combination with the listener's own experience.[94]

In the second part of *Time and Narrative*, Ricoeur contends that the logic of emplotment informs the writing of history, even history that ostensibly rejects a narrative structure. In the third, he discerns the logic of emplotment in fictional texts, primarily novels of the twentieth century. Despite their different truth claims, he argues, history and fiction draw on the same intuitive preunderstanding of narrative, and both depend for their intelligibility on the capacity to synthesize disparate elements, the 'grasping together' that characterizes emplotment. There is a 'profound kinship' between a historical change, construed as part of an analytical discourse, and a narrative event in a plot, he writes.[95] Ricoeur describes history and fiction in a relationship of '*référence croisée* [interweaving reference]' as each informs the reader's expectations of the other, and both refigure the reader's perception of the world.[96] From history, he argues, we derive the capacity to recognize patterns of coherence in past events, while from fiction we derive the capacity to explore alternative courses of action and to imagine different kinds of temporal experience as they might unfold in the time to come.

In the fourth and final part, Ricoeur proposes that narrative discourse can mediate between two seemingly incompatible understandings of time: the subjective experience of 'phenomenological time', described by Augustine in the *Confessions*, and 'cosmological time' that derives from motion and change in the physical universe, as defined by Aristotle in the *Physics*. Ricoeur identifies an 'unbridgeable gap' between these two understandings of time, neither of which can account for the other: 'the distension of the soul alone cannot produce the extension of time', he writes, and 'the dynamism of movement alone cannot generate the dialectic of the threefold present'.[97] Ricoeur describes a series of 'reflective instruments' that connect lived experience to longer spans of history: calendars and chronicles, direct encounters with people of other generations, and the 'traces' (documents and artefacts) left by people who died before the present generation was born.[98] Each of these produces what he calls the 'reinscription' of phenomenological time onto cosmological time, making it possible to think about both orders of time at once.[99] Calendars, for example, are organized around an 'axial moment', perhaps the birth of Christ or the coronation of a new king, which serves as the zero-point for the calculation of other times and intervals. The axial

---

[93] Ricoeur, *Time and Narrative*, 1: 73.
[94] Ricoeur, *Time and Narrative*, 1: 77.
[95] Ricoeur, *Time and Narrative*, 1: 229.
[96] Ricoeur, *Time and Narrative*, 1: 32, 82.
[97] Ricoeur, *Time and Narrative*, 3: 19, 21.
[98] Ricoeur, *Time and Narrative*, 3: 104.
[99] Ricoeur, *Time and Narrative*, 3: 99.

moment coincides with a specific instant in cosmological time, but its significance arises in the phenomenological present, as a break with the past that inaugurates new conditions for the future. Using the calendar, it is possible to speak about an experience of the past, present, and future that unfolds in relation to measurable dates and intervals of time, and so in a temporal relation to the experiences of others.[100] To encounter a 'trace' involves reckoning with cosmological and phenomenological time in a similar way. The 'trace' is both a present phenomenon and a product of another moment in time; it can be dated with reference to a calendar, but it must also be understood in relation to the concerns and investments of the people who made it and used it.[101] With reference to 'reflective instruments' like these, then, it is possible to project new narratives into what Ricoeur calls the 'third time' of public history, where the time of subjective experience can be measured against the observable time of the world.

As it mediates between the time of the soul and the time of the world, emplotment enables self-knowledge and social action. Emplotment makes it possible to speak about a coherent personal identity, to grasp disparate events and experiences together as part of an individual life, and to assert that a single self endures even as the body and its circumstances change. Ricoeur describes a 'discordant concordance' of selfhood, a 'dynamic identity' that is formed through the mediation of narrative.[102] Emplotment also allows people to make and evaluate ethical choices, by recognizing the relationship between intentions, actions, and consequences. Narrative allows readers and listeners to evaluate the moral implications of their past actions and to embark on new initiatives with a realistic sense of what their outcomes might be. Emplotment also enables people to understand themselves as ethical actors in a world that antedates and outlasts them. Each of the 'reflective instruments' that Ricoeur describes in part four make it possible to imagine how lived experience might extend through different eras and epochs, beyond the limits of an individual lifetime.

Ricoeur's account of emplotment as a process that draws patterns of coherence out of the simple succession of events, that frames and directs ethical decisions, that places historical analysis in dialogue with speculative, imaginative fiction, and that enables self-understanding in relation to an interpreted history that extends beyond the self, provides rich resources for thinking about late medieval sermons and about Langland's creative engagement with them. In essays that develop the argument of *Time and Narrative*, Ricoeur himself considered the sermon as a narrative form. In 'Interpretative Narrative' he proposes that biblical narratives are already engaged in a form of interpretation that the exegete can take up and

---

[100] Ricouer, *Time and Narrative*, 3: 105–9.   [101] Ricoeur, *Time and Narrative*, 3: 116–26.
[102] Ricoeur, 'Narrative Identity', 188–99 in *On Paul Ricoeur: Narrative and Interpretation*, ed. David Wood (London: Routledge, 1991), 195. Ricoeur develops these claims about narrative interpretation and personal identity in *Oneself as Another*, trans. Kathleen Blamey (Chicago: University of Chicago Press, 1992), esp. at 113–39, 140–68.

continue. These narratives can be said to explicate a core 'kerygmatic' statement (from 'kerygma', preaching or proclamation), which functions as the 'single thought', the *res*, or 'gist', that holds their disparate elements together, establishing a relation of 'discordant concordance' between them.[103] The preacher's task, he writes in 'Philosophical Hermeneutics and Biblical Hermeneutics', is not simply to identify and articulate the 'kerygmatic' statement that informs the biblical narrative, but to extend and elaborate the work of emplotment, so that the 'world of the text' continues to unfold before the listener, reshaping the listener's horizon of expectations: 'what is thereby opened up in everyday reality', he writes, 'is another reality, the reality of the *possible*'.[104] Langland, I argue, would surely recognize the narrative dimension of preacherly exegesis, which redescribes the present moment as part of a larger, interpreted plot.

When Langland represents preaching as part of the allegorical action of *Piers Plowman*, he explores the way that emplotment worked in practice. The poem depicts preachers engaged in this dynamic, creative activity, and shows how the narratives they composed reconfigured their listeners' lived experiences in turn. I will argue that this kind of interpretative labour was at the heart of the preacher's vocation for Langland and was central to his own interest in sermons as a narrative poet: through the work of emplotment, preachers could render daily life newly comprehensible and ethical action both urgent and achievable. The best preaching in the poem achieves these effects with dramatic and consequential results. Ricoeur develops his theory of emplotment through an extended engagement with ancient and patristic authors, and with other practitioners of twentieth-century hermeneutic phenomenology, elaborating his argument in abstract, speculative terms. Langland, however, is interested in the situations where emplotment takes place, in the complicated social circumstances where speakers and listeners interact, and in the hierarchies of power and knowledge that structure those interactions.

Ricoeur's account of time and narrative has made occasional but illuminating appearances in recent studies of medieval literature. In her study of the 'heterogeneous temporalities' that could co-exist in the medieval 'now', for example, Carolyn Dinshaw draws on Ricoeur's account of Augustine's distended soul, and the 'extended and dialectical present' that it perceives.[105] More recently, Gillian Adler has used Ricoeur's theory of emplotment to frame her own discussion of the way that Chaucer's narratives reconfigure temporal experience, posing ethical

---

[103] Ricoeur, 'Interpretive Narrative', 181–99 in *Figuring the Sacred: Religion, Narrative, and Imagination*, ed. Mark I. Wallace, trans. David Pellauer (Minneapolis: Fortress Press, 1995).

[104] Ricoeur, 'Philosophical Hermeneutics and Biblical Hermeneutics', 89–101 in *From Text to Action: Essays in Hermeneutics II*, trans. Kathleen Blamey and John B. Thompson (Evanston: Northwestern University Press, 2007), 95–6, 97 (emphasis original).

[105] Carolyn Dinshaw, *How Soon is Now? Medieval Texts, Amateur Readers, and the Queerness of Time* (Durham, NC: Duke University Press, 2012), 7–16 (quotations at 4 and 13 note 45).

questions about the profitable use of time.[106] In a study I return to in the coda of this book, Raschko cites Ricoeur to show how the four daughters of God, who debate Christ's atonement in the sixth vision of *Piers Plowman*, are engaged in a collective effort to integrate disparate elements into a single narrative, performing the work of emplotment.[107] Studies like these have begun to answer calls for a renewed and extended engagement with Ricoeur that have recently emerged in literary theory and cultural studies. In *The Limits of Critique*, Rita Felski associates the 'mood and method' of much twentieth- and twenty-first century criticism with the 'hermeneutics of suspicion', a phrase Ricoeur applied to readings that sought to decode or decipher the text, uncovering latent forms of unspoken or partially acknowledged significance.[108] Felski advocates for a 'post-critical' alternative that would acknowledge the 'coconstitution of texts and readers', attending to the way that texts themselves can move, engage, and act on the readers who interpret them, rather than imagining the reader as a privileged, sceptical interrogator of the text.[109] As she formulates this new, 'post-critical' approach, she seeks to recuperate several important aspects of Ricoeur's hermeneutics, notably his sense that literary texts might 'reconfigure' the way their readers perceive their own experience in generative ways.[110] Thinking with Ricoeur about preaching in *Piers Plowman* suggests that Felski's 'post-critical' approach might have pre-modern antecedents. Langland's poem, as I will argue, is closely engaged with the way that sermons shape and inform their listeners' perception of the present moment, with what Felski might call their capacity 'to recontextualise what we know and to reorient and refresh perception'.[111]

* * *

In the chapters that follow, I present five studies of preaching and narrative in *Piers Plowman*, and a brief, final coda. Each is concerned with a particular context or occasion for preaching as represented in the poem, and each reveals new aspects of Langland's thought about the way that sermon narratives could reconfigure lived experience. In choosing these passages for analysis, I have sought to address all the scenes in the poem where speakers deliver a sermon or where preaching is a central topic of discussion, alongside passages in the allegorical action where sermons are recalled or where their impact on their listeners can be seen. I do not attempt to address every speech that has been likened to a sermon in the critical literature, however, not least because almost every extended passage in

---

[106] Gillian Adler, *Chaucer and the Ethics of Time* (Cardiff: University of Wales Press, 2022). For discussion of Ricoeur, see 9, 16–21.
[107] Raschko, 'Storytelling at the Gates of Hell: Narrative Epistemology in *Piers Plowman*', *Studies in the Age of Chaucer* 44 (2022): 172.
[108] Rita Felski, *The Limits of Critique* (Chicago: University of Chicago Press, 2015), 1–2, 6. Felski discusses the origins of this phrase and situates it in Ricoeur's thought at 30–2.
[109] Felski, *Limits of Critique*, 154.   [110] Felski, *Limits of Critique*, 17.
[111] Felski, *Limits of Critique*, 181.

the first person has at some point been described in this way. My analysis focusses primarily on the B text, where many of these preaching scenes appear in their most interesting forms, but I also consider C-text revisions that extend and develop the poem's thought about preaching and narrative. I read these scenes from *Piers Plowman* alongside late medieval sermons in Latin and Middle English, texts that theorize the practice of preaching, and records of sermons that were actually delivered, offering new contexts and analogues for passages in *Piers Plowman*, as well as revisiting some well-known parallels for the poem in this literature. These materials show that the poem represents forms of preaching that contemporary audiences would recognize and addresses itself to challenges and complexities that preachers faced themselves. When Langland locates the work of emplotment as an essential component of the preacher's task, he draws on a detailed and wide-ranging knowledge of the preaching culture of his time.

In Chapter 1, I read the coronation scene from the poem's prologue and Conscience's account of Christ's nativity from the seventh vision, two interrelated scenes where preachers identify a turning point in public life and explain its significance in the context of a larger narrative. In Ricoeur's terminology, the coronation and the nativity can each be described as an axial moment, a dateable instant in cosmological time that also marks a break with the past in the phenomenological present and that inaugurates a new set of historical conditions. In these two scenes, Langland shows how preachers interpret these moments for the people who live through them, explaining their significance in narrative terms: in the Prologue, a lunatic, an angel, and a goliard deliver three sermon-like speeches, expressing their hopes and fears for the coming reign, while in the seventh vision Conscience employs the exegetical forms of preaching to explain how Christ will institute and maintain a new law for his people, changing the conditions of salvation. These preachers locate their listeners in an interpreted present that is also part of a shared, public history, establishing a narrative discourse in which the *commune* can express their aspirations for good governance and articulate their mutual responsibilities to one another under a just and merciful law. I also read the angel's speech from the Prologue in the context of Lambeth Palace Library MS 61, where it was copied at the end of a sermon on Thomas Becket by the Oxford theologian Henry Harclay. Harclay's sermon presents an extended historical narrative to show how God has punished English kings for Becket's martyrdom, organizing its own story of good and bad governance around this axial moment, and the angel's speech offers an elliptical reply, considering each new coronation as a potential turning point in England's fortunes.

In Chapter 2, I read the poem's second vision as a study of the way that preaching motivates reforming action. At the start of this vision, Reason preaches to the whole community, redescribing recent storms and plagues as punishments for sin and as signs of the apocalypse, and revealing the strict but comprehensible standard of God's justice in the apparent chaos of recent history. This sermon exemplifies the operations of emplotment as Ricoeur understands them, configuring disparate events from its listeners' direct experience into an interpreted whole and reconfiguring their understanding of the possibilities that confront them in the present time. It provokes the penitential action that unfolds through the subsequent passūs, as the people resolve to go on pilgrimage, motivated by the fear of God's punishments, and by hope for his mercy. Later in the second vision, Piers Plowman offers to lead the people on their pilgrimage, and, as the pilgrimage is recast as agricultural labour on the half-acre, Piers himself becomes a kind of preacher, configuring narratives from the events of his own life to reinforce the lessons of Reason's sermon. For all the ingenuity of his preaching, however, Piers faces hostility from some members of his audience, who no longer understand their lives in the terms that Reason offered them. The ploughman's experience, I argue, shows that, for Langland, the transformative effects of a sermon like Reason's must be sustained through an ongoing effort of narrative interpretation, a demanding, pastoral endeavour that constitutes a lifetime's work. I read the sermons of the second vision alongside sermons by Thomas Brinton and an anonymous Middle English preacher that also interpret storms and plagues as apocalyptic signs. These texts, which offer parallels to Reason's sermon, show how emplotment transforms paralysing terror into galvanizing fear, but they also call for the ongoing interpretative effort in which Piers Plowman is engaged, urging their listeners to seek out new signs of God's judgement in the world around them.

In Chapter 3 I address the poem's critique of corrupt, self-interested preaching through a reading of Study's complaint in the third vision and the feast of Conscience in the fourth. These parts of the poem describe clerics at St Paul's Cross in London who preach on esoteric topics to impress their powerful patrons and then encourage them to debate difficult theological questions after dinner in the halls of great houses; Study compares these preachers to scurrilous entertainers, who also debase their wisdom and wit to indulge the desires of wealthy lords. Study describes the effect of this preaching on the wider community, who lapse into sin and doubt as preachers neglect the work of emplotment. Still more fundamentally, I argue, she suggests that sermons on esoteric subjects erode the capacity for narrative interpretation itself: encouraging an indiscriminate desire for knowledge of all kinds, they make it harder for people to distinguish patterns of significance in the simple succession of events. As she develops her critique, Study also imagines virtuous forms of minstrelsy that might provide a model for the reform of preaching, offering narratives from the Bible and calling for penance and for charity; at the feast of Conscience, where the guests include a gluttonous doctor, known for his ostentatious sermons at St Paul's, Conscience and Patience offer minstrelsy of this kind, culminating in a riddle contest that establishes the priority of love above other forms of knowledge. In these scenes, I argue, Langland discovers that the most elementary operations of emplotment have an ethical dimension: where Ricoeur identifies the capacity to discern and prioritize significant events as a form of practical wisdom, Langland suggests that it arises through patience, study, and love. This chapter also reads contemporary accounts of a dispute between William Taylor and Richard Alkerton, who preached at St Paul's Cross in the early fifteenth century, and who echoed elements of Langland's polemic in their sermons.

In Chapter 4, I consider the resources that sermons provide to think about personal identity in *Piers Plowman*. I read a series of scenes in the poem where the dreamer's interlocutors encourage him to consider his life as an interpreted whole: his encounter with Holy Church in the first vision; his double encounter with Scripture, before and during the first inner dream; his meeting with Ymaginatif after the inner dream concludes; and his meeting with Elde and Kynde in the final passus. Holy Church and Scripture deliver sermons themselves in these scenes, but all of these interlocutors urge the dreamer to understand his present moment in relation to the preaching and teaching that he has heard over the course of his life, to make sense of his life story using the discursive resources that preaching provides. In *Oneself as Another*, Ricoeur shows how narrative interpretation, applied to the events of a human life, enables people to make ethical commitments that express their 'self-constancy' over time. Langland, too, I argue, understands the interpreted life to be structured around promises: the dreamer's interlocutors remind him of his baptismal vows, and encourage him to configure a narrative of his life around them, a strategy that can also be found in surviving sermon texts. These scenes also show how clerical instruction becomes part of 'kynde' experience in the poem, as the dreamer recovers the lessons of preaching from his own memory and employs the techniques of preaching to interpret his life: Langland reveals that the most dissolute experience can be recuperated as a source of exemplary instruction, and the most demanding doctrine can be balanced against the consolations of early, catechetical teaching, when considered as part of a narrative. This chapter also considers the links between narrated self-understanding and the composition of poetry, a question that arises when Will defends his 'makynges' to Ymaginatif and when John But presents his own account of the dreamer's biography in a posthumous conclusion to the A text.

In Chapter 5, I turn to the dreamer's encounter with Anima, which culminates in the second inner dream and the vision of the Tree of Charity. Anima encounters the dreamer at a moment of personal crisis, and helps him to recover a sense of his own identity, encouraging him first to narrate the story of his own life, and then to understand his biography in the larger context of salvation history. In this part of the poem, the personal and eschatological narratives considered in previous chapters are synthesized and integrated in new ways. Anima's speech is characterized by the recurrent use of preacherly *distinctiones* and of *figurae* that serve as a visual guide to the relationships between them, and it shows how these exegetical forms can provide a stimulus for emplotment, demanding and facilitating narrative interpretation. At the Tree of Charity itself, the poem shows how historical time unfolds in newly comprehensible ways from exegetical structures like these, as Piers Plowman construes the tree as a schematic *figura*, but the dreamer's request to eat the fruit of charity leads to a re-enactment of the Fall. I read this scene alongside a closely analogous allegorical episode from the prologue to Robert of Gretham's sermon collection, the *Mirour des Évangiles*, where fruit falling from a tree figures the effects of preacherly exegesis. The speech of Anima also contains the poem's only sustained depiction of non-Christian preaching: a story about the sermons of the Prophet Mohammed. Anima considers different examples from the history of Christian preaching and evangelism that might serve to counter Mohammed's sermons, drawing on a narrative of the past to offer radical, experimental prescriptions for the present and future. Here, as the dreamer's own experience is integrated by stages into the overarching narrative of Christian history, Anima models another way of thinking with narrative, as a source of alternative possibilities.

The coda to this book considers the poem's sixth vision, which describes the crucifixion of Christ and the harrowing of hell. This vision of the poem combines many different elements that were familiar from sermons, as well as from other literary contexts, notably the image of Christ as a jousting knight and the debate between the four daughters of God. Yet, it also describes a moment in time when Christian preaching as Langland's contemporaries practiced it was not yet possible, when the central narrative to which sermons gave expression was still taking shape. In his triumphant speech at the gates of hell, I argue, Christ himself performs an act of emplotment that explains the narrative significance of the atonement, and establishes, as though for the first time, the narrative that the poem's preachers strive to make visible in the daily experience of their listeners.

1
Preaching on the Coronation
The Prologue and the Sermon of Conscience

In this chapter I consider two historical turning points in the action of *Piers Plowman* and the preaching voices that seek to interpret them. The first is the appearance of a king in the poem's Prologue, a scene that has long been identified with the coronation of Richard II, and which, in the B text, prompts preacherly interventions from a lunatic, an angel, and a goliard. The second is the incarnation of Christ, imagined in different ways in the fifth and sixth visions of the poem and then explained in a sermon by Conscience in the seventh. Langland and his contemporaries were accustomed to thinking about these events together: in Richard's coronation ceremony, the king's arrival was imagined as a Christ-like *adventus*, while the liturgy of Advent figured the coming of Christ as the arrival of a new king. The political ceremony and the liturgical feast were both occasions for preaching. They prompted sermons that sought to define the ideals of good kingship, looking to past precedents and imagining their future application. These were sermons that sought to locate the *adventus* of a new king as a turning point in the life of the community and to explain its implications in narrative terms. When *Piers Plowman* dramatizes the coronation and the incarnation, it also considers the role of preachers who must translate and interpret these events for the people who live through them; the work of emplotment is required to make the significance of these moments visible. These two parts of the poem show that a transformation in the conditions of history, brought about by a new king or by Christ himself, must be followed by a transformation in the people's understanding, brought about by preaching.

In the fourth part of *Time and Narrative*, Ricoeur describes the incarnation of Christ and the coronation of a new king as two examples of an 'axial moment', an historical turning point that inaugurates a new era or a new set of historical conditions. Represented on a calendar, the axial moment provides a 'zero point' for the calculation of other dates and times: the statutes for the reign of Richard II number the years since his coronation, the *anni Ricardi*, as well as the *anni Domini* on the Gregorian calendar, for example. For Ricoeur, as we saw in the Introduction, the axial moment allows the calendar to function as a 'reflective instrument' that connects the phenomenological time of human perception to cosmological time that arises from motion in the physical world. An axial moment occurs at a particular instant in the regular succession of days and years, but its significance arises as a moment in human experience, a present that constitutes a break from the past and creates new possibilities for the future.[1] To understand an axial moment, then, is to think about both orders of time together. With reference to an axial moment, moreover, it is possible to imagine how the experience of past, present, and future might map onto measurable dates and intervals at other times. For Ricoeur, the axial moment itself becomes thinkable through the mediation of narrative. To recognize the significance of a moment like this requires an act of emplotment that confers the status of a narrative event on a particular point of historical change. Once an axial moment is established, moreover, it enables the production of new narratives that give shape to collective experience, allowing individuals to understand their own lives in relation to the story of their community. It is in this intersubjective time, which Ricoeur calls 'properly historical time', that political life takes place and communities act on their obligations to one another.[2] As I will argue in this chapter, the preachers of the Prologue and Conscience in the poem's seventh vision are concerned with historical turning points of precisely this kind, with the narratives that make them visible, and with the stories that can be told in the shared, historical time that unfolds around them.

Many readers of *Piers Plowman* have understood the coronation scene as an early effort to formulate a common or public voice in the poem. Studies by Emily Steiner and Matthew Giancarlo, for example, have shown how the poem experiments with contemporary parliamentary forms for the expression of common assent when characters speak on behalf of the *commune* in this scene.[3] The sermon of Conscience, too, elaborates a discourse for the *commune* to speak about their mutual obligations under the new law: while it begins as a private response to the dreamer, it ends as an address to the larger community, at a moment when the institutions of church and state are refashioned and social bonds are reaffirmed. Langland shows that preachers have a crucial role to play in facilitating this kind of public discourse: marking the king's coronation as an axial moment in the life of the community, they begin to elaborate narratives for the *commune* to speak about their shared past and future.

The poem is also conscious of the political risks and practical difficulties facing preachers who sought to intervene in public life, however. As Fiona Somerset has shown, the preachers of the Prologue have to negotiate different languages and

---

[1] Ricoeur, *Time and Narrative*, 3: 108–9.   [2] Ricoeur, *Time and Narrative*, 3: 99.
[3] Emily Steiner, 'Commonality and Literary Form in the 1370s and 1380s', *New Medieval Literatures* 6 (2003): 199–221; Matthew Giancarlo, *Parliament and Literature in Late Medieval England* (Cambridge: Cambridge University Press, 2007), 179–208. For other formulations of the 'common voice', see also Galloway, 'The Common Voice in Theory and Practice in Late Fourteenth Century England', 243–86 in *Law, Governance, and Justice: New Views on Medieval Constitutionalism*, ed. Richard W. Kaeuper with Paul Dingman and Peter Sposato (Leiden: Brill, 2013). All these studies invoke Middleton's influential essay, 'The Idea of Public Poetry in the Reign of Richard II', *Speculum* 53 (1978): 94–114, which describes an 'ideal of literary eloquence' shared by Langland and many of his contemporaries, where the poet sought to speak with a 'common voice' to serve the 'common good' (94, 95).

registers as they address the king on behalf of the *commune*, fashioning a common voice from a range of interested and exclusionary discourses.[4] In the allegorical drama of the poem, moreover, these three counsellors face an uncertain future, as they wait to see how their narratives of good governance will inform the king's decisions in the reign to come. In the seventh vision, meanwhile, Conscience will see his account of Christ's new law co-opted and exploited by a tyrannical king, who uses it to justify the exercise of power in accordance with his own will. Here, as David Aers has recently argued, the hopeful discourse of his sermon becomes entangled in the compromised discursive realities of the late medieval present day.[5] Public, political preaching often had to negotiate difficulties like this and, while preachers expressed confidence in their own capacity to guide and direct royal government, Langland's poem treats these claims with scepticism. Langland's ambivalence about this kind of public preaching has implications for his own project, in turn. *Piers Plowman*, too, confronts the risks of making a discursive intervention in public life and the difficulties of speaking in a common voice.[6] As he acknowledges the difficulties of establishing a public discourse in his own moment, Langland allows us to see Ricoeur's account of an intersubjective, 'historical time', mediated by narrative, in a more complex way.

Stephen Barney and Sarah Wood have described the close affinities between the Prologue coronation scene and the sermon of Conscience as a product of the sequence in which the B text of *Piers Plowman* was composed. According to a theory first advanced by Aubrey Gwynn and more recently endorsed by Ralph Hanna, Langland began the B text as a continuation from the end of A before returning to the start of A to revise his existing material; as Barney and Wood observe, this means that the sermon of Conscience in B.19 would have been fresh in the poet's mind when he added the coronation scene to the Prologue.[7] Lawrence Warner, however, has argued for an alternative history of the B text, which holds that B was released for copying much later than previously thought and was contaminated at an early stage in its circulation with C-text material. Warner argues that passūs 19–20 were not part of Langland's original B text at all,

---

[4] Somerset, '"Al þe comonys with o voys atonys": Multilingual Latin and Vernacular Voice in *Piers Plowman*', *YLS* 19 (2005): 107–36.

[5] Aers, *Beyond Reformation? An Essay on William Langland's Piers Plowman and the End of Constantinian Christianity* (Notre Dame: University of Notre Dame Press, 2015).

[6] Indeed, readers have sometimes asked whether these coronation scenes might constitute the poem's own contribution to the 'mirrors for princes' tradition. See, for example, Anna Baldwin, 'The Historical Context', 67–86 in *A Companion*, ed. Alford; and Maura Nolan, 'The Fortunes of *Piers Plowman* and its Readers', *YLS* 20 (2006): esp. 2–3.

[7] Stephen A. Barney, *The Penn Commentary on Piers Plowman, vol. 5: C Passūs 20–22; B Passūs 18–20* (Philadelphia: University of Pennsylvania Press, 2006), 102. Sarah Wood, *Conscience and the Composition of Piers Plowman* (Oxford: Oxford University Press, 2012), 82–3. For this account of the composition of B, see A. Gwynn, 'The Date of the B-Text of *Piers Plowman*', *Review of English Studies* 19 (1943): 1–24; Hanna, *Pursuing History: Middle English Manuscripts and their Texts* (Stanford, CA: Stanford University Press, 1996), 233–4.

but were originally composed for C, and appended to the ancestor of all surviving B-text manuscripts by a scribe.[8] On this account, the B-text Prologue and the sermon of Conscience were never part of the same authorial version of the poem, so the affinities between them should be understood as Langland's reconsideration of the same issues across different iterations of the text. While the present chapter does not make an argument about the sequence of the poem's composition, I do treat the position of these episodes at the beginning and end of the B text as we have it (Warner's 'received B') as significant. For readers who encountered the poem in this version, these scenes frame a large swathe of intervening action, whether Langland composed them close together or years apart. After many passūs, the poem returns to the contemporary moment with which it began, and to the role it first imagined for preachers, and re-evaluates the task of elaborating narratives for the *commune* as a whole.

This chapter does take up another aspect of the poem's textual history, however. Sometime in the fifteenth century, the angel's speech from the Prologue to *Piers Plowman* was copied onto the last page of London, Lambeth Palace, MS 61, at the end of a sermon on the feast of Thomas Becket by the fourteenth-century theologian Henry Harclay. In this manuscript context, an excerpt from *Piers Plowman* appears alongside the text of a real medieval sermon, and an allegorical act of preaching from Langland's poem comments on a text that was delivered from the pulpit. Harclay's sermon offers an extended narrative of English political history, as he argues that successive English kings have been punished for Thomas Becket's martyrdom and warns the present king not to persecute the church like his predecessors. This sermon, that is, identifies Thomas's martyrdom as an axial moment in the life of the realm, and elaborates narratives to explain its significance, and its larger implications for policy in the present time. In this context, I will argue, the angel's speech from *Piers Plowman* offers an elliptical echo of Harclay's address to the king, mapping out the precedents and opportunities for just rule in the reign still to come.

'To counseillen þe Kyng and þe Commune saue'

After his initial account of the field of folk in the B-text Prologue, a vision of contemporary society in all its complexity and diversity, the dreamer witnesses two allegorical scenes where the church and the state are constituted as though for the first time: the election of a new pope, where 'Cardinals at court' confer the

---

[8] Warner, *The Lost History of Piers Plowman: The Earliest Transmission of Langland's Work* (Philadelphia: University of Pennsylvania Press, 2011). Warner first developed his case about the final passūs in 'The Ur-B *Piers Plowman* and the Earliest Production of C and B', *YLS* 16 (2002): 3–39; and 'The Ending, and End, of *Piers Plowman* B: The C-Version Origins of the Final Two Passus', *Medium Ævum* 76 (2007): 225–50.

powers once granted to St Peter on one of their own number (B.Prol.107), and the coronation of a new king. The poem stages an allegorical coronation ceremony that explains how the different estates first came into being and allows them to reaffirm their mutual obligations under the law. The king is led in by 'Kny3thod' and 'made...to regne' by the 'communes'; Kynde Wit establishes the clergy, whose role is 'to counseillen [counsel] þe Kyng and þe Commune saue [protect]'; the king, the clergy, and Knighthood together determine that 'þe commune' should provide food for everyone, using the 'craftes' that Kynde Wit has given them; finally, representatives from each estate agree the principles of 'lawe and leaute [loyalty, justice, fidelity]' that will regulate their social lives, enabling 'ech lif to knowe his owene' (B.Prol.112–22).[9]

Once the coronation is complete, three preachers arrive to explain its significance. The lunatic, angel, and goliard address the king in the presence of the *commune*, counselling him for the common good in the role that Kynde Wit has just ordained for clerics. In their sermon-like speeches, they reveal the significance of this event as a turning point in the life of the realm, establishing it as an axial moment, and they tell new narratives in the public history that coheres around it, looking back to past precedents and imagining how 'lawe and leaute' might be instantiated in the reign to come. These speeches exemplify a common characteristic of late medieval 'public poetry', as Anne Middleton describes it, where an address to the king creates 'an occasion for gathering and formulating what is on the common mind'.[10] Yet, they also serve another political purpose, establishing the discursive context where the king and the *commune* can understand their mutual obligations in what Ricoeur would call the intersubjective 'third time' of public life. If the coronation scene formulates political relationships in theory, these three conflicting, competing sermons provide the resources to imagine them in practice, by interpolating them into a larger narrative.

The speeches of the lunatic, the angel, and the goliard have an important place in the history of scholarship on *Piers Plowman* and medieval preaching as I noted in the Introduction. In his article for the *Modern Language Review*, and in both of his subsequent books, G. R. Owst identified the angel as a figure for Thomas Brinton, preaching at the convocation of clergy before the Good Parliament of 1376, and the goliard as Peter de la Mare, who echoed Brinton's calls for reform in his role as speaker for the commons.[11] With this heroic portrait of Brinton, Owst argued, Langland revealed his deep respect for the 'social message' of the English pulpit, and signalled his intention to echo it in *Piers Plowman*.[12] Owst's

---

[9] On the meanings and origins of 'leaute', see *C Text*, ed. Pearsall, 51–2; Galloway, *Penn Commentary*, 1: 123–5.
[10] Middleton, 'Public Poetry', 107.
[11] Owst, 'The "Angel" and the "Goliardeys",' 270–9; Owst, *Preaching in Medieval England*, 18–19; Owst, *Literature and Pulpit*, 548–93.
[12] Owst, *Literature and Pulpit*, 549.

interpretation of this scene was challenged first by Cyril Brett and then later by E. Talbot Donaldson on the grounds that, while de la Mare agreed with Brinton, the angel and the goliard are apparently at odds.[13] Owst's reading is open to a more fundamental challenge than this, however, because it rests entirely on his perception of a shared social attitude and polemical tone in the speech and the sermon, rather than on any precise correspondences between the two. Brinton's convocation sermon certainly includes some striking parallels with other parts of *Piers Plowman*: as Dorothy L. Owen was the first to note, and as Owst goes on to observe, both Langland and Brinton tell the story of the rodent parliament, where the mice propose to hang a bell on the cat that has been hunting them.[14] As we will see in Chapter 2, moreover, Brinton also preaches on the maxim that forms the text of Piers's pardon in the second vision, 'Bene fac et bene habe [Do well and have well]', a correspondence that Owst does not mention.[15] Yet neither parallel offers grounds to identify the angel in the Prologue with Brinton himself, or to read his speech as a summary of the convocation sermon as a whole.

In his own reading of the Prologue, Donaldson established a different set of topical reference points for this scene. Taking up a hypothesis first advanced by J. A. W. Bennett, Donaldson showed that the coronation scene and the speeches that follow it contain a series of allusions to the coronation of Richard II in 1377.[16] When they speak about the duties and obligations of kingship, the lunatic, the angel, and the goliard echo the language of the coronation service, as recorded in the *Liber Regalis* (the coronation *ordo*), in chronicle accounts by Thomas Walsingham and the *Anonimalle* chronicler, and in a record of the ceremony entered in the court rolls on the orders of John of Gaunt.[17] The shout of common

---

[13] Cyril Brett, 'Notes on Old and Middle English', *Modern Language Review* 22 (1927): 261–2, and E. Talbot Donaldson, *Piers Plowman: The C-text and its Poet* (New Haven: Yale University Press, 1949, repr. London: Cass, 1966), 112–15.

[14] Owst, 'The "Angel" and the "Goliardeys",' 276, and see also Dorothy L. Owen, *Piers Plowman: A Comparison with Some Earlier and Contemporary French Allegories* (London: Hodder & Stoughton, 1912), 86–7. While most scholars have treated Brinton's sermon as a potential source for Langland's poem, Hanna has considered the possibility that Brinton was responding to Langland: Hanna, *London Literature, 1300–1380* (Cambridge: Cambridge University Press, 2005), 251–2. On the history of the rodent parliament fable, and its frequent appearance in sermons and compendia for preachers, see Galloway, *Penn Commentary*, 1: 133–4; Elizaveta Strakhov, '"But who will bell the cat?": Deschamps, Brinton, Langland, and the Hundred Years' War', *YLS* 30 (2016): 253–76; and Strakhov, 'Political Animals: Form and the Animal Fable in Langland's Rodent Parliament and Chaucer's *Nun's Priest's Tale*', *YLS* 32 (2018): 289–313.

[15] Pearsall, 'G. R. Owst', notes that Owst knew the poem primarily from Skeat's student edition of the B text *visio*, and that he rarely quotes from the later *passūs* (20, n. 20). The surprising omission of 'Bene fac et bene habe' from his discussion of Brinton's convocation sermon might suggest that he was less familiar with the later parts of the *visio*, too.

[16] Donaldson, *Piers Plowman*, 116–18. J. A. W. Bennett had suggested that the king's arrival might allude to Richard's coronation among other possibilities; 'The Date of the B-text of *Piers Plowman*', *Medium Ævum* 12 (1943): 57.

[17] For the coronation *ordo* and the court rolls, see *English Coronation Records*, ed. and trans. by Leopold G. Wickham Legg (Westminster: Constable, 1901), 81–112, 112–30 (*Liber Regalis*); 131–50, 150–68 ('court of claims rolls'). For the chronicle accounts, see *The St Albans Chronicle: The Chronica*

assent during the coronation service informs the dreamer's opening claim that the king reigns through the 'Might of þe communes' and is dramatized in turn as the 'crye' of the 'commune' that concludes this scene (B.Prol.113, 143). The Prologue also alludes to the pageantry that surrounded Richard's coronation: the angel who addresses the king resembles the mechanical 'angelus aureus [golden angel]' that greeted Richard when he rode through London on the day before the ceremony, leaning forward from a tower in Cheapside to offer the king a crown.[18] More recent scholarship has tended to endorse the claim that this scene alludes to Richard's coronation. Hanna, for example, links the angel's discussion of *nudum ius* to the moment in the service when the archbishop strips away the king's outer clothes to anoint him with holy oil, a ceremony that the reminds the king of his human vulnerability even as it invests him with political power.[19] Andrew Galloway cautions that critical attention to the topical references in this scene has sometimes distracted readers from the theoretical account of kingship and governance that it offers.[20] Yet, it seems significant that the poem develops its theoretical claims in part as a response to events that its readers could identify. The elaboration of public, historical narratives begins by marking a turning point in contemporary history. This is also a moment when theory is tested in practice: the *commune* recalls the principles of 'lawe and leaute', and waits to see how the new king will enact them.

Preaching was an essential part of the coronation ceremony and of the pageantry that surrounded it; in Westminster, and again in the streets of London, senior churchmen explained the significance of this event in the public life of the realm. During the service, Archbishop Simon Sudbury delivered a sermon on the mutual obligations of the king and the *commune*. As Walsingham reports, 'episcopus sermonem fecit de materia regis et regni ad populum, qualiter rex se haberet in populo, et in quibus populus sibi debuit obedire [the bishop preached a sermon to the people on the subject of the king and the kingdom, how the king should behave among the people, and in what respects the people should

---

Maiora of Thomas Walsingham, ed. and trans. John Taylor, Wendy R. Childs, and Leslie Watkiss, 2 vols (Oxford: Oxford University Press, 2003–11), 1: 136–56, 137–57; and *The Anonimalle Chronicle, 1333–1381*, ed. V. H. Galbraith (Manchester: Manchester University Press, 1927, repr. 1970), 107–15.

[18] Donaldson, *Piers Plowman*, 118. For contemporary accounts of Richard's coronation riding and the golden angel in Cheapside, see Walsingham, *St Albans Chronicle*, ed. and trans. Taylor, Childs, and Watkiss, 1: 140, 141; *Anonimalle Chronicle*, ed. Galbraith, 107–8. The *Anonimalle* chronicler's account of Richard's coronation entry is translated as an appendix to Richard Maidstone, *Concordia (The Reconciliation of Richard II with London)*, ed. David R. Carlson, trans. A. G. Rigg (Kalamazoo, MI: Medieval Institute Publications, 2003). E. R. Truitt compares the 'angelus aureus' of Richard's coronation to a similar spectacle that marked the entry of Queen Isabel of Bavaria into Paris, where a man dressed as an angel was lowered by machinery from the towers of Notre Dame to place a crown on the queen's head: *Medieval Robots: Mechanism, Magic, Nature, and Art* (Philadelphia: University of Pennsylvania Press, 2015), 136–7.

[19] Hanna, *London Literature*, 248–9. As Hanna acknowledges, these correspondences were first observed by Bennett, 'Date of the B-text', 57.

[20] Galloway, *Penn Commentary*, 1: 118–19. Galloway writes, 'This section in *Piers Plowman* is political and social theory rather than topical reportage.'

obey him]'.[21] Thomas Brinton was also involved: on the day after the coronation, he preached to a large assembly of lords, prelates, and commoners who took part in a procession through the city. Preaching *ad populum* to the *commune* as a whole, Brinton urged the three estates to set aside dissent and discord, and to emulate the virtues of their new king, who was still 'puero et innocenti [a boy and an innocent]'.[22] As Walsingham's account suggests, the preacher's role in these events was to explain the significance of the coronation for the king and the *commune* in their own historical moment, to translate the ancient language of the *ordo* into a call for good governance and social cohesion in the present time. The angel's speech may not echo Brinton's convocation sermon as Owst once thought, but, along with speeches of the lunatic and the goliard, it does resemble the kind of preaching that took place at the coronation, addressing the king and the *commune* at this transitional moment, reminding them of their mutual obligations, and urging reform in their social and spiritual lives.[23]

Coronation preaching identified an axial moment in the political life of the realm, but it also linked this turning point to other events in the larger narrative of Christian history, comparing the *adventus* of the new king with the twofold advent of Christ. As Gordon Kipling has shown, the language and conventions of the Roman triumph informed the earliest development of the Advent liturgy, and civic and ecclesiastical authorities drew on this liturgy in turn to celebrate the investiture of new kings in the Middle Ages.[24] In patristic and medieval exegesis, moreover, Christ's first advent at his incarnation was understood to foreshadow his second advent at the Last Judgement and to prefigure his coming to individuals, as an advent in the soul.[25] Medieval pageant organizers developed these associations, too, so that the king's coronation would recall the gospel narrative while also looking forward to the apocalypse. If Richard's royal entry

---

[21] Walsingham, *St Albans Chronicle*, ed. and trans. Taylor, Childs, and Watkiss, 1: 142, 143.

[22] Walsingham, *St Albans Chronicle*, ed. and trans. Taylor, Childs, and Watkiss, 1: 154, 155. The text of Brinton's procession sermon has not been identified conclusively. Devlin argued that sermon 44 in the Harley manuscript was the best match for Walsingham's description, but Wenzel casts doubt on this identification, noting that the sermon treats only two of the four points in Walsingham's summary, and that its complaint about poor attendance at processions seems hard to reconcile with Walsingham's claim that this event was attended by 'plebis multitudine copiosa'. Brinton, *Sermones*, ed. Devlin, 1: xxvii–xxviii; Wenzel, *Latin Sermon Collections*, 46, n. 6. Sermon 44 is edited by Devlin, 1: 194-200, and translated by Jeanne Krochalis and Edward Peters in *The World of Piers Plowman* (Philadelphia: University of Pennsylvania Press, 1982), 115–24.

[23] Criticism since Owst has sometimes misrepresented his argument about the angel's speech, claiming that he identified it with Brinton's procession sermon in 1377, and not with his convocation sermon in 1376. This mistake perhaps originates in an unconscious effort to synthesize Owst's reading with Donaldson's. See *Piers Plowman: The Prologue and Passus I–VII of the B text*, ed. J. A. W. Bennett (Oxford: Clarendon Press, 1972), 99; Krochalis and Peters, *The World of Piers Plowman*, 112–13; Somerset, 'Multilingual Latin and Vernacular Voice', 119.

[24] Gordon Kipling, *Enter the King: Theatre, Liturgy, and Ritual in the Medieval Civic Triumph* (Oxford: Clarendon, 1998), 21–3.

[25] Kipling, *Enter the King*, 25–6.

was designed to recall the incarnation of Christ, it also prefigured Christ's coming in judgement, with the city recast as the earthly Jerusalem of the gospels and the New Jerusalem of the apocalypse. The angel of the goldsmiths' pageant resembles the angels who herald the incarnation, and the angels who herald the second coming.[26] The coronation ceremony itself invoked the advent of Christ in the soul, as the archbishop sang the antiphon 'Veni Creator Spiritus [Come creator spirit]'. The chroniclers do not record whether Sudbury or Brinton developed these connections in their preaching for the coronation, but the clerical speakers in the Prologue to *Piers Plowman* certainly allude to them. The significance of the coronation is established with reference to other events in salvation history, a narrative relationship reinforced by typological connections.

The lunatic, the angel, and the goliard contribute to an evolving, multivocal act of emplotment in the Prologue to *Piers Plowman* as they each describe the king's coronation as part of a longer history. These are brief, elliptical speeches, allegorical representations of the extended sermons that were actually delivered at the coronation.[27] Yet individually and in combination they perform the kinds of configuration that Ricoeur associates with *mimesis*², drawing patterns of coherence out of the simple succession of events and construing a range of choices and actions as part of an interpreted whole. Through their successive interventions, these three preachers mark the coronation as an axial moment and elaborate a narrative discourse around it, looking back to past precedents and imagining future possibilities. At the same time, however, the poem registers tensions between these figures. Speaking from different postures and in different languages, they reveal the complex and sometimes contentious situation of preaching in Langland's contemporary moment.

The lunatic is the first to speak after the coronation and the first to locate this event in a larger narrative. In his short speech, he commends the king to Christ, and asks for blessings on his rule:

---

[26] Scott Lightsey has argued that the goldsmiths exploited these typological connections for their own ends, transforming the city into a New Jerusalem in a display of their own skill and ingenuity: *Manmade Marvels in Medieval Culture and Literature* (Basingstoke: Palgrave Macmillan, 2007), 43–4.

[27] Owst, who read the angel's speech as a precis of Brinton's convocation sermon, described these lines as a *recapitulacio in metro* of the longer text, a technique employed by the Carmelite John Haynton in an academic sermon, delivered in 1432, which begins and ends with a summary of its argument, presented in hexameter lines ('The "Angel" and the "Goliardeys",' 273, n. 6, citing Haynton's sermon from London, British Library, Harley MS 5398; Owst identifies Haynton as the author of this sermon in *Preaching in Medieval England*, 260–6). A similar use of Latin hexameter can be found in a Middle English sermon by Hugh Legat, where each principal part concludes with verses that summarize its subdivisions: *Three Middle English Sermons from the Worcester Chapter Manuscript F.10*, ed. D. M. Grisdale (Kendal: Wilson, 1939), 1–21. In *Latin Sermon Collections*, Wenzel discusses Haynton's sermon as an example of Carmelite preaching (292), and notes that Haynton and Legat made similar use of Latin verses to summarize their arguments (153, n. 10). Here then, *Piers Plowman* adopts a form that suggests a condensed report of a longer sermon, the distillation of a more elaborate narrative.

'Crist kepe þee, sire Kyng, and þi kyngryche,	*protect; kingdom*
And lene þee lede þi lond so Leaute þee louye,	*grant; govern; may love you*
And for þi riȝtful rulyng be rewarded in heuene!'	*(may you) be*
	(B.Prol.125–7)

The lunatic is an ambivalent figure: he adopts a deferential posture, 'knelynge to þe Kyng' (B.Prol.124), but addresses him in familiar terms, using the informal 'þee' form.[28] He speaks 'clergially' but without any clear institutional authorization. The next figures to be identified as lunatics in the poem will be the 'lunatyk lollares and lepares aboute' who are named in Truth's pardon in the C text (C.9.107, 137), charismatic figures who 'preche nauht [do not preach]', but who serve, even so, as 'mesagers' from God (C.9.112, 136). In his three-line intervention after the coronation ceremony, the lunatic calls on Christ to prolong the king's life and extend his rightful rule, and then to reward him for that rule in heaven, in language that echoes the archbishop's blessing from Richard's coronation service: 'Presta ei prolixitatem uite per tempora ut in diebus eius oriatur iustitia; a te robustum teneat regiminis solium, et eum iocunditate et iustitia eterno glorietur in regno [Give him a long life that during his time justice may grow; with your help may be keep the seat of government strong, and be glorified by you in your eternal kingdom with joy and justice]'.[29] This short speech establishes a narrative framework that the subsequent speakers will elaborate. The lunatic identifies the coronation as a turning point in the life of the realm and imagines the forms of 'riȝtful rulyng' that might follow from it, anticipating the reign to come. He also invokes a larger eschatological context, alluding to the incarnate Christ as a model for kingship, and to the final judgement that awaits the king at the apocalypse. Framed as a prayer, by a 'clergial' speaker whose clerical status is hard to determine, this narrative enters the poem in a precarious, uncertain way.

The angel, who appears next, speaks in an authoritative register from an authoritative position, descending from 'þe eyr on heiȝ [the air on high]' to address the king 'in Latyn' (B.Prol.128–9). He delivers seven hexameter lines that both complement and complicate the lunatic's act of emplotment, marking the significance of the coronation and mapping out its implications for the future:

'"Sum Rex, sum Princeps"; neutrum fortasse deinceps!
O qui iura regis Christi specialia regis,
Hoc quod agas Melius—iustus es, esto pius!
Nudum ius a te vestiri vult pietate.

---

[28] See David Burnley, 'Langland's Clergial Lunatic', 31–8 in *Langland, the Mystics and the Medieval English Religious Tradition: Essays in Honour of S. S. Hussey*, ed. Helen Phillips (Cambridge: Brewer, 1990); Somerset, 'Multilingual Latin and Vernacular Voice', 119; Galloway, *Penn Commentary*, 1: 122–3.

[29] Walsingham, *St Albans Chronicle*, ed. and trans. Taylor, Childs, and Watkiss, 1: 142, 143.

> *Qualia vis metere, talia grana sere:*
> *Si ius nudatur, nudo de iure metatur;*
> *Si seritur pietas, de pietate metas.'.*
>
> (B.Prol.132–8)

["I am king, I am ruler": perhaps you will be neither hereafter. O you who rule by the laws of Christ the king, so that you may do this better, as you are just, so be merciful! Naked law needs to be clothed by you with mercy. Sow the sort of grain that you wish to reap. If you strip the law bare, then may naked law be used on you; if mercy is shown, then may the same be measured out to you.][30]

Like the lunatic, the angel echoes the language of the coronation service: the injunction to temper justice with mercy, in emulation and anticipation of God's own judgement, resembles Richard's own promise that he 'iudicium rectum inter uirum et uirum faceret, et precipue misericordiam obseruaret, sicut suam indulgeat misericordiam clemens et misericors Deus [would judge fairly between one man and another, and would above all show mercy, just as the compassionate and merciful God granted His mercy to him]'.[31] The angel also elaborates on the lunatic's act of emplotment as he imagines how the king might temper *ius* with *pietas* as part of the exercise of 'riȝtful' rule. As he speaks about the coronation, the angel looks back to the incarnation of Christ and forward to the last judgement, establishing these events in a typological relationship even as he links them together as episodes in a single narrative. The incarnate Christ who, as *rex Christus*, provides a model for the kings who follow him, also stands as the ultimate arbiter of their rule on judgement day. The angel himself is present at all these events, announcing the incarnation, heralding the apocalypse and, as the 'angelus aureus' of the goldsmith's pageant, proffering his crown to the king.

The third speaker, the goliard, offers an argument from the etymology of the king's new title that extends this narrative in significant ways: '*Dum "rex" a "regere" dicatur nomen habere,/ Nomen habet sine re nisi studet iura tenere* [Inasmuch as a king has his name from (the fact of) being a ruler, he possesses the name (alone) without the reality unless he is zealous in maintaining the laws]' (B.Pr.141–2). Will describes the goliard as a 'gloton of wordes', suggesting a deep if worldly involvement in intellectual discourse (B.Prol.139). He assumes a contentious posture when he first appears ('Thanne greued hym a goliardeis'), which might imply that he speaks from a legal or academic milieu, as Somerset argues.[32]

---

[30] I use Somerset's translation of these lines, presented with commentary in 'Multilingual Latin and Vernacular Voice', 118, n. 26. Schmidt's translation renders 'pius' as 'godly', which obscures the important opposition between justice and mercy that is introduced in these lines. For a discussion of the issues involved in this translation, see Jill Mann, 'Some Observations on Structural Annotation', *YLS* 25 (2011): 5–6.

[31] Walsingham, *St Albans Chronicle*, ed. and trans. Taylor, Childs, and Watkiss, 1: 142, 143.

[32] Somerset, 'Multilingual Latin and Vernacular Voice', 120–1.

Like the lunatic and the angel before him, the goliard is concerned with how the king will rule in the reign to come, enacting the principles of justice that have been reaffirmed at his coronation. In this sense, his brief interjection projects a narrative into the intersubjective, public time elaborated by the previous speakers. As he offers this argument from etymology, however, the goliard also invokes the kinds of narrative that often unfold in sermons, where the preacher would explicate the words of a short, authoritative text, by tracing their derivation, concatenating them with other texts on the same topic, and showing them instantiated in historical examples. Although the goliard only hints at this kind of exegetical narrative, his text offers suggestive clues as to how it might unfold.

The goliard's argument from the etymology of *rex* had its own long history of citation and application. Patristic exegetes employed it to distinguish rightful rule from tyranny and to associate good governance with the rule of law. In *De civitate Dei*, for example, Augustine notes that *rex* derives from *regere*, a term for just rule, and not from *regnare*, which implies arbitrary domination.[33] In the *Enarrationes in Psalmos*, meanwhile, he argues that the king should govern by a strict moral standard, symbolized by his sceptre, which is like a carpenter's rule, a 'uirga directionis', or 'rod of correction'; through this reading of the sceptre, Augustine recalls the derivation of *rex*, and explains the forms good rule should take.[34] These arguments were rehearsed in medieval advice to princes, codified in manuals of law, and anthologized in resources for preachers; they were also alleged in polemical contexts, where kings were accused of tyranny and misrule.[35] Archbishop Sudbury invoked them at Richard's coronation ceremony: presenting the king with his sceptre, Sudbury called it 'uirgam scilicet regni rectam [the

---

[33] Augustine, *De civitate Dei*, ed. Bernard Domart and Alfons Kalb, 2 vols, CCSL, 47–8 (Turnhout: Brepols, 1955), 1: 142–3 (5.xii). Augustine's account of this etymology may be a response to a passage from Cicero's *De republica* that is now lost; see Cicero, *On the Republic, On the Laws*, trans. Clinton W. Keyes, LCL 213 (Harvard: Harvard University Press, 1928), 162–3, note to 2.xvii.31.

[34] Augustine, *Enarrationes in Psalmos*, ed. Eligius Dekkers and Johannes Fraipont, 3 vols, CCSL 38–40 (Turnhout: Brepols, 1956), 1: 505–6 (44.xvii); translation from *Expositions of the Psalms, 33–50*, ed. John E. Rotelle, trans. Maria Boulding, WSA 3, no. 16 (Hyde Park, NY: New City Press, 2000), 294–5.

[35] For these etymological arguments in advice to princes literature, see Gerald of Wales, *Instruction for a Ruler (De Principis Instructione)*, ed. and trans. Robert Bartlett (Oxford: Clarendon, 2018), 42 (1.i), 188 (1.xvi), 320–2 (1.ix); John of Salisbury, *Policraticus: Of the Frivolities of Courtiers and the Footprints of Philosophers*, trans. Cary J. Nederman (Cambridge: Cambridge University Press, 1990), 191 (8.xvii). For legal contexts, see Henry of Bracton, *De Legibus et consuetudinibus Angliæ (On the Laws and Customs of England)*, ed. George E. Woodbine, trans. Samuel E Thorne, 2 vols (Cambridge, MA: Belknap Press of Harvard University Press, 1968), 2: 304, 305; *Fleta*, ed. and trans. H. G. Richardson and G. O. Sayles, 3 of 4 vols (London: Quaritch, 1955–84), 2: 35, 36 (1.17). Among resources for preachers, the etymology is found in Bromyard, *Summa praedicantium*, 2 vols (Venice: Nicolini, 1586), 2: 303r (R.iiii.5), and Robert of Basevorn, *Forma praedicandi*, in *Artes praedicandi*, ed. Charland, 315 (49). Polemical uses of this etymology are preserved in chronicle accounts. See, for example, Matthew Paris, *Chronica Majora*, ed. Henry Richards Luard, 7 vols (London: Longman, 1872–80; repr. Cambridge: Cambridge University Press, 2012), 5: 339; and *Vita Edwardi Secundi: The Life of Edward II*, ed. and trans. Wendy R. Childs (Oxford: Clarendon Press, 2005), 128–30, 129–31.

proper staff of kingship]', exhorting him to govern himself and rule his people with it.[36]

When the goliard cites this etymology in the Prologue, then, he locates the moment of the king's coronation in a long history of Christian kingship and English law. Yet, the claims of his argument must also await future confirmation. In his own speech to the king, the angel had already suggested that he might not retain the titles he claims for himself: '"Sum Rex, sum Princeps"; neutrum fortasse deinceps!'. The angel, however, is thinking about the instability of life and politics in a fortune-governed world. His opening declaration, '"Sum Rex, sum princeps"' invokes conventional depictions of the wheel of Fortune, as Galloway has noted, where the king declares 'ero rex' as he ascends the wheel, 'sum rex' when he reaches the top, and 'eram rex' as he falls off the other side.[37] The goliard's point, by contrast, is that a king who does not implement the law renders his title meaningless, because his actions contradict the primary sense of *rex*. This is a narrative that follows the changing significance of words rather than the turns of fortune. The goliard, then, cites an etymology that suggests its own proof texts, but that must also await confirmation in the coming reign. This is an exegetical strategy that unfolds in the time of public history and that enriches the narratives that the angel and the lunatic have sketched out with many new instances of exemplary rule.

In this scene, closely identified with the study of preaching in *Piers Plowman* from the first formulation of this topic in twentieth-century criticism, the poem begins to identify the preacher's task with the discursive labour of emplotment. After the formalities of the coronation itself, these three speakers explain the significance of the new king's *adventus* in the context of English law and political history and in the larger historical frame of Christian eschatology. Marking this axial moment in the history of the realm, each new speaker elaborates a public, historical discourse in which the others can participate, expressing their hopes and fears for the future. The final voice in this scene is the voice of the people, as 'gan al þe commune crye [all the commons cried out] in vers of Latyn [. . .] "*Precepta Regis sunt nobis vincula legis!*" [The king's bidding has for us the binding force of law]' (B.Prol.143–5). This cry of the assembled 'commune' is expressed in the language of the coronation *ordo*, where a statement of allegiance follows the king's oath, and precedes the antiphon 'Veni Creator Spiritus'. In the Prologue to *Piers*, however, it takes place after the coronation ceremony, once the meaning of this moment has been interpreted by three clerical speakers, through three successive

---

[36] Walsingham, *St Albans Chronicle*, ed. and trans. Taylor, Childs, and Watkiss, 1: 148, 149. These same qualities might be praised in a king after his death: David D'Avray discusses a funeral sermon for Edward I, which defines good governance as the proper combination of justice and mercy. See D'Avray, *Death and the Prince: Memorial Preaching before 1350* (Oxford: Clarendon, 1994), 71–2, with further discussion at 139–40.

[37] Galloway, *Penn Commentary*, 1: 127.

acts of emplotment. The preachers have identified the coronation as an axial moment, a turning point in the life of the *commune*, a date on the calendar that coincides with an experiential present. Expressing their hopes and fears for the reign to come, they have sketched the outlines of a narrative in which the people can reflect on their social obligations, as actors in a social and eschatological history. When the people assent to the king's rule, they participate in a public discourse, where narratives of good governance, and of the king's obligations to the law of Christ, serve to structure a shared experience of historical time.

Conflicted Voices

Medieval preachers spoke with confidence about their own capacity to direct the government of the realm and to shape a public discourse in which the *commune* might speak about their shared past and future. In a sermon delivered at St Paul's Cathedral on the Third Sunday after Easter in 1375, for example, Brinton considered the preacher's role in directing public policy.[38] This sermon elaborates a narrative of recent history, contrasting the present state of the realm with an earlier time in the reign of Edward III when England could be called the 'regnum regnorum [kingdom of kingdoms]'. Catherine Royer-Hemet has argued that Brinton was trying to revive the people's enthusiasm for their elderly and ailing king in this sermon, recounting his past achievements in the declining years of his rule.[39] Brinton also reads the past as a template for the future, anticipating the restoration of former glories through good government in the years to come. Brinton delivered this sermon to a mixed audience of 'militares' and 'clericales', as his closing address makes clear, and he argues that both groups have a role to play in directing affairs of state.[40] Brinton's *thema* for this sermon was 1 Peter 2:17, 'Regem honorificate [Honour the king]', and in the first division he argues that the king's honour derives from his own good government of the realm ('iusto regimine populi'). Citing the etymology of *rex*, he reminds his listeners that a king who does not govern well does not deserve his title: 'Rex eris si recte viuas et facias. Si non recte facias, non eris rex [You will be king if you live and act correctly; if you do not act correctly, you will not be king]'.[41] In two further *divisiones*, however, he adds that the king also derives honour from the prowess of his 'militares', who fight to defend him, and from the wisdom of 'clericales' who

---

[38] This is one of three sermons delivered 'Apud Sanctum Paulum' according to the rubric in MS Harley 3760. On the date, see Devlin's introduction: Brinton, *Sermones*, ed. Devlin, 1: xxxii.

[39] Catherine Royer-Hemet, *Prédication et Propagande au Temps D'Édouard III Plantagenêt* (Paris: University of the Sorbonne Press, 2014), 125–6.

[40] Brinton, *Sermones*, ed. Devlin, 1: 48.

[41] Brinton, *Sermones*, ed. Devlin, 1: 46. Wood notes the play on *rex* and *regere* in this sermon: *Conscience and the Composition of Piers Plowman*, 85.

offer him counsel: 'honor regis stat in sano consilio et sapiencia clericali, quia regis consiliarii debent...pro commodo republice feruidi [the honour of the king resides in good counsel and in the wisdom of the clergy, for the king's counsellors must be...anxious for the good of the state]'.[42] Brinton's own account of English history in the first part of the sermon, and his exhortations to the king to govern well, can themselves be understood in these terms, as a demonstration of the preacher's role in guiding the practice of government.

Preaching in the early fifteenth century, Robert Rypon argued that the preacher himself might serve as an example of good rule. In an Advent sermon on Matthew 21:5 and Zechariah 9:9, 'Ecce rex tuus venit tibi [Behold your king shall come to you]', Rypon imagines the preacher as an exemplary model for the king. Rypon explains that Christ embodies the essential virtues of kingship, 'iusta potencia, vera sapiencia, et bona clemencia [just power, true wisdom, and good mercy]', and that he displays them in his threefold *adventus*, acting with 'iusta potencia' at the incarnation, coming into the minds of men with 'vera sapiencia', and granting 'bona clemencia' to the faithful at the last judgement.[43] These are the turning points in Christian history that were invoked in the coronation *ordo*, the axial moments to which the preachers of the Prologue refer. Like Brinton and the goliard, Rypon also considers the derivation of *rex* from *regere*, citing the etymology from Robert Grosseteste, but unlike them, he applies it to preachers, who govern themselves and impose a rule on the souls in their care, an application that originates in the work of Gregory the Great.[44] Rypon explains that the preacher should be 'rector spiritualis populi cui predicat et eos docere qualiter animas suas regant [a spiritual rector for the people to whom he preaches, and he should teach them how to rule their own souls]'. He goes on to explain that 'omnes rectores animarum, si populum vobis subiectum recte regitis reges et vocamini et estis [all rectors of souls, if you properly rule the people subjected to you, are both called kings and are kings]'.[45] For Brinton, the preacher participates in the 'riȝtful' rule of the realm as he counsels the king, but for Rypon he models and exemplifies this rule in the way he performs his office, ruling himself and governing others.

---

[42] Brinton, *Sermones*, ed. Devlin, 1: 46.

[43] Rypon, *Selected Sermons*, ed. and trans. Johnson, 1: 50, 51.

[44] Gregory the Great applies the etymology of *rex* to preachers in his *Moralia in Iob*, in a passage that provides an important precedent for Rypon's exegesis here. Gregory explains that preachers are both kings and rulers, in that they govern themselves and the souls in their care: 'Reges sunt quia semetipsos regere sciunt; terrae sunt consules quia terrenas mentes per exhortationis suae consilium ad caelestia pertrahunt [As kings they know how to rule over themselves; as rulers of the world they lead worldly minds to heaven by their advice and exhortations]' (4.xxix.56). Gregory the Great, *Moralia in Iob*, ed. Marc Adriaen, 3 vols, CCSL 143–143B (Turnhout: Brepols, 1979–85), 1: 201; translation from Gregory the Great, *Moral Reflections on the Book of Job*, trans. Brian Kerns, 6 vols (Collegeville, MN: Cistercian Publications, 2014–22), 1: 285–6.

[45] Rypon, *Selected Sermons*, ed. and trans. Johnson, 1: 40, 41. Wenzel discusses the extended treatment of preaching in this sermon as an example of Rypon's characteristic concern with the *officium predicatoris*; *Latin Sermon Collections*, 71.

The Prologue to *Piers Plowman* is much more ambivalent about the preacher's ability to counsel the king than these late medieval sermons are. It also suggests that the language of preaching itself may be fractured and exclusionary in ways that make it harder to shape an inclusive, public discourse. As we have seen, the three preachers of the Prologue speak in different languages and registers, and stand in different relationships to institutional authority. The discursive mediation they offer includes and excludes different parts of the *commune*, so that individuals understand the significance of this moment in different ways: when the angel speaks 'in Latyn', the dreamer observes that his speech is inaccessible to the 'lewed': 'lewed men ne koude [did not know how to] / Iangle [argue] ne iugge þat iustifie hem sholde [what would justify them]' (B.Prol.129–30), a claim that has implications for the goliard's etymology, too. Somerset argues that the lack of a common voice reveals the lack of common assumptions in this scene.[46] Steiner, meanwhile, notes that this exchange delays and displaces the cry of *Precepta Regis sunt nobis vincula legis* that ends the scene, as though to illustrate the tensions between individual interests and the common good that complicate such efforts at collective expression.[47] Even as it dramatizes the transformative work of emplotment, where three successive preachers explain the historical significance of the coronation, the poem shows how preaching, in its different modes and registers, might exacerbate the existing divisions in a general audience.

The preaching angel embodies some of the tensions that surround the presentation of sermon discourse in this scene. Preachers were often compared with angels in patristic and medieval writing because preachers, like angels, carried messages from God.[48] Augustine, who notes that the Latin *angelus* derives from the Greek *angelos* or 'messenger', argues that anyone who proclaims God's word can be said to imitate the angels, who are 'nuntii ueritatis' ('messengers of truth').[49] Gregory the Great, similarly, expresses his hope that preachers might prove themselves worthy to be called angels through their commitment to disseminating the gospel.[50] The analogy was commonplace in *artes praedicandi* and in medieval sermons: Humbert of Romans refers to preaching as an angelic office ('est angelicum'), while his fellow Dominican Thomas Waleys argues that the

---

[46] Somerset, 'Multilingual Latin and Vernacular Voice', 117–23.

[47] Steiner, 'Commonalty and Literary Form', 218–19.

[48] On the angelic office of preaching, see Claire M. Waters, *Angels and Earthly Creatures: Preaching, Performance, and Gender in the Later Middle Ages* (Philadelphia: University of Pennsylvania Press, 2004), 3–8.

[49] Augustine, *De civitate Dei*, ed. Domart and Kalb, 108 (15.xxiii); Augustine, *Enarrationes in Psalmos*, ed. Dekkers and Fraipont, 1: 55 (8.xii).

[50] Gregory the Great, *Homiliae in Evangelia*, ed. Raymond Étaix, CCSL 141 (Turnhout: Brepols, 1999), 42–3 (5.vi). A Middle English translation of this passage from Gregory's homily appears as part of the lollard tract 'Anoþer sentens schewynge þat þe peple may haue holy writ in her moder-tunge lefully', 110–16 in *The Earliest Advocates of the English Bible: The Texts of the Medieval Debate*, ed.

preacher should present himself as an angel, a messenger who has come down from heaven ('tanquam angelus et nuntius quidam de coelo lapsus'); the author of *Dives and Pauper*, whose sermons are preserved in Longleat House MS 4, declares that 'euery prechour of goddys word...is goddis aungil & goddis messager to mennys soulis'.[51] This analogy arises in precisely the liturgical contexts that Richard's coronation ceremony invoked. Like Gregory before him, the Longleat friar drew this comparison in a sermon for Advent while, at different moments in his *ars*, Humbert likens preachers to the angels who announced the incarnation, and to the angels of the apocalypse.[52] The preacher, who speaks God's word in a singular, authoritative voice, appears, like the angels, to herald turning points in Christian history, revealing their significance to the faithful.

Langland's angel also invokes a parallel exegetical tradition, which emphasizes the preacher's obligation to adapt God's message for different audiences and occasions. In the *Contra Faustum*, and again in his sermons on the Gospel of John, Augustine likens preachers to the angels of Jacob's vision, who ascend and descend a ladder between earth and heaven; preachers ascend and descend when they address different topics, he explains, turning from God the Father to the incarnate Christ, or from heavenly mysteries to simple instruction.[53] Alan of Lille offers his own version of this idea in the preface and first chapter of his *Ars praedicandi*. For Alan, preachers ascend when they speak about rational theology, which seeks out knowledge of the divine ('quae de divinis scientiam prosequitur'), and descend to speak about moral theology, concerned with good and bad conduct in the world.[54] On this account, the angel's downward gesture in *Piers* (from the 'eyr on heiȝ' he 'Lowed to speke') might seem to anticipate the political

---

Mary Dove (Exeter: University of Exeter Press, 2010), at 111: 'An aungel in Grek and Latyn is a messegere in Englische, þerfore he þat is sent to schewe þe hiȝe Iuge is riȝtly clepid an aungel, þat he kepe þe dignite and name which he fillith in worchynge.'

[51] Humbert of Romans, *Liber de eruditione praedicatorum*, 2: 373–484 in *Opera de vita regulari*, ed. Joachim Joseph Berthier, 2 vols (Rome: Befani, 1888–89; repr. Rome: Marietti, 1956), 2: 374 (1.ii). Waleys, *De modo componendi sermones*, 1.v, ed. Charland, 332. Warminster, Longleat House MS 4, fols 6r–6v; on the authorship of this cycle see Hudson and Spencer, 'Old Author, New Work: The Sermons of MS Longleat 4', *Medium Ævum* 53, no. 2 (1984): 221–38. On this analogy in Waleys's *ars*, see Owst, 'The "Angel" and the "Goliardeys",' 274, and Waters, *Angels and Earthly Creatures*, 49. John Dygon likens preachers to angels in a sermon for the feast of St Michael and the Holy Angels, part of which is transcribed and translated in Wenzel, *Latin Sermon Collections*, 268.

[52] Humbert of Romans, *Liber de eruditione praedicatorum*, 1.i, 1.vii, 2.xiii, ed. Berthier, 2: 374, 394, 408.

[53] Augustine, *Contra Faustum Manichaeum*, 249–797 in *De Utilitate credendi* [...], ed. Joseph Zycha, Corpus Scriptorum Ecclesiasticorum Latinorum, 25, no. 1 (Vienna: Tempsky, 1891), 354–5 (12. xxvi), and *In Iohannis Evangelium tractatus CXXIV*, ed. Radbodus Willems, CCSL 36 (Turnhout: Brepols, 1954), 80–1 (7.xxiii). On Augustine's account of Genesis 28:10–19, and his reading of these angels as preachers, see M.-F. Berrouard, OP, 'Saint Augustin et le ministère de la prédication', *Recherches Augustiniennes* 2 (1962): 447–501.

[54] Alan of Lille, *De arte praedicatoria*, 210: cols 111–98 in *PL*, ed. J. P. Migne, 217 vols (Paris: Migne, 1844–55), 210: col. 112 (1). Alan's account of Genesis 28 was echoed in other, later *artes*. See, for example, the Pseudo-Aquinas, *Tractatulus solemnis de arte et vero modo predicandi*, trans. Harry Caplan, 'A Late Medieval Tractate on Preaching', 61–90 in *Studies in Rhetoric and Public Speaking in*

preoccupations of his sermon. Alan's *ars* offers a practical address to the problem that Augustine identifies, describing appropriate sermons for many different audiences, on the model of Gregory's *Regula pastoralis*. In doing so, it illustrates the kind of flexibility that preaching demanded, imagining new constituencies of listeners in every chapter. This account of the preacher as an angel draws attention to what Claire Waters has called the preacher's 'hybrid position' as a human speaker with a divine message who must modulate his words and modify his appearance in order to deliver that message effectively.[55] In Langland's Prologue, these forms of modulation create complex patterns of inclusion and exclusion, as speakers articulate the common interest in language that excludes particular groups within the *commune*.

The Prologue admits other forms of anxiety, too, in that all the sermons it depicts await validation in the reign to come. Although the poem does not introduce the language of 'preching' and 'preuing' here, it nevertheless makes clear that each of these sermons will be 'tried' in future against the realities of political experience. While the *commune* express their allegiance to the king, the king himself remains silent and inscrutable in response to the counsel of these preachers. This scene of public preaching and royal counsel is followed 'at ones' by the fable of the rodent parliament (B.Prol.146), which illustrates the practical difficulty of imposing restraints on royal power. In this fable, the rats and mice agree, 'for þe commune profit', to hang a bell on the cat who hunts them, exercising his tyrannical power 'whan hym liked', and preying on them 'at his wille' (B.Prol.148–50), but once the bell is brought in, none of the rodents are brave enough to put this plan into practice, calling the value of their earlier 'counseil' into question (B.Prol.180). A mouse appears, who suggests another, more pragmatic solution, directing the cat's predatory energies into catching 'conynges [rabbits]' (B.Prol.189), perhaps, as Elizaveta Strakhov has suggested, a figure for renewed military efforts in France.[56] In his sermon to the convocation of clergy before the Good Parliament, Brinton deployed this fable as part of a strident call for political action: 'non simus tantum locutores sed factores [let us be not merely talkers but doers]', he says, 'sed ne parliamentum nostrum comparetur fabuloso parliamento murium et ratonum [lest our parliament be compared to that parliament of rats and mice in a fable]'.[57] In *Piers Plowman*, by contrast, it suggests the difficulties confronting counsellors who would seek to influence public policy in this way. The dreamer declines to interpret the fable, in a gesture that seems to

Honor of James A. Winans, ed. A. M. Drummond (New York: Century, 1925); repr. at 40–79 in Caplan, *Of Eloquence: Studies in Ancient and Mediaeval Rhetoric*, ed. Anne King and Helen North (Ithaca, NY: Cornell University Press, 1970), 56.
[55] Waters, *Angels and Earthly Creatures*, 1.
[56] Strakhov, 'Bell the Cat', 268; 'Political Animals', 299–300.
[57] Brinton, *Sermones*, ed. Davlin, 2: 317; translation from Wenzel, *Preaching in the Age of Chaucer: Selected Sermons in Translation* (Washington, DC: Catholic University of America Press, 2008), 241–54 (246).

distance the poem itself from direct participation in such 'advice to princes', saying 'What þis metels bymeneþ [dream signifies], ye men þat ben murye,/ Deuyne ye [you interpret], for I ne dar' (B.Prol.209–10).

The lunatic, the angel, and the goliard disappear from the C-text version of the coronation scene. Here, the lunatic's address to the king is reassigned to Kynde Wit and the angel's speech is reassigned to Conscience who addresses it 'to Clergie' as well as 'to þe Kynge' (C.Prol.151). The goliard's argument from the etymology of *rex* and the cry of the assembled people are removed altogether. One effect of these changes, as Galloway notes, is to diminish the 'topical interest' of the passage: the angel, with his links to Richard's coronation cavalcade, and two speeches with direct references to the coronation *ordo* are now absent.[58] The coronation still constitutes a turning point in the allegorical action, but its links to a real event in the recent experience of the poem's readers are no longer clear. Langland's revisions to this scene also seem to downplay the tensions between the different preachers and between the different modes of address they employ: Kynde Wit counsels the king in his own voice, rather than delegating this task to three embodied preachers with different claims on institutional and discursive authority, and Conscience no longer figures the difficulties of bearing God's messages to different constituencies of listeners as the angel does. While Kynde Wit speaks in English and Conscience in Latin, moreover, the poem no longer draws attention to the way that Latin preaching excludes 'lewed' listeners. When Kynde Wit and Conscience explain the significance of the coronation, they offer a narrative discourse that speaks with confidence 'to þe Kynge and to þe Comune' (C.Prol.147), without the kinds of contention and contradiction that are present in the B-text version of this scene.

Even in the C text, however, Langland makes clear that preachers are under an obligation to speak in moments like this, and that counselling rulers involves personal risk. By this point in the C-text Prologue, Conscience has already appeared in the poem, and has issued some stern warnings to the clergy. In a new passage, perhaps incompletely revised at the time of Langland's death, Conscience rebukes covetous priests on the field of folk, invoking the story of Hophni, Phineas, and Eli from the first book of Samuel. The 'fals prestis [false priests]' Hophni and Phineas appropriated the offerings that people brought to the temple, Conscience explains, and their corruption brought about the defeat of Israel by the Philistines, the loss of the Ark of the Covenant, and the death of their father Eli who had failed in his duty to discipline them (C.Prol.106). Conscience reads the story of Hophni and Phineas as a warning against clerical covetousness and the fate of Eli as a reminder that priests should discipline those in their care: 'ȝe shulde be here [their] fadres and betre hem techen [teach them better]' (C.Prol.120). Repeatedly in this passage, Conscience inveighs against 'soffraunce

---

[58] Galloway, *Penn Commentary*, 1:11–12, 119.

[toleration, lenience]' (C.Prol.101, 109, 119, 125). Contemporary clerics have failed in their permissive attitude to wrongdoing, he argues, and their failure to criticize the sins of others. Conscience's reading of Hophni and Phineas finds many parallels in sermons addressed to clerical audiences, as Siegfried Wenzel has shown, but Conscience delivers his rebuke in front of all the estates on the field, showing his own willingness to offer strident criticism in public: 'Conscience cam and cused [accused] hem—and þe comune herde hit' (C.Prol.95).[59] This polemical passage forms the context for Conscience's next speech in the poem, when he delivers the lines '*Sum Rex, sum Princeps*'. While, in the B text, the angel speaks to the king alone, Conscience speaks 'to Clergie and to þe Kynge' (C.Prol.151), as though the political counsel he offers also models the brave, principled speech required from clerics. In this way, the C text continues to acknowledge the moral effort and personal risk required to counsel the powerful, and to speak in narrative terms about the past and future of good governance.

Henry Harclay and the Crown of England

The Latin lines '*Sum Rex, sum Princeps*', spoken by the angel in the B-text Prologue, and by Conscience in C, are also copied on the last page of Lambeth Palace Library, MS 61, at the end of a sermon for the feast of Thomas Becket by the theologian Henry Harclay (Figure 1.1). The headnote records that Harclay delivered this sermon in the year when Piers Gaveston was buried in the king's chapel at Langley, which probably means that he preached it on 29 December 1314, the feast of St Thomas Becket, five days before Gaveston's burial on 2 January 1315.[60] Bennett, who first identified the Latin lines in Lambeth Palace MS 61 as the angel's speech from *Piers Plowman*, assumed that the verses were contemporary with the sermon, and argued on this basis that Langland was quoting a pre-existing Latin poem in his Prologue.[61] As Traugott Lawler has

---

[59] Wenzel, 'Eli and His Sons'.
[60] The headnote and colophon are reproduced in M. R. James and Claude Jenkins, *A Descriptive Catalogue of the Manuscripts in the Library of Lambeth Palace*, 2 vols (Cambridge: Cambridge University Press, 1930–32, repr. 2011), 97–9. Another copy of Harclay's sermon survives without attribution in Hereford Cathedral Library, MS P 5 XII, a manuscript that also contains sermons by John Stratford, Archbishop of Canterbury from 1333–48, and it has sometimes been misattributed to Stratford as a result. See, for example, W. D. Macray, 'Sermons for the Festivals of St. Thomas Becket, etc., Probably by Archbishop Stratford', *English Historical Review*, 8, no. 29 (1893): 85–91. E. W. Kemp was the first to recognize that the Hereford and Lambeth manuscripts preserve the same sermon, and to establish that Harclay, not Stratford, was the author: 'History and Action in the Sermons of a Medieval Archbishop', 349–65 in *The Writing of History in the Middle Ages: Essays Presented to Richard William Southern*, ed. R. H. C. Davis and J. M. Wallace-Hadrill with R. J. A. I. Catto and M. H. Keen (Oxford: Clarendon, 1981).
[61] J. A. W. Bennett, '"Sum Rex, sum Princeps, etc": Piers Plowman B, Prologue 132–8', *Notes and Queries* 205 (1960): 364; *Piers Plowman B*, ed. Bennett, 99. See also Alford, *Guide to the Quotations*, 33, and Galloway, *Penn Commentary*, 1:127.

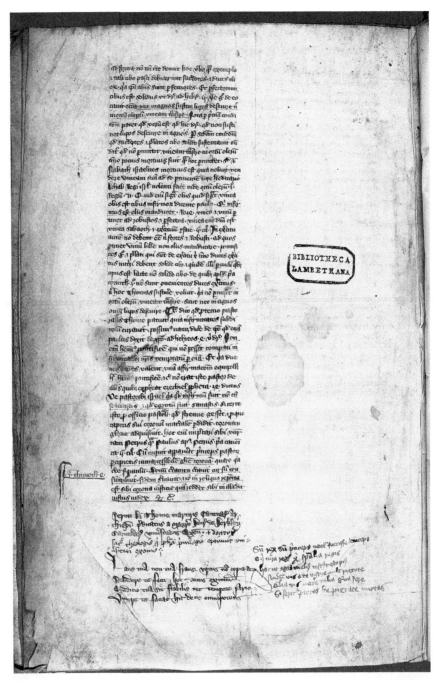

Figure 1.1 The final page of Henry Harclay's sermon for the feast of Thomas Becket, London, Lambeth Palace, MS 61, fol. 147v.

noted, however, the verses were added to this manuscript in a fifteenth-century hand, so their appearance here does not preclude Langland's authorship.[62] The inclusion of these verses in Lambeth Palace MS 61 resembles other instances where scribes copied Latin lines excerpted from Langland's poem, a phenomenon recently discussed by Warner.[63] I have recently considered the possibility, first raised by M. R. James, that the copy of Harclay's sermon in Lambeth Palace MS 61 was originally bound together with the copy of Ranulph Higden's *Polychronicon* in British Library, Royal MS 14 C XII; this book was held in the hospital of St Thomas of Acre in Cheapside in the early fifteenth century, at the time when these verses were copied. The hospital had strong links with the Mercer's Guild, who held regular meetings there, and whose members and affiliates included several readers and owners of *Piers Plowman*. Readers like this would have recognized the lines at the end of the sermon as a quotation from the poem, and remembered the context where they appear in the Prologue.[64]

Harclay's sermon has clear affinities with the kind of public preaching that Langland sought to dramatize in the Prologue coronation scene. This sermon, too, attempts to frame a new understanding of political relations in its contemporary moment through an elaborate historical narrative, focussed on questions of kingship and governance. The sermon begins with an introduction where Harclay defends Thomas against writers like William of Newburgh who had criticized him, and it concludes with a virtuosic exposition of the *thema*, where Harclay offers a new *distinctio* on each word in turn.[65] The long, central section, however, unfolds as an extended narrative account of English history, where Harclay explains the misfortunes of successive English kings as divine retribution for the martyrdom of Thomas Becket. Here, Harclay performs an elaborate act of emplotment, configuring events from a century and a half of English history into a narrative that articulates the fearful logic of divine retribution. The death of Thomas supplies an axial moment for Harclay's account of English history: it inaugurates a new era where new conditions prevail. Like the preachers of Langland's Prologue, Harclay not only articulates the significance of this historical turning point but also configures new narratives around it, tracing past precedents and future possibilities into the intersubjective time of public life. These narratives establish the context for his own intervention in public policy, as he counsels the king not to persecute the church like his forefathers.

---

[62] Lawler, 'Langland Versificator', *YLS* 25 (2011): 63, citing Hanna's assessment of the scribal hand.
[63] On Langland's Latin excerpted in other contexts, see Warner, *Myth of 'Piers Plowman'*, 67–71; at 58–9, however, Warner distinguishes the lines beginning 'Sum rex, sum princeps' from the kinds of Latin that appear elsewhere in the poem.
[64] Alastair Bennett, 'An Excerpt from *Piers Plowman* in the Hospital of St Thomas of Acre', *Medium Ævum*, 92, no. 1 (2023): 104–20.
[65] Macray, 'Sermons for the Festivals of St. Thomas Becket', prints most of Harclay's exposition of *cecidit* and *corona* from the Hereford MS at 89–91.

In this central section of his sermon, Harclay construes disparate historical events as part of a single plot that describes the consequences of Thomas Becket's martyrdom. Here, he interprets the loss of English territories as punishments for Thomas's murder: during the reign of Henry II, he writes, the king of England held Ireland and Aquitaine and claimed lordship over Scotland, but by the middle of the reign of John, 'totum hoc dominium regni et coronae Anglicanae fuit confractum et diminutum [this whole dominion, kingdom and crown of England, was broken up and diminished]'.[66] He argues that God continues to punish the kings of England for Henry's crimes, reading the English defeat at the battle of Bannockburn, only six months before this sermon was preached, as a sign of ongoing divine displeasure. Harclay appeals to political prophecy to reinforce the central claims of this narrative. He cites approvingly from Joachim of Fiore, whose prophecies confirm that the kings of England would be punished for Thomas's murder: 'Quod contricio et infelicitas venerunt super nostrum regnum et nostram gentem pro sancto Thome probatur per prophetiam abbatis Joachim... [That grief and misfortune came to our kingdom and our people for St Thomas is proved by a prophecy of the abbot Joachim...]'.[67] He also quotes a prophecy recorded in Henry of Huntingdon's *Historia Anglorum*, which predicts that the English will be subject to French lordship and will suffer humiliation at the hands of the Scots, 'ex scelerum suorum inmanitate [because of the enormity of their crimes]'.[68] The logic of prophecy and fulfilment bolsters the coherence of Harclay's narrative and helps to explain why the disparate events he describes should be understood as part of a single *holos*.

Although this is not a coronation sermon, the image of the king's crown serves as an important organizing conceit, and one that recurs in the narrative of the central section. Harclay preached on Lamentations 5:15, 'Cecidit corona capitis

[66] London, Lambeth Palace Library, MS 61, fol. 144v. The full text of Harclay's sermon has not been edited, but Kemp includes a detailed summary of its contents in 'History and Action', 350–5. For further discussion, see Phyllis B. Roberts, *Thomas Becket in the Medieval Latin Preaching Tradition: An Inventory of Sermons about St Thomas Becket c.1170–c.1400*, Instrumenta Patristica, 25 (The Hague: Nijhoff, 1992), 34–42 (Harclay's sermon is no. 34 in this inventory), and Roberts, 'University Masters and Thomas Becket: Sermons Preached on St Thomas of Canterbury at Paris and Oxford in the Thirteenth and Fourteenth Centuries', *History of Universities* 6 (1986): 65–79. Henry Wharton printed a short extract from the Lambeth MS in *Anglia sacra, sive Collectio historiarum* [...], 2 vols (London: Chiswell, 1691), 2: 523–4, and further extracts from the Hereford MS are printed in Owst, *Literature and Pulpit*, 126–32, and Macray, 'Sermons for the Festivals of St. Thomas Becket'.

[67] Lambeth Palace MS 61, fol. 145v. The prophecy comes from the pseudo-Joachite *De Oneribus Prophetarum*. Marjorie Reeves discusses the account of the *De Oneribus Prophetarum* in this sermon as evidence for 'a considerable vogue for Joachimist prophecies' in late medieval England, although, following Macray, she attributes the sermon to Stratford, preaching in the 1340s. Reeves, *The Influence of Prophecy in the Later Middle Ages: A Study in Joachimism* (Oxford: Oxford University Press, 1969), 82–3. In his *Quaestiones Ordinariae*, Henry criticized Joachim of Fiore for attempting to calculate the date of judgement day, as we will see in the next chapter.

[68] Lambeth Palace, MS 61, fol. 146r-v, citing the *Historia Anglorum*, vi.1. In the *Historia*, this prophecy anticipates the Norman conquest, but Harclay reads it in relation to the defeat at Bannockburn. See Henry, Archdeacon of Huntingdon, *Historia Anglorum (History of the English People)*, ed. and trans. Diana Greenway (Oxford: Clarendon, 1996), 338–41.

nostri [The crown is fallen from our head]', an unusual *thema* for the feast of St Thomas when John 10:11 was more commonly used.[69] Defending this choice in his opening remarks, Harclay links the text to the circumstances of Thomas's martyrdom, when Henry's knights cut off the crown of the archbishop's head: 'ista uerba possunt applicari ad sanctum Thomam Cantuariensis cuius corona ad litteram cecidit amputata [these words can be applied to Saint Thomas of Canterbury whose amputated crown literally fell]'.[70] When he relates the history of England in the central part of his sermon, Harclay uses his *thema* to describe the falling crowns of English kings, explaining political instability and national misfortune as the consequences of Thomas's martyrdom. The connection is most explicit when he describes the ceremony of reconciliation that followed the papal interdict on England under King John: Harclay explains how 'corona auulsa fuit a capite suo per legatum pape Nicholum Tusculanum Episcopum in subieccionis signum et postea fuit reponita per eundem [the crown was torn from his head by the papal envoy bishop Nicholas of Tusculum in a sign of subjection and was then put back again by him]'. Underlining the point, Harclay asks, 'Nonne ergo vere corona nostra cecidit pro corona quam Thomas perdidit? [Has our crown not truly fallen then, for the crown that Thomas lost?]'.[71] The development of the *thema* enables the work of emplotment in this sermon, as these repeated references to the crown reinforce the connections between narrated events. While Harclay reserves the more elaborate, word-by-word exegesis of this *thema* for the final part of his sermon, his account of English history is nevertheless informed by an exegetical logic.

The act of emplotment that forms the centrepiece of Harclay's sermon provides the context for his direct advice to the king. God has punished the kings of England not only for their fathers' crimes, Harclay argues, but also because they re-enact those crimes themselves. John's territorial losses, for example, result directly from Thomas's martyrdom, but also from John's persecution of his own archbishop Stephen Langton. Citing Deuteronomy 5:9, Harclay notes that God punishes children for their fathers' sins into the third and fourth generation, with

---

[69] On the choice of this unusual *thema*, see Roberts, 'Thomas Becket: The Construction and Deconstruction of a Saint from the Middle Ages to the Reformation', 1–22 in *Models of Holiness in Medieval Sermons: Proceedings of the International Symposium (Kalamazoo, 4–7 May 1995)*, ed. by Beverly Mayne Kienzle and others (Louvain-la-Neuve: Fédération Internationale des Instituts d'Études Médiévales, 1996), 8–9.

[70] Lambeth Palace, MS 61, fol. 143r. The amputation of Thomas's crown was described in eyewitness accounts of his martyrdom, and preachers often discussed the significance of this detail; see Roberts, *Becket in the Medieval Latin Preaching Tradition*, p. 38. John Mirk offers a grisly description of this moment in his own sermon on Thomas Becket: 'Reynald wyth hys swerdes poynt put of Thomas cappe þat he hadde on hys hed, and smot at hym, and kutte half hys crowne. Þen anoþur smot aftur, and hutte in þe same stroke, and smot hys croune al of, þat hyt honget by as hyt hadde ben a dysch.' Finally, at the door of the church, 'Robert Brok ȝede aȝeyn, and set hys fot in Thomas necke, and scrypput out þe brayn of þe skolle abouten on þe pament'; Mirk, *Festial*, ed Powell, 1: 42.

[71] Lambeth Palace, MS 61, fol. 145v.

fearful implications for the present king, Edward II (this calculation treats the brothers Richard and John as a single generation). He concludes that Edward can avoid his forefathers' fate if he also turns from their example: 'Caueant ergo illi vel ille qui est in 4 generatione ab Henrico quod non sit imitator paterni sceleris et proculdubio peccatum paternum in persona sua impune transibit [Therefore let those, or he, who is in the fourth generation after Henry take care that he be not an imitator of the father's villainy, and the father's crimes will surely pass over his person unpunished]'.[72] The preachers of Langland's Prologue urge the king to emulate historical examples as he works to implement the laws of Christ, but Harclay encourages Edward to break with the past so as to avoid the fate of his forefathers. Yet, in this sermon, as in *Piers*, the work of emplotment helps to frame the choices that confront the ruler and to reveal their larger implications for the *commune* as a whole. As he traces this narrative of English history, Harclay locates his own moment in a larger constellation of public events, mapping out the historical time in which political decisions are made.

While *Piers Plowman* dramatizes the response of the *commune*, at least in the B-text version, we do not know how Harclay's original audience reacted to his sermon, or how it shaped their perception of contemporary political events. Yet, several annotations to the sermon in Lambeth MS 61 reveal the reactions of later readers, who responded to Harclay's narrative with their own reflections on kingship and governance. After the colophon, a supplementary annotation in the distinctive hand of Thomas Gascoigne adds further details about Harclay himself, and about the privileges he enjoyed as Chancellor of Oxford University.[73] Underneath this annotation, at the foot of the column, another hand has copied a four-line poem 'Laus tua, non tua fraus':

Laus tua, non tua fraus, virtus, non copia rerum
Scandere te fecit hoc decus eximium.
Conditio tua sit stabilis! Nec tempore paruo
Viuere te faciat hic Deus omnipotens![74]

[Your good reputation, not your deceit, your good character, not your abundant possessions, raise you up to this great honour. May your condition be permanent! May almighty God ensure that you live here for a long time!]

---

[72] Lambeth Palace MS 61, fol. 145r.
[73] James and Jenkins, *Descriptive Catalogue*, 98, and see Bennett, 'Thomas of Acre', 110.
[74] These verses are transcribed from Lambeth MS 61 in James and Jenkins, *Descriptive Catalogue*, 99; punctuation follows the edition in Georg Capellanus, *Sprechen Sie Lateinisch? Moderne Konversation in lateinischer Sprache*, 10th edn by Hans Lamer (Berlin: Dümmler, 1929), 125, cited in Thomas Haye, *Päpste und Poeten: Die mittelalterliche Kurie als Objekt und Förderer panegyrischer Dichtung* (Berlin: de Gruyter, 2009), 11-12.

This was a well-known poem, anthologized in collections of Latin epigrams including Richard of Segbrok's *Liber sententiarum* and jotted in the margins and flyleaves of other manuscripts.[75] Compilers would sometimes draw attention to its central trick: as a note in Segbrok's anthology explains, 'Relegantur isti versus et est sensus contrarius [Go over these in reverse, and the meaning is contrary]'.[76] Read backwards, the encomium is transformed into an excoriating critique:

Omnipotens Deus hic faciat te viuere paruo
Tempore! Nec stabilis sit tua conditio!
Eximium decus hoc fecit te scandere, rerum
Copia, non virtus, fraus tua, non tua laus.

[May almighty God ensure that you only live here for a short time! May your condition be temporary! Your abundant possessions, not your good character, your deceit, not your good reputation, raise you up to this great honour.]

This short poem has its own narrative logic that complements the more extensive narrative in Harclay's sermon: addressing a ruler who has just assumed his position, it looks back to recall the way he obtained his power and forwards to imagine what he will do with it. It also offers a guarded alternative to Harclay's outspoken intervention in public life, encoding criticism in the form of praise. This short poem allows an attentive recipient to imagine the alternative futures that might unfold in the time of public history, to hear the praise that might follow from good government, and the condemnation that will follow from tyranny. It invites a powerful addressee to think about the narrative context of his own rule, and to imagine the stories that others might tell about it, without itself committing to praise or critique.

The lines '*Sum Rex, sum Princeps*', spoken by the angel and by Conscience in *Piers Plowman*, are copied next to the poem '*Laus tua, non tua fraus*' at the bottom of the otherwise empty second column on this page (Figure 1.1a). Here, they respond to the act of emplotment in Harclay's sermon, and also to the complex and elliptical form of public address that is manifest in the palindrome. The verses were most likely copied from a C text of the poem since, like all C-text

---

[75] The poem is no. 10203 in Hans Walther, *Initia carminum ac versuum medii aevi posterioris latinorum* (Göttingen: Vandenhoeck & Ruprecht, 1959), 519. The text of Segbrok's *Liber Sententiarum* is edited by Carl Horstmann, in *Yorkshire Writers: Richard Rolle of Hampole and his Followers*, 2 vols (London: Sonnenschein, 1895-6, repr. Cambridge: Brewer, 1976), 1: 420-34 (the poem is at 427). See also W. Leonard Grant, 'The *Liber Sententiarum* of Richard of Segbrok', *Phoenix* 3.3 (1949): 94-101. In the sixteenth century, George Puttenham included this poem in his *Art of English Poesy*, where he attributed it to a 'gibing monk' from the time of Charlemagne. See Puttenham, *The Art of English Poetry*, ed. Frank Whigham and Wayne A. Rebhorn (Ithaca, NY: Cornell University, 2007), 105-6 (1.7).

[76] *Yorkshire Writers*, ed. Horstmann, 1: 427. See also Puttenham, *Art of English Poetry*, ed. Whigham and Rebhorn, 105-6.

60 PREACHING AND NARRATIVE IN *PIERS PLOWMAN*

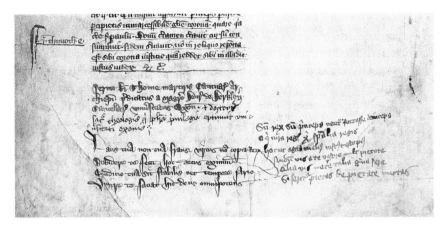

Figure 1.1a Detail showing annotations by Thomas Gascoigne, the poem 'Laus tua, non tua fraus' and the verses '*Sum Rex, sum Princeps*', London, Lambeth Palace, MS 61, fol. 147v.

manuscripts, they lack the line 'Si ius nudatur, nudo de iure metatur', although, if they were added to the Lambeth Palace sermon in the library at St Thomas of Acre, then the annotator may also have had their B-text context in mind: the goldsmith's pageant that apparently inspired Langland's preaching angel was staged in front of the hospital building, on a scaffold constructed over the Cheapside conduit.[77] Read in this manuscript context, the angel's speech seems to echo Harclay's address to the king, preserving the lessons that emerge from Harclay's act of emplotment without reproducing the complex detail of his narrative. These lines encourage the king to reflect on the fragility of political power. They also remind him of his own obligations to God, in a narrative context that looks back to earlier precedents and forward to the final judgement on his soul. Like the palindrome 'Laus tua, non tua fraus', however, the verses from *Piers* might seem to present an alternative to Harclay's outspoken intervention in public life, offering a discourse of counsel and advice that is both revealing and withholding, that invites the king to imagine the possible futures that might unfold in the context of a public history but without threatening disaster in concrete, imminent terms.

If the scribe knew these lines from *Piers Plowman*, then his decision to copy them at the end of this sermon may reflect his understanding of their context in Langland's poem: the choice of a coronation address, for example, provides an ironic counterpoint to a sermon where the kings of England are constantly at risk of losing their crowns. Yet, the angel's association with a coronation episode also points to an alternative history of English kingship, where each new monarch

---

[77] Bennett, 'Thomas of Acre', 112–13.

reaffirms his obligations to the law and to God. Copied after Harclay's sermon, where the martyrdom of Thomas Becket supplies an axial moment for English history, the speech insists that each new coronation might constitute another kind of turning point in political life, when the principles of good government are reaffirmed. Read together in this manuscript, Harclay's sermon, the poem 'Laus tua, non tua fraus' and the angel's speech from *Piers Plowman* offer their own, multivocal address to the king and the *commune* that echoes the situation of Langland's Prologue. Like Langland's speakers, they articulate the same essential message but with different emphases and in variously veiled and outspoken forms. Perhaps the scribe who added Langland's lines to this manuscript recognized them as a poetic representation of the kind of public preaching in which Harclay was engaged; in placing them here, he reproduced something of the complex, qualified, and multivocal situation of that preaching as Langland represented it.

Conscience and the 'lawe of lif'

The later visions of *Piers Plowman* trace the outlines of eschatological history, beginning in the fifth vision with a version of the Fall and concluding in the eighth with the impending apocalypse. The poem relates the story of Christ on at least four occasions in the context of this larger narrative: the dreamer observes the events of Christ's life from the foot of the Tree of Charity, anticipating the atonement in the immediate aftermath of the Fall; later, he watches the crucifixion in Jerusalem and descends into hell to witness the harrowing; then, at the start of the seventh vision, he meets Conscience, who recounts two new versions of the life of Christ, presenting them in the form of a sermon. The sermon of Conscience marks a return to the specific concerns of the Prologue coronation scene. As Wood has shown, Conscience draws on the conventions of Advent preaching as he tells the story of Christ, treating his birth as a royal *adventus*, explicating his royal titles, and seeking out examples of 'riȝtful rulyng' in his life. Like the preachers of the Prologue, moreover, he thinks about the inauguration of a new reign as a turning point in the life of the community, which establishes a new law for the people who live after it. Conscience positions Christ's *adventus* as an axial moment in Christian history, and elaborates new narratives in the intersubjective, historical time that unfolds around it.[78]

---

[78] John Burrow has argued that Wood's reading of Conscience's sermon places undue emphasis on Christ's role as king at the expense of his role as conqueror. Wood draws particular attention to the moment of Christ's resurrection, where angels proclaim '*Christus Rex resurgens*', as though heralding a royal *adventus*, but Burrow notes that '*Rex*' in this line is a conjectural emendation, found in the Athlone editions, with minority support in the C-text tradition and no witnesses in B (Schmidt rejects this reading in the parallel text edition, cited here). More generally, Burrow argues that an emphasis on conquest rather than kingship is appropriate to the Eastertide setting of this sermon. As Wood

The sermon of Conscience is structured as a series of *distinctiones* that explicate the names and titles of Christ, and that describe the events of his life in relation to the Do-wel triad: Do-Wel, Do-Bet, and Do-Best. In this sense, as Barney writes, Conscience 'renders in expository discourse what the preceding passus realized dramatically'.[79] Yet, this part of the poem also reaffirms that, for Langland, preacherly exegesis could express a narrative logic. When Conscience explicates the names and titles of Christ, he also articulates 'the narratives and histories through which God is revealed', as Aers has observed.[80] Mary Raschko, who draws on Ricoeur's account of emplotment in her own analysis of this scene, has described the overlapping, reiterative narratives in the sermon of Conscience as an expression of the poem's ongoing commitment to 'understanding God through story'.[81]

Conscience delivers his sermon to the dreamer but also to the wider Christian community, explaining the implications of Christ's atonement for the *commune* as a whole. In the waking episode that follows the harrowing of hell, Will goes to church to hear mass. His visionary encounter with Conscience takes place in the middle of the service, in the place where a sermon might occur: 'In myddes of þe masse.../ I fel eftsoones aslepe [asleep again]' (B.19.4–5). The narratives that Conscience will offer in his sermon draw on the traditions and discourses that were available in this liturgical context, linking the advent of Christ at the incarnation to his *adventus* in the souls of individual believers and at the last judgement, and associating these events with the pageantry of coronation. Although the sermon begins as a dialogue between Will and Conscience, it follows a eucharistic miracle where Christ appears 'bifore þe comune peple' (B.19.7), and after it concludes the dreamer finds himself among 'manye hundred' worshippers (B.19.212) who have also apparently heard it. Isabel Davis argues that the explication of ranks and titles in this speech marks a 'turn toward the human world', which enables Will to understand the significance of the atonement in his own social and historical moment.[82] Marking the incarnation as an axial moment in Christian history, moreover, Conscience makes it the basis for a public discourse in which the whole community can participate, imagining their own lives in relation to the life of the institutions that are being established around them.

---

observes, however, and as contemporary sermons demonstrate, it was commonplace for Advent preachers to anticipate the events of Easter, and to explain the significance of the incarnation with reference to the coming atonement. Burrow, 'Conscience on Knights, Kings, and Conquerors: *Piers Plowman* B.19.26–198', YLS 23 (2009): 85–95 (Burrow was responding to an earlier version of Wood, *Conscience*, 70–86, that was published as Wood, '"Ecce Rex": *Piers Plowman* B.19.1–212 and its Contexts', YLS 21 (2007): 31–56); for Wood's own reply, see *Conscience*, 82, n. 49.

[79] Barney, *Penn Commentary*, 5: 114.   [80] Aers, *Beyond Reformation?*, 4.
[81] Raschko, 'Storytelling at the Gates of Hell', 188.
[82] Isabel Davis, 'Calling: Langland, Gower, and Chaucer on Saint Paul', *Studies in the Age of Chaucer* 34 (2012): 83.

Here, as Raschko writes, 'Conscience...shows how *vitae Christi* can define the boundaries of a Christian community'.[83]

This part of the poem also responds to the Prologue's complex and ambivalent account of the preacher's role in public life. While the lunatic, the angel, and the goliard express their hopes and fears for the coming reign, Conscience speaks with confidence about the life of Christ, explaining the significance of the incarnation with reference to the atonement, where Christ will 'preue' the qualities that are encoded in his names and titles. Yet, Conscience, too, will find it difficult to speak with certainty about the future of good government as the poem's allegorical action catches up with its contemporary moment. After the sermon of Conscience concludes, the dreamer will witness the foundation of the Christian community and of the institutions that guide and regulate it in scenes that echo the foundation of the commonwealth in the Prologue. As Aers has argued, however, the later part of passus 19 and the final vision in passus 20 also trace the gradual corruption of these Christian institutions, as the church becomes involved in the exercise of secular power, and as the language of virtuous rule is undermined.[84] At the end of the seventh vision, Conscience confronts a contemporary king who announces his intention to govern according to his own will rather than according to the law of Christ, and who casts the future of rightful rule into doubt.

When Conscience describes Christ as a new king, he develops a central metaphor from the dreamer's vision of the harrowing of hell in the preceding passus. Twice in this vision, Will hears a voice proclaiming Christ as the king of glory, in the words of Psalm 23:29 (B.18.261a–4, 317–21), and when Christ appears at the gates of hell, he defends the atonement as the proper exercise of his royal prerogatives. This speech follows two scenes where the four daughters of God and then the parliament of devils debate the logic of salvation: these speakers struggle to reconcile the strict standard of God's justice, manifest in his judgement on Adam and Eve at the Fall, with the mercy promised by the prophets and patriarchs who predict that Adam and Eve and their descendants will be redeemed. One devil in the parliament implies that, if Christ rescues them from hell, then he acts as a tyrant, enforcing his will in violation of the law: 'if he reue [deprive] me of my riȝt, he robbeþ me by maistrie [sheer force]...For hymself seide, þat sire [lord] is of heuene,/ That if Adam ete þe appul, alle shoulde deye' (B.18.276–80). When Christ announces his *adventus* at the gates of hell, however, he explains how justice and mercy can be reconciled. The atonement can be justified under 'þe Olde Lawe', he says, because it is a trick on the devil, which answers the devil's deception of Adam and Eve ('Þe Olde Lawe graunteþ/ That gilours [deceivers] be bigiled'), and because Christ gives his life in exchange for

---

[83] Raschko, 'Storytelling at the Gates of Hell', 189.
[84] Aers, *Beyond Reformation?* On the 'malicious distortion of the gifts of language' (40) in these passūs, see esp. 85–90.

theirs: 'Membre for membre was amendes [satisfaction] by þe Olde Lawe' (B.18.339-40, 343). This, then, is mercy that satisfies the requirements for justice: '*Dentem pro dente et oculum pro oculo* [Tooth for tooth, and eye for eye]' (B.18.340a, based on Exodus 21:24). Christ also affirms his commitment to rightful rule in this speech by invoking the privileges of kingship. He notes that a felon who survives hanging cannot be hanged again, and that a king may pardon a criminal if he is present at the execution.[85] On this logic, he argues, 'it liþ [lies] in my grace/ Wheiþer þei deye or deye noȝt' (B.18.387-8). Finally, Christ claims a 'kynde' relationship to human beings as a consequence of his incarnation, which changes the way he rules them. Christ argues that the natural law of 'kynde' compels him to show mercy to his 'kyn' and, through a pun, he identifies this 'kyndenesse' as a quality of kingship: 'I were [would be] an vnkynde kyng but I my kyn holpe [if I did not help my kin]' (B.18.399).[86] Where the preachers of the Prologue urged the new king to follow Christ's example, moderating *ius* with *pietas* as he implements the law, in passus 18 Christ looks to the example of English kings in order to defend the new law he institutes at the harrowing, where justice and mercy are integrated. As a king, he declares, 'I may do mercy þoruȝ rightwisnesse, and alle my wordes trewe [(remain) true]' (B.18.390).

The sermon of Conscience places this triumphant moment in the narrative context of Christ's incarnation, life, and ministry, to show how the harrowing of hell fulfils the promise of his first *adventus* at the incarnation. Conscience begins his sermon in response to the dreamer's question about the name of Christ: recalling Philippians 2:10, the lection for Palm Sunday, Will observes that all creatures 'sholden knelen and bowen' at the name of Jesus, and presses Conscience to explain whether Christ is 'moore of myȝt [of greater power]' or a 'moore worþiere name' (B.19.17-18, 24).[87] This verse from Philippians acts as the *thema* for the sermon to follow, as Conscience elaborates a double narrative of Christ's life through a series of *distinctiones* on Christ's name.[88] He first explains that one person can have many names, as when the same individual is called

---

[85] On these related legal principles, see Alford, *Piers Plowman: A Glossary of Legal Diction* (Cambridge: Brewer, 1988), 67, s.v. 'hangen'. Skeat observed that these two principles were combined in practice in 1363, when Edward III pardoned Walter Poynant of Hambledon: *The Vision of William Concerning Piers the Plowman in Three Parallel Texts*, ed. W. W. Skeat, 2 vols, (Oxford: Oxford University Press, 1886) 2: 263-4; he also lists other, later examples where medieval kings pardoned convicted criminals who survived execution. The case of Walter Poynant (aka 'Walter Wynkenburn') is recorded by Henry Knighton: *Knighton's Chronicle, 1337-1396*, ed. and trans. by G. H. Martin (Oxford: Oxford University Press, 1995), 188-91. See also Steiner, 'William Langland', 121-34 in *The Cambridge Companion to Medieval English Law and Literature*, ed. Candace Barrington and Sebastian Sobecki (Cambridge: Cambridge University Press, 2019), 130; and Steiner, 'Neck Verse', *New Literary History* 53 (2022): 340-2.

[86] On the wordplay in this passage, see Davlin, '*Kynde Knowynge*', 14-15, and Davis, *Books of Nature*, 4.

[87] On the allusion to Philippians in these lines, see Barney, *Penn Commentary*, 5: 110.

[88] Barney (*Penn Commentary*, 5: 109) refers to these *distinctiones* as the 'distributive scheme' of Conscience's discourse.

knight, king, and conqueror, then retells the story of the crucifixion to explain how Christ obtained these titles: Christ appeared as a knight to joust with the devil, was crowned as a king on the cross, and won the title of conqueror when he harrowed hell. This narrative concludes when Christ, as conqueror, institutes a new 'lawe of lif that laste shal evere [shall last forever]' (B.19.45), bestowing new lands and titles on his followers, while depriving the Jews of their 'gentil' status in a bleak expression of the poem's supercessionist logic (B.19.34).

Next, Conscience tells the whole story of Christ's life from the nativity to the resurrection, a second, more expansive narrative that encompasses the events of the first. This narrative is organized around the Do-wel triad: Conscience explains that Christ 'comsede [began]' to 'Dowel' when he performed his first miracle at the wedding feast in Cana (B.19.123), earned the 'gretter name' of Do-bet through his ministry and his acts of healing (B.19.128–9), and finally achieved the name of Do-best after the resurrection, when he delegated his powers on earth to Piers Plowman in the poem's version of the Petrine commission.[89] At the conclusion of this second narrative, Christ decrees that the whole of the *commune* should live under his law, and appoints Piers Plowman to administer it on earth. In the sermon of Conscience, as James Simpson writes, '[t]o understand the names of Jesus Christ is to recount the whole life, a life that resolves into its immediate institutional upshot in the England of a newly-made papal figure, Piers Plowman'.[90]

Wood compares the speech of Conscience with medieval sermons on Matthew 21:5, 'Ecce rex tuus venit tibi [Behold thy king cometh to thee]', a common *thema* for the First Sunday in Advent. Medieval preachers would often explicate this text by listing Christ's qualities as king and making each of these the basis for a new division, much as Conscience does with the titles knight, king, and conqueror. This is how Robert Rypon structures one of his Advent sermons, as we saw in the second part of this chapter. Wood notes another example in an Advent sermon by Nicholas of Aquavilla, who attributes 'quinque conditiones [five qualities]' to Christ the king, 'iustitiam, sapientiam, potentiam, mansuetudinem et humilitatem [justice, wisdom, power, mildness, and humility]', and offers a *divisio* on each.[91] Aquavilla's sermons, composed in the early fourteenth century, were often cited and adapted by later preachers: Wood notes that John Felton incorporates these

---

[89] On the poem's reimagining of the Petrine commission, see Barney, *Penn Commentary*, 5: 126–31. As Aers has shown, this is a distinctive, Langlandian version of the Petrine commission, which makes the pope's power to pardon conditional on the penitent's efforts to make restitution: *Beyond Reformation?*, 6–11. Aers argues (29–37) that this version of the Petrine commission gives no warrant for the exercise of secular power by the institutional church.

[90] Simpson, 'The Power of Impropriety: Authorial Naming in *Piers Plowman*', 145–65 in *William Langland's Piers Plowman: A Book of Essays*, ed. Kathleen M. Hewett-Smith (New York: Routledge, 2001), 156.

[91] Wood, *Conscience*, 80–1. For the text, see *Sermones dominicales reverendi patris Nicolai ab Aquevilla* (Paris: Badium Ascensium and de Marnef, 1519).

divisions on Christ's kingly qualities into his own Advent sermon, for example.[92] They also formed the basis for a Middle English collection, produced by a compiler with lollard sympathies, where the whole sermon for Advent 2 is based on Aquavilla's *divisiones* on Christ's kingly qualities.[93] In a departure from Aquavilla, the lollard compiler invokes the derivation of *rex* from *regere*, as explained by the goliard in the Prologue to *Piers Plowman* ('Cryst is cleypd [called] owre kyng ffor þat [because] he gouernyt vs'), and develops it to suggest that the qualities of good kingship can be found in the man who governs himself: 'þys king had fyue condicions, þe weche eche good kyng schul haue, and euery good crystyn man þat is kyng of himself: ryȝtwysnesse, wysdam, power, myldenes and mekenesse, for al theys were yn Crist'.[94]

An Advent sermon from the macaronic collection in Oxford, Bodleian Library, MS Bodley 649, attributed to Hugh Legat by Alan Fletcher, offers even closer parallels with the sermon of Conscience.[95] This sermon, too, lists Christ's qualities as a king but Legat, like Conscience, instantiates them in a narrative, disclosing the principles of 'lawe and leaute' through an act of emplotment. Legat introduces Christ as 'A blissful rex', in whom 'misericordie' and 'iusticie' are like the two poles of a magnet: his mercy draws sinful souls towards heaven, while his justice pushes them away to hell.[96] He then divides his *thema* by listing three royal virtues found 'souerenlich [pre-eminently, regally]' in Christ: strength to resist his enemies, wisdom to rule his subjects, and prudence in making judgements. In the subsequent divisions, Legat offers an exegetical narrative, showing how Christ displayed these virtues in his life and death. Christ is both king and conqueror in this sermon: Legat explains that he was crucified with a crown on his head and a lance at his side ('Habuit coronam in capite, lanceam in latere'), and that he conquered the devil at the harrowing of hell: 'Christ[us] nostri regis...vicit inimicum nostrum, demonem inferni [Christ our king...conquered our enemy, the devil of hell]'.[97] As he claimed his crown, moreover, Christ established a new law, 'lex caritatis et amoris [the law of charity and love]', by which Christians should 'be lad and gouerned'.[98] Legat urges his listeners to conform their lives to this law, in service to Christ the king: 'precipue quod sitis in amore et caritate vnusquisque cum alio [you should

[92] Wood, *Conscience*, 80–1. On Felton's extensive borrowings from Aquavilla, see Fletcher, *Preaching, Politics and Poetry*, 59, n.7, and Wenzel, *Latin Sermon Collections*, 54.

[93] Ruth Evans, 'An Edition of a Fifteenth Century Middle English Temporale Sermon Cycle in MSS Lambeth Palace 392 and Cambridge University Library Additional 5338', 2 vols (PhD thesis, University of Leeds, 1986), 1: 134–41, 2: 2–25. On this and other English translations of Aquavilla, see Spencer, *English Preaching*, 128, 250–1.

[94] 'Temporale Sermon Cycle', ed. Evans, 1: 137.

[95] For this attribution, see pp. 15–16 above; in '*Piers Plowman* and the Benedictines', Fletcher argues that Legat was a reader of *Piers Plowman*.

[96] *Macaronic Sermon Collection*, ed. and trans. Horner, 369.

[97] *Macaronic Sermon Collection*, ed. and trans. Horner, 374, 375; 378, 379.

[98] *Macaronic Sermon Collection*, ed. and trans. Horner, 382–4, 383–5.

especially be in love and charity each one with the other]'.[99] Like the sermon of Conscience, then, Legat's sermon first explains how Christ's kingly qualities were manifest in his life, and then extrapolates from them a law for others to live by.

The second narrative in the sermon of Conscience begins with a coronation scene, where angels herald the birth of Christ and the Magi appear with gifts that represent the qualities of kingship: 'Reson' in the form of frankincense, 'Rightwisnesse vnder reed gold', and 'Pitee, apperynge by mirre' (B.19.86, 88, 92). These are the qualities of *ius* and *pietas* that a king must reconcile in the practice of 'riʒtful' rule; gold, which figures righteousness, is also 'likned to Leautee', Conscience explains (B.19.89), the principle that informs the law and enables 'ech lif to knowe his owene' in the Prologue. Here too, Langland alludes to late medieval ceremonial: coronation entries would often include Epiphany scenes, where the king was presented with gifts that symbolized his virtues, as Kipling notes.[100] Conscience, however, insists that none of the gifts that Christ receives confers kingship by itself. Instead, like the titles conferred at the king's coronation, they must be 'preued' through the king's own actions in the reign to come:

Ac for alle þese preciouse presentʒ Oure Lord Prynce Iesus
Was neiþer kyng ne conquerour til he comsede wexe   *began to grow*
In þe manere of a man, and þat by muchel sleighte.   *great cunning*
(B.19.96–8)

In the Prologue, the lunatic, the angel, and the goliard described the qualities of good kingship that were represented in the coronation ceremony and encoded in the etymology of the king's new titles, in the hope that the new king would manifest these qualities in the coming reign. When Conscience describes the *adventus* of Christ, however, he is able to show how Christ went on to earn these titles through his subsequent actions: in his *distinctiones* on the Do-wel triad, Conscience explains how *ius* and *pietas* are manifest in the life, death, and resurrection of Christ, configured as narrative of 'riʒtful' rule.

Throughout this second narrative, Conscience continues to prioritize the moments when Christ earns his titles through his actions above the moment when these titles were first conferred on him. In his account of the crucifixion, for example, Conscience claims that 'Christ' derives from 'conqueror', and that Jesus has earned this title by harrowing hell: 'He may wel be called conquerour—and þat is "Crist" to mene' (B.19.62). In fact, as was well known from Augustine, Isidore,

---

[99] *Macaronic Sermon Collection*, ed. and trans. Horner, 392, 393.
[100] Kipling, *Enter the King*, 115–20. See also Barney, *Penn Commentary*, 5: 102. Barney (*Penn Commentary*, 5: 117) argues that the scene contains a precise topical allusion to the three kings of Spain, Navarre, and Portugal, who visited the infant Richard II, according to the chronicle of William Thorne.

and other authorities including the *Glossa ordinaria*, the name of 'Christ' derives from *chrisma*, a term for the holy oil that was used to anoint the priests of Israel.[101] The same holy oil formed part of the coronation ceremony: the *Liber custumarum* records that Sudbury anointed Richard II with 'oleo sancto atque chrismate [holy oil and chrism]' at his coronation.[102] Insisting on this derivation, Conscience invokes a familiar etymology with explicit links to the coronation of medieval kings and then overwrites it with a new one that emphasizes Christ's act of conquest. Later, when Christ performs his healing miracles, the 'comune peple' proclaim him '*Fili Dauid*', 'kyng of þe kingdom of Iuda' (B.19.132–3, 138), with a shout of affirmation that echoes the coronation ceremony and the 'crye' of the 'commune' in the Prologue. Yet, Conscience insists that the 'comune' make Jesus their king 'For þe dedes þat he did', noting that these 'dedes' confirm his royal lineage, since David, too, was 'doughtiest of dedes in his tyme' (B.19.133–4). Here again, Conscience is able to describe Christ's *adventus* in terms of the subsequent events that 'preue' his titles, conclusively and unambiguously.

In his account of Christ's *adventus*, Conscience revisits the analogy between angels and preachers that appeared in the Prologue. Where in the earlier coronation scene the angel was one of three preachers who revealed the difficulty of speaking for the *commune* in the multiple languages and registers of late medieval preaching, however, the angels in the sermon of Conscience speak in a confident, unified, public voice that reflects the distinctive confidence of this historical moment.[103] Conscience relates how 'kynges and aungeles' pay homage to Christ, marking his *adventus* and proclaiming its significance (B.19.72). The angels come 'out of heuene' with their songs of praise while the Magi offer 'richesses of erþe' as gifts (B.19.73–4), an opposition that recalls the contrasting postures of the angel and the lunatic in the Prologue, but both groups then adopt the same posture, kneeling before the new king in a collective display of reverence (B.19.75, 81). Later, the angels will counsel the kings, in an echo of the role that Kynde Wit assigns to the clergy: the Magi return to their kingdoms 'by counseil of aungeles' (B.19.79), without reporting their discovery to Herod. Here, too, the scene resembles the situation in the Prologue, as kings and angels, who are in turn identified

---

[101] On this etymology, see for example Augustine, *De civitate Dei*, ed. Domart and Kalb, 2: 543–5 (16.xxxviii); Augustine, *Enarrationes in Psalmos*, ed. Deckers and Fraipont, 3: 1598–9 (108.xxvi); Isidore of Seville, *Etymologiarum*, ed. W. M. Lindsay, 2 vols (Oxford: Clarendon Press, 1911), unpaginated (7.2.2–9). On the *glossa* and for other citations, see also Barney, *Penn Commentary*, 5: 111.

[102] *Munimenta Gildhallae Londoniensis*, vol. 2: *Liber Custumarum, with Extracts from the Cottonian MS. Claudius D.II*, ed. Henry Thomas Riley (London: Longman, 1860; repr. Cambridge: Cambridge University Press, 2012), 479. Walsingham refers to 'oleum sanctificato' but not to 'chrismate' in his own account of this ceremony; *St Albans Chronicle*, ed. and trans. Taylor, Childs, and Watkiss, 1: 144, 145.

[103] Angels perform their preacherly role as heralds and messengers in the earlier iterations of Christ's life, too: the inner dream contains an annunciation scene, where Gabriel, described as 'þe messager', tells Mary that Jesus 'moste iouke in hir chambre' (B.16.97, 92); the angels proclaim Christ's atonement after the harrowing of hell, singing lines from the hymn *Æterne Rex altissime* (B.18.408–9).

with preachers, affirm their obligations to one another, following the advent of a new king.

As he describes the kings and angels kneeling together, Conscience returns to Philippians 2:10, the text that Will invoked in his original question, and that formed the *thema* for his sermon: '*Omnia celestia, terrestria, flecantur in hoc nomine Iesu* [That in the name of Jesus every [knee] should bow, of those that are in heaven, on earth...]'. As the kings and angels speak with their unified voices, Conscience arrives at a moment of structural agreement in his own discourse:

And þere was þat word fulfilled þe which þow of speke—	*spoke*
Omnia celestia, terrestria, flecantur in hoc nomine Iesu.	
For alle þe aungeles of heuene at his burþe knelede,	
And al þe wit of þe world was in þo þre kynges.	*wisdom, those*
	(B.19.80–2)

Conscience adds his own preacherly voice to the voices of the kings and angels, articulating the significance of an axial moment for the life of the Christian community. In his reading of Philippians 2:10, moreover, he takes the kings and angels to represent a much larger community of which he is himself a part, a *commune* that encompasses all of creation, on earth and in heaven. Here, then, the analogy between angels and preachers, which previously suggested strains and tensions in the preacher's voice, is now recuperated in a triumphant image of harmonious, collective speech, lucid interpretation, and shared understanding.

At the end of his sermon, Conscience invites the dreamer to participate in these gestures of reverence, and to speak with this singular voice of praise, as an individual member of the contemporary *commune*. Conscience and the dreamer kneel together, singing the antiphon 'Veni Creator Spiritus' as they welcome the arrival of the Holy Spirit, and are joined by a large crowd of worshippers: 'Thanne song I þat song, and so dide manye hundred,/ And cride wiþ Conscience, "Help vs, God of grace!"' (B.19.212–13). This Pentecostal scene marks the advent of Christ in the soul and provides an opportunity for the *commune* to speak together, affirming their allegiance to the new king, and their submission to his new law. Barney notes that the 'Veni Creator Spiritus' was sung at the Offertory during mass, returning the action to the liturgical context where the dreamer first fell asleep.[104] Simpson, meanwhile, links this scene to a moment in London civic pageantry, when the mayor, aldermen, and sheriffs processed from Cornhill to St Paul's for a service where vicars sung 'Veni Creator Spiritus' while 'an angel censed from above'.[105] As

---

[104] Barney, *Penn Commentary*, 5: 132.
[105] Simpson, '"After Craftes Conseil clotheth yow and fede": Langland and London City Politics', 109–27 in *England in the Fourteenth Century: Proceedings of the 1991 Harlaxton Symposium*, ed. Nicholas Rogers (Stamford: Paul Watkins, 1993), 109.

we saw in the earlier parts of this chapter, moreover, the antiphon 'Veni Creator Spiritus' formed part of Richard's coronation ceremony where, after the anointing, the archbishop prayed that the king would rule with justice and moderation ('iustis moderaminibus'), and called on God to guide his judgements.[106] The collective cry that follows this hymn echoes the cry of assent from the coronation *ordo*, and its allegorical depiction in the Prologue to *Piers*, where the 'commune' cried out 'in vers of Latyn', expressing their fealty to the king (B.Prol.143). Here as in the Prologue, the poem looks to public, liturgical, and ceremonial contexts to imagine the *commune* speaking together, declaring their commitments to one another in an interpreted present, reconfigured through the mediation of narrative.

The Prologue does not dramatize the king's response to the lunatic, the angel, and the goliard, or show how their preaching at the coronation informs the subsequent reign, except insofar as the conditions of this new era might be represented in the fable of the rodent parliament. Once Conscience concludes his sermon in the seventh vision, however, the poem shows how public life unfolds in the present time, reconfigured by the act of emplotment he has performed. After he describes Christ's *adventus* as an axial moment in the life of the community, and explains the new 'lawe of lif' that will follow from it, Conscience witnesses the foundation of the institutions that will administer this law in the world. The poem imagines the Christian community remade in the aftermath of his sermon as Grace advises Piers Plowman to summon 'þe comune', and distributes the skills and talents that will allow each estate to perform its social function (B.19.215). This distribution of gifts leads once more to the creation of preachers, who receive 'wit to wissen oþere [instruct others] as grace hem wolde teche' (B.19.234), continuing the work that Conscience has begun, elaborating new narratives from within the institution of the church.

Even before he gives these gifts to the people, however, Grace predicts a time when Conscience will have to fight against the forces of the Antichrist, when kings will fall under the influence of flatterers and false prophets, and when Pride will be installed as Pope, with Coueitise and Vnkyndenesse as his cardinals. In the later part of this passus, the dreamer watches as Pride appears on the field with his 'greet oost [army]' to 'greuen [harass]' Conscience, and to undermine the public life of the community, subverting the law that Christ has instituted (B.19.338–9). Conscience continues to preach in this part of the poem, offering 'conseil' to 'al þe comune' (B.19.397, 395), but he finds himself addressing a divided community in a debased and contested language: Conscience confronts the realities of the schismatic late medieval church with popes 'At Auynoun [Avignon]' and 'in Rome' (B.19.426–7), he meets hostility from different individuals within the *commune*, like the brewer who declares that 'I wol noȝt be ruled' (B.19.400), and

---

[106] Walsingham, *St Albans Chronicle*, ed. and trans. Taylor, Childs, and Watkiss, 1: 144, 145.

encounters a discourse where vice can be redescribed as virtue, in forms that Aers identifies with the figure of *paradiastole*.[107]

The challenges facing Conscience come into sharp focus at the end of this vision, when he meets a contemporary king and advises him on the administration of justice. The king arrives with a line that echoes the Prologue coronation scene ('þanne cam þer a kyng'), but he proposes a form of government that is strikingly different from the 'riȝtful rulyng' envisaged by the preachers in that scene. Swearing 'by his croune', the king declares that he will rule according to his own desires, as though *rex* was derived from *regnare*, and not from *regere*:

> And þanne cam þer a kyng and by his croune seide,
> 'I am kyng wiþ croune þe comune to rule,
> And Holy Kirke and clergie fro cursed men to defende.   *evil*
> And if me lakkeþ to lyue by, þe lawe wole I take it
> Ther I may hastilokest it haue—for I am heed of lawe: *most promptly*
> For ye ben but members and I aboue alle.'
>
> (B.19.469–74)

Aers reads this speech as an example of the paradiastolic redefinition of virtues as vices that characterizes this part of the poem: the king goes on to redefine '*Spiritus Iusticie*' as a rationale for tyrannical domination, using it to justify his own 'unqualified domination of the "commune".'[108]

Conscience responds to the king in a short, three-line speech, with only the faintest echo of his earlier sermon—a discourse that had occupied nearly two hundred lines at the start of this vision. He concedes that the king may 'haue þyn asking [request], as þi lawe askeþ [requires]', on the condition that he 'rule þi reaume in reson, right wel and in truþe', and concludes with a veiled warning in Latin: '*Omnia sunt tua ad defendendum set non ad deprehendendum* [Everything is yours to defend, but not to despoil]' (B.19.481–3a).[109] These lines contain a subtle echo of the lunatic's prayer for 'riȝtful rulyng', and mirror the angel's turn to Latin as they warn about the limits of royal power; the singular voice of Conscience now moves between the multiple and potentially exclusionary registers of contemporary preaching and royal advice. Like the preachers of the Prologue, Conscience offers a guarded account of the king's obligations under the law and imagines alternate possibilities for his rule in the future. This brief and hesitant interjection falls far short of the transformative, discursive work that Conscience performed in his earlier narratives about the life of Christ. Preaching at the foundation of the Christian community, Conscience was able to show how

---

[107] Aers, *Beyond Reformation?*, 85.   [108] Aers, *Beyond Reformation?*, 79.
[109] For this translation see Barney, *Penn Commentary*, 5: 184. This quotation may be an adapted form of lines from the *Summa de vitiis* of Peraldus; see Alford, *Guide to the Quotations*, 116.

Christ's royal qualities of *ius* and *pietas*, figured by the gifts he received at his coronation, became manifest in his life, ministry, and death. Configuring disparate events from the gospels into a cohesive narrative of good governance, he was able to extrapolate from them a 'lawe of lif' that would govern the community in his own time. At the end of passus 19, however, he finds himself in the position of the lunatic, the angel, and the goliard in the Prologue, seeking 'to counseillen þe Kyng and þe Commune saue' in a discursive context characterized by risk and uncertainty about the future.

* * *

In these two episodes from the Prologue and the seventh vision of *Piers Plowman*, Langland explores the role of preaching at important moments in public, political life. The preachers in these episodes establish the significance of the king's coronation and the *adventus* of Christ by reconfiguring them as part of a larger narrative of good governance and 'riȝtful' rule, looking back to earlier precedents and forward to imagine the implementation of law in the coming reign. Drawing on the coronation *ordo* and the Advent liturgy, they locate these inaugural events as 'axial moments', turning points in the life of the community that mark a break from the past and establish new possibilities for the future. For Ricoeur, the 'axial moment' marks the 'reinscription' of cosmological and phenomenological time, as a significant present experience coincides with a dateable instant on the calendar; moments like this provide a point of orientation for the 'third time' of public history, where individuals understand their own experiences in relation to those of their forebears, contemporaries, and successors. Langland's preachers, too, work to establish a narrative discourse that enables their respective audiences to speak collectively about their shared investments and obligations under the law, expressing their hopes and fears for the future. The lunatic, the angel, and the goliard in the Prologue, and Conscience in the seventh vision, perform acts of emplotment that are followed by collective expressions of agreement and assent, by the establishment of new laws and institutions, or by the renewal of old ones. In each case, the preacher's work of emplotment enables a community to speak and act together in the context of an interpreted present.

As he imagines the work that preaching could perform for the *commune* as a whole in these scenes, however, Langland also acknowledges the challenges facing preachers who sought to intervene in public life. While preachers like Brinton and Rypon spoke with confidence about their public role, guiding and directing royal policy and promoting good governance, *Piers Plowman* locates risks and difficulties in counselling the king on behalf of the *commune*. In the Prologue, Langland imagines contentious, conflicting voices engaged in a shared interpretative project, as the lunatic, the angel, and the goliard work to fashion a common, narrative discourse from the different languages and registers of contemporary preaching. Conscience, too, generates multiple narratives to explain the *adventus* of Christ, drawing out different aspects of the same story as he deploys the exegetical techniques of the preacher. The preachers of the Prologue offer advice on good government that will be tried and tested in the reign to come, projecting narrative possibilities against a shared horizon of expectations, and their interventions are answered by a fable that calls the value of counsel into question. In the seventh vision, by contrast, Conscience is able to interpret the events of Christ's *adventus* in the light of his victory on the cross, gesturing ahead to a time when the hopeful aspirations that are encoded in the symbolism of Christ's nativity will be born out in clear, conclusive ways by his decisive actions as king. Yet Conscience, too, confronts the uncertain situation of the Prologue's preachers as the institutions of contemporary life are established around him, and he addresses himself to a tyrannical king who seems determined to govern according to his own will. These scenes from the poem suggest that preachers might fashion a common discourse for the larger community through the interpretative labour of emplotment, but they seem sceptical, even pessimistic about the preacher's capacity to guide and direct the policy of government.

These preaching scenes from the Prologue and the seventh vision demonstrate some of the many ways that sermon discourse could give rise to narrative, as elliptical maxims about good government unfold their temporal logic, as etymologies of kingship suggest relationships between past precedent and future practice, and as a discussion of names and titles establishes the premise for multiple *distinctiones* that reveal new aspects of the same story. In Lambeth Palace MS 61, where the angel's speech from the Prologue is appended to Harclay's sermon on Thomas Becket, it serves as a concise, if cryptic, summary of an extended narrative discourse that traces the history of English kingship from Becket's martyrdom until the present day, and offers direct advice to the present king. Like the palindrome 'Laus tua, non tua fraus', these excerpted lines from *Piers Plowman* reiterate the narrative logic of Harclay's sermon in other terms, imagining a past that contains instructive precedents for the future.

2
Preaching on the Half-Acre
Fear, Hope, and Narrative in the Second Vision

In the second vision of *Piers Plowman*, Langland considers the power of preaching to motivate and sustain reforming effort. This vision begins with a sermon, as Reason preaches to the king and the whole community. He explains the natural disasters they have lived through as divine retribution for human sin and as warning signs of the coming apocalypse, and calls on them to repent before the end of the world. This sermon performs a powerful and compelling act of emplotment, taking up a range of events from recent history, configuring them into a narrative, and so reconfiguring its listeners' perceptions of the world they inhabit: here, the threefold *mimesis* that Ricoeur describes takes place in the dramatic action of the poem. The effects it achieves can be seen in the action that follows: Reason moves the people to contrition, which leads in turn to the confession of the Sins, a penitential pilgrimage, and the receipt of a pardon. Through the act of emplotment it performs, Reason's sermon discloses the strict but comprehensible standard of God's justice at work in recent history, transforming his listeners' sense of their obligations and capacities: if the people are responsible for the storms and pestilences they have suffered, then perhaps they can also avert future disasters through their own efforts. It also locates contemporary events in the broader scheme of eschatological time, so that recent disasters portend an imminent apocalypse, creating powerful imperatives to reform. This sermon produces a sense of dread that is galvanizing and enabling, fear for the future that is tempered by hope.

Reason's sermon is among the most effective in the whole poem. Emily Steiner observes that it is 'universally affecting'.[1] Alan Fletcher, who describes it as 'preaching's benchmark' in *Piers Plowman*, notes that '[n]othing impugns it' and 'no dissenting voices detract from it'.[2] In the fraught and conflicted action that unfolds in the later parts of the second vision, however, Langland will suggest that even this exemplary sermon cannot sustain the people's efforts for the duration of their pilgrimage to Truth. After the confessions of the sins, Piers Plowman himself appears on the field to guide and direct the people in their penitential activities. Piers, I argue, takes up the task that Reason began, offering

---

[1] Steiner, *Reading Piers Plowman* (Cambridge: Cambridge University Press, 2013), 69.
[2] Fletcher, *Preaching, Politics, and Poetry*, 202–3.

new acts of emplotment that keep the strict standard of God's justice and the implications of the imminent apocalypse in view, interpreting the lived experience of history as it unfolds. In this sense, as the other pilgrims are increasingly aware, Piers himself becomes a preacher. As the pilgrimage to Truth is subsumed into labour on the half-acre, however, and this labour evolves into a site of social conflict, narratives of the kind that Reason had offered become harder to articulate, and the people less receptive to hearing them. The memory of recent disasters begins to fade, threatened punishments and promised rewards are repeatedly deferred, and the ploughman's own authority to preach comes under critical scrutiny. Taken as a whole, then, the second vision develops a contrast between the preaching of Reason, imagined as a single, decisive intervention in public life, and the preaching of Piers Plowman, imagined as an ongoing project of spiritual guidance and pastoral care. As we will see, the work of emplotment proves more difficult for the ploughman, who must keep the large-scale implications of history in view amid the distractions and preoccupations of daily life.

In making this argument, I seek to re-open a critical debate about the structure of this part of the poem that has long seemed settled. In a 1965 article recently described as 'one of the most influential essays ever written' on *Piers Plowman*, John Burrow argued for the unity of Langland's second vision, which earlier critics had understood as a series of discontinuous episodes.[3] Burrow traced an 'arc of penitential action' through this part of the poem, beginning with Reason's sermon and concluding with the pardon, and described the stages of the penitential process as the beginning, middle, and end of an Aristotelian plot.[4] He then argued, however, that the poem obscures the logic of this narrative through a series of metaphorical 'substitutions,' which reflect Langland's scepticism about penitential practice: the pilgrimage to Truth is reimagined by stages as work on the half-acre, while the pardon, for which no satisfactory substitute can be found, is ultimately torn and discarded. In this chapter, I offer a challenge to Burrow's reading and a new paradigm for thinking about the second vision. The most important narrative structures in this part of the poem, I argue, are those that are spoken as part of the dramatic action, when preachers seek to interpret the world around them. The 'arc of operations' that Ricoeur describes takes place repeatedly within Burrow's 'arc of penitential action', as Reason and Piers reveal how God's justice operates in history, and urge their listeners to reform. Where Burrow describes a narrative logic that is gradually eroded by substitution and negation, I will show that the poem dramatizes the ongoing efforts of different preachers to discern this logic in

---

[3] Burrow, 'The Action of Langland's Second Vision', *Essays in Criticism* 15 (1965): 247–68, repr. as 79–101 in Burrow, *Essays on Medieval Literature* (Oxford: Clarendon, 1984). On the lasting influence of this essay, see Hanna, *The Penn Commentary on Piers Plowman, vol. 2: C Passūs 5–9; B Passūs 5–7; A Passūs 5–8* (Philadelphia: University of Pennsylvania Press, 2017), 48. Schmidt directs his readers to Burrow for an account of the structure of the second vision: *Parallel Text*, ed. Schmidt, 2: 520.

[4] Burrow, 'Langland's Second Vision', 70–80 (quotation at 80).

the world around them, and to make it visible to their listeners. On Burrow's account of the second vision, Reason's sermon, while structurally important, is largely peripheral to Langland's satirical concerns. Burrow's reading has tended to direct critical attention away from the sermon, and to focus it on the later stages of this vision, where penitential structures come under attack.[5] This chapter, however, will show that the transformative effects of Reason's sermon are key to the vision as a whole, as Piers attempts to sustain and extend the work of emplotment it performs.

Reason's sermon finds many analogues in preaching from the late fourteenth and early fifteenth centuries: surviving sermon texts perform similar acts of emplotment, explaining recent disasters as punishments for human sin and as forerunning signs of judgement day. Sermons on Luke 21, where Christ predicts the signs that will herald the end of the world, might also attempt to locate these signs in the lived experiences of their listeners, 'preuing' the claims of scripture with evidence from the observable world. These sermons offer their own reflections on the effects that Reason achieves in the second vision, considering the spiritual value of *timor* and 'drede,' and showing how they emerge through the mediation of narrative. Construed as part of a plot, these preachers suggest, 'Principium sapientiae timor Domini [The fear of the Lord is the beginning of wisdom]' (Proverbs 9:10). Yet, they also describe the kind of ongoing, interpretative labour that Piers Plowman will undertake and that will prove so problematic in the later parts of the second vision, urging their listeners to seek out new apocalyptic signs in the world around them, and to reconfigure their everyday experience in terms of the narrative resources they have provided. The difficulties that the ploughman encounters are difficulties that many late medieval preachers might recognize.

Storm Damage

In his sermon at the start of passus 5 in the B text, Reason preaches about the recurrent outbreaks of plague in England since 1348 and St Maur's wind, 'þe south-west wynd on Saterday at euen [in the evening]' which struck during the second of these, on Saturday 15 January 1362. He configures these events into a narrative, explaining them as punishments from God for human 'pride' and as a foretaste of the judgement that will follow for 'dedly synne' on 'domesday':

---

[5] '[T]o put it bluntly', Burrow writes, Langland did believe 'in sermons and confessions' but he 'did not believe in pilgrimages'; thus, the poem reserves its critical attention, and its satirical comment, for the later parts of the vision: 'Langland's Second Vision', 83–4. More recently, Steiner has described 'three discreet episodes' in the second vision: 'the Confession of the Seven Deadly Sins', 'the Plowing of the Half-Acre', and 'Truth's Pardon'; this overview disregards the sermon, except as a prompt for the confessions that follow it; *Reading Piers Plowman*, 61.

And þanne sauȝ I muche moore þan I bifore tolde—	*described*
For I seiȝ þe feld ful of folk þat I before of seide,	
And how Reason gan arayen hym al þe reaume to preche,	*prepare*
And wiþ a cros afore þe Kyng comsede þus to techen.	*began*
He preued þat þise pestilences was for pure synne,	*demonstrated; solely*
And þe south-west wynd on Saterday at euen	*in the evening*
Was pertliche for pride and for no point ellis.	*manifestly; other reason*
Pyries and plum-trees were puffed to þe erþe	*Pear-trees*
In ensample, segges, þat ye sholden do þe bettre;	*As a sign; men*
Beches and brode okes were blowen to þe grounde	*Beach trees; broad oaks*
And turned vpward here tail in tokenynge of drede	*roots; fear*
That dedly synne er domesday shal fordoon hem alle.	*before; destroy*

(B.5.9–20)

As Reason delivers this sermon, the threefold *mimesis* that Ricoeur describes takes place in the dramatic action of the poem.[6] Reason discerns the logic of divine retribution in this apparently chaotic sequence of events and configures them into a plot that gives this logic expression, 'grasping [them] together' in a relation of 'discordant concordance'.[7] In doing so, he reconfigures his listeners' perception of their own moment in time, changing their understanding of the recent past and their expectations about the imminent future. The sermon produces what, borrowing from Gadamer, Ricoeur describes as a 'fusion of horizons', as the 'world of the text', or in this case the interpreted world of Reason's oratory, unfolds in front of his listeners.[8] The 'folk' on the field experience 'the shock of the possible' as his sermon discloses new possibilities for reforming, penitential action, in the context of their interpreted present time.[9]

Contemporary chroniclers described the aftermath of St Maur's wind in similar terms to Reason and sometimes imagined the storm as an apocalyptic sign. The anonymous Canterbury Chronicler, for example, says that 'arboresque fructifere in gardinis et locis aliis, et arbores alie in nemoribus et alibi existentes, cum magno sonitu a terra radicitus euulse fuerunt, ac si dies iudicii adueniret [fruit trees in gardens and other places, along with other trees standing in woods and elsewhere, were wrenched from the earth by their roots with a great crash, as if the Day of Judgement were at hand]'.[10] The imagery of upturned trees was also associated with apocalyptic prophecy in the tradition of the 'Fifteen Signs Before Doomsday',

---

[6] Ricoeur, *Time and Narrative*, 1: 52–87.   [7] Ricoeur, *Time and Narrative*, 1: 41, 66.
[8] Ricoeur, *Time and Narrative*, 1: 77.   [9] Ricoeur, *Time and Narrative*, 1: 79.
[10] *Chronicon Anonymi Cantuariensis: The Chronicle of Anonymous of Canterbury, 1346-1365*, ed. and trans. Charity Scott-Stokes and Chris Given-Wilson (Oxford: Oxford University Press, 2008), 118, 119. See also *Knighton's Chronicle,* ed. and trans. Martin, 184, 185, and *The Anonimalle Chronicle*, ed. Galbraith, 50.

which was often rehearsed in medieval sermons.[11] In the final, apocalyptic passus of *Piers Plowman*, the dreamer will describe how Antichrist turned 'al þe crop [branches, foliage] of truþe/... vp-so-doun, and ouertilte [upended] þe roote' (B.20.53-4), in an allusion to this familiar imagery.[12] Reason's sermon elaborates the narrative logic that informs these readings of recent disasters, drawing out the causal connections between individual sin, divine retribution, and the coming apocalypse, as he construes them as part of an interpreted *holos*. His sermon shows how this kind of emplotment might be a source of pastoral consolation, revealing a narrative logic in the apparent chaos of recent experience, and a source of spiritual inspiration, encouraging new efforts to turn from sin.

Reason in *Piers Plowman* embodies a universal standard of equity and order, reflected in human laws and social institutions and manifest in the design of the natural world, as John Alford has shown.[13] At the end of the previous vision, where Reason is called to the court to advise on the trial of Mede, he expresses this principle in a maxim of canon law: 'nullum malum inpunitum, nullum bonum irremuneratum [no evil unpunished, no good unrewarded]' (B.4.143-4).[14] In this earlier scene, the logic of the maxim seems obscure and difficult and its claim on contemporary realities uncertain. Reason recasts it as a miniature personification allegory, where *Nullum malum* 'þe man' demands of *Inpunitum* that *Nullum bonum* should not be rewarded, so that its central claim becomes an expression of desire, rather than a statement of fact (B.4.139-44).[15] He adds that the maxim will require further translation and exegesis in a private and exclusive setting, as though its Latin form obscures its meaning: 'Lat þi confessour, sire Kyng, construe

[11] For a recent reading of the 'Fifteen Signs' from an ecocritical perspective, see Shannon Gayk, 'Apocalyptic Ecologies: Eschatology, the Ethics of Care, and the Fifteen Signs of Doom in Early England', *Speculum* 96, no. 1 (2021): 1-37. Gayk considers Reason's moralizing sermon as an outlier in this tradition, where the signs were more commonly presented as a numbered list, an invitation to observe environmental change on its own terms (20).

[12] See Barney, *Penn Commentary*, 5: 206-7.

[13] Alford, 'The Idea of Reason in *Piers Plowman*', 199-215 in *Medieval Studies Presented to George Kane*, ed. Edward Donald Kennedy, Ronald Waldron, and Joseph S. Wittig (Cambridge: Brewer, 1988). See also Alford, *Glossary of Legal Diction*, 134-5, s.v. 'Resoun'. For Reason as a legal concept, see Galloway, *Penn Commentary*, 1: 377-8, and for reason as a psychological power that participates in these larger patterns of rational order, see Zeeman, *Arts of Disruption*, 169.

[14] The maxim is translated and discussed in Galloway, *Penn Commentary*, 1: 411-12. Alford argues that this maxim encapsulates the principles that Reason stands for; 'The Idea of Reason', 208-10. On the maxim as a principle of canon law, see Nick Gray, 'Langland's Quotations from the Penitential Tradition', *Modern Philology* 84 (1986): 55-6; Alford, *Guide to the Quotations*, 42-3; Thomas, *Piers Plowman and the Reinvention of Church Law*, 164-205. Versions of this maxim were rehearsed in medieval sermons. See, for example, Brinton, *Sermons*, ed. Devlin, 2: 480, and Mirk, *Festial*, ed. Powell, 1: 75.

[15] This moment offers an example of the 'vertiginous use of personification allegory' that Michael Calabrese describes in the poem, where 'a "character"... might spring briefly into animated form before vanishing back into the poetic discourse'; 'Posthuman Piers?: Rediscovering Langland's Subjectivities' *YLS* 32 (2018): 5. Galloway explains that the meaning of the *nullum malum* phrase emerges obliquely in this allegorical encounter, through a series of negations: 'an entity "No Evil"... meets with the figure "Not Punished" and requests that "No Good" not be rewarded (or even that No Good *become* another entity, "Not Rewarded")'; *Penn Commentary*, 1: 412.

þis on Englissh' (B.4.145). Preaching in the second vision, however, Reason uncovers this essential principle in the events of recent history and discloses it to the king and the whole community, stridently and in the vernacular, through an act of emplotment. The maxim becomes what Ricoeur would call the 'single thought' that governs his narrative, and that confers coherence on its disparate elements. The dreamer introduces his *reportatio* of this sermon with the 'prechen' and 'preuen' collocation—having prepared himself 'to preche', he says, Reason 'preued þat þise pestilences was for pure synne' (B.5.11, 13), as though the sermon offers an exegetical narrative elaborated from the book of nature, rather than a reading of canon law texts.[16] Principles of justice that were difficult to discern and dangerous to articulate at court, emerge clearly and incontrovertibly in Reason's account of the natural world. The dreamer discerns the same clarity in Reason's sermon as Reason discerns in the storm: Reason, he says, preaches 'pertly [openly, forthrightly] afore þe peple' (B.5.23), just as, on Reason's own account, 'þe south-west wynd on Saterday at euen/ Was pertliche [openly, manifestly] for pride and for no point ellis' (B.5.14–15).[17]

Reason's sermon inspires a kind of 'drede' that is consistent with the principles of rationality he embodies and that emerges through the act of emplotment he performs. As Mary Carruthers has shown, Langland uses 'drede' in contexts like this to translate the concept of *timor Domini*, 'the fear of the Lord'.[18] Carruthers describes a widespread distinction in medieval culture between *timor Domini*, which produces understanding and devotion, and *terror Dei*, where thought and sensation are suspended. *Timor domini* is characteristically rational, a reasonable reaction to the revelation of divine power, while *terror* strips rationality away and removes a person's capacity to think or act.[19] *Piers Plowman* offers its fullest account of *timor Domini* in the third vision, where Wit aligns the 'drede' of God with Do-wel. Wit quotes Psalm 110:10, 'the fear of the Lord is the beginning of wisdom', but adds that, from these beginnings, new actions follow: '*Inicium sapiencie timor Domini./* That dredeþ God, he dooþ wel' (B.9.94a–95).[20] At the

---

[16] Reason appears again as an exegete of the natural world in the poem's first inner dream, B.11.334–404. See Alford, 'Idea of Reason', 210–14; Davis, *Books of Nature*, 156–64.

[17] See *MED* 'pertli' (a), 'openly, clearly, plainly, publicly', citing both these instances from B.5 as examples of the same sense. Alan of Lille suggests that a preacher might project the force of a storm when reprimanding his listeners. He writes that a strident sermon 'compluat doctrinis' and 'tonet minis' ['rains down doctrines' and 'thunders forth admonitions']; *De arte praedicatoria*, 1, ed. Migne, 210: col. 113, translation adapted from Alan of Lille, *The Art of Preaching*, trans. Gillian R. Evans (Kalamazoo: Western Michigan University Press, 1981), 20.

[18] Carruthers, '*Terror, Horror*, and the Fear of God, or, Why There Is No Medieval Sublime', 17–36 in '*Truthe is the beste*': *A Festschrift in Honour of A. V. C. Schmidt*, ed. Nicholas Jacobs and Gerald Morgan (Oxford: Peter Lang, 2014), 29–30.

[19] Carruthers, '*Terror, Horror*, and the Fear of God', 21.

[20] Paul Megna has shown how the poem's thought on 'drede' evolves through the different versions of this passage, where love first counterbalances then finally supplants fear as the impetus to ethical action. Megna, 'Dread, Love, and the Bodies of *Piers Plowman* A.10, B.9 and C.10', *YLS* 29 (2015): 61–88.

start of the second vision, the fear of God emerges through the discursive mediation of narrative, as Reason interprets recent events in his sermon. The direct, phenomenological experience of storms and plagues is one of paralysing *terror*, but Reason recasts these experiences as a source of *timor* by locating them in a larger plot, disclosing their significance in relation to the sins of individuals and the overarching shape of eschatological history. As punishments for 'pride' and as forerunning signs of the apocalypse, these fearful events become a source of 'drede', creating imperatives to reform and producing a new resolve to 'do þe bettre'.

Like the sermons of the B-text Prologue, Reason's sermon is delivered to 'al þe reaume', and in the presence of the king, and like them it invites its listeners to understand their own present moment in history, as part of a narrative that unfolds in public, intersubjective time. In Chapter 1, I argued that the preachers of the Prologue sought to identify the king's coronation as a point of orientation for a public history like this, where phenomenological experience coincides with dateable instants in cosmic time, an 'axial moment' in Ricoeur's terminology. Reason's sermon imagines the 'pestilence' in a similar way. As Andrew Galloway notes, the first outbreak of plague in 1349 was 'inscribed deeply in later fourteenth century culture', and several speakers in *Piers Plowman* offer a 'construction of history "before and after the plague"'.[21] Although Reason's sermon refers directly to the recurrence of plague that coincided with St Maur's wind in the early 1360s, he understands it as part of a series of disasters, 'þise pestilences', stretching back to the original outbreak that inaugurates the contemporary moment.

Alongside the axial moment, Ricoeur describes other 'connective instruments' that link phenomenological and cosmological time and serve to orient a public history. These include the 'traces' and 'vestiges' of the past, the material and documentary records of events that unfolded at other points in time, where they once formed part of direct, phenomenological experience; to 'reckon with' traces and vestiges like this, Ricoeur observes, is to think about both orders of time together.[22] Reason's sermon locates traces and vestiges of God's displeasure in the landscape. When he recollects the storms, in particular, he draws attention to the damage they leave behind, describing 'Pyries and plum-trees... puffed to þe erþe'; 'Beches and brode okes... blowen to þe grounde'. If the pestilence offers an ultimate point of orientation, these traces and vestiges establish more immediate reference points in the shared social space of the field and the collective memory of Reason's listeners. In the context of Reason's sermon, moreover, the pestilence and the storms that follow it encode warnings about the future: this record of past

---

[21] Galloway, *Penn Commentary*, 1: 95, and see also Galloway, 'Latin England', 41–95 in *Imagining a Medieval English Nation*, ed. Kathy Lavezzo (Minneapolis: University of Minnesota Press, 2004), 46–7. For an argument that Langland is largely silent about the plague and its effects, however, see Smith, *Arts of Dying: Literature and Finitude in Medieval England* (Chicago: University of Chicago Press, 2020), 131–2.

[22] Ricouer, *Time and Narrative*, 3: 120–6.

experience can also be read to foreshadow the apocalypse, to make it vivid and tangible in the experiential present.

In the main divisions of his sermon, Reason offers reforming injunctions to each estate in turn, inviting the people to think afresh about their shared past and their collective future. Members of each estate are encouraged to reconsider their mutual obligations in the light of the narrative that Reason elaborates. Reason's sermon has often been described as a *sermo ad status* because it addresses different social groups in this way.[23] This claim, however, rests on a mischaracterization of *ad status* sermons, which typically addressed one group to the exclusion of others rather than many groups together. James of Vitry's *ad status* collection, for example, distinguishes twenty-nine categories of people and presents multiple sermons tailored specifically to each of them.[24] As both Fletcher and Ralph Hanna have argued, Reason's sermon more closely resembles a late medieval sub-genre of preaching on the three estates, exemplified by Thomas Wimbledon's widely disseminated sermon on Luke 16:2, delivered at St Paul's Cross in c.1387.[25] Like Reason on the field, Wimbledon addresses each social group in the shadow of the impending apocalypse. In the first part of his sermon, he declares that 'euery staat [estate] shul loue oþer [the others] . . . siþ þey beþ so nedeful [necessary, beneficial] euerych to oþer'; then, in a series of subdivisions, he imagines how each estate will answer the same three questions, which Christ will put to them on doomsday: 'þe firste questioun, how hast þou entred; þe secunde, how hast þou reulid [ruled]; and þe þridde, how hast þou luyuyd'.[26] In the second part, he performs an act of emplotment, locating his present moment near the end of eschatological history: here, he describes the 'þre somoners [summoners]' who will call people to the 'special' judgement after death, and the forerunning signs that herald the 'vniuersal' judgement on doomsday, before calculating the date when the apocalypse will fall.[27]

---

[23] On Reason's sermon as a *sermo ad status* see, for example, *Piers Plowman B*, ed. Bennett, 151–2; Wenzel, 'Medieval Sermons', 162; Simpson, *Introduction*, 58; *Piers Plowman Parallel Text*, ed. Schmidt, 2: 559. Bloomfield, citing Bennett's definition of the *sermon ad status*, argued that the poem as a whole resembles a sermon *ad status* more than any other type of sermon; *Fourteenth Century Apocalypse*, 33.

[24] Jacques de Vitry, *Sermones vulgares vel ad status 1*, ed. Jean Longère, CCCM 225 (Turnhout: Brepols, 2013), 7 (Prol.6). The other major thirteenth century *ad status* collections, by Humbert of Romans and Guibert of Tournai, are structured in a similar way. The twelfth-century 'Sermo generalis' by Honorius of Autun is a rare example of a sermon *ad status* that addresses several social groups on a single occasion: *Speculum ecclesiae*, 172: cols 813–1108 in *PL*, ed. Migne, 172: cols 861–70. On *ad status* preaching and social theory, see Carolyn Muessig, 'Audience and Preacher: Ad status Sermons and Social Classification', 255–76 in *Preacher, Sermon and Audience in the Middle Ages*, ed. Muessig (Leiden: Brill, 2002).

[25] Fletcher, *Preaching, Politics, and Poetry*, 208; Hanna, *Penn Commentary*, 2: 49–50.

[26] *Wimbledon's Sermon*, ed. Knight, 65–6, 70. Ann Killian notes that these three questions, plus a fourth, are found in Bromyard's *Summa praedicantium*, where they are posed exclusively to clerics, and also appear in the eight-part *Prick of Conscience*, addressed to 'alle manere of men/ That othere shulden reule, teche and ken'; Killian, 'Menacing Books: *The Prick of Conscience* and the Rhetoric of Reproof', *YLS* 31 (2017): 17–20.

[27] *Wimbledon's Sermon*, ed. Knight, 98.

Reason calls on each estate to enforce the strict standard of justice that he embodies, and which he has discerned in his reading of recent disasters. He commands 'Tomme Stowue' to fetch his wife home from 'wyuene pyne [wives' punishment, the "pining stool"]' taking 'two staues [sticks]' to beat her with (B.5.28–9) and he tells 'Bette' to 'kutte a bouȝ [bough] ouþer tweye [or two] / And bete Beton þerwith but if she wolde werche' (B.5.32–3).[28] He also tells merchants to 'chasten hir children', quoting Proverbs 13:24 in support of corporal punishment: '*Qui parcit virge odit filium:*/ Whoso spareþ þe spryng [rod] spilleþ [spoils] hise children' (B.5.39a–40). In the C text, Reason also threatens clerics with a beating. Speaking words that were first composed for Study's complaint in B, he tells the professed religious that 'a kyng' will come to 'bete ȝow ... for brekynge of ȝoure reule' (C.5.168–9), and will give 'þe Abbot of Engelonde and the Abbesse his nese [niece] ... a knok vppon here crounes [tonsured heads]' (C.5.176–7), an apocalyptic prediction that imagines the last judgement in terms of corporal punishment.[29] With these violent beatings, Reason suggests, husbands, parents, and rulers will affirm the principle of the maxim 'nullum malum inpunitum, nullum bonum irremuneratum' and prolong the instructive *timor* that arises from divine retribution. Indeed, as it rips up trees and scatters them through the landscape, the storm supplies people with the 'staues', the 'bouȝ', and the 'spryng' to emulate and extend its violence.[30] In the A text, when Wit describes Do-wel as the 'drede of God', he likens Do-bet to a student's fear of beatings from his schoolmaster: 'Þanne is Dobet to ben ywar for betyng of þe ȝerde' (A.10.79, 85).[31] For Reason, too, the fear of the Lord is the beginning of wisdom, a precondition and a starting point for instruction.

In drawing these connections, Reason interpolates the lived experiences of individuals into the larger narrative of Christian eschatology: corporal punishment in the household creates its own traces and vestiges in the mind and on the body, which reinforce the lessons of the upturned trees in the landscape. His sermon contains a series of embedded references to lyrics and proverbs that mandate corporal punishment, as though calling to mind the formative experiences of childhood instruction in this context. In his instructions to merchants, for example, Reason quotes the first line of a lyric, 'Chasteȝ ȝoure chyldren quyl þay

---

[28] On the 'pining stool', also described at B.3.78, see Galloway, *Penn Commentary*, 1: 300, Hanna, *Penn Commentary*, 2: 56.

[29] Alford, 'The Idea of Reason in *Piers Plowman*', 209–10, argues that the poet reassigns this material in the C text in order to provide still more illustrations of the *nullum malum inpunitum* idea, and to 'connect that idea even more forcefully with the figure of Reason'.

[30] These various forms of domestic and pedagogical violence were authorized to different ends in different discursive and institutional contexts, as Ben Parsons has shown, but in each case writers appealed to an ideal of 'reason' in order to legitimate and delimit their use; Parsons, 'Beaten for a Book: Domestic and Pedagogic Violence in *The Wife of Bath's Prologue*', *Studies in the Age of Chaucer* 37 (2015): 163–94.

[31] On this passage, and its complex evocation of the 'rod' and 'staff' of Psalm 22.4, see Megna, 'Dread, Love, and the Bodies', 70.

ben yonge', also found in the *Fasciculus morum* and in contemporary sermons, which reminds parents that 'if ʒe lett hem to be bold,/ Þay wol yow greve when þay ben old'; he then cites one of the Proverbs of Hendyng, which follows the lyric in *Fasciculus morum*, as though recalling it from his own childhood: 'My sire seide so to me, and so dide my dame,/ That þe leuere child þe moore loore bihoueþ' (B.5.37–8).[32] In this moment, Reason presents himself as the adult product of such childhood instruction, as though the imposition of these strict standards might produce not a person, but a personification. Stern parental discipline shapes an individual life story in this example, just as divine retribution has shaped the story of the *commune* as a whole. 'Tomme Stowue', who Reason enjoins to discipline his wife, is another familiar figure from the discourses of proverbial instruction. In a macaronic sermon from British Library, Cotton MS Faustina A V, the preacher cites a proverb naming Tom as an idle husband, who fails to enforce discipline in the household: 'Þar [Where] Thome Stouue es at ham [is at home], God gif þe husband schame'.[33] He names him first as 'Thomas þe Thome (id est, vacuus)' (ll. 29–30), with a play on Middle English *tome*, meaning 'empty' or 'idle', then later as 'Thome Stowe', a name that refers to lopping the branches from a tree, and which figures the way that idleness cuts down virtue.[34] In Reason's sermon, by contrast, Tom's name refers to his reformed role as a strict disciplinarian; it not only recalls the uprooted trees that move him to 'do þe bettre' but also refers to the action of taking 'two staues', fashioning the instruments of household discipline from the debris of divine retribution. With these examples, Reason invokes the fearful experience of childhood instruction and domestic discipline and integrates these experiences into the larger narrative with which he began, encouraging his listeners to understand their own lives in relation to the intersubjective time of public history.

Reason also offers injunctions to other preachers. Speaking to parish priests and to the bishops who oversee pastoral care, he commands them to 'preue' their

---

[32] The lyric and proverb appear in the *Fasciculus morum: A Fourteenth-century Preacher's Handbook*, ed. and trans. Wenzel (University Park, PA: Pennsylvania State University Press, 1989), 90 (1.xi). For the text of the Proverbs of Hendyng, see 'Mon that wol of wysdam heren', in *The Complete Harley 2253 Manuscript*, ed. Susanna Greer Fein, 3 vols (Kalamazoo, MI: Medieval Institute Publications, 2014–15), 3: 220–36 (this proverb is at p. 222, ll. 40–1). Wenzel, 'Medieval Sermons', 162, notes the coincidence of the lyric and the proverb in *Fasciculus Morum* and *Piers Plowman*; he also discusses the lyric in *Verses in Sermons*, 146. Owst, *Preaching in Medieval England*, 272, identified versions of this lyric in Latin sermons from Worcester Cathedral Library MS F 19 and Lincoln Cathedral Library MS A 6 19.

[33] On the complex history of this manuscript, see Fletcher, *Preaching, Politics, and Poetry*, 21–30. I cite the text from Fletcher's edition and translation at 32–40. Fletcher links the character 'Tomme Stowue' in this sermon to the character in *Piers Plowman* in *Preaching, Politics, and Poetry*, 209, and also in 'The Essential (Ephemeral) William Langland', 73. See also Hanna, *Penn Commentary*, 3: 56.

[34] *MED*, 'tome', a, b, c, and d; *OED*, 'stow' v.2, 'to crop, cut close', and cf. *OED*, 'stow' n.4, 'the stump of a tree or shrub' and *MED* 'stoue' n.2, 'a short piece left on a tree after a branch has broken off, a stub'.

preaching from the evidence their own lives: 'That ye prechen to þe peple, preue it on yowselue,/ And dooþ it in dede—it shal drawe yow to goode' (B.5.42-3). He adds that 'If ye leuen [live] as ye leren [teach] vs, we shul leue [believe, accede to] yow þe bettre' (B.5.41-4), punning on two senses of 'leue' as he identifies the preacher's conduct as a source of persuasive power.[35] Like the rest of the *commune*, the prelates and priests receive these admonitions in an interpreted present, surrounded by the traces and vestiges of divine retribution and the forerunning signs of judgement day; to 'preue' their preaching in their lives is to submit themselves to discipline, to guard against the sin of pride. Yet, these clerical figures are also charged with continuing the work that Reason begins, extending the interpretative labour of emplotment in their own sermons and reinforcing it in their exemplary lives. When Reason employs the 'prechen' and 'preuen' collocation in these lines, he echoes the dreamer's description of his own preaching at the start of this passus: 'He preued þat þise pestilences was for pure synne' (B.5.12). Of all the groups on the field, the priests and prelates have a special obligation to interpret the ongoing experiences of the people, using the discursive resources of narrative.

At the start of the second vision, then, Reason's sermon offers a powerful demonstration of what preaching might achieve. It confers a compelling clarity on events that once seemed complex and chaotic, by grasping them together as related episodes in a unified plot. It reveals the strict but comprehensible standard of divine justice at work in recent history, as God inflicts punishments for human sin, and it discerns in that history the signs of the impending apocalypse, where the people will face their final judgement. Reason's sermon locates the subjective experience of individuals in the intersubjective time of public life: the choices and actions of each estate have implications for the others, and these implications play out in history, both in the contemporary world and in relation to the larger, eschatological story. This historical time finds points of orientation in the traces and vestiges that recent disasters leave behind, the uprooted, overturned trees that record the terror of past experiences, and that now supply a source of *timor domini*, as Reason interprets them. This sermon initiates the action to follow, as Reason moves his audience to confess, beginning the penitential sequence that will lead in turn to the pilgrimage to Truth. It does so by locating the people in an interpreted present, where the need for action, and its possible consequences, are clearly defined.

---

[35] Some C-text manuscripts replace 'leue' with 'love' in their readings of this line, so that preaching by word and example becomes a way of capturing the audience's goodwill: British Library MSS Royal 18 B XVII (R) and Cotton Vespasian B XVI (M), which Russell and Kane describe as an 'unmistakable genetic pair' have 'Lyueth 3e as 3e lerne vs; we shulleþ love 30w þe bettere' and 'Lyueþ as 3e lerne vs; we shall love 30w þe bettere', respectively, while British Library, Harley MS 2376 (N) has 'Lyueth 3e as 3e lerne vs; we shulleþ love 30w þe bettere'. *Piers Plowman: The C Version*, ed. George Russell and George Kane (London: Athlone, 1997), 37.

Signs of the Times

Surviving sermons from late medieval England also construe the storms and pestilences of the 1360s as punishments from God and as signs of the approaching apocalypse, much as Reason does in the second vision of *Piers Plowman*. These sermons, too, are engaged in the work of emplotment, reading the traces and vestiges of the past as warnings about the future, and locating their present time in a larger, eschatological narrative. In this section, I consider two sermons on natural disasters, both of which respond in different ways to the apocalyptic preaching of Gregory the Great, adapting a passage from his homily for the Second Sunday in Advent where he locates the fearful 'signa' of Luke 21:25–33 in the events of his own time. The medieval preachers adapt this passage so that it refers to contemporary disasters, storms and plagues that their listeners have experienced directly. These sermons are themselves engaged in the kinds of interpretative labour that Reason performs on the half-acre and that Piers Plowman will later take up as he leads the people on their pilgrimage to Truth. Both sermons elaborate on the spiritual benefits of 'drede', and explain how this kind of instructive, enabling fear emerges through the discursive mediation of narrative. The second, meanwhile, also recognizes that the narrative interpretation of contemporary history will be an ongoing project, where preachers and listeners collaborate, seeking out the signs of the apocalypse in the unfolding events of lived experience.

The first of these sermons was delivered by Thomas Brinton to the monks of Rochester Priory on the third Sunday after Easter in 1374. The fear of God was Brinton's primary subject. His *thema*, from 1 Peter 2:17, is 'timere Deum [fear God]', and, as he explicates it, he cites a range of confirmatory authorities that identify *timor* with wisdom and virtue, including Ecclesiasticus 1:20, 'Plenitudo sapientiae est timere Deum [To fear God is the fullness of wisdom]', and Ecclesiasticus 15:1: 'Qui timet Deum faciet bona [He that feareth God, will do good]'. In his opening account of this *thema*, Brinton asserts that the fear of God serves to initiate reforming action and to sustain people in their virtuous endeavours: 'bene timorem Domini, quia non solum *timor Domini expellit peccatum, Ecclesiastici primo*, sed custodit animam ne redeat ad peccatum [the fear of the Lord is good, not only because "the fear of the Lord driveth out sin" (Ecclesiasticus 1:27), but also because it guards the soul so that it might not turn back towards sin]'.[36] As the sermon goes on, Brinton will consider the circumstances that produce *timor Domini*, and will argue that, before it can become instructive, the experience of fear must be mediated by narrative.

---

[36] Brinton, *Sermons*, ed. Devlin, 1: 181.

Brinton distinguishes two forms of 'drede' in this sermon, echoing the distinction between *timor* and *terror* that Carruthers describes (although Brinton uses *timor* for both). The first of these arises from a direct encounter with God, as a response to his 'maiestatis'. This is like the fear that an animal feels when it encounters a predator, or that a soldier fears in the presence of the king. This kind of *timor* is confined to the phenomenological present, an instinctive, intuitive reaction to power. It becomes even more intense when people realize the limits of their phenomenological perception by comparison with God's omniscience; to underline this point, Brinton quotes the poet Sedulius, who observes that God perceives all times at once: 'dicente poeta *Cernit cuncta Deus, presencia, prisca, futura* [as the poet says, "God perceives past, present, and future as a whole"]'.[37] The second kind of 'drede', closely aligned with Carruthers' account of 'timor Domini', emerges when direct encounters with fearful events are reconfigured by narrative. To exemplify this kind of fear, Brinton recalls the storm of 1362 and construes it as a warning of the coming apocalypse, much as Reason does in *Piers Plowman*:

> Si timor fuit magnus nobis Anglicis paucis annis elapsis vidisse per ventum arbusta erui, domos opprimi, pinnacula et ecclesias dirui, et in pestilencia homines ad vesperam sanos in mane sepeliri, quomodo in iudicio non erit maior timor quando *Arescent homines pre timore que superuenient vniuerso orbi. Luce 21.*[38]
>
> [If great fear came to us Englishmen only a few years ago when, during the storm, we saw orchards ripped up, houses destroyed and spires and churches demolished and, in the pestilence, men who were healthy in the evening buried early the next morning, then how should there not be greater fear at the Last Judgement when 'Men shall wither away for fear of what shall come upon the whole world'. (Luke 21:26)

In this example, the fear of God arises not from a direct encounter with divine 'maiestatis', but through a subsequent act of interpretation, where events from the past are construed as warnings about the future. Experienced in the phenomenological present, such disasters create a paralysing *terror*, but configured and mediated by narrative, they provoke the kind of fear that motivates reform.

Brinton's account of these natural disasters echoes a passage from Gregory the Great's homily for the Second Sunday in Advent. Preaching on Luke 21, where Christ predicts the signs that will herald the apocalypse, Gregory identifies some

---

[37] Brinton, *Sermons*, ed. Devlin, 1: 181, citing the *Paschale carmen*, book 2, l. 99. See Sedulius, *The Paschal Song and Hymns*, ed. and trans. Carl P. E. Springer (Atlanta: Society of Biblical Literature, 2013), 50. (The source of this quotation was unknown to Devlin.)

[38] Brinton, *Sermons*, ed. Devlin, 1: 184.

of these signs in the events of his own time. Early in this sermon, he construes the sack of Rome in 546, along with recent plagues and earthquakes, as the signs that Christ predicts in Luke 21:10-11. Later, in the passage that serves as Brinton's model, he explains how a recent storm anticipates the events of judgement day:

> Nudius tertius, fratres, agnouistis quod subito turbine annosa arbusta eruta, destructae domus atque ecclesiae a fundamentis euersae sunt. Quanti ad uesperum sani atque incolumes acturos se in crastinum aliquid putabant, et tamen nocte eadem repentina morte defuncti sunt, in laqueo ruinae deprehensi?... Quid ergo iudex iste facturus est cum per semetipsum uenerit et in ultionem peccatorum ira eius exarserit, si portari non potest cum nos per tenuissimam nubem ferit?

> [The day before yesterday, my friends, you heard that an old orchard was uprooted by a sudden hurricane, that homes were destroyed and churches knocked from their foundations. How many persons who were safe and unharmed in the evening, thinking of what they would do the next day, suddenly died that night, caught in a trap of destruction?... What will that Judge do when he comes in person, when his anger is burning to punish sinners, if we cannot bear him when he strikes us with an insignificant cloud?][39]

Brinton follows Gregory as he explains how the storm ripped up orchards and tore down houses and churches, as he reflects on the fate of people who died unexpectedly overnight, and as he positions these disasters as forerunning signs of the coming apocalypse. Yet, he also adapts this model to speak about events in his own time: in Brinton's sermon, it is the pestilence that kills overnight, rather than the storm. His specific reference to the ruined 'pinnacula', meanwhile, seems to draw on his personal experience: Brinton was resident in Norwich in 1362, when the storm tore down the cathedral spire, destroying the presbytery roof and the clerestory, creating damage that took many years to repair.[40]

These references to real events are essential for the point that Brinton seeks to illustrate: the immediate terror that natural disasters inspire gives way to instructive, galvanizing *timor* when those disasters are construed as part of a narrative, which draws in turn on other texts. Like Reason in *Piers Plowman*, Brinton draws

---

[39] Gregory the Great, *Homiliae in Evangelia*, ed. Étaix, 9–10 (I.i.5); translation from Gregory the Great, *Forty Gospel Homilies*, trans. David Hurst (Kalamazoo, MI: Cistercian Publications, 1990), 19. This sermon is homily 1 in Étaix, who follows the sequence of the *Patrologia Latina* edition, where the homilies of book 1 appear in random order; it is homily 3 in Hurst, who rearranges the homilies to follow the sequence of the liturgical year.

[40] Brinton, *Sermons*, ed. Devlin, 1: 180. On the damage to the cathedral spire, see Francis Woodman, 'The Gothic Campaigns', 185–96 in *Norwich Cathedral: Church, City and Diocese, 1096–1996*, ed. Ian Atherton, Eric Fernie, Christopher Harper-Bill, and Hassell Smith (London: Hambledon Press, 1996), 170–71, 179, 196, and Roberta Gilchrist, 'Norwich Cathedral Tower and Spire: Recording and Analysis of a Cathedral's *Longue Durée*', *Archaeological Journal* 158, no. 1 (2001): 296–7.

attention to the traces and vestiges of these events, which persist into the present as a record of the past, and that seem to call for narrative interpretation. The damage to the cathedral spire, for example, could still be seen in 1374, as a record of the storm in 1362. Preaching more than a decade later, he describes the storm and the pestilence as though they happened only recently, 'paucis annis elapsis', acknowledging their vivid presence in the memory, as well as in the landscape. For Brinton, as for Langland's Reason, these events serve as orientation points for a public history; Brinton demands that his listeners 'reckon with' them, as records of phenomenological experience at different points in cosmological time. It is in this moment of reckoning that 'drede' arises, for Brinton. The fear of the lord arises when these encounters are construed in narrative terms, as retribution for sin, and as signs of God's impending judgement.

Another account of these natural disasters appears in a Middle English sermon for the second Sunday in Advent, from a cycle preserved in Trinity College Dublin, MS 241 and partly in Cambridge, St John's College, MS G.22 and Cambridge University Library Additional MS 5338. The cycle as a whole borrows extensively from the *English Wycliffite Sermons*, as Anne Hudson and Pamela Gradon have noted, while some of its sermons also appropriate material from lollard pastoralia, as H. Leith-Spencer observes.[41] This Advent sermon, however, is based primarily on Gregory's homily for this occasion, amplified with passages of exegesis from Bede and some well-known exempla.[42] As such, the sermon offers an unusual example of patristic preaching repurposed for delivery in the late medieval pulpit.

Like Brinton, the Trinity 241 compiler adapts Gregory's account of contemporary disasters so that it speaks to events in his own time. Gregory's first discussion of plagues and earthquakes, with its specific reference to the sack of Rome, is removed in the Middle English and replaced with a comment from Bede's commentary on Luke, linking the apocalyptic signs that Christ predicts with the 'tribulatio magna [great tribulation]' that heralds the coming of Antichrist in Matthew 24:21. Gregory's account of the hurricane, however, prompts an expanded account of recent catastrophes in the Middle English sermon:

> Sires, bute litil while siþen ȝe han seyen diuerse tribulacions, as erþe donyng [eathquakes], grete wyndes and wedres, þe whiche han turned vpsodoun houses and trees, and also rising of puple, and alle þese ben signes of þe ende of þis world, and al is synne þe cause. Also ȝe han seyen [you have seen] stronge men go

---

[41] *English Wycliffite Sermons*, ed. Hudson and Gradon, 1: 99–106; Spencer, *English Preaching*, 224–7.

[42] On the sermon and its sources, see Alastair Bennett, 'A Middle English Sermon Based on Gregory the Great's Homily for the Second Sunday in Advent', *Mediaeval Studies* 83 (2021): 27–57.

to þer beddes hool and sound and amorewe ded [dead the next day] bi pestilence, and al þis is in vengeaunce of synne. And þis is þat [what] Crist seide to his disciplis, and seide hem of wondres and tokenes þat shulden come tofore [before] þe gret and dredful day of dom.'[43]

For the Middle English preacher, translating Gregory's text involved updating its contemporary allusions for an audience at a later point in time. Like Brinton, he recasts the men who die suddenly overnight as victims of 'pestilence', rather than of the storm. He also refers to earthquakes and 'rising of puple' alongside the 'grete wyndes and wedres' that Gregory described. These references to recent 'tribulacions' are insufficiently precise to help with dating the sermon collection, as Veronica O'Mara and Suzanne Paul observe.[44] Yet, all of them occurred in the later decades of the fourteenth century: storms and pestilence in the 1360s, the 'rising of puple' in the revolt of 1381, and 'erþe donyng' in the earthquake of 1382. The sermon marks a clear turn from scriptural exegesis to direct observation when this section begins: 'Lo sires, now we han herd what þat haþ be spoken of oure lord þat is almyȝti God, now speke we a litil of þe world'; and, as he lists these tribulations, the preacher invites his listeners to recall them for themselves, presenting them as things that 'ȝe han seyen'.[45] Although these disasters have unfolded over many decades, this preacher, like Brinton, insists on their imminence, locating them 'bute litil while siþen'; as traces and vestiges, they remain vivid and perceptible, demanding narrative interpretation. The preacher configures them into a plot that extends the logic of Luke 21, reading them as 'vengeaunce' for human sin and as 'tokenes' of the 'dredful day of dom'. Here as in Brinton's sermon, narrative discloses the larger significance of fearful events, so that the terror of immediate experience gives way to instructive *timor*.

Gregory observes that his own sermon is designed to promote and prolong this experience of fear, in order to motivate his listeners in their spiritual efforts, and to prevent them sliding back into sin: 'Haec nos, fratres carissimi, idcirco dicimus ut ad cautelae studium uestrae mentes euigilent, ne securitate torpeant, ne ignorantia languescant, sed semper eas et timor sollicitet et in bono opere sollicitudo confirmet'; or, in the Middle English version: 'Þese þingis to þis entente ben seid [are said for this purpose]: þat ȝe shulen wiþ al þe bisinesse of ȝoure wittis be war þat ȝe ne tristen not [do not trust] to þe falsnesse of þis world ny to þe veyn ioye þerof, bute euer wiþ drede þat ȝour bisinesse be to kepe þe commaundementes of God and louen his lawes and fle al maner of synne.'[46] As Gregory goes on to acknowledge, however, and as the Middle English translator demonstrates through his own adaptation of the text, the work of extending this apocalyptic narrative is an

---

[43] Bennett, 'Middle English Sermon', 54.   [44] O'Mara and Paul, *Repertorium*, 1: lviii.
[45] Bennett, 'Middle English Sermon', 53, 54.
[46] Gregory, *Homiliae in Evangelia*, ed. Étaix, 6 (I.i.2); Bennett, 'Middle English Sermon', 48–9.

ongoing, collaborative project. Christ himself urges his disciples to seek out the signs of doomsday in their own experience in the gospel text, and, as his sermon draws to a close, Gregory continues this work, urging his listeners to keep the coming apocalypse 'ante oculos [before their eyes]'.[47] The Middle English sermon introduces new material at this point, citing an exemplum about St Jerome, who heard the trumpet calling him to judgement wherever he went and whatever he was doing:

> Þat day sires, prentiþ [imprint] hit in ȝoure soules and lettiþ it not passe out of ȝoure mynde, for þe holi doctour Seynt Ierom dredde [feared] þat day as it is writen when he seide wheþer he eete or dronk or slepte, or what oþer þing þat he dide, euer him þouȝte þat he herde þe dredeful sown of þe laste trompe in his ere, seying 'Rys vp, wretche, and come to þe dredeful iugement.' Certes, þis ouȝte to stire eche Cristene mannes soule for to leue his synnes and amende his lif...[48]

Through this spiritual exercise, Jerome understands every moment of his own experience in relation to the larger narrative of Christian eschatology; the mundane acts of eating, drinking, and sleeping, which might otherwise follow as a simple succession of events, are continually configured as part of this larger plot. Jerome maintains himself in a continual state of fear (the passage repeats 'dredde' and 'dredeful' on three occasions), and of spiritual vigilance.

Searching out the signs of the apocalypse could bring risks as well as benefits. Thomas Wimbledon, whose sermon to the three estates presents an important analogue for the sermon of Reason, as we have seen, went so far as to predict the date of judgement day, citing 'a doctor in a book' who has deduced that 'þe grete Anticrist schulde come in þe fourtenþe hundred ȝeer fro [after] þe birþe of Crist'. On this calculation, the final phase of human history would begin less than twelve years after the sermon was preached.[49] This kind of prediction had recently been condemned and suppressed in academic circles, as Kathryn Kerby-Fulton observes.[50] Henry Harclay, who cited prophetic writers like Joachim of

---

[47] Gregory, *Homiliae in Evangelia*, ed. Étaix, 10, trans. Hurst, 19 (I.i.6).

[48] Bennett, 'Middle English Sermon', 56-7. This story combines elements from two sources: a passage in Jerome's Epistles where Jerome urges Pammachius to listen for the sounding horn of Christ's love (Jerome, *Epistulae 1-70*, Ep. 66.10, ed. Isidorus Hilderg and Johannes Divjak, rev. Margit Kamptner, CSEL 54 (Vienna: Tempsky, 1996), 660), and a passage from the twelfth-century *Regula monachorum*, widely attributed to Jerome in the Middle Ages, which instructs readers to keep the last judgement in their minds as they perform the *opus dei*: 'Semper tuba illa terribilis vestris perstrepat auribus: "Surgite, mortui, venite ad iudicium" [The terrible trumpet should always resound in your ears, saying "Get up, you who are dead, and come to judgement"]'; Pseudo-Jerome, *Regula monachorum*, 30: cols 391-426 in *PL*, ed. Migne, 30: col. 417. It also appears in a cluster of interrelated sermons edited and discussed by Fletcher, *Late Medieval Popular Preaching*, 161-240.

[49] *Wimbledon's Sermon*, ed. Knight, 116.

[50] Kerby-Fulton, *Books Under Suspicion*, 79. On the question of Wimbledon's orthodoxy, see also Wenzel, *Latin Sermons Collections*, 172-3, O'Mara, 'Thomas Wimbledon's Paul's Cross Sermon', 166, and Killian, 'Menacing Books', 13.

Fiore in his sermon on Thomas Becket, as we saw in Chapter 1, nevertheless wrote against Joachim's eschatological calculations in his *Quaestiones Ordinariae*. Here, Harclay cites Gregory's comments on *timor* from his homily for the Second Sunday in Advent and argues that the spiritual benefits of 'drede' arise when doomsday is understood to be imminent, but its precise hour unknown:

> Et subdit Gregorius: 'Haec nos, fratres karissimi, idcirco dicimus, ut ad cautelae studium nostras mentes vigilent, ne securitate torpeant, ne ignoratia languescant, sed semper eas et timor sollicitet et in bono opere solicitudo confirmet.' Ergo secundum Gregorium magis expedit ad salutem nescire horam adventus quam scire, dum tamen certum est quod venturus sit.
>
> [Gregory then adds: 'These things I say, my dearest brethren, that our minds may be vigilant in the pursuit of caution, lest they slumber in complacency, be slothful in ignorance; rather, let fear ever urge them on and careful attention confirm them in good deeds.' According to Gregory, then, it is more help to our salvation not to know the hour of Christ's coming than to know it, although all the time it is certain that he will come].[51]

Wimbledon himself equivocates about the value of eschatological prediction, explaining that his primary purpose is not to establish the precise date of judgement day, but rather to insist on its imminence, and so to inspire 'drede' in his listeners: 'Þis resoun put I not as to schewe any certeyn tyme of his comynge, siþ y haue not þat knowlechynge [knowledge], but to schewe þat he is nyȝ, but how nyȝ I wote neuere [do not know]'.[52] This qualification might be a response to ecclesiastical censorship, but it also distinguishes controversial apocalyptic calculation from the legitimate purpose of apocalyptic preaching, which is to provoke 'drede' in the present, as people reckon with the traces and 'tokens' of divine justice in their own time.

Brinton's sermon on *timor* and the Middle English translation of Gregory's homily on Luke 21 echo Reason's sermon not only in their direct address to the disasters of the late fourteenth century but also in the acts of emplotment they perform: each locates its present moment in relation to a larger, public history, reading the traces of recent disasters to foreshadow the approach of doomsday. Both explain the spiritual benefits of *timor*, which arise when fearful events are construed as part of a narrative. The phenomenological experience of disaster and tribulation may be petrifying, but experiences like this become a source of instructive 'drede' when people reckon with the traces they leave behind and with their implications for the future. Gregory's sermon, moreover, recognizes

---

[51] Henry of Harclay, *Ordinary Questions*, ed. Mark G. Henninger, SJ, trans. Raymond Edwards and Mark G. Henninger, SJ, 2 vols (Oxford: Oxford University Press, 2008), 1: 22, 23 (I.31).
[52] *Wimbledon's Sermon*, ed. Knight, 116–17.

that these acts of reckoning must continue after the preacher concludes, a point that the Middle English translator would demonstrate many centuries later, applying the discursive resources of Gregory's narrative to the events of his own time. As they reconfigure their listeners' experiences, locating the experiential present in a larger, interpreted narrative, these sermons recognize that their listeners must now deploy the resources of narrative themselves, searching out the signs of the apocalypse in the unfolding events of their own lives.

Piers Plowman and the Hope of 'Hire'

In the immediate aftermath of Reason's sermon, the Deadly Sins make their confessions, beginning the next stage of the penitential process. The sins who appear early in the sequence have powerful, emotional reactions to what Reason has said: Pernele Proude-herte throws herself to the ground in sorrow, while Lechour says 'Allas!' and cries out to the Virgin Mary before his confession begins (B.5.62, 71).[53] The confessions that follow introduce their own problems and complexities, as contrition proves easy to confuse with other, sinful forms of regret ('"I am euere sory", quod Enuye, "I am but selde ooþer [only seldom anything else]"' [B.5.126]), and as the practical demands of restitution prove difficult to understand and to meet. Even so, as Steiner observes, the confession scene allows the personified Sins 'to participate in ritual community', sometimes 'despite themselves', as each confession works to reinforce and facilitate the others.[54] These confessions are framed by speeches from Repentance, who reiterates the central message of Reason's sermon, so that the narrative context for these new efforts at penance remains in view. As Reason concludes, the dreamer reports that Repentance ran forward 'and reherced his teme', as though reiterating the *thema* that Reason explicated (B.5.60). After the confessions conclude, Repentance offers a condensed account of salvation history, running from the creation and the Fall to the incarnation and atonement, to explain the origins of sin and reaffirm the possibilities for penance. This is the narrative that Reason elaborated, but in a hopeful rather than a fearful aspect: if the coming apocalypse creates the imperatives to reform, Christ's atonement for human sin creates the opportunities. Once again, the people on the field understand their present moment as part of a larger narrative, with clear implications for their own choices and actions.

Reason's sermon continues to motivate the later action of the second vision, as the people take up his concluding injunction to 'Sekeþ [Seek] Seynt Truþe, for he may saue yow alle' (B.5.57). This is to be a penitential pilgrimage, the next stage in

---

[53] On these responses to preaching, see Spencer, *English Preaching*, 102–3.
[54] Steiner, *Reading 'Piers Plowman'*, 74.

Burrow's 'arc of penitential action'. As they assemble to 'go to Truþe' after the confession scene, however, they quickly discover that none of them knows 'þe wey þider' (B.5.512–13). In their efforts to 'do þe bettre', the people respond to the act of emplotment that Reason performs and to the sense of 'drede' that it inspires, but their confusion in this moment reveals their need for ongoing pastoral instruction to direct and motivate their action. It is in this context that Piers Plowman makes his first appearance in the poem, promising to direct the pilgrims on their journey. As I will argue in this section, the ploughman takes up the interpretative project that Reason began, locating the principles of God's justice and the signs of the coming apocalypse in the events of his own life and offering his life story as a paradigm for others to follow. As he does so, however, he will also discover the difficulties of sustaining the work of emplotment, as an interpreted present is gradually reabsorbed into the simple succession of events.

Piers himself will come to resemble a preacher in this part of the poem, but a different kind of preacher from Reason. Reason's sermon is imagined as a major public occasion in all versions of the poem: in the B text, he preaches with a crozier, like a visiting bishop; later in the poem, both Thought and Anima will read the crozier as a symbol of the bishop's obligation to preach and teach in his diocese (B.8.96–8; B.15.569–72); in the C text, meanwhile, he appears 'yreuestede [vestmented] ryht as a pope', with Conscience as his cross-bearer (C.5.112–13) (Figure 2.1).[55] Piers Plowman, however, engages in the kind of preaching that formed part of the regular life of the parish, interpreting the lived experience of the people on the field as part of an ongoing project of pastoral care. The challenges that confront him are those that parish priests encountered as they urged their parishioners to spiritual reform.

Piers arrives in the poem in a moment of confusion, as the pilgrims 'blustreden forþ [wander aimlessly]' across the landscape, uncertain of the way to Truth (B.5.514). He intrudes suddenly and unexpectedly into the phenomenological present, stepping forward with an oath: '"Peter!" quod a Plowman, and putte forþ his heued [head]' (B.5.537).[56] As he begins to speak, however, Piers supplies a narrative context for this sudden appearance, telling the story of his 'fourty wynter' in service to Truth (B.5.543). Piers explains how Conscience and Kynde Wit first 'kenned [directed] me to his place', and how he promised to serve Truth 'for euere' on their first meeting (B.5.539–40), and he describes all of his subsequent work, ploughing the land, sowing seed, digging ditches and threshing corn, as the fulfilment of this first contract. In this speech, then, Piers himself performs an act of emplotment, configuring the disparate activities of his long working life

---

[55] On preaching with a cross, see Spencer, *English Preaching*, 76, and 390 n. 240.
[56] Middleton describes this moment as a genuine innovation, a dramatic interruption without precedent in *Piers Plowman*, or in any other English writing; 'Playing the Plowman', 113–42 in *Chaucer, Langland, and Fourteenth-Century Literary History*, ed. Steven Justice (Farnham: Ashgate, 2013), 123.

Figure 2.1 Archbishop Arundel preaching from a pulpit with a cross bearer standing to his left, from Jean Creton's *Histoire rimée de Richard II* (*La Prinse et mort du roy Richart*). London, British Library, Harley MS 1319, fol. 12r.

into a coherent *holos* and presenting them as evidence of his personal integrity and of his longstanding relationship to Truth. This narrative confers new significance on the present moment for both Piers and his listeners: the pilgrims understand the ploughman's sudden appearance in relation to their own search for Truth, while Piers construes this encounter as another act of service in his long life of faithful labour.

Like Reason before him, Piers reveals the principles of divine justice at work in the world and reminds his listeners of the imminent approach of judgement day. Piers affirms that Truth will reward people for their labour, and promises that all who serve him will receive their 'hire...at euen':

For þou3 I seye it myself, I serue hym to paye;	*to (his) satisfaction*
I haue myn hire of hym wel and ouþerwhiles moore.	*pay; from him*
He is þepresteste paiere þat pouere men knoweþ:	*promptest paymaster*
He wiþhalt noon hewe his hire þat he ne haþ it at euen.	*workman*
	(B.5.549–52)

Reason and Piers emphasize different aspects of God's justice: while Reason threatens divine retribution, Piers promises prompt and equitable 'hire'. Yet, despite this change in emphasis, both speakers insist on the same essential standard, where human efforts will be properly rewarded: while Reason warns that 'nullum malum inpunitum', Piers affirms that 'nullum bonum irrenumeratum'. Like Reason, Piers discerns these principles at work in recent history and locates that history in a broader, eschatological context. Referring to the wages that people will receive each day, 'hire...at euen', he declares that Truth is a fair employer, who follows the law of Leviticus 19:13.[57] He also invites his listeners to think about God's final judgement on their works, at the point of death, and at the end of the world.

This connotation becomes more explicit elsewhere in *Piers Plowman*, as when Patience invites Haukyn to imagine salvation as 'hire' for his 'trauaille' (B.14.153–4). It was also commonplace in vernacular sermons. The Longleat friar, for example, refers to the particular judgement on individual souls as the 'hyre' that Christians receive 'in þe euyn': 'Alle men and wommen of þe newe lawe in þe euyn of here deth [their death] þey ben payd here hyre, and takin to here mede [as their reward] þe peny of endeles blysse if þey ben clene clenside of synne.'[58] Wimbledon develops the same idea in his address to the different estates, urging 'eueri man' to 'trauayle in his degre', in the expectation of payment 'whanne þe euen is come þat is þe ende of þe world'. He cites 1 Corinthians 3:8, 'þanne euery man shal take reward, good oþer euyl, aftir þat he haþ trauayled here', a verse that reaffirms the logic of the 'nullum malum' maxim.[59] At this point in the second vision, then, the ploughman recounts the story of his own life in terms that also suggest the imminence of judgement day, holding out the hope of 'hire' in language that also contains the possibility of divine retribution. The narrative that offers grounds for hope also contains reasons to be fearful, a rationale for *timor* and 'drede'.

The ploughman draws on his own experience, and his own manifest integrity, to 'preue' the narratives that he offers in this scene. Piers presents his physical body as the starting point for a sermon-like, exegetical discourse when he first appears the poem, 'putt[ing] forþ his heued' and swearing an oath.[60] This gesture recalls the moment when Peace displays his head during the trial of Lady Mede to demonstrate the injuries he has suffered (B.4.78–9).[61] The display of physical

---

[57] 'Non morabitur opus mercenarii tui apud te usque mane [The wages of him that hath been hired by thee shall not abide with thee until the morning]'. On this and other biblical verses that relate to this discussion of 'hire', see Hanna, *Penn Commentary*, 2: 191.

[58] Longleat House, MS 4, fol. 26v. In his sermon for the second Sunday after Easter (fol. 51v) the Longleat friar distinguishes between 'wordly hyre', the 'gold and syluer and wardly mede þat men heer takin for here trauayle', and 'gostly hyre', which is 'heuene blisse'.

[59] *Wimbledon's Sermon*, ed. Knight, 68.

[60] Later in the second vision, Piers swears 'by myn heed' (B.5.628), as though restating this initial oath, once more alleging his body as proof of his words.

[61] Elsewhere in the poem, speakers *putte forþ* logical arguments and textual authorities, as when Holy Church imagines a time when the dreamer might 'put forþ þi Reason' (B.2.49), and Study complains that 'lewed' men 'puten forþ presumpcion to preue þe soþe' (B.10.55) when they speculate about theology at the dinner table.

injuries was 'a traditional part of complaints of assault', as Galloway observes, and was 'codified in legal theory by the maxim *res ipsa loquitur* ["the facts speak for themselves"]', a maxim that makes strong claims for experiential proof.[62] In this context, then, the body itself offers 'traces and vestiges' of past events, demanding narrative interpretation. The head of a man was also a common metaphor for the *thema* of a scholastic sermon: both Thomas of Chobham and Martin of Cordoba say that the *thema* is related to the sermon as the head is related to the body.[63] In this context, too, the ploughman's appearance seems to invite discursive elaboration. Chobham argues that, if a sermon is well constructed, then its listeners should be able to anticipate the parts that will follow from the *thema*, just as 'si uidet aliquis caput alicuius hominis ingredientis, naturaliter intelligere debet quod sequuntur pectus et manus et pedes et cetera membra [if we see the head of a man coming forward, we should naturally understand that there is also a torso, hands, feet and other members]'.[64] For Chobham, the sight of a man's head coming forward suggests the beginning of an exegetical discourse, whose integrity is guaranteed by the integrity of the body. Presenting his head, Piers Plowman offers himself as a subject for exegesis, and encourages his listeners to anticipate the form it will take.[65]

As he relates his biography, moreover, Piers captures the goodwill of his audience, 'preuing' his knowledge of Truth from the evidence of his own life. The people address him as 'leue Piers' (B.5.556), recalling Reason's comment that people will 'leue' preachers who 'leuen as [they] leren vs', and drawing out the connections between living, believing, and loving that emerge in the scribal variants on this line. Rita Copeland has discovered remarkable evidence of Piers Plowman's appeal to sermon audiences in Cambridge, Peterhouse, MS 57, a copy of Aristotle's *Rhetoric* in the Latin translation by William Moerbeke.[66] In book 2, where Aristotle discusses the kinds of people who provoke *philia* or 'friendly feeling' in an audience, including agricultural labourers, one fifteenth-century reader has added a couplet about Piers Plowman: 'O pers plwman, iust is thi

---

[62] Galloway, *Penn Commentary*, 1: 397.

[63] Thomas of Chobham, *Summa de arte praedicandi*, ed. Franco Morenzoni, CCCM 83 (Turnhout: Brepols, 1987), 296 (vii, 2.2). Martin of Cordoba's *ars* is edited in Fernando Rubio, '*Ars praedicandi* de Fray Martin de Cordoba', *La Ciudad de Dios* 172 (1959): 327–48 (on the *thema* as head, see 332). See also Wenzel, *Medieval Artes Praedicandi*, 51.

[64] Chobham, *Summa de arte praedicandi*, ed. Morenzoni, 296 (vii, 2.2); translation from Chobham, *Summa de arte praedicandi*, 614–38 in *Medieval Grammar and Rhetoric: Language Arts and Literary Theory, AD 300–1475*, ed. and trans. Rita Copeland and Ineke Sluiter (Oxford: Oxford University Press, 2009), 632.

[65] Spearing proposed that Piers might serve as an embodied *thema* for Langland's poem as a whole: 'The poem is so fiercely concerned with action rather than doctrine that its theme can hardly be formulated, but only embodied in a living and acting person—the enigmatic figure of Piers himself'; 'The Art of Preaching and *Piers Plowman*', 117–18.

[66] Copeland, '*Pathos* and Pastoralism: Aristotle's *Rhetoric* in Medieval England', *Speculum* 89, no. 1 (2014): 96–127; now revised and expanded in Copeland, *Emotion and the History of Rhetoric in the Middle Ages* (Oxford: Oxford University Press, 2021), see esp. 328–38.

life/ thw [you] livist of thi labor with owt ani strife [discord].'[67] Copeland suggests that this reader may himself have been a parish priest, looking to Aristotle for advice on public oratory that would also be applicable to preaching.[68] His marginal annotation offers a creative response to Aristotle and a perceptive reading of *Piers*, imagining the people's response to the ploughman as an example of *philia*. The couplet in this manuscript might even seem to link this kind of response to the narrative that Piers relates, and to the principle of justice it affirms, at this point in *Piers Plowman*: the ploughman earns the goodwill of his audience as he tells the story of his 'iust...life', and as the evidence of his life authenticates the message of his preaching.

In the subsequent lines, Piers transforms this narrative of his own experience into a guide for others to follow, mapping out an allegorical journey through the Ten Commandments to Truth. A journey through the commandments was a familiar metaphor in preaching: in a macaronic sermon from the collection in Oxford, MS Bodley 649, for example, Hugh Legat describes the 'via mandatorum [the path of the commandments]' as 'recta via versus celum [the right path to heaven]', and imagines them as waymarks on a journey through the 'woful desert' of the world.[69] Piers Plowman's itinerary, however, retains close links to his life story. As Katharine Breen observes, the journey has a biographical shape: the people will begin at a brook that suggests the water of baptism, then come to a ford called 'Honora patrem et matrem', before proceeding to the commandments that govern adult life.[70] It also recalls the ploughman's own journey to Truth, guided by Conscience and Kynde Wit. More generally, this catechetical journey promises to reaffirm the lessons that Piers has learned during his forty years of service: if the people follow Truth's commandments, then they will receive their equitable 'hire'. As Piers extrapolates direction from his own biography, moreover, the poem figures the power of emplotment to guide and inform new action. The pilgrims are wandering aimlessly in the landscape when Piers arrives, but Piers now makes the landscape intelligible, and offers to direct them through it. Like Reason before him, Piers makes a confusing landscape seem comprehensible by performing an

---

[67] Copeland, '*Pathos* and Pastoralism', 114–15; *Emotion and the History of Rhetoric*, 332–3. The couplet on Piers Plowman is written in the margin of Peterhouse MS 57, fol. 65r, and copied again in the bottom right margin of this page.

[68] Copeland notes that many of the English owners and donors of the *Rhetoric*, including Walter de Blacollisley who donated this manuscript to Peterhouse, were men with pastoral responsibilities, including preaching. The fifteenth-century annotator who added this couplet also copies out a list of maxims from book 2 in the back of the manuscript, perhaps for use in sermons, along with a comment on speaking before a large crowd from book 3. See Copeland, '*Pathos* and Pastoralism', 106–13; *Emotion and the History of Rhetoric*, 328–31.

[69] *A Macaronic Sermon Collection*, ed. and trans. Horner, 240, 241. Fletcher cites this passage as evidence that Hugh may have known *Piers Plowman*, and drawn on it in his preaching: '*Piers Plowman* and the Benedictines', 54–5.

[70] Katharine Breen, 'Reading Step by Step: Pictorial Allegory and Pastoral Care in *Piers Plowman*', 90–135 in *Taxonomies of Knowledge: Information and Order in Medieval Manuscripts*, ed. Emily Steiner and Lynn Ransom (Philadelphia: University of Pennsylvania Press, 2015), 115–16.

act of emplotment, transforming past experience into a guide for future action, but where Reason construes the traces of storm damage as divine retribution and as forerunning signs of the apocalypse, Piers configures his own labouring life as a map that leads towards heavenly rewards. Breen argues that, when Piers maps out this journey, he constructs and manipulates an instructive *pictura* of the kind that many preachers used, imagining the commandments as a diagram with roots and branches like a tree, and then laying it out to form a path for people to follow.[71] In this sense, perhaps, both Reason and Piers imagine branches spread across the field, but where Reason invokes the aftermath of St Maur's wind as a fearful incentive to 'do þe bettre', Piers lays out an instructive diagram, showing how such reforming action might be achieved.

At this point in the second vision, then, Piers Plowman has reaffirmed the message of Reason's sermon by performing his own act of emplotment, disclosing the operations of God's justice in contemporary experience and looking ahead to a final reckoning with Truth at the end of the world. Encountering the people in a state of confusion, he has reconfigured their understanding of the present moment, and channelled their unfocussed desires into a collective effort at reform. In the action that follows, however, Piers resolves to stay with the company of pilgrims, and to lead them on the journey he has mapped out, a journey that is quickly subsumed into labour on his half-acre of land. He fulfils the aspiration that Gregory expresses in the *Regula Pastoralis*, 'ut praedicator quisque plus actibus quam vocibus insonet, et bene vivendo vestigia sequacibus imprimat potius, quam loquendo quo gradiantur ostendat [that every preacher should make himself heard rather by deeds than by words, and that by his righteous way of life should imprint footsteps for men to tread in, rather than show them by word the way to go]'.[72] With this crucial decision, Piers not only expresses his commitment to 'preuing' his preaching by his own way of life but also acknowledges that preaching like this involves a long-term investment in the life of a particular community. It is at this moment in the poem that Piers departs from Reason's example, and takes up an ongoing project of narrative interpretation, as an obligation of spiritual leadership, and as an expression of pastoral care.

Throughout this next phase in the action of the second vision, Piers will recognize the signs of God's justice, and of the coming judgement, in the world around him. Assigning the people their tasks on the field, for example, he promises them gleaning rights in reward for their labour: 'whoso helpeþ me to erie [plough] or sowen...Shal haue leue, by Oure Lord, to lese [glean] here in

---

[71] Breen, 'Reading Step by Step', 107–19.
[72] Gregory the Great, *Regula Pastoralis*, ed. Floribert Rommel, trans. Charles Morel, 2 vols, Sources chrétiennes (Paris: Editions du Cerf, 1992), 2: 381–2 (3.xxix); translation from Gregory the Great, *Pastoral Care*, trans. Henry Davis, SJ, Ancient Christian Writers, 11 (New York: Newman Press, 1950), 232.

heruest' (B.6.66–7).[73] Promising rewards at harvest time, the ploughman invokes a widely instantiated scriptural metaphor for doomsday, even as he describes the business of ordinary life.[74] Later, the ploughman makes his will, imagining a final encounter with Truth when he will have to 'come to hise acountes', like a manorial official answering to his lord (B.6.89). This is the metaphor that Wimbledon uses to describe the general judgement in his sermon on Luke 16:2: 'eueriche man' will have to 'answere of þe goodis þat God haþ bytaken [entrusted to] hym', like a reeve or bailiff called before his master.[75] This part of the poem also offers a brief description of the ploughman's family: his wife, 'Dame Werchwhan-tyme-is', his daughter, 'Do-riȝt-so-or-þi-dame-shal-þee-bete', and his son, 'Suffre-þi-Souereyns-haue-hir-wille-:/ Deme-hem-noȝt-for-if-þow-doost-þow-shalt-it-deere-abugge' (B.6.79–81). These names suggest that Piers imposes strict discipline in the household, recreating the effects of divine retribution in miniature; his son and daughter, in particular, have learned to fear corporal punishment, and now endeavour to 'do riȝt' in order to avoid future beatings.[76] This glimpse at the ploughman's domestic life confirms that, for Piers, the 'drede' of punishment is consistent with the hopeful expectation of 'hire', an extension of the same rational principles, disclosed through the mediation of narrative. As he exercises these different forms of responsibility, personal, familial, and manorial, the ploughman continues to interpret them in relation to the narrative that Reason first set out.

The people recognize that the ploughman is preaching to them as he pursues this interpretative project. When the knight offers to help Piers at the plough, for example, he admits that 'on þe teme, trewely, tauȝt was I neuere' (B.6.22), confessing his need for practical and pastoral instruction through a pun on 'teme', the main beam of a plough and the *thema* of a sermon.[77] These connections are more fully elaborated in the penultimate vision of the poem, where Piers, who has received the Petrine commission, sets to work on the field once more, driving a 'teeme' of the four evangelists, harrowing the ground with four horses, Augustine, Ambrose, Gregory, and Jerome, who act as confirmatory authorities, and sowing the seeds of the cardinal virtues, which take root in men's souls (B.19.269–77). The image of the preacher as a ploughman was widely instantiated in scripture, in

---

[73] On gleaning rights and harvest regulations in the poem, see Ellen Rentz, 'Half-Acre Bylaws: Harvest-Sharing in *Piers Plowman*', *YLS* 25 (2011): 95–115, and Rentz, *Imagining the Parish in Late Medieval England* (Columbus: Ohio State University Press, 2015), 110–12.

[74] Barney, *Penn Commentary*, 5: 154, lists some of the scriptural verses where the harvest appears as a metaphor for doomsday. Hanna, *Penn Commentary*, 2: 14–15 and 214, also notes the apocalyptic connotations of the harvest time.

[75] *Wimbledon's Sermon*, ed. Knight, 68–9. Hanna, *Penn Commentary*, 2: 234–35, argues that Piers alludes to Luke 16:2 when he imagines giving an account of himself to Truth.

[76] On the link between these names and the injunctions of Reason's sermon, see Breen, 'Reading Step by Step', 115–16, and Hanna, *Penn Commentary*, 2: 232. Galloway, *Penn Commentary*, 1: 380, proposes that long 'sententious names' like these allegorize the 'moral burden' that such characters have to carry.

[77] On this pun, see Fletcher, *Preaching, Politics, and Poetry*, 227, and *C Text*, ed. Pearsall, 157.

patristic exegesis, and in medieval pastoralia, as Stephen Barney has shown.[78] It served to explain how preaching cultivates the soul and prepares the mind to receive new knowledge, but it also served to reinforce the connections between spiritual labour and equitable 'hire', harvest and doomsday, that Piers is concerned to promote. The 'Sermon of Dead Men', which forms part of a vernacular sermon collection composed in the late fourteenth century, figures God as an 'an erþe tilier [farmer] ... in whose teme alle Cristen men shulden draw as oxen', and explains that priests should help to drive the plough by preaching God's word.[79] Like the knight in the second vision, the preacher associates the plough team with his sermon *thema*, proposing 'to dryue þis worþi teme', by 'seying þe wordis þat I toke to my teme'. The 'teme' he has chosen, from Ecclesiasticus 7:40, concerns the imminence of divine judgement: '*Memorare nouissima tua, etc,* þat is: "Haue mynde on þi laste þingis"'; this *thema*, he argues, will spur God's people to draw his plough 'spedily and euen'; no other text in scripture is so 'sharply pricking to moue ȝow [move you]'.[80] If the labour of ploughing supplies a metaphor for preaching, it also contains a reminder of the harvest to come, when the labourers on the field will be called to account; the 'drede' of judgement emerges in this sermon alongside the hope of 'hire'.

In the later action of the second vision, however, Piers Plowman will find it increasingly difficult to sustain this kind of interpretative labour, and his efforts to discern the principles of justice, and to locate the signs of the apocalypse, in the lived experience of the community will provoke resistance and hostility rather than *filia*. The configurational work of emplotment that Ricoeur describes takes place for Langland in an increasingly contentious and hostile social environment. Piers pauses his plough to 'ouersen' the people and finds that some of them are drinking and singing rather than working. In an outburst of 'pure tene', he threatens these 'wastours' with punishments if they do not return to work, promising to withhold their 'hire' at harvest time:

At heiȝ prime Piers leet þe plowȝ stonde,	
To ouersen hem hymself; whoso best wroȝte,	*oversee; whoever*
He sholde be hired þerafter, whan heruest tyme come.	*accordingly*
And þanne seten somme and songen atte nale,	*sat; drinking ale*
And holpen ere his half-acre wiþ 'How trolly lolly!'	*helped plough*
'Now, by þe peril of my soule!' quod Piers al in pure tene,	*anger*

---

[78] Barney, 'The Plowshare of the Tongue: The Progress of a Symbol from the Bible to *Piers Plowman*', *Mediaeval Studies* 35 (1973): 261–93.

[79] *Lollard Sermons*, ed. Gloria Cigman, EETS, os 294 (Oxford: Oxford University Press, 1989), 211. On the date of this sermon collection, see Cigman, '*Luceat Lux Vestra*: The Lollard Preacher as Truth and Light', *Review of English Studies*, new series 40, no. 160 (1989): 482.

[80] *Lollard Sermons*, ed. Cigman, 211. Gayk discerns Langlandian affinities in the way these sermons valorize physical labour as a source of spiritual knowledge: '"As Plouȝmen Han Preued": The Alliterative Work of a Set of Lollard Sermons', *YLS* 20 (2006): 49.

'But ye arise þe raþer and rape yow to werche,	*hasten*
Shal no greyn þat here groweþ glade yow at nede,	*grain*
And þou3 ye deye for doel, þe deuel haue þat recche!'	*hunger-pains; should care*
	(B.6.112–20)

In this pivotal scene, Piers, whose own lived experience has been reconfigured by narrative, confronts the wasters, who no longer perceive their lives in this way. Surveying the field at 'hei3 prime', Piers identifies the phenomenological present with a particular instant in cosmological time and positions it in a narrative that looks forward to the coming harvest. The wasters, by contrast, inhabit an uninterpreted present, with no recollection of the past and no concern for the future; they experience time as a simple succession of events, unmediated by narrative. The implications of Reason's sermon, and the promises of Piers Plowman's biography, are no longer real for them. Indeed, as they abandon their work on the field, the wasters ignore Reason's first injunction to the different estates in his audience: 'He bad Wastour go werche what he best kouþe [knew how to] / And wynnen his wasting [earn what he spent] wiþ som maner crafte' (B.5.24–5). Piers addresses the wasters 'al in pure tene' at this moment (B.6.117). This richly polysemous term describes the anger of a manorial official observing recalcitrant labourers, but also the weary frustration of a preacher whose listeners have forgotten the message of his sermons.[81] 'Tene' can also describe the pain of hard work: Piers will use it in this sense when he complains that idle workers 'wasten þat men wynnen wiþ trauaille and wiþ tene' (B.6.133).[82] As he confronts the wasters, the ploughman realizes that the work of emplotment must begin again and that it may never be finished: pastoral labour, and the project of narrative interpretation that lies at its heart, now appear as a lifetime's 'trauaille' in service to Truth.

The ploughman's rebuke restates the logic of his earlier narrative, with a new emphasis on 'drede' to counterbalance the hope of 'hire'. Those who 'trauaille as Truþe wolde' may still take 'mete and hyre [food and wages]' for their labours, Piers explains (B.6.139). As he describes the work that remains to be done, digging ditches and threshing corn, he recalls his own biography, his life of service to Truth, and the principles of justice and equity that it expresses. At the same time, Piers warns that Truth will punish those who do not work and who undermine the efforts of the larger community, restating the *thema* of his preaching in final and absolute terms: 'Truþe shal teche yow his teme to dryue' (B.6.134). Far from inspiring the wasters to work, however, Piers moves them to dissimulation and to anger: some pretend to be blind or maimed and call on the ploughman for alms,

---

[81] *MED*, 'tene' (n.2), 4 and 3.   [82] *MED*, 'tene' (n.2), 5.

while others threaten to fight with him and tell him to 'go pissen with his plow3' (B.6.155). In place of the willing pilgrims who formed his earlier audience, and who responded with *philia* to his life story, Piers confronts the recalcitrant workforce who were imagined in contemporary labour legislation: fraudulent beggars, who subvert the operations of charity through their feigned abjection, and defiant, aggressive workmen on the cusp of revolt, who resist his authority with menaces.[83] The ploughman now faces a series of interpretative challenges. In his role as overseer, he must distinguish these imposters from the 'blynd or brokelegged', and from 'ancres and heremites', who really do deserve alms (B.6.136, 145).[84] In his role as preacher, he must explain this situation with reference to the narrative that Reason first set out. Piers protests that the present moment offers little evidence of divine justice and few signs of the coming judgement. It is difficult to assert the maxim 'nullum malum inpunitum' in a world where wasters thrive by subverting people's charitable impulses. As he condemns the wasters, Piers protests God's forbearance: 'al is þoru3 suffraunce [toleration, lenience] þat vengeaunce yow ne takeþ!' (B.6.144).

Piers will ultimately abandon the task of narrative interpretation and will force the wasters to work by other means. He turns first to the knight, who threatens them with judicial punishments but proves to be ineffective, and then to Hunger, who inflicts physical torments on them, and drives them back to their labours. Here, as Steiner writes, 'Hunger fills a vacuum of coercive agency left by lordship and law.'[85] Piers abandons his efforts to prolong the transformative effects of Reason's sermon, exchanging instruction, explication, and exhortation for the exercise of coercive force. The arrival of Hunger is itself a kind of natural disaster, akin to the storms and pestilences that Reason described in his sermon: famine and crop failure were recurrent experiences in the fourteenth century, 'familiar and menacing facts of life', as Robert Worth Frank observes.[86] Langland figures the painful effects of hunger as a kind of beating ('He buffetted þe Bretoner...'

---

[83] Middleton describes the way that both these groups were defined in the 1388 Statute of Labourers, and traces the 'genealogy' of this definition back into the earlier legislation; 'Acts of Vagrancy: the C Version "Autobiography" and the Statute of 1388', 208–317 in *Written Work: Langland, Labor, and Authorship*, ed. Justice and Kerby-Fulton (Philadelphia: University of Pennsylvania Press, 1997), 235–44. On 'wasters' and the discourse of contemporary labour legislation, see Aers, *Community, Gender, and Individual Identity: English Writing 1360–1430* (London: Routledge, 1988), 35–49. Aers writes that '[i]n Piers Plowman (unlike *Winner and Waster*) the term "waster" is developed to classify those who resist the pieties and discipline of the employers', a group that was defined and condemned in the labour ordinances of 1349, and in subsequent legislation (40).

[84] Aers, *Community, Gender, and Individual Identity*, 43, explains how the labour statutes, which forbade almsgiving to false beggars, created an obligation to distinguish between the deserving and the undeserving poor. Hanna, *Penn Commentary*, 2: 261, argues that the specific requirements of this labour legislation are ultimately subordinated to the larger, 'gospel-focused' question of 'discrimination in charity' in the second vision.

[85] Steiner, *Reading Piers Plowman*, 85.

[86] Robert Worth Frank Jr, '"The Hungry Gap", Crop Failure, and Famine: The Fourteenth-Century Agricultural Crisis and *Piers Plowman*', YLS 4 (1990): 88. See also Hanna, *Penn Commentary*, 2: 220, 278.

'He bette hem so boþe...'), recalling the corporal punishment that Reason enjoined, and which Piers himself enforces at home (B.6.176, 178). Crucially, however, the ploughman makes no effort to discern the operations of God's justice in these events, to construe them as divine retribution or as forerunning signs of the apocalypse. Instead, he employs the pressing, physical pain of hunger to 'amaistren [govern]' the people 'and make hem to werche' (B.6.211). Piers has harnessed the visceral *terror* of hunger to motivate the hostile wasters but, without the discursive mediation of narrative, these natural disasters cannot serve as a source of *timor*, or motivate reforming action in better times. For the rest of this passus, the people work when Hunger threatens them, and return to vagrancy and acts of defiance while Hunger is satisfied.[87]

The poem registers the inherent dangers that arise from the ploughman's choices in the moment, warning that Hunger will soon return, and predicting famine, floods, storms, and crop failures within the next five years. This dark prophecy equates the return of Hunger explicitly with the natural disasters that Reason addressed in his sermon. In the C text, it echoes the language of his sermon precisely, predicting 'foule wederes' and 'pestilences' in response to 'pruyde' (C.8.347–8).[88] The prophecy concludes with a riddle, sent as a message from Saturn, a planet associated with 'famine, flood and pestilence', as well as with 'social upheaval' as A. V. C. Schmidt observes.[89] In the B-text version, it refers to signs in the heavens, recalling the 'signa in sole, et luna, et stellis' of Luke 21:25. In all versions of the poem, this prophecy construes the events of the second vision as an extension of the narrative that Reason first elaborated, reading the arrival of Hunger as divine retribution for human sin and as a warning of further disasters still to come. The prophecy also comments on the absence of effective preaching on the field, however. These lines are spoken as an apostrophe to the 'werkmen' (B.6.319), who experience the privations of hunger, but take no instruction from them.

In the second vision of *Piers Plowman*, then, Langland charts the ploughman's efforts to continue the work that Reason began, offering new narratives that disclose the operations of divine justice in the lived experience of recent history, and that remind his listeners of the immanence of judgement day. Piers finds innovative ways to 'preue' these claims from the evidence of his own life and offers his own biography as an exemplary map for others to follow. He also translates Reason's arguments about divine retribution and natural disaster into terms that

---

[87] As Kate Crassons has shown, Hunger acts in unpredictable and indiscriminate ways in this passus, which are not easy to explain as expressions of social justice. Crassons, *The Claims of Poverty: Literature, Culture, and Ideology in Late Medieval England* (Notre Dame: University of Notre Dame Press, 2010), 35–40.
[88] On the link between these new lines in the C text and Reason's sermon, see *Parallel Text*, ed. Schmidt, 2: 559, and Hanna, *Penn Commentary*, 2: 276.
[89] *Parallel Text*, ed. Schmidt, 2: 559.

relate to the daily experience of work, promising equitable 'hire' when the harvest comes. In doing so, he assumes the role of a preacher, driving his 'teme' through exegesis and instruction, even as he leads the people in their agricultural labour. As so often in this poem, however, the allegorical action continues until tensions emerge in the project of reform, and conflict breaks out among the participants in this penitential project. Piers confronts an increasingly hostile audience, in a contemporary context that offers few signs of God's exacting justice, or of his impending return. In the end, other imperatives that arise from the simple need to survive crowd out the ploughman's concern with narrative interpretation, his efforts to render lived experience meaningful through the creative, expository labour of emplotment.

Piers the Pardoner

In the final passus of the second vision, Truth sends a pardon to Piers and all the people on the field, granting them remission for their sins. The receipt of the pardon seems at first to conclude the 'arc of penitential action' that Burrow once described: the people have fulfilled the injunction that emerged from Reason's first act of emplotment, to seek 'Seynt Truþe, for he may saue yow alle' (B.5.57). It soon becomes clear, however, that the pardon will depend on the people's ongoing efforts to 'do þe bettre', to promote and enforce the strict standard of God's justice in their own lives. Truth will pardon kings and knights who 'rulen þe peple' (B.7.10), bishops who 'preche' the 'lawes' to 'þe lewed' (B.7.14) and labourers who 'treweliche taken [receive payment] and treweliche wynnen [prosper],/ And lyuen in loue and in lawe' (B.7.61–2). Far from bringing the people's work to an end, then, the pardon restates the terms on which it must continue. Truth also demands new labour from Piers. At the start of this passus, Truth tells the ploughman to 'taken his teme and tilien þe erþe', giving him a new commission, perhaps even a licence, to preach (B.7.2). If the people are to receive their 'hire' at the harvest time, then Piers must continue to interpret the world in which they labour, to sustain their fear of punishment and their hope of reward. In this coda to the second vision, then, the poem reaffirms what Piers has learned about preaching on the half-acre. The preacher's task is to locate the operations of divine justice and the signs of the coming judgement in the lived experience of his listeners, disclosing patterns of narrative coherence in the simple succession of events.

For the first hundred lines of this passus in the B text, the poem elaborates on the contents of the pardon from Truth in terms that echo Reason's sermon at the beginning of the second vision: the document, like the sermon, is addressed to all the people on the field and sets out the duties and obligations of each estate in turn. The logic of 'nullum malum inpunitum, nullum bonum irremuneratum' informs this document too, although here, as in the ploughman's preaching, the emphasis falls on the hope of 'hire', rather than on the fear of retribution. It is not clear who reads the pardon out, although it is clear from the people's reactions that it has been read to them (the merchants weep for joy at their inclusion). If it is Piers himself who expounds the document, then the ploughman comes closer than ever to rehearsing the kind of discourse that Reason offered in passus 5; the movement between the third and first person in this passage might suggest a situation where the ploughman's voice reaches us via the dreamer's *reportatio*, just as Reason's did. To adopt the role of a preaching pardoner has other, more troubling connotations, however. At this moment in the poem, the ploughman begins to resemble the pardoner from the Prologue who 'preched... as he a preest were' (B.Prol.68), using his documents to deceive his audience, and promising them absolution in exchange for gifts and donations; a similar pardoner has already parted ways with the pilgrim company in the second vision, abandoning the quest for Truth at the end of passus five (B.5.639–40).[90] The pardoner of the Prologue is a figure who exceeds the bounds of his own authority, speaking as a preacher in contravention of canon law.[91] He is also a preacher who appeals to the people's desire for easy absolution, promising them their 'hire' before the harvest, indulging what Anne Middleton has called their 'strange and malleable' desire to believe in an obvious deception.[92] From the beginning of the passus, then, the poem hints that the ploughman's position is becoming untenable, and that the pardon from Truth might not really be able to offer the narrative conclusion that it seems to promise.

At the very end of this vision, Piers is obliged to defend his preaching from an attack by a priest, a figure who has been absent from the field for much of the second vision and whose role as preacher and pastor the ploughman has usurped. Demanding to see the text of the pardon, the priest reveals that it contains only two lines of the Athanasian Creed: '*Et qui bona egerunt ibunt in vitam eternam;/ Qui vero mala, in ignem eternum* [And those who have done well shall go into eternal life; but those who have done evil will go into eternal fire]' (B.7.110a); he quickly recasts these lines as a proverb, an English equivalent to the pastoral

---

[90] On the consequences of the Pardoner's deception, see Alastair Bennett, 'Covetousness, "Unkyndenesse", and the "Blered Eye" in *Piers Plowman* and *The Canon's Yeoman's Tale*', YLS 28 (2014): 29–64.

[91] Canon 62 of the Fourth Lateran Council made clear that pardoners should do nothing more than read out their letters and documents, and prohibited them from preaching; English bishops continued to reiterate these rules, and to complain about pardoners who broke them, in the later Middle Ages. See *Disciplinary Decrees of the General Councils*, ed. and trans. H. J. Schroeder, OP (St Louis: Herder, 1937), 581–2 (text), 286–7 (translation); Arnold Williams, 'Some Documents on English Pardoners, 1350–1400', 197–207 in *Medieval Studies in Honor of Urban Tigner Homles, Jr*, ed. John Mahoney and John Esten Keller (Chapel Hill: University of North Carolina Press, 1965); Minnis, *Fallible Authors: Chaucer's Pardoner and Wife of Bath* (Philadelphia: University of Pennsylvania Press, 2008), 36–97.

[92] Middleton, 'Commentary on an Unacknowledged Text: Chaucer's Debt to Langland', YLS 24 (2010): 117.

dictum 'bene fac et bene habe': 'Do wel and haue wel, and God shal haue þi soule' (B.7.112). He challenges the ploughman's understanding of this document, which offers 'no pardon' at all (B.7.111). The priest also questions the ploughman's authority as a preacher. Although Piers is 'lettred [educated] a litel' (B.7.132), as the priest is surprised to discover, he is not authorized to expound the gospel, and the priest condemns his preaching as a foolish parody of licenced, clerical discourse: '"Were þow a preest, Piers", quod he, "þow myȝtest preche where þow woldest/ As diuinour [expositor] in diuinite, wiþ *Dixit insipiens* ['The fool hath said...', Psalm 13:1] to þi teme'" (B.7.134–5). In response to this challenge, the ploughman tears the pardon apart with a new expression of 'pure tene', in one of the poem's most controversial and enigmatic gestures (B.7.115).

The priest provokes the ploughman's anger in part because he denigrates the work of emplotment, which Piers has recognized as central to the preacher's task. The text he discovers in the pardon resembles the maxim 'nullum malum inpunitum, nullum bonum irremuneratum', as Alford observes, expressing the principle of justice that Reason embodies.[93] When he expounds it, however, he overlooks the way that Reason 'preued' this principle in his sermon, reconfiguring the lived experience of his listeners to show God's justice at work. The priest proposes to 'construe ech clause' of this text and explain it 'on Englissh' (B.7.106) echoing the private and exclusive discussion that Reason had imagined in the king's court—'Lat þi confessour, sire Kyng, construe þis on Englissh' (B.4.145)— rather than the open demonstration he achieved in his sermon on the field. Piers has learned that in order to motivate good action the preacher must reveal the principles of 'nullum malum inpunitum' at work in the world, discerning the signs of God's impending judgement in the traces and vestiges of recent events. For the priest, however, preaching can be reduced to a display of clerical skill, the concatenation and explication of texts. Piers, who has been preaching since his first appearance in this vision, confronts one of the priests who Reason had enjoined to 'prechen to þe peple', and to 'preue' that preaching through the work of emplotment, and finds that he has only a superficial understanding of his vocation (B.5.42–3).

In his *Similitudinarium*, an alphabetical repository of images, metaphors, similes and examples for use in preaching and instruction, William de Montibus cites the proverb 'bene fac et bene habe' to critique a reductive approach to preaching and pastoral care. Middleton has claimed this passage as the 'ultimate "pretext"' for Langland's use of the proverb in the pardon scene.[94] William presents the proverb in his entry on preaching, as 'a defining example

---

[93] Alford notes the close resemblance between this maxim and the text of the pardon; 'The Idea of Reason in *Piers Plowman*', 206, 208.

[94] Middleton, 'Do-wel, the Proverbial, and the Vernacular: Some Versions of Pastoralia', 143–69 and 231–8 in *Medieval Poetics and Social Practice: Responding to the Work of Penn Szittya*, ed. Seeta Chaganti (New York: Fordham University Press, 2012), 151.

of a pastoral adage that is memorable but inadequate to its purpose', a truism that requires elaboration and instantiation:

> Aiunt aliqui, summa totius predicationis hec est, bene fac et bene habebis. Set hec est ac si uiatori uiam querenti dicatur: Recta semper uia gradere, et sic poteris ad metam peruenire. Numquid sufficit hic dictum? Item dicunt quidam: Scio totam summam predicationis: Declina a malo et fac bonum.... Sufficit hoc dicere?
>
> [Some say that the sum of all preaching is this: 'Do well, and have well.' But this is as if one said to a traveller seeking directions: 'Always follow the right road and you will reach your destination.' Does this suffice? Again, some say: 'I know the sum of all preaching: avoid evil and do good.' ... Is it enough to say this?][95]

For William, as Middleton writes, the value of maxims like this emerges only through the application of the 'pastoral arts', which 'give them their bearing, experiential amplification, and spiritual utility'.[96] The work of emplotment is key to this kind of applied, interpretative pastoral instruction, as Piers has discovered on the half-acre. The priest is concerned to discern and articulate the essential 'gist' of the ploughman's preaching, or what Ricoeur in his essay on 'Interpretative Narrative' calls the central 'kerygmatic statement' of a sermon.[97] As Ricoeur goes on to argue, however, and as Piers has learned through his own endeavours, the preacher's task is to elaborate the logic of this central claim through ongoing acts of narrative interpretation, so that listeners can recognize it in their own interpreted experience and in relation to their own projected future actions.

In his convocation sermon of 1376, Brinton demonstrates what this maxim could achieve when fully instantiated in narrative.[98] He cites it to confirm the divisions of his *thema*, 'Factor operis hic beatus [The doer of the work shall be blessed]' (James 1:25), and concatenates it with other texts that illustrate the forms this work should take, calling for penitence and reform. Like William de Montibus, Brinton notes that this proverb might be said to encapsulate the central message of every sermon: '*Benefac et bene habe* et ad illum finem sit omnis sermo vt discant auditores quomodo bene debeant operari et iuxta bona opera premiari

---

[95] Joseph Goering transcribes and translates this passage from Oxford, New College MS 98, fol. 135r in *William de Montibus (c.1140–1213): The Schools and the Literature of Pastoral Care* (Toronto: Pontifical Institute of Mediaeval Studies, 1992), 305–6. Cited by Middleton, 'Some Versions of Pastoralia', 150–1. I have silently adapted Goering's translation.

[96] Middleton, 'Some Versions of Pastoralia', 152.   [97] Ricoeur, 'Interpretative Narrative'.

[98] Owst does not mention this proverb when he argues, in 'The "Angel" and the "Goliardeys"' and in *Literature and Pulpit*, that Langland knew Brinton's convocation sermon. This might seem to bear out Pearsall's suspicion that Owst did not read the whole of Langland's poem: Pearsall, 'G. R. Owst', 20, n. 20. Burrow notes the appearance of this proverb in Brinton's sermon ('Langland's Second Vision', 96), and see also Hanna, *Penn Commentary*, 2: 330–1. In *London Literature*, 251–2, Hanna argues that Brinton's sermon may be a response to Langland's poem, since it treats the rodent parliament and the proverb 'bene fac, bene habe' close together.

["Do well and have well". May every sermon be to that end, so that those who hear it may learn how they should do well and be rewarded according to their good works].'[99] Yet, he also elaborates on this proverb to issue specific, reforming injunctions, urging his listeners to abandon their sins and engage with clerical instruction, and calling for the reform of royal government, which has fallen under the influence of corrupt councillors. In his final peroration, Brinton promises that heavenly rewards will follow from good works, using the language of equitable 'hire' that Piers Plowman employs on the half-acre: '*Dum tempus igitur habemus, operemur bonum* vt in die iudicii cum bonis operariis in perpetuum muneremur, dicente patre ad filium, *Voca operarios et redde illis mercedem* ["Therefore, while we have time, let us work good" (Galatians 6:10), that on the day of judgement we may be rewarded with the good workers for all eternity, when the Father will say to the Son, 'Call the laborers and pay them their hire' (Matthew 20:8)"].'[100]

Recent readings of the pardon scene have argued that, in tearing the pardon, Piers seeks to instantiate it, to show how the implications of the maxim 'bene fac et bene habe' might play out in his own particular circumstances. Steiner argues that the pardon from Truth recalls the 'chirographum dei' of patristic and medieval exegesis on Colossians 2:14–15, a written deed or charter that expresses the conditions of salvation. The tearing of the pardon, meanwhile, resembles the formal enactment of an indenture in medieval legal practice, where a scribe would cut or tear up a duplicate copy of the document and distribute the parts to the legal actors. When Piers tears the pardon, Steiner proposes, he also implements it, so that its general claims become 'literally relevant [in his] own moment'.[101] Curtis Gruenler reads the tearing of the pardon as an enigmatic allusion to the tearing of the temple veil at the moment of Christ's death ('velum templi scissum est in duas partes', Matthew 27:51). This event, which figured the transition from the Old Law to the New, recalled the moment when Moses broke the tablets containing the Ten Commandments, and prefigured the face-to-face encounter with God that Paul imagines at the Last Judgement (1 Corinthians 13:12); in this way, it stands as a reminder that God reveals himself over time, in the particular circumstances of lived experience. For Gruenler, then, the tearing of the pardon marks a rejection of 'static doctrine' in favour of an ongoing 'process of interpretation based on the action of God in history'.[102] Both these readings are consistent with an understanding of this moment as a reaffirmation of the work of emplotment. When Piers tears the pardon, he calls for new

---

[99] Brinton, *Sermones*, ed. Davlin, 2: 318; trans. Wenzel, *Age of Chaucer*, 247.
[100] Brinton, *Sermones*, ed. Davlin, 2: 321, trans. Wenzel, *Age of Chaucer*, 254.
[101] Steiner, *Documentary Culture and the Making of Medieval English Literature* (Cambridge: Cambridge University Press, 2003), 141.
[102] Gruenler, *Poetics of Enigma*, 238.

acts of narrative interpretation that might locate the abstract principles of the maxim 'bene fac et bene habe' in historical reality.

If Piers defends his preaching project in this moment, however, he also responds to the priest's objections by thinking through the different forms it might take in the future. He distances himself from the practical work of providing food for the community, proposing to 'cessen of my sowyng' and 'swynke [work] noȝt so hard,/ Ne aboute my bely ioye [delight in food] so bisy be na moore', and declares that he will use 'preieres' and 'penaunce' as his plough in future (B.7.118–20). This is the labour that he first performed for Truth, the experience he configured into a biographical narrative when he appeared on the field; it is also, by allegorical extension, the role in which he led the people on their pilgrimage, combining the work of priest and overseer. It has also attracted criticism from the priest, however, who understands the work of a ploughman to be incompatible with the work of a preacher, and Piers now tries to reimagine it in a more acceptable form. The dreamer, too, will seek out new forms of preaching after this vision ends. In the subsequent passus, he will elicit a series of sermons, from a range of speakers, on the different forms that 'Do-wel' might take, in the particular circumstances of his own historical moment. Reflecting on his vision, however, he articulates the central lesson that has emerged from the sermon of Reason, echoed and amplified by Piers in his long endeavours on the field, calling for grace to do good works before the final judgement arrives: 'God gyue vs grace here, er we go hennes,/ Swiche werkes to werche, þe while we ben here,/ That after oure deþ day, Dowel reherce [might declare] / At þe day of dome, we dide as he hiȝte [commanded]' (B.7.198–201).

* * *

In the second vision of *Piers Plowman*, Langland shows how a single sermon can motivate a large-scale effort at reform. Preaching on the field at the start of this vision, Reason provides the impetus for the penitential activities that will unfold in the subsequent allegorical action, revealing the operations of divine justice in the chaotic events of recent history, and establishing powerful imperatives to 'do þe bettre' as 'domesday' approaches (B.5.17, 20). This is a decisive intervention in the life of the community, one that reconfigures the people's shared understanding of the recent past and of the imminent future. The later action of this vision, however, reveals that no single sermon can permanently transform its listeners' understanding of their capacities and obligations in the present time. Piers Plowman, who reaffirms the narrative logic of Reason's sermon from the evidence of his own experience, commits himself to a lifetime of interpretative labour as he offers to lead the people on their pilgrimage. The work of emplotment becomes an essential part of pastoral care on the half-acre, as Piers locates new evidence of God's justice, and new signs of his coming judgement, in the ordinary lives of his fellow labourers. This part of the poem dramatizes an ongoing effort to render lived experience comprehensible, to locate patterns of narrative coherence in the simple succession of events, and to establish people in an interpreted present where they can perceive the incentives and the opportunities to 'do wel'.

Burrow's influential account of this vision allowed readers to see, for the first time, the penitential logic that informs the movement from Reason's sermon to the confession of the sins, the pilgrimage to Truth, and the receipt of the pardon, but it also directed critical attention towards the later stages of this sequence, where Langland's scepticism about contemporary penitential practice produces metaphorical 'substitutions' and finally a moment of episodic rupture, as the pilgrimage is reimagined as agricultural labour, and as the pardon is torn. My own reading has focussed on the acts of emplotment that take place as part of the allegorical action, as Reason and Piers present the people with new narratives to explain their recent experience and guide their future efforts, and has sought to reconsider the vision as a whole as a response to the sermon that initiates it.

Reading *Piers Plowman* alongside Brinton's sermon on the fear of God and the Middle English reworking of Gregory's Advent homily, it is possible to see how Langland thinks in the second vision about issues that engaged contemporary preachers. As Brinton observes, it is the labour of emplotment that renders paralysing *terror* into galvanizing *timor* by assigning new meanings to fearful events, while Gregory and his later adaptor recognize the need to seek out new signs of the coming apocalypse and to interpolate them into an ongoing narrative, applying the discursive resources of emplotment to lived experience. In the ploughman's final encounter with the priest, meanwhile, Langland shows how preaching falls short of these pastoral requirements when it reduces the labour of emplotment to the simple restatement of familiar maxims, abstracting the *res* or 'gist' of a narrative from the narratives in which it has been instantiated. For Piers, the injunction to 'do wel and haue wel' becomes meaningful only in the context of an interpreted present where direct experience is mediated by narrative. In the subsequent visions of *Piers Plowman*, Langland will extrapolate new narratives from this dictum, as the dreamer asks a series of interlocutors how to find 'Do-wel', and each of them explains the forms that 'Do-wel' might take, in speeches that often resemble sermons. The ploughman abandons his pastoral labour on the field, but the work of emplotment continues in new forms.

3
Preachers and Minstrels
Study's Complaint and the Feast of Conscience

As I have argued in the previous chapters of this book, *Piers Plowman* imagines that sermons could produce new forms of understanding and action through their characteristic use of narrative, reconfiguring their listeners' perception of their present moment in order to shape and direct their spiritual efforts. In its many passages of anticlerical criticism and topical complaint, however, the poem also shows how covetous, self-interested preachers could use their sermons to advance their private interests at the expense of the larger community, leading their listeners into spiritual confusion or even encouraging their sins. In this chapter, I consider scenes from the third and fourth visions of *Piers Plowman* that describe this kind of preaching, and that detail its effects on the people who hear it. In the third vision, Dame Study complains about 'freres [friars] and faitours [deceivers, impostors]' who preach on difficult, academic topics at St Paul's Cross, appealing to the intellectual vanity of their wealthy patrons in exchange for praise and preferment (B.10.71). In the fourth, when the dreamer attends a feast at the house of Conscience, he encounters a preacher like this, a friar who has recently delivered a sermon at St Paul's and who now eats rich food at the high table, enjoying the social and material rewards that accrue from his preaching.[1] The 'freres and faitours' in these scenes have succumbed to the intellectual vice of *curiositas*—a covetous and indiscriminate desire for knowledge as an end in itself, which patristic and medieval authors identified with pride and with the desire for money—and they encourage this sin in their elite listeners. At the same time, they neglect their pastoral obligations to the *commune* as a whole: the ordinary people who hear their sermons are deprived of essential spiritual instruction and of the narratives that might make sense of their present moment (B.10.74).

Study considers these curious preachers alongside scurrilous minstrels, the 'iaperis [jesters] and iogelours and iangleris of gestes [chattering storytellers]' (B.10.31) who perform in the halls of great houses, and her complaint invites comparisons between these groups. Like preachers at St Paul's Cross, she suggests, these 'iaperis' and 'iangleris' indulge the tastes and appetites of powerful men in

---

[1] The close relationship between these episodes has often been noted by readers of the poem, as Traugott Lawler observes: *The Penn Commentary on Piers Plowman, vol 4: C Passūs 15–19; B Passūs 13–17* (Philadelphia: University of Pennsylvania Press, 2018), 8.

exchange for material rewards while withholding more edifying entertainment from the rest of their audience (B.10.31). When preachers themselves appear in the hall, debating curious topics as an extension of the meal-time entertainment, Study shows that both groups exploit their intelligence for private profit in similar ways. As she develops this critique, however, Study also imagines alternative forms of minstrelsy that could supply the instruction, and the narrative interpretation, that are missing from sermons at St Paul's Cross. At the feast of Conscience, the poem explores what this kind of minstrelsy might look like: while the dreamer agitates to challenge the doctor, engaging him in clerical disputation, Conscience tells stories from scripture and proposes a discussion of Do-wel, while Patience, who has been the dreamer's dinner companion, engages the other guests in a riddle contest, where the answers reveal the importance of love. Virtuous minstrelsy performs its own acts of emplotment, offering 'murye [merry] tales' that disclose new opportunities for action in the interpreted present (B.13.57). Over the course of these two connected scenes, the analogy with minstrels, first introduced to critique self-interested preaching, comes to supply a model for its reform.

The work of emplotment remains essential to the preacher's task in the third and fourth visions of *Piers Plowman*, where virtuous minstrels supply the narrative interpretation that corrupt, acquisitive preachers neglect and withhold. As it confronts the damaging effects of curious preaching, moreover, and as it works to counter them, *Piers Plowman* also discovers that the most elementary operations of emplotment have an ethical dimension. In his reading of Aristotle's *Poetics*, Ricoeur observes that the composition of narratives requires the capacity to discern some essential, atemporal logic in the simple succession of events and to reconfigure those events so that they articulate that logic in a compelling way.[2] In Study's complaint and again at the feast of Conscience, however, *Piers Plowman* shows that *curiositas* erodes the forms of discrimination and discernment that make emplotment possible; this covetous appetite for knowledge is by definition indiscriminate and observes no limits or priorities. In these parts of the poem, I will argue, Langland identifies the capacity to distinguish significant events and construe them as a narrative with the capacity to distinguish essential knowledge from knowledge that is vain and frivolous; these are capacities that curious preachers lack and which they undermine in their listeners, but that virtuous minstrels possess and seek to encourage in theirs. Ricoeur explains that for Aristotle the capacity to discern patterns of narrative significance in events as they unfold is a kind of *phronesis*, or 'practical wisdom'.[3] In *Piers Plowman*, however, it arises through the careful cultivation of knowledge and through submission to different kinds of instruction, that is, through study and patience. While *curiositas* is rooted in covetousness, moreover, the forms of discernment that give rise to narrative are also expressions of love, which Piers Plowman

[2] Ricoeur, *Time and Narrative*, 1: 40.   [3] Ricoeur, *Time and Narrative*, 1: 41.

himself has set above 'alle sciences' (B.13.125), and which Study recognizes as the 'science' that is 'souereyn [most important] for þe soule' (B.10.208).

This chapter also considers a dispute between the lollard William Taylor and the parish priest Richard Alkerton that unfolded at St Paul's Cross in the early fifteenth century. Only Taylor's sermon survives, but the chronicler Thomas Walsingham summarizes what Alkerton said in reply, and a further account of the dispute and its aftermath appears in the *Testimony* of the lollard William Thorpe, which records Thorpe's own interrogation for controversial preaching. The language of this dispute contains revealing echoes of Study's complaint: both Taylor and Alkerton were accused of preaching to please wealthy lords, while hostile listeners in Alkerton's audience sought to expose him as a kind of entertainer, performing for praise and promotion. This episode also reveals the innovative quality of the solutions that Langland imagines for curious, contentious preaching, however. The preachers in this dispute arrived at a kind of impasse, contesting one another's authority in similar terms until the ecclesiastical authorities intervened to suppress the debate. Langland, by contrast, turns to minstrelsy as a model for the reform of preaching that might avoid this kind of contentiousness and the deadlock it produces.

Curious Preaching

Early in the third vision of *Piers Plowman*, Dame Study launches an outspoken attack on people who use their 'wisdom and wit' to enrich themselves, turning their natural intelligence and their accumulated knowledge into commodities for sale (B.10.17).[4] Study reserves some of her strongest criticism for preachers who deliver ostentatious sermons at St Paul's Cross, competing with one another for prestige and for the patronage of 'proude men':

Freres and faitours han founde vp swiche questions	*thought up*
To plese wiþ proude men syn þe pestilence tyme,	*since*
And prechen at Seint Poules, for pure enuye of clerkes,	
That folk is no3t fermed in þe feiþ, ne free of hire goodes,	*strengthened; generous*
Ne sory for hire synnes...	

(B.10.71–5)

---

[4] Study compares the commodification of knowledge to the way that clothiers card their woollen cloth, raising its market value: 'Wisdom and wit now is no3t worþ a kerse' she declares, 'But if it be carded wiþ coueitise as cloþeres kemben hir wolle' (B.10.17–18). For an argument that these lines refer to the process of combing finished cloth, rather than to combing out the tangled fibers of raw wool in preparation for spinning, see Alastair Bennett, 'Carding with Covetousness in *Piers Plowman*', *Notes and Queries* 65, no. 1 (2018): 5–8. For a sceptical response, see Galloway, 'Langland and the Reinvention of Array in Late Medieval England', *Review of English Studies*, new series 71, no. 301 (2020): 612–14.

Preaching at St Paul's has become indistinguishable from academic debate on intellectual *questiones*, Study argues, except that this debate is performed in public, and it encourages lay lords with no formal training to speculate on difficult points of theology. As they appeal to the tastes of 'proude men' with these difficult, academic sermons, moreover, the 'freres and faitours' neglect the pastoral needs of ordinary 'folk', who receive no encouragement or instruction in the faith.[5] As her complaint unfolds, Study will suggest that this kind of preaching makes it difficult for either group to understand their present circumstances in relation to a larger narrative, obscuring the imperatives and opportunities for social and spiritual reform that emerge through the work of emplotment.

Other speeches in *Piers Plowman* anticipate and echo this passage from Study's complaint. During the confessions of the sins, Wrath says that he fosters competition between the friars and other clerics, teaching the friars how to 'plese' 'lordes' with their learning until their pursuit of their own interests brings them into conflict with the beneficed clergy and each group attacks the other from the pulpit (B.5.138). Later, in the fifth vision, Anima attacks 'Freres and fele oþere maistres' who preach on 'materes vnmesurables [unfathomable subjects]', while neglecting the essentials of the catechism (B.15.70–71). These preachers, too, display their 'heigh clergie [advanced clerical knowledge]' in order to 'plese' 'lordes': 'That I lye no3t, loo!—for lordes ye plesen,/ And reuerencen þe riche þe raþer for his siluer' (B.15.78–81).[6] When Study, Wrath, and Anima refer to preachers who 'plese' 'lordes' and 'proude men' (B.10.72, B.5.138, B.15.80), they echo the language of Psalm 52:6, 'Deus dissipavit ossa eorum qui hominibus placent [God has scattered the bones of them that please men]', and Galatians 1:10: 'Si adhuc hominibus placerem, Christi servus non essem [If I yet pleased men, I should not be the servant of Christ].'[7] All three speakers describe preaching that no longer fulfils its primary purposes, because it has been co-opted for other ends: lords experience this preaching as a flattering invitation to participate in academic discourse, and their patronage of preachers produces contention and competition in turn.

---

[5] On the critique of friars in Study's complaint, see for example Penn R. Szittya, *The Antifraternal Tradition in Medieval Literature* (Princeton, NJ: Princeton University Press, 1986), 251–2, 265, 267; Lawrence M. Clopper, *'Songes of Rechelesnesse': Langland and the Franciscans* (Ann Arbor: University of Michigan Press, 1997), 74–7; David Strong, 'Illumination of the Intellect: Franciscan Sermons and *Piers Plowman*', 197–220 in *Speculum Sermonis: Interdisciplinary Reflections on the Medieval Sermon*, ed. Georgiana Donavin, Cary J. Nederman, and Richard Utz (Turnhout: Brepols, 2004), 214–16. On the antimendicant connotations of 'faitours', see Wendy Scase, *Piers Plowman and the New Anticlericalism* (Cambridge: Cambridge University Press, 1989), 70–2.

[6] On the echoes of Study's complaint in Anima's critique of proud, acquisitive preaching, see Fletcher, *Preaching, Politics, Poetry*, 206–7; Lawler, *Penn Commentary*, 4: 155.

[7] The Wycliffite Bible refers to 'plesing men' in its translations of these verses: 'For God scaterede the bones of hem, that plesen to men' (Psalm 52:6); 'If Y pleside 3it men, Y were not Cristis seruaunt' (Galatians 1:10). *The Holy Bible…by John Wycliffe and his Followers*, ed. Josiah Forshall and Sir Frederic Madden, 4 vols (Oxford: Oxford University Press, 1850).

St Paul's Cross, which stood outside the cathedral to the north east, was a famous site of outspoken and controversial preaching in the fourteenth and fifteenth centuries.[8] Richard FitzRalph delivered sermons against the friars here and Thomas Wimbledon preached his sermon on Luke 16:2, with its wide-ranging social criticisms and its provocative calculation of the date of doomsday.[9] Thomas Brinton, in his convocation sermon of 1377, complained that preachers had been arrested and arraigned before the king's court for criticizing the aristocracy in their sermons at the cross.[10] Sermons at the preaching cross were also identified with ostentatious intellectual display. In his 1598 *Survey of London*, John Stow described a longstanding tradition where the cathedral authorities appointed one cleric to preach on the passion at St Paul's Cross on Good Friday, three more to preach on the resurrection at the cross outside the Hospital of St Mary Bishopsgate on the days after Easter, and a final preacher to synthesize and evaluate all four previous sermons at St Paul's Cross on Low Sunday, 'either commending or reproving them', in an impressive feat of memory and improvisatory analytical skill.[11] These sermons were addressed to powerful and influential audiences: Stow records that the mayor and aldermen attended in their violet gowns on Friday and Wednesday and in their scarlets on other days. In *Piers Plowman*, Study identifies St Paul's Cross as a site for sermons that might address the *commune* as a whole, but where the lure of contentious academic debate and proud intellectual display have created fractures in this audience, prioritizing the pleasure of a small elite above the needs of the larger community.

Study accuses the 'freres and faitours' at St Paul's Cross of *turpis curiostias*, a covetous and materialistic attitude to knowledge that was associated with pride and with the desire for profit.[12] Patristic and medieval authors developed a sophisticated theory of this intellectual vice, as Richard Newhauser has shown.[13]

---

[8] On the location of the preaching cross, and its growing significance as a site of public pronouncements, see Derek Keene, 'From Conquest to Capital: St Paul's *c*.1100–1300', 17–32 in *Saint Paul's: The Cathedral Church of London 604–2004*, ed. Keene, Arthur Burns, and Andrew Saint (New Haven: Yale University Press, 2004), 20, and Caroline M. Barron and Marie-Hélène Rousseau, 'Cathedral, City, and State, 1300–1540', 33–44 in *Saint Paul's: The Cathedral Church*, 44.

[9] For an overview of preaching at St Paul's Cross in the later Middle Ages, see Horner, 'Preachers at Paul's Cross: Religion, Society, and Politics in Late Medieval England', 261–82 in *Medieval Sermons and Society: Cloister, City, University*, ed. Jacqueline Hamesse, Beverly Mayne Kienzle, Debra L. Stoudt, and Anne T. Thayer (Louvain-La-Neuve: Fédération Internationale des Instituts d'études médiévales 1998).

[10] Brinton, *Sermons*, ed. Devlin, 2: 317; trans. Wenzel, 246.

[11] John Stow, *A Survey of London*, ed. C. L. Kingsford, 2 vols (Oxford: Clarendon, 1908, repr. Cambridge: Cambridge University Press, 2015), 1: 167. Horner cites this passage from Stow as evidence for a long-standing tradition of 'public debate among the preachers' at St Paul's Cross; 'Preachers at Paul's Cross', 266–7. See also O'Mara, 'Thomas Wimbledon's Paul's Cross Sermon', 157–8.

[12] Richard K. Emmerson, '"Coveitise to Konne", "Goddes Pryvetee", and Ambiguous Dream Experience in *Piers Plowman*', 89–121 in *'Suche Werkis to Werche': Essays on Piers Plowman in Honor of David C. Fowler*, ed. Mí·eál F. Vaughan (East Lansing: Colleagues Press, 1993), 94–5.

[13] Richard Newhauser, 'Curiosity', 849–52 in *The Oxford Guide to the Historical Reception of Augustine*, ed. Karla Pollmann and Willemien Otten (Oxford: Oxford University Press, 2013), 849. See also Newhauser, 'Augustinian *Vitium curiositas* and its Reception', 99–104 in *Saint Augustine and*

In his *Sermones super Canticum Canticorum*, for example, Bernard of Clairvaux distinguishes students who are motivated by prudence and charity from those who are motivated by curiosity. Bernard writes that 'fructum et utilitatem scientiae in modo sciendi constituit [the fruit and usefulness of knowledge is determined by the manner in which one knows]'.[14] A prudent person learns to prioritize the knowledge that leads to salvation above all other kinds of knowledge, and a charitable person seeks to learn in order to teach other people; these attitudes to learning demonstrate sound judgement. The curious person, however, pursues all forms of knowledge indiscriminately, seeking knowledge as an end in itself ('fine tantum').[15] Bernard associates 'turpis curiositas' with other sinful motives for learning: the desire to become well known, which is 'turpis vanitas [shameful vanity]', and the desire to earn money or praise, which is 'turpis quaestus [shameful profiteering]'.[16] These are the interrelated vices that animate the commodification of 'wisdom and wit' in Study's account, and which find their public expression in sermons at St Paul's Cross. As they compete with each other to 'plese...proude men', the 'freres and faitours' are able to profit from their own *curiositas*, burnishing their intellectual reputations and seeking out material rewards.[17] Yet, they also erode those capacities for discrimination and discernment that Bernard associates with prudence, and which, as I will argue, are fundamental to the creative, interpretative activity of emplotment.

Late medieval *artes praedicandi* warn preachers not to encourage *curiositas* in their listeners: Ranulph Higden tells preachers not to seek 'lucri temporalis [worldly profits]' or 'sui ostentacionem [the ostentation of self]' by preaching on things that are 'impertinens ad salutem pocius aurem quam animam demulcens [irrelevant to salvation, attracting the ear rather than the soul]', tracing the same connections between curiosity, pride, and profiteering that Bernard describes.[18]

---

his *Influence in the Middle Ages*, ed. Edward B. King and Jacqueline T. Schaefer (Sewanee, TN: Press of the University of the South, 1988), and 'The Sin of Curiosity and the Cistercians', 71–95 in *Erudition at God's Service: Studies in Medieval Cistercian History*, ed. John R. Sommerfeldt (Kalamazoo, MI: Cistercian Publications, 1985), both reprinted in Newhauser, *Sin: Essays on the Moral Tradition* (Aldershot: Ashgate, 2007).

[14] Bernard of Clairvaux, *Sermones super Canticum Canticorum*, vols 1–2 in *Sancti Bernardi opera*, ed. J. Leclercq, C. H. Talbot, and H. M. Rochais, 8 vols (Rome: Editiones Cistercienses, 1957–8), 2: 5 (Sermon 36, 3.II.3); translation from Bernard of Clairvaux, *Sermons on the Song of Songs*, trans. Killian Walsh, 4 vols (Kalamazoo: Cistercian Publications, 1971–80), 2: 176.

[15] Bernard of Clairvaux, *Sermones super Canticum Canticorum*, Sermon 36, 3.III.3, ed. Leclercq, Talbot, and Rochais, 2: 5.

[16] Bernard of Clairvaux, *Sermones super Canticum Canticorum*, Sermon 36, 3.III.3, ed. Leclercq, Talbot, and Rochais, 2: 5–6; trans. Walsh, 2: 176.

[17] The situation at the preaching cross illustrates the fine distinction 'between flattery and self-aggrandizement' that Amanda Walling describes in Langland's account of friars who appeal to powerful men through the display of their own learning. Walling, 'Friar Flatterer: Glossing and the Hermeneutics of Flattery in *Piers Plowman*', YLS 21 (2007): 65.

[18] Ranulph Higden, *Ars componendi sermones*, ed. Jennings (Leiden: Brill, 1991), 7–8, trans. adapted from Higden, *Ars componendi sermones*, trans. Jennings and Sally A. Wilson (Leuven: Peeters, 2003), 35–6.

Other *artes*, however, acknowledge a powerful appetite among some audiences for preaching on obscure, arcane material. Robert of Basevorn criticizes preachers who encourage 'curiositatem et vanitatem [curiosity and vanity]' in their sermons, rather than offering 'aedificationem [edification]', but he also acknowledges that, if listeners demand this kind of material, then preachers may have to include it: 'Modo, tanta est vanitas hominum, praecipue anglicorum, quod tantum ad curiosa respiciunt nec alia commendant; ideo oportet talibus insistere [Indeed, so great is men's vanity, especially that of the English, that they only consider the curious and do not commend anything else; that makes it necessary to lean on such methods]'.[19] Thomas Waleys writes that the preacher 'non conetur sic hominibus...placere ut sequatur aliquorum vanitatem qui frequentantes sermones ea quae sunt curiositatis commendant [should not try to please men... to the point where he indulges the vanity of those who attend sermons frequently, and who will only commend them for their curiosity]'.[20] Yet, Waleys too acknowledges that even those preachers who object to preaching on 'vanitates' have included them for fear that 'sermones suos minus appretiari si a priorum consuetudine deviarent [their sermons would be valued less if they deviated from the previous custom]'.[21]

Late medieval preachers described these tensions, too. In a sermon for Ascension Day, for example, the Longleat friar criticizes 'clerkys þese days' who prefer 'veyn fablys and coryouste' to the words of scripture, and who 'han... leuere [prefer] to prechyn phylosophye, astronomye, geometrie þan cristis theologye'.[22] These clerics 'schewin here [their] wyt' in order 'to magnyfyin hemself', the friar says, 'more sekin [seeking] in here preching here owene worschepe þan goddys worschepe'.[23] They also appeal to the rich at the expense of the poor: they 'raþere wyl prechin [prefer to preach] to ryche folk to getyn with here fayre wordys and with flaterie wordly wynnyng, þan to pore folk to wynnyn mannys sowle'.[24] Like Study, the Longleat friar describes a divided audience: 'ryche folk' who delight in 'coryouste' and 'pore folk' who are abandoned to their sins. In his sermon for the Fourth Sunday in Lent, however, the Longleat friar reflects that people who come to sermons to hear 'coryouste & newe þyngis' will not listen to a preacher who does not satisfy them; when Jesus preached on the mountain near the sea of Galilee, his listeners sat down to hear him (John 6:10), but listeners now remain

---

[19] Basevorn, *Forma praedicandi*, 7, ed. Charland, 244; trans. Krul, 127. I have silently modified the punctuation.
[20] Waleys, *De modo componendi sermones*, 1.9, ed. Charland, 336. Translation adapted from Martin Camargo, 'How (Not) to Preach: Thomas Waleys and Chaucer's Pardoner', 146–78 in *Sacred and Profane in Chaucer and Late Medieval Literature: Essays in Honour of John V. Fleming* (Toronto: University of Toronto Press, 2010), 171–2. These passages from Basevorn and Walleys are also considered together by Fletcher, *Preaching, Politics, and Poetry*, 261–2, in a discussion of Chaucer's pardoner.
[21] Waleys, *De modo componendi sermones*, 1.9, ed. Charland, 336–7; trans. Camargo, 172.
[22] Longleat House, MS 4, fols 59v–60r.   [23] Longleat House, MS 4, fol. 59v.
[24] Longleat House, MS 4, fol. 60r.

standing 'þat þey moun redely [easily] gon awey ȝif þe prechour plese hem nout'.[25] Study's complaint expresses its own version of these concerns. The 'freres and faitours' at the preaching cross have created an appetite they must continue to satisfy, indulging 'proude men' in their taste for arcane knowledge. If curious preaching is to be reformed and recuperated, Study suggests, then this will require a transformation in the desires of these influential listeners, too.

As they cater to the appetites of wealthy lords, the preachers at St Paul's Cross withhold valuable and necessary instruction from the *commune* as a whole. Later in the poem, Anima will identify this instruction with elementary catechesis, saying that 'doctours' should preach on 'þe ten comaundementȝ' and 'þe seuene synnes', rather than on 'materes vnmesurables' (B.15.71–4). For Study, however, it takes the form of emplotment: the people who listen to curious sermons are deprived of the discursive resources of narrative. Study continues her critique of 'freres and faitours' with a description of the lives of their listeners, the 'folk' who listen to their sermons, but who are not 'fermed in þe feiþ, ne free of hire goodes,/ Ne sory for hire synnes' (B.10.70–75):

... so is pride woxen	*grown*
In religion and in al þe reme amonges riche and pouere	*religious orders; realm*
That preieres haue no power þise pestilences to lette.	*prayers; prevent*
For God is deef nowadayes and deyneþ noȝt vs to here,	*does not condescend*
That girles for hire giltes he forgrynt hem alle.	*children; sins; destroys*
And yet þe wrecches of þis world is noon ywar by ooþer,	*take no instruction from*
Ne for drede of þe deeþ wiþdrawe noȝt hir pride,	*plague*
Ne beþ plenteuouse to þe pouere as pure charite wolde,	*generous*
But in gaynesse and in glotonye forglutten hir good hemselue,	*extravagance; eat up*
And brekeþ noȝt to þe beggere as þe Book techeþ:	*do not share their bread*

Frange esurienti panem tuum...

(B.10.75–84a)

['Deal thy bread to the hungry', Isaiah 58:7]

The friars have abandoned these ordinary listeners in an uninterpreted present, where they are unable to recognize the imperatives or opportunities for ethical action and spiritual reform. This part of Study's complaint looks back to the second vision, where Reason and Piers engaged in the interpretative labour of emplotment. These preachers offered a narrative interpretation of lived experience

---

[25] Longleat House, MS 4, fol. 41v. The relevant passage from this sermon is transcribed and discussed in Hudson and Spencer, 'Old Author, New Work', 223.

and recent history that served to guide and direct new action, establishing a public discourse in which the *commune* could understand their obligations to one another, and to God. When preaching becomes a commodity for a small elite, however, it no longer serves its function for the larger community, as Study makes clear. Without the mediation of narrative, the people at the preaching cross lapse into sin and spiritual inertia.

Study's description of the disengaged 'folk' at the preaching cross contains complex and ironic echoes of Reason's sermon in particular. Preaching on the field of folk, Reason performed one of the poem's most striking and revelatory acts of emplotment, as I argued in Chapter 2, revealing the strict standard of God's justice at work in the world: his sermon reimagined the disasters of the recent past, including 'þise pestilences', as divine retribution for 'pride', and as portents of an imminent apocalypse, reconfiguring the lived experiences of his listeners, and offering powerful imperatives to 'do þe bettre' (B.5.13–17). Like the 'folk' on the field, the people at the preaching cross inhabit a world that has been shaped by the effects of the 'pestilence'. Without the discursive mediation of narrative, however, they are unable to perceive these disasters as punishments from God or as forerunning signs of the last judgement. Reason's listeners engage in a sustained, communal effort at reform, motivated by the fear of God, but the people at St Paul's, who feel no 'drede of þe deeþ', see no reason to 'wiþdrawe...hir pride' or to exercise charity towards one another. Reason shows how God intervenes in the world to punish human sin and reward human effort, but the audience at the preaching cross have come to think that God is indifferent to their actions. Study recalls them saying that 'preieres haue no power þise pestilences to lette', and that 'God is deef nowadayes and deyneþ noȝt vs to here'. When Study declares that 'þe wrecches of þis world is noon ywar by ooþer', she affirms that, without the mediation of narrative, they take no instruction from their own experiences.

In her later advice to the dreamer, Study begins to imagine how education and preaching might be reformed, in order to arrest the spread of *curiositas* and to supply the *commune* with more beneficial forms of instruction and direction. As Nicolette Zeeman has shown, Study herself personifies the hardships and privations that form part of basic instruction, that serve to cultivate a disciplined, attentive, and discriminating attitude to knowledge.[26] This is the virtue of *studiositas*, the disciplined attitude to learning that Bernard associates with prudence and charity: to be studious is to prioritize the knowledge that leads to salvation, and seek to share it with others. *Studiositas*, which is generous and discriminating and directed towards the good, counteracts the vice of *curiositas*, which is covetous, indiscriminate, and directed towards arcane, esoteric knowledge as an end in itself. Bernard writes that a studious person seeks knowledge 'non ad inanem

---

[26] Zeeman, *Discourse of Desire*, 109–31.

gloriam, aut curiositatem, aut aliquid simile, sed tantum ad aedificationem tuam, vel proximi [not through vain-glory or *curiositas* or any base motive, but for the welfare of oneself or one's neighbour]'.[27] In the final part of her speech, Study shows how *studiositas* can shape and direct a lifetime of learning that is directed towards salvation, and how learning like this might find expression in preaching for the benefit of the whole of the *commune*. She also shows that the virtue of *studiositas* is essential to the work of emplotment and to the forms of narrative understanding that give shape to an ethical life. What becomes clear in the last section of this speech is that the forms of clerical covetousness that characterize preaching at St Paul's Cross are not merely a distraction from the work of emplotment, but actually erode the kind of discernment that makes emplotment possible.

After Will submits to her instruction, Study directs him on 'þe heighe wey' to Clergy, mapping out an allegorical itinerary that resembles Piers Plowman's directions to Truth (B.10.157).[28] The journey leads through the hardships that Study represents, 'Suffre-/ Boþe-wel-and-wo, if þat þow wolt lerne' (B.10.159–60), and it skirts round a country called 'richesse' (Study warns the dreamer not to 'rest...þerinne'), avoiding the acquisitive desires that give rise to *curiositias* (B.10.161). The dreamer should avoid the 'likerous [lascivious] launde' of lechery, until he arrives at a court called 'Kepe-wel-þi tunge', where he will see Sobriety and Simplicity of Speech and be introduced to Clergy, with Study's recommendation (B.10.163–6). Like the ploughman's directions in the second vision, Study's map of the learning life constitutes, if not a form of emplotment, then at least a metaphor for the way emplotment works, configuring the disparate experiences of education into a narrative of progress through the curriculum. Study directs the dreamer on to other, more sophisticated forms of learning that offer many enticements to *curiositas*, as she frankly acknowledges in her parting words; here, Study warns the dreamer against astronomy, geometry, geomancy, sorcery, and alchemy, which she describes as 'fibicches in forceres', tricks in boxes, designed to 'deceyue' the 'folk' (B.10.213–17).[29] Yet, the discipline of *studiositas* will help the dreamer to navigate the risks and temptations that are associated with advanced study, because it will allow him to prioritize those forms of knowledge that lead to salvation. Study acknowledges that academic theology seems difficult and obscure to her: 'The moore I muse þerinne [think about it], þe mystier it semeþ', she says; 'It is no science, forsoþe, for to sotile inne [contemplate, reflect on]' (B.10.183, 185). Yet, she navigates its obscurities by focussing on love, which is the central lesson that theology has to teach: 'A ful leþi

---

[27] Bernard of Clairvaux, *Sermones super Canticum Canticorum*, Sermon 36, 3.II.3, ed. Leclercq, Talbot, and Rochais, 2: 5; trans. Walsh, 2: 176.

[28] On the parallels between these journeys, see Zeeman, *Arts of Disruption*, 366–7.

[29] Schmidt glosses 'fibicches' as 'tricks': *Piers Plowman B*, ed. Schmidt, 151, and see also the discussion in Schmidt, *Parallel Text*, 2: 589. This line from the B text supplies the only example of this term in the *MED*: see *MED*, s.v. 'febicches'.

[empty] þyng it were if þat loue þerinne nere [was not in it];/ Ac for it leteþ best by loue, I loue it þe bettre' (B.10.186–7). This is the discrimination that arises from *studiositas*, the capacity to prioritize the most essential knowledge. It is the essential principle that should direct the learning life, the *res*, or 'gist' of the intellectual biography that Study maps out for Will.

In this final part of her speech, Study explains how studious discipline might give rise to beneficial preaching, animated by prudence and charity, drawing a contrast between the 'freres and faitours' at St Paul's Cross and the apostle Paul himself. The Longleat friar offers a similar contrast in his sermon for Ascension Day, where he juxtaposes 'clerkys þese days' who prefer 'veyn fablys and coryouste' to the words of scripture, with Paul, who 'knew mor of goddys pryuytes þanne ony maystyr of dyuynyte' but declared that he was not ashamed of the gospel (Romans 1:16).[30] Study offers Will an example of how the *studiosus* discriminates between different kinds of knowledge, comparing Cato's advice to dissemble against dissemblers ('*sic ars deluditur arte* [thus art is beguiled by art]', B.10.193), with Paul's injunction '*operemur bonum ad omnes* [let us work good to all men]' (B.10.201a, citing Galatians 6.10); Study prefers Paul's advice because it is animated by love: 'For he biddeþ vs be as breþeren, and bidde [pray] for oure enemys,/ And louen hem þat lyen on [slander] us' (B.10.199–200).[31]

Study quotes the injunction '*operemur bonum ad omnes*' from Paul's Epistle to the Galatians: this epistle, which began with a warning against those who preach to please men, concludes in this verse with an exhortation to charity. Study pursues this thought into an account of Paul's own preaching, which she construes as an expression of the apostle's 'parfitnesse' (Figure 3.1):

Poul preched þe peple, þat parfitnesse louede,	who
To do good for Goddes loue, and gyuen men þat asked,	
And to swiche, nameliche, þat suwen oure bileue;	especially; follow
And alle þat lakkeþ vs or lyeþ vs, Oure Lord techeþ vs to louye,	disparage; slander
And noȝt to greuen hem þat greueþ vs—God hymself forbad it:	injure
Michi vindictam et ego retribuam.	
Forþi loke þow louye as longe as þow durest,	see to it that; survive
For is no science vnder sonne so souereyn for þe soule.	beneficial, salvific
	(B.10.202–8)

['Vengeance is mine, and I will repay', Deut. 32:35, cited Rom 12:19]

---

[30] Longleat House, MS 4, fols 59v–60r.
[31] Cato's advice reappears in a recuperated form much later in the poem, however, as part of an argument in defence of the atonement. See Christopher Cannon, *From Literacy to Literature: England, 1300–1400* (Oxford: Oxford University Press, 2016), 188–9.

Figure 3.1 St Paul preaching, from the Breviary of John the Fearless and Margaret of Bavaria, London, British Library, Additional MS 35311, fol. 238v.

Early in his *Forma praedicandi*, Robert of Basevorn considers the merits of several exemplary preachers, including St Paul. Basevorn commends the wide range of topics that Paul addressed in his sermons, which seem to comprehend 'totum evangelium, legem et prophetas [the entire Gospel, the Law and the prophets]', and remarks on the way he adapted his sermons to the needs of his audiences, consoling them, rebuking them, and reasoning with them as the occasion demanded. Yet, the essential point for Basevorn is that all these subjects and methods of preaching were movitated by *caritas*: 'In omnibus semper ostendit quod ex magna caritate quam ad auditores habuit illa dixit et scripsit [In all things and all ways he showed that his writings and words flowed from the great charity which he had towards his listeners].'³² Study's account of Pauline preaching has the same emphasis: she offers an overview of a lifetime's ministry, sermons delivered on many occasions to many audiences, that nonetheless affirms a single message and expresses a central principle: calling on the people 'To do good for Goddes loue'. Unlike Basevorn, however, Study uses this central principle to organize a narrative of Paul's evangelism, a preacher's biography that extends from her own, earlier map of the learning life.

This Pauline preaching offers the essential instruction that is missing from sermons at St Paul's Cross. While the 'freres and faitours' indulge their own *curiositas* and appeal to 'proude men' for praise and rewards, Paul, through his *studiositas*, prioritizes love, the 'science' that is 'souereyn for þe soule', and seeks to share it with his listeners. While the 'faitours' preach against each other, 'for pure enuye of clerkes', Paul advocates love for 'alle þat lakkeþ vs or lyeþ vs'. And while sermons at the preaching cross leave ordinary people disengaged, 'noȝt fermed in þe feiþ, ne free of hire goodes,/ Ne sory for hire synnes', Paul tells his congregations 'To do good for Goddes loue', offering clear instruction and moral direction, with an echo of Reason and Holy Church, who urge their listeners to 'do þe bettre'. Study does not elaborate on the content of Paul's preaching, or the narratives it might contain, but it is clear from her own map of the dreamer's learning life, and from her biography of Paul, that the capacity for discrimination that emerges from disciplined study is also central to the work of emplotment. Curious preachers do not simply neglect the kind of explanatory narratives that Reason offered on the field of folk; rather, their indiscriminate desire for esoteric knowledge makes it impossible for them to articulate narratives like this, to distinguish and prioritize the most important lessons that emerge from the simple succession of events. Paul's capacity to distinguish love as the 'souereyn' science allows him to engage in the kind of narrative interpretation that the poem locates as vital to the preacher's task.

In this part of her complaint, then, Study combines a critique of clerical *curiositas*, which echoes the language of contemporary *artes* and sermons, with an attack on preachers who neglect the work of emplotment, as defined and illustrated in the previous part of the poem. The 'freres and faitors' at St Paul's betray a disorderly attitude to knowledge that arises from failures in their own early instruction, using their 'wisdom and wit' to enrich themselves through an appeal to the appetites of proud men, and, as they do so, they divert these intellectual resources away from the elementary instruction, and from the narrative interpretation, that might benefit the *commune* as a whole. As she directs the dreamer away from this clerical *curiositas*, towards a life of learning that is ordered

---

[32] Basevorn, *Forma praedicandi*, 9, ed. Charland, 246; translation from Basevorn, *The Form of Preaching*, trans. Leopold Krul, 109–215 in *Three Medieval Rhetorical Arts*, ed. James J. Murphy (Berkeley and Los Angeles: University of California Press, 1971), 129–30.

and regulated by love, Study also begins to imagine the kind of preaching that might emerge from a reformed education like this, Pauline sermons that would urge 'þe peple.../To do good'. This kind of preaching, driven not by covetousness but by charity, might supply the kind of narrative interpretation that Reason and Piers Plowman had offered to the people on the field of folk. Yet questions remain about the form this preaching should take, and about who should deliver it, in a world where the discourse at the preaching cross has been so thoroughly corrupted. Answers begin to emerge when Study develops another part of her argument, likening preachers at the cross to entertainers in the dining hall.

Tales of Tobit

As her complaint unfolds, Study draws frequent comparisons between acquisitive preachers and secular entertainers, 'iaperis and iogelours and iangleris of gestes'. She locates these preachers and performers in the same extended networks of patronage and preferment: 'iaperis' and 'iangleris' receive their 'yeresȝeue[s] [annual gifts]' from 'kyng[es]', 'knyȝt[es]' and 'canon[es] of Seint Poules' (B.10.45–6), the same elite listeners who enjoy intellectual sermons at the preaching cross. Study argues that they also exploit their 'wisdom and wit' in closely analogous ways: like the 'freres and faitours' at St Paul's, 'iaperis' and 'iangleris' use their intelligence to enrich themselves, contriving performances to 'plese... proude men', and like them, they withhold more edifying narratives from the *commune* at large, depriving ordinary people of stories and instruction that might bring them spiritual benefits. Study employs these comparisons to extend her critique of curious preaching and of the way it erodes the capacity for narrative understanding. As she does so, however, she also discovers some surprising possibilities for the reform of preaching, modelled on a turn to other, more virtuous forms of minstrelsy.

Medieval *artes praedicandi* caution their readers to distinguish themselves from minstrels and entertainers when they preach. Alan of Lille warns preachers not to use poetic ornaments or obscene language in their sermons, noting that 'quae predicatio theatralis est et mimica [such preaching is theatrical and histrionic]'; listeners who recognize these techniques will think that the preacher has devised his sermons to win their praise ('elaborata ad favorem hominum') and not for their spiritual benefit.[33] The preacher should announce that he does not seek 'inanibus vulgi clamoribus [the foolish acclaim of the mob]', or to provoke 'theatrali applausu [applause, as in a theatre]', distinguishing his motives from those of secular entertainers. Instead, he should appeal to his

---

[33] Alan of Lille, *De arte praedicatoria*, 1, ed. Migne, 210: col. 112, trans. Evans, 18–19.

listeners through the display of his authentic virtues: 'praedicator debet captare benevolentiam auditorum a propria persona per humilitatem [the preacher must win the goodwill of his audience through the humility he shows in his own person]'.[34] Later *artes* proscribe theatrical gestures, which also suggest dishonest motives, and imply that the preacher projects a *persona* that is different from his authentic nature.[35] In this tradition, preachers resemble entertainers when they contrive their sermons to 'plese... proude men', the accusation levelled at curious, contentious preachers by Wrath, Study, and Anima. This is an easy way to capture the goodwill of an audience, but one that undermines a preacher's capacity to 'preue' his sermon from the evidence of his own life, because it tacitly reveals his proud, acquisitive motives for preaching.

Study draws precisely the connections that the *artes* encouraged preachers to avoid, and develops further parallels between preachers and entertainers to extend the logic of her own critique. Study says that popular entertainers 'spitten and spuen [vomit] and speke foule wordes' when they perform, comparing obscene speech to other grotesque excesses of the mouth (B.10.40). This kind of speech seems very different from the rarefied, academic discourse that was available at St Paul's Cross. As Study goes on to make clear, however, the obscenity of 'foule wordes' arises not from their semantic content but from the acquisitive desires that motivate them, desires that preachers and performers have in common. Here as elsewhere in the poem, the phrase 'foule wordes' offers a Middle English equivalent for Latin *turpiloquium*.[36] The poem's references to *turpiloquium* contain a pun on 'turpe lucrum [filthy profit]', as Ralph Hanna notes, linking the 'foul speech' of entertainers with the 'filthy lucre' they hope to earn from it.[37] This, in

---

[34] Alan of Lille, *De arte praedicatoria*, 1, ed. Migne, 210: col. 114, trans. Evans, 20–1 (adapted). Paradoxically, as Waters has observed, the preacher who follows Alan's advice must invoke and negotiate theatrical precedents in order to project his authentic self: 'he must create a persona by rejecting the suggestion that he is an actor'; *Angels and Earthly Creatures*, 45–6.

[35] Thomas of Chobham says that those who gesticulate while they preach 'uidentur esse histriones quam predicatores [will seem to be actors rather than preachers]'; *Summa de arte praedicandi*, 2.v, ed. Morenzoni, 301–3, trans. Copeland and Sluiter, 637–8. Higden identifies excessive and disorderly gestures with 'placitatores [flatterers]' and 'ypocrita [hypocrites]'; *Ars componendi sermones*, 4, ed. Jennings, 10, trans. Jennings and Wilson, 37. Higden draws this material from Hugh of St Victor's instructions to novices, book 12: 'De institutione novitiorum', 58–74 in *L'œuvre de Hugues de Saint-Victor, 1: De institutione novitiorum, De virtute orandi, De laude caritatis, De arrha animae*, ed. H. B. Feiss and P. Sicard, trans. D. Poirel, H. Rochais, and P. Sicard (Turnhout: Brepols, 1997). Thomas Waleys also warns against the use of theatrical gestures ('motus inordinatus'); *De modo componendi sermones*, 1.v, ed. Charland, 332, trans. Camargo 167. Minnis, *Fallible Authors*, 120–21, notes that Chaucer's Pardoner confesses to making many of the disorderly movements that Waleys condemns, turning his head left and right, and stretching out his arms, in 'The Pardoner's Prologue', VI, ll. 395–9.

[36] *Turpiloquium* is first identified with 'iaperis' and 'iangleris' in the Prologue (B.Prol.39). Later, in a passage of direct address to patrons, Langland says that entertainers lead their listeners to hell with their 'foule wordes', singing 'turpiloquio, a lay of sorwe' (B.13.455–7). See Edwin D. Craun, *Lies, Slander, and Obscenity in Medieval English Literature: Pastoral Rhetoric and the Deviant Speaker* (Cambridge: Cambridge University Press, 1997), 157–86.

[37] Hanna, *Penn Commentary*, 2: 173. See also *DMLBS*, s.v. 'turpilucrum'.

turn, was an important category in medieval canon law where, as Arvind Thomas has shown, any activity undertaken from a desire for 'turpe lucrum' might be condemned as usurious.[38] The speech of 'iangleris' also comments on curious preaching at St Paul's because it is characteristically indiscriminate. Richard Rolle, who renders the 'uir linguosus' of Psalm 139:12 as a 'man iangelere' in his translation of the Psalms, explains in the revised version of his Psalter commentary that a jangler pays no attention to his own speech, pronouncing truths and falsehoods without differentiating between them.[39] Study's use of this epithet implies that obscene entertainers, like curious preachers, are unable to distinguish what is valuable or important from what is trivial and inessential.

Study does not describe 'iaperis' and 'iangleris' performing at St Paul's, although contemporary legislation suggests that some attempted to do so: statutes drawn up while Ralph de Baldock was dean (1294–1304) required vergers to guard the precinct entrances so that 'beggars and minstrels' could not enter.[40] However, she does describe 'freres and faitours' in the halls of great houses where 'iaperis' and 'iangleris' performed.[41] The preachers are seated at the high table, as the honoured guests of great lords. As they engage their hosts in academic conversation, however, they continue the work of minstrels, providing entertainment for their patrons 'at mete [meal times] in hir murþes [when they are enjoying themselves] whan mynstrals beþ stille' (B.10.52). The lords participate in these debates as clerical disputants, alleging authorities and adducing arguments, but, without the proper clerical training, they stray into dangerous theological error. Study describes them disputing the logic of the Fall, and directing 'fautes [charges of blame]' at God (B.10.105); here, the narrative of salvation that emerges from the best preaching in *Piers Plowman* is subsumed into confusing academic speculation that obscures its significance.

---

[38] Thomas, *Piers Plowman and the Reinvention of Church Law*, 69–70, 79. Szittya (*Antifraternal Tradition*, 254) observes that '[m]instrelsy for gain' is often imagined as 'a secular form of simony' in *Piers Plowman*, 'selling a divine gift for "mede"'.

[39] *Two Revisions of Rolle's English Psalter Commentary and the Related Canticles*, ed. by Anne Hudson, EETS, os 340, 341, 343, 3 vols (Oxford: Oxford University Press, 2012–14), 3: 1075–6. On the 'uir linguosus' in pastoral writings on deviant speech, see Craun, *Lies, Slander, and Obscenity*, 220–1. Linda J. Clifton, who notes this example from Rolle, argues that the third vision of *Piers Plowman* responds to the treatment of 'japing and jangling' in contemplative writings, which often warn against the idle and worldly speech that distracts the soul from its ascent to God. Clifton, 'Struggling with Will: Jangling, Sloth, and Thinking in *Piers Plowman* B', 29–52 in *'Suche Werkis to Werche'*; see also Galloway, *Penn Commentary*, 1: 67.

[40] Barron, 'London and St Paul's Cathedral in the Later Middle Ages', 126–49 in *The Medieval English Cathedral: Papers in Honour of Pamela Tudor-Craig*, ed. Janet Backhouse (Donington: Shaun Tyas, 2003), 135–6.

[41] *Piers Plowman* repeatedly imagines entertainers performing in the great hall of the medieval manor house. The address to patrons imagines performers 'at festes', and commands that 'noon harlot' should 'haue audience in halle' (B.13.438, 434), while Haukyn relates how he struggled to compete with obscene entertainers 'at festes' (B.13.232).

Study employs commonplace figurative associations between eating, speaking, and learning as she describes the scene in the hall.[42] In conversation with their clerical guests, the 'proude men' at the high table regurgitate partially digested knowledge, spitting and spewing like obscene minstrels: 'Thus þei dryuele at hir deys [daïs] þe deitee [divine nature] to knowe,/ And gnawen [chew] God wiþ þe gorge [throat] whanne hir guttes fullen [fill up]' (B.10.56–7).[43] The effects of *curiositas* were often compared to the excessive consumption of indigestible food like this. In his *Sermones super Canticum Canticorum*, for example, Bernard of Clairvaux asks, 'It et multa scientia ingesta stomacho animae, quae est memoria, si decocta igne caritatis non fuerit, et per quosdam artus animae,... transfusa atque digesta,... nonne illa scientia reputabitur in peccatum, tamquam cibus conversus in pravos noxiosque humores? [If a glut of knowledge stuffed in the stomach of the mind, which is the memory, has not been cooked on the fire of love, and transfused and digested by certain skills of the soul... will not that knowledge be reckoned sinful, like the food that produces irregular and harmful humours?].'[44] Humbert of Romans uses similar metaphors in his advice to preachers. The preacher who prioritizes useful knowledge is like a host who prepares a nourishing meal for his guests, he argues, but a preacher who includes too many 'subtilita [subtleties]' and 'philosophica [philosophical points]' in his sermons offers them a meal that is hard to digest: 'Et sicut cibus modiocris confert sanitatem stomacho, sic nimius subvertit stomachum [A moderate amount of food is good for the stomach, but too much revolts it].'[45]

In the symbolic space of the dining hall, the gluttonous overindulgence of lords and clerics also appears as a failure of charity to the larger community. The hall of the medieval manor house was organized to facilitate displays of generosity and largesse: the lord of the manor would be served more food than he could eat in deference to his social position and would then redistribute a portion to other members of his household. Many noble households also arranged to feed the poor at the gates, extending these formal acts of generosity to the community as a whole.[46] This largesse might also extend to the provision of entertainment and

---

[42] See Mann, 'Eating and Drinking in *Piers Plowman*', *Essays and Studies* 32 (1979): 34–5. Lawler, *Penn Commentary*, 4: 15–16, 19. On the origins and development of this imagery, see Jean Leclercq, *The Love of Learning and the Desire for God: A Study of Monastic Culture*, trans. Catharine Misrahi, 3rd edn (New York: Fordham University Press, 1982), 72–3; Carruthers, *The Book of Memory: A Study of Memory in Medieval Culture* (Cambridge: Cambridge University Press, 1990), 164–220.

[43] These lines recall Study's first appearance in the poem, where she rebuked her husband Wit for sharing 'wisdomes' with the dreamer before he had cultivated the proper mental discipline; citing Matthew 7:6, she accused him of casting pearls before swine, who 'doon but drauele þeron' (B.10.11).

[44] Bernard of Clairvaux, *Sermones super Canticum Canticorum*, Sermon 36, 3.III.4, ed. Leclercq, Talbot, and Rochais, 2: 6; trans. adapted from Walsh, 2: 176–7.

[45] Humbert of Romans, *Liber de eruditione praedicatorum*, 1.ii (vii.86), ed. Berthier, 2: 394–5, translation from Humbert of Romans, *Treatise on the Formation of Preachers*, 179–384 in *Early Dominicans: Selected Writings*, trans. Simon Tugwell (London: SPCK, 1982), 205–6.

[46] Mark Girouard, *Life in the English Country House: A Social and Architectural History* (New Haven: Yale University Press, 1978), 49–50.

instruction for the other people in the hall. In the second vision, Piers Plowman tells the knight to 'eschewe [avoid]' 'harlotes [obscene entertainers]' 'at þe mete', but encourages him to employ virtuous minstrels whose 'tales' are 'of wisdom or of wit, þi werkmen to chaste [correct]' (B.6.51–4). The 'iaperis' and 'iangleris' who Study describes actively subvert the flow of charity to the poor, taking 'goodes' and 'yiftes' from their patrons, while the needy are shut outside: 'þe carefulle [wretched] may crie and carpen at þe yate,/ Boþe afyngred [hungry] and afurst [thirsty]' (B.10.30, 42, 58–9).[47] The 'freres and faitours' participate in the same activity, appropriating food that might otherwise be redistributed. Their patrons, meanwhile, are guilty of a related failure of charity, withholding beneficial instruction from the household in order to indulge their own desires. The situation in the dining hall helps to clarify the situation that unfolds at the preaching cross, where 'proude men' exert their influence to promote curious sermons, to the detriment of the larger community.

In all these ways, then, the analogies between acquisitive preachers and scurrilous entertainers serve to deepen and extend Study's critique of preaching at St Paul's Cross. As she develops these comparisons, however, Study also imagines forms of minstrelsy that might serve as a corrective to curious preaching, offering the religious instruction and the narrative interpretation that have long been abandoned at St Paul's. These virtuous minstrels recall the 'joculatores Domini' of the early Franciscan tradition: the *Speculum perfectionis* records that Francis himself sent his followers out to preach and sing, with instructions to announce themselves as minstrels of the lord.[48] They might also resemble those members of the cathedral clergy who composed their own poetry in this period, producing serious, sophisticated work in the alliterative tradition of *Piers Plowman*. Ruth Kennedy proposed John Tickhill, collector of rents for the Dean and Chapter of St Paul's, as the likely author of 'A Bird in Bishopswood', while Hanna has argued that *St Erkenwald* might also be a product of this milieu.[49] Kathryn Kerby-Fulton has

---

[47] This criticism was also rehearsed in material for preachers: in the *Summa praedicantium*, for example, John Bromyard imagines a scene at the Last Judgement where the poor complain about the rich, who spend extravagantly on 'histriones, et turpes persone [performers and shameful people]' while neglecting their charitable obligations. Entertainers cry out '"ad largitatem ad largitatem" ["for largess, for largess"]' as they take their rewards, while the poor, who receive nothing, cry '"ad fugam, ad fugam" ["run away, run away"]'. Bromyard, *Summa Praedicantium*, 1: 308r (F.8); translation adapted from Owst, *Literature and Pulpit*, 301. Donaldson, *Piers Plowman: The C-text*, 143–4, notes the relevance of this passage for *Piers Plowman*.

[48] *Speculum perfectionis*, ed. Charles Sabatier (Paris: Fischbacher, 1898), 198; translated as 'A Mirror of the Perfection of the Status of a Lesser Brother (The Sabatier Edition, 1928)', 3: 253–372 in *Francis of Assisi: Early Documents*, ed. Regis J. Armstrong, J. A. Wayne Hellmann, and William J. Short, 3 vols (Hyde Park, NY: New City Press, 1999–2001), 3: 348. On the relationship between the Franciscan *joculatores Domini* and *Piers Plowman*'s account of 'Goddes minstrales', see Donaldson, *Piers Plowman: The C-text*, 146–7, Szittya, *Antifraternal Tradition*, 251–7, and Clopper,'*Songes of Rechelesnesse*', 200–1; Clopper notes that Jusserand was the first to argue for this connection (16).

[49] Ruth Kennedy, '"A Bird in Bishopswood": Some Newly-Discovered Lines of Alliterative Verse from the Late Fourteenth Century', 71–87 in *Medieval Literature and Antiquities: Studies in Honour of*

recently considered these poets as representatives of a wider class of precariously employed clerics, who were drawn to cathedral communities by the prospect of chantry positions and other related work, and who 'contributed disproportionately' to the composition and dissemination of Middle English literature.[50]

Early in her complaint, Study observes that 'iaperis' and 'iangleris' have displaced other kinds of performer in the hall. While wealthy lords reward 'harlotes' for their obscenities (B.10.30), they overlook virtuous entertainers who tell stories from the Bible:

Ac he þat haþ Holy writ ay in his mouþe	*always*
And kan telle of Tobye and of þe twelue Apostles	*Tobit*
Or prechen of þe penaunce þat Pilat wro3te	*suffering; caused*
To Iesu þe gentile, þat Iewes todrowe—	*noble; mutilated*
Litel is he loued or lete by þat swich a lesson sheweþ...	*loved; esteemed*
	(B.10.32–6)

This kind of minstrelsy offers a secular analogue to the preaching of St Paul, which Study commends at the end of her encounter with the dreamer. In his selection and treatment of biblical texts, the virtuous minstrel displays the prudence and charity that Bernard associated with *studiositas* and that Study herself will go on to identify with love. He prioritizes scripture over other kinds of narrative, telling stories about the passion of Christ and the acts of the Apostles, and he speaks from a desire to instruct others, rather than seeking out the 'goodes' that 'iaperis' and 'iangleris' desire. Study returns to the imagery of eating and speaking in this passage when she describes the virtuous minstrel with 'Holy writ ay in his mouþe'. Here, however, it suggests thoughtful rumination on well-chosen and properly assimilated knowledge, rather than the greedy consumption of indigestible curiosities. This image points to the minstrel's authenticity, too. The man with scripture 'ay in his mouþe' is always consistent in what he says, while 'iaperis' and 'iangleris', like 'freres and faitours', assume a persona to 'plese...proude men'. This virtuous minstrel has cultivated a discriminating attitude to knowledge, born of a concern with salvation, and taken up a vocation that allows him to share it, a secular equivalent to the life of Pauline 'parfitnesse' that Study will later recommend for studious preachers.

Study hints that this kind of minstrelsy might answer to the spiritual needs of the people at St Paul's by supplying new acts of emplotment. The virtuous minstrel reaffirms the tenets of the faith through his selection of biblical stories

---

Basil Cottle, ed. Myra Stokes and T. L. Burton (Cambridge: Brewer, 1987). Hanna, 'Alliterative Poetry', 488–512 in *The Cambridge History of Medieval English Literature*, ed. David Wallace (Cambridge: Cambridge University Press, 1999), 510.

[50] Kerby-Fulton, *Clerical Proletariat*, 2; for discussion of Tickill, see 97–102, and for the *Erkenwald*-poet see 261–97.

and encourages 'penaunce' through his account of the passion. In his allusion to the book of Tobit, meanwhile, the minstrel encourages charity, as Study will later go on to make clear. Later in her complaint, Study herself cites Tobit in a rebuke to rich men who 'brekeþ noȝt to þe beggere', in lines that suggest what the message of this minstrelsy might be:

> Tobye techeþ yow noȝt so! Takeþ hede, ye riche,
> How þe book Bible of hym bereþ witnesse:
> *Si tibi sit copia habundanter tribue; si autem exiguum,*
> *illud impertiri libenter stude.*
> Whoso haþ muche, spende manliche—so meneþ Tobye –   *generously*
> And whoso litel weldeþ, loke hym þerafter...   *behave accordingly*
> (B.10.87–90)

['If thou have much, give abundantly; if thou have little, take care to bestow willingly even a little', Tobit 4:9]

This quotation, from Tobit 4:9, forms part of Tobit's advice to his son, which includes repeated injunctions to charity and warnings against indulgence and excess. Tobit says, 'Panem tuum cum esurientibus et egenis comede [Eat thy bread with the hungry and needy]' (Tobit 4:17), advice with particular resonance in the symbolic space of the hall. He also counsels his son against pride, which proliferates at the preaching cross: 'Superbiam numquam in tuo sensu, aut in tuo verbo, dominari permittas [Never suffer pride to reign in thy mind, or in thy words]' (Tobit 4:19). Tobit locates these injunctions in a narrative frame, reminding his son to 'spende manliche' in order to receive a heavenly reward on the day of judgement. Citing Tobit in this apostrophe to 'proude men', then, Study hints at the kind of emplotment the virtuous minstrel might perform: this is a narrative that explains the imperatives to 'do wel', that encourages people to 'wiþdrawe... hir pride' and 'beþ plenteuouse to þe pouere', in the expectation of an imminent encounter with God. Stories about love and charity are already preconfigured in the symbolic operations of the manor house hall, awaiting minstrelsy that can articulate them. In this social space, where the *curiositas*, *vanitas*, and *turpis quaestus* of 'proude men' and worldly preachers currently appear as glutinous overindulgence and as failures of charity to other people, warnings against pride and injunctions to 'spende manliche' reaffirm the need for largesse and generosity.

Although they do not gratify contemporary lords, Study insists that these tales of Tobit can still delight and entertain. She describes this 'mynstralcie' as a source of 'murþe' (B.10.48), and identifies it with musical skill, noting that 'iaperis' and 'iangleris' 'konne na moore mynstralcie ne music men to glade/ Than Munde þe Millere of *Multa fecit Deus*' (B.10.43–4). These lines recall a distinction, found in Peter the Chanter's *Summa de sacramentis* and elsewhere, between musicians, who delight, console, and edify, and other performers who rely on obscene words and gestures.[51] They also recall Francis' injunction to the 'ioculatores Domini' to preach and sing. Humbert of Romans, who drew a favourable comparison between preaching and minstrelsy in his *ars*, placed musical skill at its heart, explaining that preaching pleases God 'sicut etiam in curiis magnates solent in cantibus joculatorum delectari [like minstrels' songs which rulers and princes enjoy in their courts]'.[52] Invoking these traditions in her complaint, Study draws attention to the question of lordly appetites, to the kinds of entertainment that 'plese...proude men'. Lords who delight in *curiositas* and *turpiloquium* dismiss the 'murþe' of 'mynstralcie', but Study insists that other forms of enjoyment are possible. Lords who cultivate them might choose to promote pious entertainments that would benefit the whole community, so that minstrelsy itself becomes available to people in the hall as a form of charity.

At the end of her encounter with the dreamer, as we saw in the first section of this chapter, Study recommends a life of learning that is focussed on love, guided by the kind of *studiositas* that can distinguish essential, salvific knowledge from knowledge that is vain or superfluous. This kind of learning results in charitable preaching and action, exemplified in the life and in the sermons of St Paul. In the midst of her complaint, however, she also identifies a kind of minstrelsy that seems to anticipate this virtuous preaching, offering warnings against pride and injunctions to charity in the manor house hall. Like the studious preacher, the virtuous minstrel has learned to prioritize essential knowledge, focussed on love and directed to salvation, and seeks to share it with other people. Study imagines that virtuous minstrelsy, like 'parfit' preaching, might take up the work of emplotment that has been neglected at the preaching cross, reconfiguring the lived experience of the *commune* to direct and encourage them in good works. She also recognizes that it creates a new role for the 'proude men' who currently indulge the 'freres and faitours' and the 'iaperis' and 'iangleris': wealthy lords who took pleasure in minstrelsy like this might also sponsor useful instruction as a kind of charity, distributing 'wisdom and wit' among the *commune*, just as they distribute food to the people in the manor house and to the beggars at the gates.

---

[51] Peter the Chanter, *Summa de sacramentis et animae consiliis*, ed. Jean-Albert Dugauquier, 3 vols in 5 fas. (Louvain: Éditions Nauwelaert, 1954-7), 3 (2a): 176-7. Thomas of Chobham, *Summa Confessorum*, ed. F. Broomfield, Analceta Mediaevalia Namurcensia, 25 (Louvain: Éditions Nauwelaert, 1968), 291-3. E. K. Chambers discussed Chobham's distinction between musicians and other performers in *The Medieval Stage*, 2 vols (London: Oxford University Press, 1903), 1: 59-62, 71, 73, and reproduced the relevant passage from his penitential as an appendix, 2: 262-3; it has often been cited since, for example by Donaldson, *Piers Plowman: The C-text*, 144, 148, who notes the 'striking similarity' between Chobham's account of virtuous minstrels and Langland's. Christopher Page, *The Owl and the Nightingale: Musical Life and Ideas in France, 1100-1300* (London: Dent, 1989), 19-33, offers a much fuller discussion of Peter the Chanter and Thomas of Chobham on minstrels and entertainers, and considers two further writers who develop their arguments: Cardinal Robert of Courçon in his *Summa* (*c.*1208-13), and the Franciscan Thomas Docking in his commentary on Galatians (*c.*1265).

[52] Humbert of Romans, *Liber de eruditione praedicatorum*, chapter 1.iii (IV 23), ed. Berthier, 2: 380, trans. Tugwell, 190.

Richard Alkerton's Curry Comb

During the parliament of 1406, as Thomas Walsingham reports in *The St Albans Chronicle*, William Taylor delivered an inflammatory sermon at St Paul's Cross where he argued that the clerics should not own property, and maintained, following the 'dampnatas opiniones' of John Wyclif, that secular lords were entitled to dispossess the clergy. The following day, a preacher called Richard Alkerton delivered another sermon at the preaching cross, where he refuted Taylor's arguments and declared that any lord who sought to deprive the church of its possessions should be excommunicated.[53] Alkerton's sermon provoked a mocking reaction from the Lancastrian squire and administrator Robert Waterton, who was in the audience, and from the lollard preacher William Thorpe, who later accosted Alkerton in the street.[54] In some ways, this polemical exchange resembles the contentious preaching that Study associated with clerical pride and ambition, a public dispute, animated by the 'enuye of clerkes'. As the surviving records make clear, however, the participants also echoed various aspects of Study's own polemic: Taylor was concerned with the commodification of knowledge, criticizing clerics who used their learning in service of secular lords, while Alkerton argued that Taylor's case for disendowment was itself designed to flatter powerful men, and was then accused of flattery himself by members of his audience. Taylor, Alkerton, and their supporters valued debate at the preaching cross, which they recognized as an arena to advocate for reforming action, yet the conclusion of this episode also illustrates the limits of what a debate like this could achieve in the climate of the early fifteenth century.

Both Taylor and Alkerton held positions at Oxford and were trained in the arts of academic disputation: Taylor was the principal of St Edmund Hall, at that time a centre of Wycliffite thought, while Alkerton was a fellow of Merton College from 1373 until at least 1398, and subsequently rented a room in Queen's College.[55] Alkerton, at least, was also a regular speaker at St Paul's Cross. Although the text of his response to Taylor is now lost, another sermon attributed to the 'worþi clerk

---

[53] Walsingham, *St Albans Chronicle*, ed. and trans. Taylor, Childs, and Watkiss, 2: 478–80, 479–81. In their translation, the editors mistakenly locate these sermons at Charing Cross, and not at St Paul's (the text situates them '*apud Crucem Londoniis*'). On the dispute between Taylor and Alkerton, see Horner, 'Preachers at St Paul's Cross', 277–82, and the introductions to the modern editions of Taylor's sermon and of a sermon for another occasion by Alkerton: *Two Wycliffite Texts: The Sermon of William Taylor, 1406; The Testimony of William Thorpe, 1407*, ed. Hudson, EETS, os 301 (Oxford: Oxford University Press, 1993), xiii–xv; O'Mara, *A Study and Edition of Selected Middle English Sermons*, Leeds Texts and Monographs, new series 13 (Leeds: School of English, University of Leeds, 1994), 28–32.

[54] On Waterton's life and career, see J. R. Whitehead, 'Waterton, Robert (d.1425)', *ODNB*, <https://doi.org/10.1093/ref:odnb/54421>

[55] Hudson, *Two Wycliffite Texts*, xvii–xxv, O'Mara, *Study and Edition*, 28–9. See also A. B. Emden, *A Biographical Register of the University of Oxford to AD 1500*, 3 vols (Oxford: Clarendon Press, 1957–9), 1: 70 for Alkerton, and 3: 1852 for Taylor; and John A. F. Thomson, 'Taylor, William (d.1423)', *ODNB*, <https://doi.org/10.1093/ref:odnb/27091>

maistir Richard Alkartoun' survives both in English, in British Library, Additional MS 37677, and in Latin, in Oxford, Trinity College, MS 42.[56] The colophon to the English version says that Alkerton preached it at 'Seint Marie Spitel', the Hospital of St Mary Bishopsgate, 'in Eestir Woke' in 1406, presumably as part of the preaching tradition that John Stow described in his *Survey of London*.[57] In this sermon, moreover, Alkterton refers to another recent sermon that he preached at the cross outside St Paul's ('As I seide late in a sermoun at Poules Cros, hou euery man þat doþ dedely sinne is an open tretour [traitor] to God…'); this suggests that his sermon in reply to Taylor was at least his second appearance at the preaching cross in this year.[58]

Taylor's sermon, which survives in a single manuscript, now Oxford, Bodleian Library, MS Douce 53, condemns the commodification of clerical knowledge in language that echoes aspects of Study's complaint. Preaching on John 6:5, 'Unde ememus panes, ut manducent hi? [Whence shall we buy bread, that these may eat?]', he uses contrasting metaphors of gluttonous consumption and charitable distribution to explain how clerics exploit their knowledge to advance themselves rather than to benefit the poor. Taylor explains that preachers should distribute the 'breed of doctryne' in their sermons as an act of charity, analogous to material almsgiving, but argues that clerics 'today' use their 'kunnyng' to advance their secular careers, 'encumbringe hemsilf in worldly ocupaciouns'.[59] Once a clerk has obtained a benefice, Taylor declares, he 'traueliþ [labours] day and nyȝt bi flateringe', and 'acumbriþ himsilf in seculer ocupacioun to plese men and to encreece his goodis'.[60] The same preachers subvert the flow of material charity to the poor, taking the 'breed of almes' for themselves, while others go hungry: Taylor describes them 'swolewinge up þe substaunce [material] of almes due bi Cristis wille to poore men', while 'wrecchid cristen men' are left to 'crye and begge' for food.[61]

---

[56] The English sermon is edited in O'Mara, *Study and Edition*, 21–80; on the Latin sermon see Wenzel, *Latin Sermon Collections*, 167, 169. The editors of the *St Albans Chronicle* mistakenly identify this 1406 sermon as Alkerton's reply to Taylor: *St Albans Chronicle*, ed. and trans. Taylor, Childs, and Watkiss, 2: 481, n. 676. Other sermons by Alkerton also survive: Alkerton's name appears in a sermon on 2 Corinthians 6:2, found in Cambridge, University Library MS Ii.3.8 and Worcester Cathedral Library MS F.10, and the abbreviated Worcester text includes a cross-reference to a further sermon by Alkerton on Luke 14:10, which Wenzel has identified in Jesus College Cambridge MS 13, Hereford Cathedral Library MS 39 and Magdalen College Oxford MS 112, and excerpted in the sermon compilation by John Felton. See Wenzel, 'Richard Alkerton's Sermon on "Amice, Ascende Superius"', *Mediaeval Studies* 83 (2021): 1–25.

[57] O'Mara considers Alkerton's sermon in relation to this Easter Week tradition; *Study and Edition*, 32–8.

[58] Alkerton, 'Easter Week Sermon', ed. O'Mara, 62.

[59] 'Sermon of William Taylor', 3–23 in *Two Wycliffite Texts*, ed. Hudson, 4.

[60] 'Sermon of William Taylor', ed. Hudson, 13. Later, Taylor compares these clerics to the Pharisees, who 'bi ypocrisie, flateringe and fals suggestioun appropren to hem þe goodis of hooly chirche' (19).

[61] 'Sermon of William Taylor', ed. Hudson, 19. Here, as Crassons has noted (*Claims of Poverty*, 152–3), Taylor satirizes clerical covetousness by 'exposing its material consequences for the poor', 'explaining that the church's covetous behaviour actually endangers the lives of those most greatly in need'.

Disendowment would solve both these problems, Taylor argues: were clerics to 'delyuere up into þe hondis of seculer men alle her poscessiouns and tresours' and 'holde hem apayd [satisfied] wiþ necessarie liiflode [the necessities of life]', then these goods could be redistributed to the poor, and the clerics themselves return to the essential tasks of preaching and pastoral care.[62]

As he develops this critique, Taylor points to failures in pastoral instruction, noting that many contemporary clerics 'can not expowne to þe puple oon [a single] article of þe feiþ'.[63] Like Study, however, he also suggests that worldly preachers neglect the task of emplotment, withholding forms of narrative interpretation that would disclose the need for action in the present time. The corrupt, self-interested use of clerical 'kunnynge' is part of a larger eschatological narrative for Taylor. Following Bernard of Clairvaux, he describes a history of the church, oppressed by tyranny in the age of the martyrs, by heresy in the age of the fathers, and by hypocrisy in the present time. The growth of clerical corruption is a sign of the coming apocalypse, Taylor argues: the devil encourages clerics in their 'vnordynat [excessive] loue to þe world', so that it will take longer to make up the number of the saved.[64] Yet, the negligence of contemporary preachers means that many people do not recognize the imminence of judgement day, or understand the imperatives it creates for reform. Like the 'folk' who Study describes at the preaching cross, and in the hall of the manor house, most people continue in their sin, without 'medicyn of sorewe, shrift and penaunce doyng', 'for defaute [lack] of þe breed Goddis lawe mynystrid to hem in ensaumple and word'.[65] Taylor offers his own sermon as a corrective, taking up the task of emplotment that other preachers have abandoned, and urging the reform of the church as the apocalypse draws closer.

Walsingham records that Alkerton appeared at St Paul's Cross the following day to refute Taylor's claims, and that he did so with a series of lucid arguments ('rationibus euidentibus'). In his own account of Taylor's sermon, Walsingham argues that Taylor was himself a flatterer or 'adulator', and that his arguments for disendowment were contrived in order to please the temporal lords who would profit from them.[66] While Taylor accused the clergy of 'swolewinge up þe substaunce of almes', Walsingham calls Taylor a glutton who belches or vomits up his arguments ('plura deliramenta alia ructauit idem ganeo die illa'), echoing the language of partial digestion and regurgitation that recur in critiques of ill-disciplined knowledge and clerical *curiositas*.[67] Walsingham notes that

---

[62] 'Sermon of William Taylor', ed. Hudson, 9.   [63] 'Sermon of William Taylor', ed. Hudson, 4.
[64] 'Sermon of William Taylor', ed. Hudson, 6.
[65] 'Sermon of William Taylor', ed. Hudson, 10–11.
[66] *St Albans Chronicle*, ed. and trans. Taylor, Childs, and Watkiss, 2: 478.
[67] *St Albans Chronicle*, ed. and trans. Taylor, Childs, and Watkiss, 2: 478. I depart from Taylor, Childs, and Watkiss's translation of this phrase, here (479), but cf. the translation in Horner, 'Preachers at St Paul's Cross', 280, and *The Chronica Maiora of Thomas Walsingham, 1376–1422*, trans. David Preest; intro and notes by James G. Clark (Woodbridge: Boydell, 2005), 343.

Alkerton's sermon provoked a hostile reaction from Robert Waterton, who accused him of flattery in turn. Waterton sent his servant to present Alkerton with a strigil, or curry comb, when he finished preaching. This satirical gift, which invoked the Middle English expression 'to correien fauvel' ('to curry favour'), implied that Alkerton was himself a flatterer, who spoke to please the listening churchmen ('uelut et ipse prelatis ecclesie adulatus fuisset').[68] At the moment when Waterton's servant presented the strigil to him, Alkerton would have appeared to his audience like one of the 'faitours' of Study's complaint, receiving his reward from a patron in the crowd.

The lollard preacher William Thorpe records that he was also present when Alkerton preached at St Paul's Cross and that he challenged Alkerton about his sermon afterwards. Thorpe's *Testimony* describes his interrogation by Archbishop Arundel, who had arrested him for preaching heretical doctrines in Shrewsbury in 1407. As Maureen Jurkowski has shown, Thorpe was detained on the authority of a 1406 statute that was itself designed to suppress controversial preaching in the aftermath of the controversy between Taylor and Alkerton.[69] As part of the examination, one of Arundel's clerks challenges Thorpe to defend his conduct during Alkerton's sermon: 'And anoon þan anoþer clerk seide to me, "How was þou so bolde at Poulis cros in London to stonde þere caproun-hardi [bold as brass], wiþ þi tepet [a shoulder covering, part of the hood] aboute þin hed and to repreue in his sermoun þe worþi clerk Alkirtoun, drawynge awei þens alle hem þat þou myʒtist?".'[70] He adds that Thorpe accosted Alkerton after his sermon was finished: 'ʒhe, and þe same daie aftir noone þou, metrynge [meeting] þat worþi doctour in Watlynge strete, clepidist [called] him fals flaterer and ypocrite'.[71] Thorpe, who accepts the facts of this account, reveals what he said during this exchange: 'Alkirtoun repreuede [reproved] þe clerk vntrewli, and sclaundride him wrongfully and vncharitabli, as I seide to hym in Watlynge strete.'[72] Like Waterton

---

[68] *St Albans Chronicle*, ed. and trans. Taylor, Childs, and Watkiss, 2: 480. For the Middle English expression, see *MED*, s.v. 'fauvel (n.)', 2: 'correien fauvel'. This idiom for flattery derived from the French satirical allegory the *Roman de Fauvel*, where the different estates compete to comb down a horse, whose name is an acrostic for the vices of *flaterie, avarice, vilanie, variété, envie*, and *lescheté*. The character of Fauel in *Piers Plowman* is named after the horse in the *Roman*. On the *Roman* as an intertext for *Piers*, see Roberta Cornelius, '*Piers Plowman* and the *Roman de Fauvel*', *PMLA* 47 (1932): 363–7, John A. Yunck, *The Lineage of Lady Meed: The Development of Mediaeval Venality Satire* (Notre Dame: University of Notre Dame Press, 1963), 221–6, and Galloway, *Penn Commentary*, 1: 219, 235–7. Galloway has shown that the *Roman de Fauvel* was closely identified with Isabella of France, widow of Edward II, and that it may have been read and performed at her court at Castle Rising in Essex, where the Rokele family had connections. See Galloway, 'Madame Meed: *Fauvel*, Isabella, and the French Circumstances of *Piers Plowman*', *YLS* 30 (2016): 227–52.

[69] Maureen Jurkowski, 'The Arrest of William Thorpe in Shrewsbury and the Anti-Lollard Statute of 1406', *Historical Research* 75, no. 189 (2002): 283–5.

[70] *The Testimony of William Thorpe*, 24–93 in *Two Wycliffite Texts*, ed. Hudson, 84. On Thorpe's account of these events, see also O'Mara, *Study and Edition*, 30. For the expression 'caproun-hardi', see Hudson's note on this passage.

[71] *The Testimony of William Thorpe*, ed. Hudson, 84.

[72] *Testimony of William Thorpe*, ed. Hudson, 85.

with his gift, Thorpe seeks to expose Alkerton as a flatterer and a hypocrite, undermining his argument by calling attention to his suspect motives.

Thorpe is strongly invested in 'preaching as agon', as Elizabeth Schirmer writes.[73] Throughout his *Testimony*, he imagines contentious sermons as a forum for public debate, and draws pointed contrasts with his own interrogation, which takes place in private. His conversation with Arundel is held in 'a priuy closet [private chamber]', after other 'secular men' are commanded to leave.[74] Yet, he returns repeatedly to scenes of public preaching, defending his own sermon in Shrewsbury, recalling a sermon by a 'a monke of Feuersam, þat men clepiden [call] Meredoun', delivered in Canterbury, and explaining his activities during Alkerton's sermon at St Paul's Cross. Thorpe associates private, academic disputations with *curiositas*. When Arundel challenges him on the eucharist, he replies that this is a discussion for specialists: 'I committee [leave] þis terme *accidentem sine subiecto* to þo clerkis which deliten hem so in curious and so sotil sofestrie, þat þei mouen [debate] ofte so difficult materis and straunge, and waden and wandren so in hem fro argument into argument.'[75] Defending Taylor's sermon against Alkerton's criticisms, however, he praises it as an open declaration of essential truths, which are suitable for everyone to hear: Taylor 'prouede clereli [clearly] alle þingis þat he...prechide', Thorpe insists, 'bi þe autorite of Goddis word and bi appreued seyntis and doctouris and bi opin resoun'.[76] For Thorpe, the preaching cross provides an important public venue to continue the labour of emplotment and pastoral instruction, in resistance to institutional authority.

The records of this dispute at St Paul's illustrate the forms that contentious preaching could take, the concerns that animated it, and the consequences that resulted from it, in the decades after *Piers Plowman* was composed. Images and ideas from Study's complaint recur in the sermons of Taylor and Alkerton and in the arguments of their supporters and detractors, although configured in different forms: Taylor complains that contemporary clerics pursue secular careers while neglecting their pastoral obligations, including the discursive labour of emplotment; Walsingham calls Taylor a glutton, vomiting up his partially digested knowledge; Alkerton identifies Taylor as a flatterer who contrives his sermons to 'plese...proude men', and is accused of flattery and self-interest in turn. Waterton's gift of the strigil, meanwhile, stands in a complex relation to the anxieties that Study voices: a lay lord intervenes in a clerical debate, but does so to censure a flattering preacher through a parodic performance of patronage. In the end, this debate arrived at an impasse and was settled in Alkerton's favour by

---

[73] Elizabeth Schirmer, 'William Thorpe's Narrative Theology', *Studies in the Age of Chaucer* 31 (2009): 295–6. For 'Meredoun', see *Testimony of William Thorpe*, ed. Hudson, 83–4.
[74] *Testimony of William Thorpe*, ed. Hudson, 29.
[75] *The Testimony of William Thorpe*, ed. Hudson, 55.
[76] *The Testimony of William Thorpe*, ed. Hudson, 85.

the intervention of the church authorities: penance was enjoined on Waterton and his servant, and Taylor himself faced successive trials for heretical preaching, which resulted in his execution in 1423. Thorpe, meanwhile, was imprisoned, although his ultimate fate is unknown. Writing in the later decades of the previous century, Langland imagined an alternative future for preaching, which turns away from disputation altogether, and looks instead to forms of minstrelsy that might model the charitable distribution of knowledge.

'Murye Tales' at the Feast of Conscience

Piers Plowman returns to the polemical concerns of Study's complaint, and to the metaphors in which she articulates them, at the start of the fourth vision, when Conscience invites the dreamer to dinner. The other guests include a doctor of divinity who has recently delivered a sermon at St Paul's Cross and who now sits with Conscience and Clergy at the high table. In this scene, the dreamer comes face to face with the kind of preacher who Study condemns, a preacher who uses his 'wisdom and wit' to advance his own interests while neglecting his pastoral obligations to the community, and he does so in the space of the dining hall, where Study had developed the analogy between preachers and secular entertainers. Will expresses a powerful desire to heckle the doctor, to expose him as a 'faitour', much as Waterton and Thorpe would later do on hearing Alkerton preach at the cross, a desire that carries spiritual risks of its own. Also in this scene, however, the dreamer encounters some of the alternative forms of preaching that Study had begun to imagine in her complaint. Patience, who joins him as a guest at the feast, will turn out to be the kind of virtuous minstrel whose tales are so often ignored by 'proude men', and Conscience, who offers some minstrelsy of his own during dinner, will also prove to be the kind of lord who values these entertainments, and who sponsors them for the edification and delight of the household.

The preaching and minstrelsy that Conscience and Patience offer serves to reaffirm the faith of their listeners, locating them in an interpreted present where the imperatives for penance and charity become clear, and where the dangers that follow from pride are also visible. As such, it begins to supply the kind of narrative mediation that was withheld at the preaching cross. As I will argue in what follows, moreover, this scene also reaffirms the more fundamental link between the virtues of *studiositas* and the labour of emplotment that began to emerge in Study's complaint. In order to recognize patterns of narrative coherence in the simple succession of events, the preacher must distinguish between essential and inessential knowledge; for the narratives that matter in *Piers Plowman*, the most essential knowledge is the knowledge that leads to salvation.

Patience and Will, who are seated together at 'a side borde [side table]' in the hall, watch while the doctor indulges himself in wine and rich food at the high table (B.13.36). Like Study in her complaint, they associate the doctor's gluttonous consumption with his other excessive and disorderly desires, so that his appetite for 'metes, mortrews [stews] and puddynges [sausages]' (B.13.62) also figures his hunger for arcane knowledge, social prestige, and private profit. Will remarks that friars like the doctor pay for 'mete of moore cost' with donations from people's ill-gotten gains, sustaining their gluttony through their pursuit of *turpe lucrum*: 'Of þat men myswonne [obtained wrongfully] þei made hem wel at ese' (B.13.41–2).[77] Patience, meanwhile, imagines that the doctor will defend his gluttony with arguments from esoteric texts, citing the 'passion of Seint Auereys' to prove that his food is fit for a penitent (B.13.91); Anne Middleton, who reads this line as a reference to Averroes, notes that critics of the friars construe their enthusiasm for this author as a sign of their materialism and 'carnality of thought'.[78] Patience goes on to predict that the doctor will adduce arguments that 'he fond in a forel', inside a bound book, or inside the binding of a book, or inside a box of books (B.13.95), once more stressing the materiality of esoteric knowledge, and recalling Study's earlier account of curious sciences as 'fibicches in forceres', or tricks in boxes (B.10.213).[79] In their running commentary on the doctor's behaviour, then, Patience and the dreamer reinforce and elaborate on the connections that Study had drawn between gluttony and *curiositas*, the indiscriminate desire for rich food and arcane knowledge, intellectual vanity and materialism.

Observing the doctor at the high table, the dreamer recalls a recent sermon he preached at St Paul's Cross on Paul's Second Epistle to the Corinthians. Here, the apostle relates events from his own life story, describing how he suffered for his preaching and evangelism, enduring hunger and thirst, whippings and beatings. Using the 'preching and preuing' collocation, Will complains that the doctor's self-indulgence in the hall undermines the message of his sermon, which had called for penitential self-discipline:

'It is noȝt foure dayes þat þis freke, bifore þe deen of   *man; St Paul's*
  Poules,
Preched of penaunces þat Poul þe Apostle suffrede—
In fame et frigore and flappes of scourges: *blows from*
Ter cesus sum et a Iudeis quinquies quadragenas...
...

---

[77] On absolution for 'miswinning', and on the imagery of eating sins on a penitent's behalf, see Lawler, 'Harlot's Holiness: The System of Absolution for Miswinning in the C Version of *Piers Plowman*', YLS 20 (2006): 141–89; and Lawler, *Penn Commentary*, 4: 17–18.

[78] Middleton, 'The Passion of Seint Averoys (B.13.91): "Deuynyng" and Divinity in the Banquet Scene', YLS 1 (1987): 36. See also Scase, *New Anticlericalism*, 115, and Lawler, *Penn Commentary*, 4: 28–31.

[79] *MED*, s.v. 'forel', 1 (b), and see Lawler, *Penn Commentary*, 4: 31.

> They [the friars] prechen þat penaunce is profitable to þe soule,
> And what mischief and maleese Crist for man þolede.   *pain; suffered*
>   'Ac þis Goddes gloton', quod I, 'wiþ hise grete chekes,
> Haþ no pite on vs pouere: he parfourneþ yuele   *enacts; badly*
> That he precheþ, and preueþ noȝt...'
>
> (B.13.65–7a, 76–80)

['In hunger and thirst...; thrice was I beaten... Of the Jews five times did I receive forty stripes...' 2 Corinthians 11:27, 25, 24]

The ironies of this scene are especially intense because the doctor's sermon so closely resembles the reformed, recuperated preaching that Study imagined in her final words to Will. This sermon tells the story of 'Poul þe Apostle', the paradigm of 'parfitnesse' who Study presents as the ideal preacher (B.10.201–2). In his preaching, and in his exemplary life, Paul was guided by love, prioritizing the scriptural knowledge that might lead to salvation and sharing it with others as an act of charity. In his sermon at St Paul's Cross, however, the doctor has advocated these virtues to serve his own acquisitive ends, encouraging penance that is 'profitable to þe soule' to obtain material rewards for himself.

The doctor's hypocrisy provokes an angry response from Will, who voices his complaints to Patience, and proposes to confront the doctor directly: 'I shal iangle to þis iurdan wiþ his iuste wombe [pot belly] / To preue me what penaunce is, of which he preched raþer [earlier]' (B.13.84–5). This moment in the poem recalls a passage from Jerome's epistles, where Jerome advises Nepotian against hypocrisy: 'non confundant opera sermonem tuum, ne cum in ecclesia loqueris tacitus quilibet respondeat: "cur ergo haec ipse non facis?" delicatus magister est qui pleno ventre de ieiuniis disputat [do not let your deeds belie your words, lest, when you are preaching in church, someone say to himself, "So why do *you* not behave like this?" He is a self-indulgent teacher who advocates the benefits of fasting when his stomach is full].'[80] H. Leith Spencer reads the gluttonous doctor alongside sermons by Odo of Cheriton and James of Vitry that offer similar warnings to hypocritical preachers.[81] Other writers, however, question the motives of listeners who react to hypocritical preaching in this way. In his *De doctrina Christiana*, Augustine notes that listeners will react with hostility to hypocritical preachers, 'respondentes corde suo, aut etiam si ad hoc erumpunt, ore suo atque dicentes: Quod mihi praecipis, cur ipse non facis? [replying in their hearts, or even bursting out with it and saying to their faces, "Why don't you yourself do what you

---

[80] Jerome, Letter 52, 7.1; text and translation from Andrew Cain, *Jerome and the Monastic Clergy: A Commentary on Letter 52 to Nepotian, with an Introduction, Text, and Translation* (Leiden: Brill, 2013), 44, 45. I have silently adapted the translation.
[81] Spencer, *English Preaching*, 98–101.

are telling me to do?"]'; yet, he also adds that 'abundant enim, qui malae uitae suae defensionem ex ipsis suis praepositis et doctoribus quaerant [there are plenty of people, after all, who seek an excuse for their bad lives in those of their very own leaders and teachers]'.[82] Similarly, in his sermon at St Paul's Cross, William Taylor notes that people use the example of sinful clerics in order to resist correction, saying '"Whi repreuest þou me of my synne?" ... "Seest þou not þis bisshop, þis persoun and þis preest, how þei doen?"'; like Augustine, Taylor argues that people make these objections in part to 'excuse her [their own] synne'.[83]

When Will proposes to challenge the doctor in this scene, he imagines himself taking part in the kind of academic disputation that Study associated with the 'enuye of clerkes' (B.10.73). Here, as Zeeman argues, the dreamer himself becomes a kind of hypocritical figure, engaging in a moral critique from questionable motives: his imagined intervention would present an opportunity for him to display his 'heigh clergie', and increase his own 'pompe'.[84] Will names the doctor as 'þis iurdan' (B.13.84), in an apparent allusion to the Dominican William Jordan who defended the friars against their critics during the controversies of the 1350s and 60s.[85] In doing so, he positions himself among the academic disputants who appeared at the preaching cross: Jordan debated FitzRalph in Avignon in 1358, shortly after FitzRalph delivered his antimendicant sermons at St Paul's.[86] Will's own reference to 'iangling', meanwhile, implies that this kind of dispute would descend into the kind of 'foule wordes' that Study condemned: undiscerning speech, motivated by profit and offered as entertainment. Will makes no reference to the central message of Paul's preaching life, that love is the 'science ... souereyn for þe soule' (B.10.208); rather, he seeks to restore to Paul's text a passage that the friars 'ouerhuppen [skip over] at ech a tyme þat þei preche', and which might serve as the basis for an antifraternal critique: 'Periculum est in falsis fratribus! [In perils from false brethren]' (B.13.68–70).[87] When Will complains about the doctor's gluttonous indulgence, he hints at his own desire for the extravagant

[82] Augustine, *De doctrina Christiana*, ed. Joseph Martin, CCSL 32 (Turnhout: Brepols, 1962), 164 (4.xxvii.60); translation from Augustine, *Teaching Christianity*, trans. Edmund Hill, OP, WSA 1, no. 11 (Hyde Park, NY: New City Press, 1996), 238.
[83] 'Sermon of William Taylor', ed. Hudson, 12, 11.
[84] Zeeman, *Arts of Disruption*, 109–10. Zeeman cites Craun, reading Will's earlier encounter with Leute, with reference to his dispute with the doctor: 'The reader recognises the truth of Will's reproof, but ... is troubled by the reprover's Will and intention.' Craun, *Ethics and Power in Medieval English Reformist Writing* (Cambridge: Cambridge University Press, 2010), 71.
[85] The allusion to William Jordan was first identified by Mildred Marcett in *Uthred de Boldon, Friar William Jordan and Piers Plowman* (New York: by the author, 1938), 62–3. Kerby-Fulton, *Books Under Suspicion*, 181, argues from this allusion that the 'þe deen of Poules' in this passage might be Richard Kilvington, who invited FitzRalph to preach at the Cross and was among his principle English supporters. See also Lawler, *Penn Commentary*, 4: 27.
[86] On Jordan's debate with FitzRalph, see Szittya, *Antifraternal Tradition*, 108–9.
[87] One of William Jordan's opponents, Uthred of Boldon, replied to him in the tract *Contra querelas fratrum*, which cites *periculum est in falsis fratribus* in its prologue, and develops the polemical implications of this verse at length in each of its subsections. See Szittya, *Antifraternal Tradition*, 109–12.

food and social prestige that the doctor enjoys in the hall, the rewards of his preaching: 'For ye han harmed vs two in þat ye eten þe puddyng,/ Mortrews and ooþer mete—and we no morsel hadde' (B.13.107-8). His last rhetorical flourish is also an unintentional confession: 'I wolde permute [exchange] my penaunce with youre' (B.13.111).

While the dreamer's attention is focussed on the doctor, however, other forms of entertainment and instruction are taking place all around him in the hall. In his role as the lord of the manor, Conscience provides material food and spiritual instruction for his guests. He redistributes these goods as an act of charity: unlike the lords and ladies of Study's complaint, Conscience 'brekeþ...to þe beggere' at his feast, inviting Patience to dine at his house. In the B text, Patience appears in a pilgrim's clothes and asks for 'mete *pur charite*' (B.13.30); the C text adds that he 'Crauede [begged] and cryede,...A meles mete [square meal] for a pore man' (C.15.35-6) so that, in this version of the poem, he is explicitly one of the 'carefulle' who 'crie and carpen at þe yate'. Conscience also takes on a preacherly role, presenting his guests with what William Taylor would later describe as the 'breed of doctryne' as well as the 'breed of almes'. Like a studious cleric, he has dined on 'sondry metes.../ Of Austyn, of Ambrose, of alle þe foure Euaungelistes', served to him by Scripture (B.13.37-8), and he acts now as the host at a feast, in Humbert of Romans' image for the preacher, serving this food to a new audience. Patience is served with texts from the penitential psalms, 'a messe [serving dish]...of/ *Miserere mei, Deus, Et quorum tecta sunt peccata* ["Have mercy on me, O God" (Psalm 50:1); "...and whose sins are covered" (Psalm 31:1) / In a disshe of derne shrift [secret confession], *Dixi* and *Confitebor tibi* ["I said I will confess", (Psalm 31:5)]', which he commends repeatedly as 'propre seruice' (B.13.53-4, 51, 59). These were elementary and essential texts, and their simplicity stands in contrast to the rich food the doctor eats and to the curious authorities he alleges in debate.[88] In selecting these materials for his guests, Conscience displays the prudence that arises from *studiositas*, distinguishing and promoting the most essential knowledge, the knowledge that leads to salvation. In distributing them, he displays the kind of charity that arises from love. Conscience also performs the work of a virtuous minstrel in this scene, entertaining his guests as they eat. Will says that 'Conscience conforted vs, and carped vs [told us] murye tales:/ *Cor contritum et humiliatum, Deus, non despicies* [A contrite and humbled heart, O God, thou wilt not despise]' (B.13.57-8, citing Ps 50:19). This is the

---

[88] As Clare Costley King'oo observes, laypeople might rehearse the seven psalms to counter their own sins in the time between confessions, as part of an assigned penance, and in the course of their prayers for the dead; *Misereri Mei: The Penitential Psalms in Late Medieval and Early Modern England* (Notre Dame: University of Notre Dame Press, 2012), 19. On the penitential psalms in late medieval England, see also Annie Sutherland, 'Performing the Penitential Psalms in the Middle Ages', 15-37 in *Aspects of the Performative in Medieval Culture*, ed. Manuele Gragnolati and Almut Suerbaum (Berlin: De Gruyter, 2010); and Sutherland, *English Psalms in the Middle Ages, 1300-1450* (Oxford: Oxford University Press, 2015), esp. 185-229.

'mynstralcie' that Study had hoped for in the hall: a man with 'Holy Writ ay in his mouþe' telling 'tales' to edify the household.

Combining the roles of generous host, studious preacher, and virtuous minstrel, Conscience supplies the instruction that 'freres and faitours' neglect at St Paul's Cross. The penitential psalms might reaffirm ordinary 'folk...in þe feiþ' and encourage them in sorrow 'for hire synnes', in the words of Study's complaint; redistributed in an act of charity, they also stand as an example to the people to be 'free of hire goodes'. As he offers Patience and Will a 'sour loof', Conscience tells them, '*Agite penitenciam* [Do penance]', echoing the central injunction of Reason's sermon from the second vision (B.13.48). As he tells his 'murye tales' in the hall, moreover, Conscience presents this vital instruction in a narrative form. Study's complaint offers clues about the content of these stories, describing tales of Tobit, the Apostles, and the passion of Christ in the mouth of the virtuous minstrel. These are stories that instantiate the principles of penitence and charity and that reveal them at work in the world. They are also stories that resonate in the symbolic space of the hall, where both penance and charity are regularly enacted. Quietly and persistently, Conscience reveals the exemplary qualities of social life, so that each person in the hall is 'ywar by ooþer'. Conscience prioritizes essential instruction in his role as a preacher and sponsors its dissemination in his role as a host, but it is in his role as a minstrel that he undertakes the work of emplotment, locating his listeners in an interpreted present, where their obligations to God, and to their community, become clear.

In the C-text version of this scene, Reason himself is present at the dinner, acting as 'steward of the hall', as Traugott Lawler notes.[89] In this role, he guides and directs the distribution of food to the guests:

Thenne was as Resoun radde, anoon riht aftur—	*directed; straight away*
That Consience comaunde sholde to do come Scripture	*make*
And bringe breed for Pacience...	

(C.15.52–4)

The poem's most effective preacher makes his presence felt at this moment, as Conscience takes up the work of his earlier sermon, articulating narratives that affirm his listeners in the faith, encourage acts of charity, and call for penitential action. In this part of the poem, Conscience finds a way to counteract the preaching of 'freres and faitours' at St Paul's Cross without engaging them in academic disputation and exposing himself to the attendant spiritual risks. As he distributes the 'breed of doctryne' to his guests, he displays and encourages the kind of studious discrimination that works to counteract the effects of *curiositas*. As he

---

[89] Lawler, *Penn Commentary*, 4: 7, 19.

tells his 'murye tales', moreover, he displays a renewed commitment to narrative interpretation, framing moral choices and encouraging moral action through the discursive labour of emplotment.

In the final part of this scene, Conscience attempts to recuperate the kinds of after-dinner conversation that Study identified with 'dreuelinge', asking each of his guests to explain the Do-wel triad. Here, as in the dining halls of Study's complaint, clerics and laymen 'at mete' engage in discourse about a trinity. In the house of Conscience, however, the conversation is not concerned with arcane curiosities, but with the knowledge that leads to salvation. Although each successive answer becomes more complex, as Curtis Gruenler has noted, each reveals a simpler and more essential truth, already familiar from Study's complaint, which is that the best forms of teaching and learning are motivated by love.[90] Reflecting on the 'propre seruice' that Conscience has performed, and in the light of the virtuous minstrelsy he provides, these speakers also draw connections between the studious ability to recognize valuable knowledge, the preacherly imperative to communicate it, and the interpretative labour of emplotment, which discerns meaningful patterns in the simple succession of events, and configures them into a narrative.

The doctor himself defines the Do-wel triad in relation to 'preching and preuing': Do-wel is to 'do as clerkes techeþ', Do-best is to teach other people, and Do-best 'doþ himself so as he seiþ and precheþ: *Qui facit et docuerit magnus vocabitur in regno celorum*' (B.13.116–18a) ['But he that shall do and teach, he shall be called great in the kingdom of heaven' (Matthew 5:19)]. This is an answer with a solid scriptural foundation, and it establishes the concern with preaching and instruction that informs the subsequent replies. Defining the object of learning as that which 'clerkes techeþ', however, the doctor sidesteps the question of how clerics themselves might learn to distinguish valuable knowledge. Clergy, who is next to answer, offers a more cautious and qualified definition, explaining that Do-wel and Do-bet are 'two infinites,/ Whiche infinites wiþ a feiþ fynden out Dobest,/ Which shal saue mannes soule' (B.13.128–30). As Middleton has shown, this grammatical metaphor explains the relationship between these terms in their 'essential, changeless, aspects', awaiting application to particular temporal circumstances.[91] Clergy's answer comes with a caveat, addressing the issue that the doctor ignores. Although his 'seuene sones', the liberal arts, serve 'þe lord of lif', Clergy explains, they are all subordinate to love: 'Piers þe Plowman haþ impugned vs alle,/ And set alle sciences at a sop saue loue one' (B.13.124–5). Like Study in her complaint, Clergy identifies love as the 'souereyn' science, which should guide and

---

[90] Gruenler, *Poetics of Enigma*, 154, reads this scene as a variation on 'a common folktale pattern', where one speaker puts the same question to three different people, 'who give increasingly riddling answers'.

[91] Middleton, 'Two Infinites: Grammatical Metaphor in *Piers Plowman*', *ELH* 39, no. 2 (1972): 171.

inform a student's engagement with all the other arts; here, the poem recalls the discipline of *studiositas*, which serves to establish the pre-eminence of love, and allows the student to negotiate the advanced curriculum while avoiding the temptations of arcane knowledge.

Clergy attributes this insight not to Study, but to Piers Plowman, who was last seen in the poem directing the people on the half-acre, extending the work of Reason's sermon with his own forms of preaching and pastoral care. Piers exemplifies the way that love can organize knowledge, both for the student and for the teacher, as he discerns God's justice in the story of his own life, and as he makes that story the basis of his preaching. It is in the work of emplotment that Clergie recognizes the application of something like *studiositas*, the capacity to distinguish essential knowledge in the ongoing experience of life, and to configure that knowledge into a narrative that will change the perception of the people who hear it. Like Reason before him, Piers himself appears in the C-text version of this scene, in order to affirm these lessons in his own voice. Appearing suddenly and enigmatically in the hall, he affirms that 'Y shal preue þat Y saide'... '*Disce, doce, dilige Deum* [Learn, teach, love God]' (C.15.140–2).[92] Like Study, Piers aligns doing well with an attitude to learning, and a life of teaching, that gives pre-eminence to love. He invokes the language of 'preching' and 'preueing', here in a multilingual formulation, anticipating an ongoing project of narrative interpretation and pastoral care that extends into the future.

In the B text, it is Patience who interprets the Do-wel triad as '*Disce... doce, dilige inimicos* [learn, teach, love your enemies]' (B.13.137–9). He attributes this lesson to Love, who taught him to 'loue leelly þi soule al þi lif tyme', and to 'louye.../Thyn enemy in alle wise eueneforþ [equally] wiþ þiselue' (B.13.140–4). This lesson closely resembles the instruction that Study derived from Paul's injunction '*operemur bonum ad omnes* [let us work good to all men]' (B.10.201a, citing Galatians 6.10), as she explained to the dreamer how the *studiosus* learns to prioritize love: 'he biddeþ vs be as breþeren, and bidde [pray] for oure enemys,/ And louen hem þat lyen on [slander] us' (B.10.199–200). In both versions of the poem, love emerges as an organizing principle that serves to discriminate between different kinds of knowledge, and that gives meaningful shape to a narrative of lived experience.

At the climax of this scene, Patience restates his answer to Conscience's question as a riddle, which he challenges the other guests to solve:

---

[92] On the ploughman's sudden appearance *in propria persona* in this scene, see Burrow, '"Quod" and "Seide" in *Piers Plowman*', *Notes and Queries* 64, no. 2 (2015): 521–4. The Latin formula he cites echoes familiar schoolroom proverbs, as Lawler has shown: Lawler, 'Langland Versificator', 72; Lawler, *Penn Commentary*, 4: 45. Invoking it here, perhaps, the ploughman once more associates love with *studiositas*, the capacity to discriminate and prioritize that is fostered by early education.

Wiþ half a laumpe lyne in Latyn, *Ex vi transicionis*,
I bere þerinne aboute faste ybounde Dowel,
In a signe of þe Saterday þat sette first þe kalender,   *as a token; established*
And al þe wit of þe Wodnesday of þe nexte wike after;   *week*
The myddel of þe moone is þe might of boþe.   *power*
And herwith am I welcome þer I haue it wiþ me.

(B.13.152–7)

In this moment, it seems, Patience turns away from the 'souereyn' science of love to indulge the *turpis curiositas* of the other guests, tempting them with arcane knowledge in its most abstract, esoteric form. The 'basic image' of Patience's riddle 'is that of a bundle tied with a strap', inscribed with the words *Ex vi transicionis*, as A. V. C. Schmidt explains.[93] The tightly bound bundle recalls Study's earlier image of curious sciences like sorcery and alchemy as 'fibicches in forceres', tricks in boxes (B.10.213); in some manuscripts, Patience says that he carries Do-well in 'a bouste', a jar or a box, the reading adopted in George Kane and E. Talbot Donaldson's B text.[94] Other characters in this scene identify the riddle with the forms of minstrelsy that Study condemns. The doctor dismisses it as a scurrilous entertainment, calling it a 'dido', and 'a disours tale!' (B.13.173). When Clergy turns on Conscience at the end of this scene, he asks 'are ye coueitous nouþe/ After yeresȝeues or ȝiftes, or yernen [long] to rede redels?' (B.13.184–5), linking an appetite for riddles to the material desires that motivate 'iaperis' and 'iangleris'.

The solution to this riddle, however, directs the dinner guests away from esoteric knowledge and back towards more elementary forms of study. R. E. Kaske argued that the riddle invokes two allegorical schemata found in Peter of Blois and elsewhere, which use the seven days of the week to map the seven virtues and the seven epochs of eschatological history. According to these schemata, 'þe Saterday' indicates *caritas*, while 'þe Wodnesday' refers to the time of Christ's atonement, and to a combination of *prudentia, saptientia, scientia*.[95] If these schemata seem esoteric in themselves, they point nevertheless to the essential principle of love, and to the central narrative of the passion in which it is exemplified. Kaske went on to explain that the phrase *ex vi transicionis*, used in elementary grammar to explain how a transitive verb governs its direct object in

---

[93] *Parallel Text*, ed. Schmidt, 2: 630.
[94] On this reading, see *Piers Plowman: The B Version*, ed. Kane and Donaldson, rev. edn (London: Athlone, 1988), 186; *Parallel Text*, ed. Schmidt, 2: 415–16.; Lawler, *Penn Commentary*, 4: 49; and Hanna, *Patient Reading*, 313, n. 39. Hanna argues that the '*bouste* keeps popping up in various metamorphoses throughout the passus', in other references to boxes and containers; *Patient Reading*, 314, n. 41.
[95] R. E. Kaske, '"*Ex vi Transicionis*" and its Passage in *Piers Plowman*', *JEGP* 62 (1963): 32–60, rev. and repr. 228–63 in *Style and Symbolism in Piers Plowman*, ed. Robert J. Blanch (Knoxville: University of Tennessee Press, 1969). Kaske was building on work by Ben H. Smith, Jr., 'Patience's Riddle, *Piers Plowman* B, XIII', *MLN* 76 (1961): 675–82.

the accusative case, suggests that patience produces these virtues, as exemplified in the 'penaunces' that Christ suffered on Good Friday.[96] More recently, Andrew Galloway has argued that Patience's 'half a laumpe lyne in Latyn' and his reference to the 'myddel of þe moone' invoke the riddle 'Lune dimidium' whose solution spells out c-o-r, the heart.[97] These parts of the riddle mark a return to the schoolroom, as Christopher Cannon has noted, and to the elementary discipline identified with *studiositas*, as Patience first presents a grammatical metaphor, and then invites the other guests to spell out the answer, letter by letter.[98] The 'Lune dimidium' riddle was itself anthologized in resources for preachers, as Galloway notes.[99] In the *Fasciculus morum*, it forms part of an exemplum, where an angel tells a man that he must offer God the new moon, the circle of the sun, and the fourth part of a wheel; the man despairs until the angel explains that these are the shapes of the letters c-o-r, and that all he need offer to God is his heart. Here, the act of solving the riddle is part of a story, where a task that seems at first to be complex and difficult turns out in fact to be simple.[100]

The answer to this curious riddle, this dubious minstrel's entertainment, is love, the 'souereyn' science that counters *curiositas* and that animates the best kinds of preaching and instruction. Working through the riddle to its solution, moreover, shows how principles of love can be discerned in history, when history is reconfigured as narrative. With its imagery of cosmic motion, and with its reference to particular dates and times, the riddle offers a comment on narrative interpretation itself; solving the riddle involves seeking out patterns of significance in the simple succession of temporal events. The riddle positions the incarnation on 'þe Saterday þat sette first þe kalender', imagining it as an axial moment, marked on one of Ricoeur's 'reflective instruments'; the *adventus* of Christ inaugurates a new set of historical conditions, and serves as a point of orientation for an intersubjective 'third time' where measurable points in cosmological time can be understood in relation to an experiential past and future. The solution to this riddle affirms that the ability to prioritize love makes emplotment possible: this is the 'souereyn' science that enables preachers and minstrels to recognize the key events in history and configure them into a narrative. The riddle alludes to the stories that Conscience tells in his role as a virtuous minstrel: narratives concerned with the passion, 'þe penaunce þat Pilat wroʒte/ To Iesu þe gentile', (B.10.34–5), and with

---

[96] Henry Bradley was the first to suggest that *ex vi transicionis* might refer to this grammatical rule: 'Some Cruces in *Piers Plowman*', MLR 5 (1910): 340–1. Kaske, '*Ex vi Transicionis*', 235–9, established that the phrase was commonly used for this purpose in twelfth- and thirteenth-century grammatical *regimen*. Cynthia Renée Bland showed that it was also widely instantiated in teaching texts that were used in late medieval English grammar schools. Bland, 'Langland's Use of the Term *Ex vi Transicionis*', YLS 2 (1988): 125–35.

[97] Galloway, 'The Rhetoric of Riddling in Late-Medieval England: the "Oxford" Riddles, the *Secretum philosophorum*, and the Riddles in *Piers Plowman*', Speculum 70, no. 1 (1995): 86–93.

[98] Cannon, *From Literacy to Literature*, 132–3.   [99] Galloway, 'Rhetoric of Riddling', 87–8.

[100] *Fasciculus morum*, ed. and trans. Wenzel, 44, 45.

the transformation of the heart itself: '*Cor contritum et humiliatum, Deus, non despicies*' (B.13.58). More than this, though, it suggests that the act of telling one story might itself produce the other: the minstrel, or the preacher, can encourage contrition and humility in the listener's heart by relating the story of Christ's atonement. In this sense, the riddle points to the way that narrative reconfigures lived experience, revealing patterns of significance in the simple succession of events that make transformative action possible.

Hanna has detected a series of allusions to 2 Corinthians 11–12 in the lines that follow the riddle itself, where Conscience declares that illness, pain, slander, and other kinds of tribulation cannot trouble the man who carries what is inside this bundle, that is love. He reads these lines as 'an implicit corrective to … the dreamer's longing for a partial reading of Paul on dangerous *fratres*', his impulse to supply the words that friars 'ouerhuppen' when they preach: '*Periculum est in falsis fratribus!* [In perils from false brethren]' (B.13.68–70).[101] Where Will seeks to restore a missing part of the text, and to engage in an interclerical debate about it, Patience seeks to restore the essential *res*, or 'gist' of this Pauline narrative, its claims about love, and its instantiation in life and preaching. As he elaborates on the solution to his riddle, then, Patience looks back to the exemplary life of preaching that Study described in her earlier encounter with the dreamer: the apostle Paul, who warns against preaching to please proud men, and who preached himself as an act of charity to others, demonstrates how disciplined study, study that distinguishes love as the 'souereyn' science, produces beneficial teaching for the *commune* as a whole.

Patience presents his riddle to Conscience, with a challenge to 'Vndo it' and 'lat þis doctour se if Dowel be þerinne' (B.13.158), encouraging this proud, acquisitive preacher to engage in penitential self-examination, to look into his own heart; this is a typical conclusion to a riddle contest, as Gruenler notes.[102] As Galloway has observed, however, to 'vndo' something in *Piers Plowman* is also to 'explicate it', so that this injunction is also a challenge to preach, to expound and disseminate what the riddle contains.[103] At the end of the second vision, as we saw in Chapter 2, the priest contests the meaning of Piers Plowman's pardon by reframing its narrative logic as a maxim, a 'kerygmatic statement' in Ricoeur's terminology: 'bene fac et bene habe'. He arouses the ploughman's 'tene' by discounting his efforts to instantiate this statement in narrative, to discern it in the simple succession of events, and to articulate it through new acts of emplotment. With this commandment to 'vndo' the riddle, by contrast, Patience invites Conscience to continue his minstrelsy, to make new narratives that reveal God's love at work

---

[101] Hanna, *Patient Reading*, 309–10.
[102] Gruenler, *Poetics of Enigma*, 159; see also Lawler, *Penn Commentary*, 4: 50.
[103] Galloway, *Penn Commentary*, 1: 185. On the multiple forms of 'undoing' at the feast of Conscience, see also Zeeman, *Arts of Disruption*, 372–81.

in history and encourage his listeners to transform their hearts. While the doctor dismisses the riddle and Clergy challenges Conscience for his interest in this minstrels' entertainment, Conscience discerns an opportunity to put virtuous 'mynstralcie' into practice, to render it into a lifelong project of the kind that Piers Plowman began on the half-acre. He pledges to go with Patience 'til I haue preued moore' (B.13.183), undertaking a life of Pauline 'parfitnesse' of the kind that Study once described, and taking this 'propre seruice' out of the hall, and into the world. This encounter with virtuous minstrelsy, in the hall of a wealthy lord who takes pleasure from the texts of scripture, produces a template for new forms of preaching, preaching that runs counter to the curious, contentious sermons at St Paul's Cross, and that offers new narratives to reveal the imperatives and opportunities for love.

* * *

In Study's complaint, and again at the feast of Conscience, *Piers Plowman* confronts corrupted forms of public preaching where clerics use their 'wisdom and wit' for their own material advantage and not for the edification of the larger community. Langland offers a nuanced account of the intellectual covetousness that motivates this kind of preaching, the forms of patronage that sustain and encourage it, and the pernicious social and spiritual effects that it produces. As I have shown in this chapter, these interlinked scenes associate the proud, acquisitive sermons of 'freres and faitours' with the intellectual vice of *curiositas*, a covetous, indiscriminate appetite for arcane knowledge, closely identified with the desire for praise and material rewards, and figured through metaphors of gluttony and excessive, disorderly consumption. The poem compares these preachers to scurrilous entertainers who debase themselves to satisfy the appetites and desires of their wealthy patrons. As Study makes clear in her complaint, moreover, this kind of preaching neglects the interpretative labour of emplotment, which the previous visions of the poem have identified as a central part of the preacher's project: listeners at the preaching cross inhabit an uninterpreted present, with no conception of the need for penance or for charity.

As it develops this critique of the 'freres and faitours' at St Paul's Cross, however, the poem also imagines an alternative in the preaching of Paul himself, who configured his sermons, and his evangelical life, as an expression of love. Minstrelsy, too, offers models for the reform of preaching: when Study compares acquisitive preachers with 'iaperis' and 'iangleris', she also imagines virtuous forms of minstrelsy, where entertainers relate stories from the Bible, and encourage penitence and charity. In the house of Conscience, where the dreamer fixates on the hypocritical preacher at the high table, the other guests engage in minstrelsy of this kind, counteracting the doctor's preaching, and supplying the forms of emplotment it withholds. The turn to minstrelsy in these scenes also allows the poem to imagine a new role for pious laymen, who might sponsor worthwhile entertainments instead of demanding esoteric sermons. Finally, perhaps, it imagines a space for a poem like *Piers Plowman* itself, thinking through the way that poetry could continue the work of preaching in new contexts and new forms.

In the process of imagining these new, more dynamic, more conversational forms of preaching, I have argued, *Piers Plowman* comes to new realizations about the work of emplotment itself. The capacity to discriminate between arcane and salvific knowledge, which arises from *studiositas*, and which serves as a check on acquisitive materialism, mirrors the ability to recognize significant events and to configure them into a narrative. Emplotment requires the kind of prudent discernment that recognizes salvation as the ultimate good, and exemplifies the kind of charity that seeks to share this knowledge with others. Insofar as preaching makes narrative discourse available to its listeners, as a structure that mediates their lived experience and renders it comprehensible, it also encourages them to distinguish the essential from the inessential in this way, to prioritize love as the 'souereyn' science. Injunctions to prioritize love will echo through the poem until its final visions: as we will see in the next chapter, when Will asks Kynde 'what craft be best to lerne?' in the final passus, Kynde tells him that he should 'Lerne to loue, ... and leef alle oþere' (B.20.207–8). In Study's complaint, and at the feast of Patience, Langland shows that the capacity to learn this lesson emerges through the mediation of narrative.

4
Preaching on the Lifetime
Sermons and the 'Self-Constant' Subject in *Piers Plowman*

Near the end of *Time and Narrative*, Ricoeur observes that the activity of emplotment, which configures disparate events into a provisional unity, might also serve to produce a coherent understanding of the human subject as an individual who possesses an essential 'self-sameness' or 'self-constancy' while retaining the capacity for evolution and change. In order to recognize ourselves, Ricoeur proposes, we must first configure the events of our lives into a *holos*, analogous to a poetic plot.[1] Ricoeur returned to this argument in a subsequent book, *Oneself as Another*, where he reaffirmed his claim that personal identity emerges through the work of emplotment. In this later study, however, Ricoeur stressed the ethical dimension of 'self-constancy'. The human subject, constituted by emplotment, is an amalgamation of habits and traits that are acquired over time as the product of their choices and actions, and the subject expresses their 'self-constancy' through their ethical commitments, by making and keeping promises, undertaking at one point in time to complete some action at another. 'Self-sameness', for Ricoeur, is a form of fidelity, not only to other people but also to oneself.[2] For Ricoeur, the work of narrative interpretation has an ethical dimension of its own when applied to the life of a human subject. In *Time and Narrative*, he proposes that the effort to construe lived experience in narrative terms answers the Socratic injunction to live an examined life.[3] In *Oneself as Another*, however, narrative interpretation provides the starting point for a larger theory of intersubjectivity: this is a form of self-understanding that draws on the stories that other people tell, and it enables relationships that are characterized by recognition and reciprocity.[4]

In this chapter, I argue that Langland comes to similar realizations about the role of narrative discourse in the constitution of personal identity. I read a series of interrelated scenes from *Piers Plowman* where the dreamer's allegorical interlocutors encourage him to think about the narrative shape of his own life: his dialogue with Holy Church from the first vision; his double encounter with Scripture, before and within the inner dream of the third vision; his dialogue with

---

[1] Ricoeur, *Time and Narrative*, 3: 246.
[2] Ricoeur, *Oneself as Another*, 123, 165.
[3] Ricoeur, *Time and Narrative*, 3: 247.
[4] Ricoeur, *Oneself as Another*, 163–8.

Preaching and Narrative in Piers Plowman. Alastair Bennett, Oxford University Press. © Alastair Bennett 2023.
DOI: 10.1093/oso/9780192886262.003.0005

Ymaginatif as that vision concludes; and his final encounter with Kynde in the poem's last, apocalyptic passus. All these interlocutors encourage Will to make sense of his experience using narrative resources derived from preaching. Holy Church and Scripture deliver their own sermons in these scenes, while Ymaginatif and Kynde recall earlier scenes of preaching and explain their application to the dreamer's present circumstances. Through these encounters, the dreamer learns that the public preaching he has observed in the poem, addressed to the needs and concerns of the *commune* as a whole, might also enable him to better understand himself, and to derive useful instruction from his lived experience. Like Ricoeur, Langland thinks seriously about the ethical implications of narrative self-understanding. When Will's interlocutors encourage him to construe the events of his own life as a plot, they often remind him of his baptism and the promises he made there, ethical commitments that extend for the duration of his life. As he reflects on his experiences in the inner dream, moreover, it becomes clear that self-examination, mediated by narrative texts, provides a crucial check on the kind of distracted absorption that might lead him into sin. Grasping the different aspects of lived experience together as a *holos* serves to mitigate against the extremes of complacency and despair, and leads instead to a productive balance of hope and fear.

In these interconnected scenes, the dreamer also comes to a new understanding of the relationship between revealed and natural knowledge, 'clergie' and 'kynde'. In his dialogue with Holy Church, Will complains that he has no 'kynde knowynge' of the things she is teaching him (B.1.138), expressing his desire for a tangible, intuitive, experiential understanding of the clerical instruction she has to offer. In her reply, however, she returns him to the scene of his earliest education, and shows how clerical instruction has long been part of his lived experience. Scripture and Ymaginatif will reinforce and extend these lessons: as Will comes to understand the shape of his own life in relation to the texts and discourses of preaching, he also recognizes that these texts and discourses are themselves interwoven with his own experiences. Preaching facilitates 'kynde' encounters with 'clergie', making clerical knowledge available in particular times and circumstances, and this knowledge, in turn, shapes the way that listeners understand their own lives. In the final passus, where instructive preaching has all but disappeared, it is Kynde himself who recalls the lessons of earlier sermons for Will.

Many readers of *Piers Plowman* have understood the poem as the story of its narrator, 'an individual who both experiences and records his experience' as Anne Middleton writes, and, perhaps especially in the third vision, a representative of the soul's volitional faculty, informed by his encounters with a series of teachers.[5] Will has been identified as a fictionalized representation of the poet on the model

---

[5] Middleton, 'Narration and the Invention of Experience', 110. For the dreamer as a representative of the 'volitional/affective power *wil*', see Zeeman, *Discourse of Desire*, 64–108.

of other dream vision narrators and on the evidence of a series of anagrammatic signatures that connect his name with Langland's.[6] Others have challenged the view that the dreamer can be seen as a coherent subject, however. David Lawton imagines Will as an 'open persona', constituted by the 'multiple and contradictory discourses' that are represented in the poem; for Lawton, '[a] plurality of voices, by no means all self-evidently "his", intersect in the subject of *Piers Plowman*'.[7] Jason Crawford, too, has described the dreamer as 'a subject extended across many selves', inhabiting 'many identities and contingencies'.[8] Lawton's account of the narrator informs recent work by Michael Calabrese on the 'continuous decompilation and reassembly' of characters in the poem, and by Tekla Bude on the way that personhood, including that of the narrator, emerges from through a series of encounters with 'agential matter'.[9] In this chapter, drawing on Ricoeur's account of the narrated self, I read the dreamer as a subject whose self-understanding is mediated by the instructive discourses he encounters and who is actively engaged in the process of interpreting his own experiences. For Langland, I argue, the capacity to formulate a single, interpreted identity from the disparate experiences of human life is an important precondition for ethical action, and he explores the development of this capacity in the represented life of the dreamer.

In what follows, as in previous chapters, I read *Piers Plowman* alongside surviving sermon texts from the later Middle Ages. Contemporary sermons on baptism show how baptismal vows might be recalled in later life as a framework to think about lived experience as a narrative whole. Passages from contemporary sermons and *artes*, meanwhile, develop the image of preaching as a mirror, a clerical discourse in which people might recognize and better understand their own experiences. As he explores the reception of preaching over the course of the dreamer's lifetime, however, Langland also tackles questions that fall outside the remit of individual sermons and the scope of many *artes*. The poem offers a searching and sustained account of the way an individual might encounter

---

[6] Middleton, 'William Langland's "Kynde Name": Authorial Signature and Social Identity in Late Fourteenth-Century England', 15–82 in *Literary Practice and Social Change in Britain, 1380–1530*, ed. Lee Patterson (Berkeley, CA: University of California Press, 1990). Kathryn Kerby-Fulton describes the emergence of a 'bibliographic ego' in the C text, where the dreamer appears as 'an authorial, rather than a simply fictional "I"', defending his literary project against misappropriation: Kerby-Fulton, 'Bibliographic Ego', 70, 79. On the 'bibliographic ego' in relation to clerical vocational crisis, see also Kerby-Fulton, *Clerical Proletariat*, 149.

[7] David Lawton, 'The Subject of *Piers Plowman*', YLS 1 (1987): 11, 16. For a counterpoint to Lawton's emphasis on voice, see Stephanie L. Batkie, 'Of Poets and Prologues', YLS 32 (2018): 245–70, who argues that the dreamer's persona emerges through a series of silences. Lawton pays particular attention to penance, as a 'discourse of power' that constitutes particular forms of selfhood, and as a public language that generates shared, social forms of interiority. Lawton, 'Subject of *Piers Plowman*', 16–21. He returns to this account of the dreamer as a 'confessional subject' in *Voice in Later Medieval English Literature: Public Interiorities* (Oxford: Oxford University Press, 2017), 103–29.

[8] Crawford, *Allegory and Enchantment*, 90.

[9] Calabrese, 'Posthuman *Piers*?' 8, and Tekla Bude, 'Wet Shoes, Dirty Coats, and the Agency of Things: Thinking Personification through New Materialism', YLS 33 (2019): 205–29.

sermons, retain them in his memory, and use them to structure his own sense of identity, to navigate moments of personal confusion and spiritual crisis. In the dreamer's encounter with Ymaginatif, Langland also asks how far the labour of emplotment, modelled in sermons, and applied to lived experience, gives rise to the distinctive and eccentric shape of his own poem. In this moment of self-theorization, I argue, the poem considers the process of its own composition in relation to the creative, interpretative practices its preachers have sought to model and encourage. In the final section of this chapter, I also read the conclusion of the A text by John But, which presents a perceptive early reader's account of the relationship between the shape of the dreamer's life and the shape of the poem as a whole.

Life Lessons

When Holy Church appears in the first passus of *Piers Plowman* and offers to explain what the dreamer has seen in the Prologue, she also performs the poem's first act of emplotment, as I argued in the Introduction. In her address to Will, Holy Church traces the broad outlines of eschatological history, describing the creation and Fall, the lives of the patriarchs, and the incarnation and atonement of Christ, and explains the implications of these events for the contemporary moment. Will, in turn, comes to recognize that the different kinds of work he has observed on the field take place in a world that has been created and provisioned by God, where the devil has introduced enticements to sin, and where Christ has created the possibility for salvation. Holy Church encounters the dreamer in an uninterpreted present moment, preconfigured with intimations of narrative, and reconfigures his understanding of the time he inhabits by integrating his experiences into a much larger plot. As we have seen, Holy Church performs this act of emplotment as part of a sermon: although her encounter with Will takes place as a private, instructional dialogue, she nevertheless employs the formal and exegetical structures of public preaching, beginning with a protheme on the axiom that 'Mesure is medicine', and then presenting a set of *distinctiones* on the dictum 'Whan alle tresors arn tried [tested] ... treuþe is þe beste', which serves as her *thema* (B.1.35, 84–5, and cf. B.1.135, 207). The stories she tells serve to exemplify and instantiate these texts, as well as to reframe the dreamer's understanding of his own time.

As she elaborates these narratives of biblical and contemporary history, however, Holy Church uncovers a surprising lacuna in the dreamer's understanding of his own life. After she explains the creation and the Fall to him, Will interrupts her to ask who she is. Holy Church replies that he should know her already, since she welcomed him at his baptism and provided his first instruction in the faith (Figure 4.1):

Figure 4.1 Baptism of an infant in a font, from a fifteenth-century English pontifical, London, British Library, Lansdowne MS 451, fol. 224v.

>   Thanne hadde I wonder in my wit what womman she were
> That swiche wise wordes of Holy Writ shewed,
> And halsede hire on þe heiȝe name, er she þenes yede,   *adjured; went*
> What she were witterly þat wised me so faire.   *certainly; counselled*
>   'Holi Chirche I am', quod she, 'þow ouȝtest me to knowe.   *recognize*
> I vnderfeng þee first and þe feiþ tauȝte.   *received; to you*
> Thow brouȝtest me borwes my biddyng to fulfille,   *sponsors, guarantors*
> And to louen me leelly þe while þi lif dureþ.'   *loyally; lasts*
>   (B.1.71–7)

In this disorientating moment, the dreamer betrays an inability to think about his lifetime as an integrated, interpreted whole: absorbed in the phenomenological present, he no longer recalls the lessons of his own past. Holy Church answers the dreamer by reminding him of his earliest commitments to her and of the early education she provided for him, and by inviting him to see his present moment in relation to these formative experiences. In doing so, she also shows how baptismal promises and early instruction supply discursive resources to perceive the self as a narrative whole, conferring those forms of 'self-constancy' that the dreamer appears to lack.

As many readers have observed, Will's confused response to Holy Church in this scene echoes the way Boethius reacts to Philosophy in the early chapters of *De consolatione Philosophiae*.[10] Boethius does not recognize Philosophy when she first appears to him and only remembers their long, shared history after she wipes his eyes with her robe: 'respicio nutricem meam, cuius ab adulescentia laribus obuersatus fueram [I saw that it was my nurse in whose house I had been cared for since my youth]'.[11] Philosophy treats Boethius' confusion as a symptom of 'lethargus', or amnesia; in forgetting his relationship to her, she suggests, Boethius has forgotten himself: 'Sui paulisper oblitus est. Recordabitur facile, si quidem nos ante cognouerit [He has forgotten for a while who he is, but he will soon remember once he has recognized me].'[12] Holy Church interprets Will's confusion in a similar way: when Will fails to recognize her, he too reveals a kind of *lethargus*, because he has forgotten the instruction that might otherwise give shape to his personal identity; like Philosophy, she uses a combination of encouragement and rebuke to bring him to his senses.[13] The instruction that Will has forgotten, however, is not a programme of philosophical study, but rather the kind of preaching and teaching that a parish priest might offer to his congregation. Holy Church represents a wide range of ecclesiastical texts and discourses over the course of this passus, as Andrew Galloway notes, but here, as Ellen Rentz has argued, she seems most strongly associated with the parish church, and with the formative instruction that takes place in this setting.[14]

---

[10] Justice, 'The Genres of *Piers Plowman*', 295–6; Nolan, 'Fortunes of *Piers Plowman*', 9–10; Galloway, *Penn Commentary*, 1: 177; Steiner, *Reading Piers Plowman*, 24–6; Frank Grady, 'Chaucer's Langland's Boethius', *YLS* 32 (2018): 271–87; Breen, *Machines of the Mind*, 286–94. Steiner and Grady have noted further allusions to Boethius elsewhere in the sermon of Holy Church: Steiner argues that the lyrical passages on the fall of Lucifer and the plant of peace resemble Boethian *metra*, because they constitute poetic interludes in a more prosaic discursive context; Grady contends that the dreamer's subsequent questions to Holy Church reflect the concerns of the opening scenes of *De consolatione*.

[11] Boethius, *Philosophiae Consolatio*, ed. Ludwig Bieler, CCSL 94 (Turnhout: Brepols, 1957; rev edn 1984), 5 (1 pr. 3); translation from Boethius, *The Consolation of Philosophy*, trans. Victor Watts (London: Penguin, 1969; rev edn 1999), 7.

[12] Boethius, *Philosophiae Consolatio*, 1 pr. 2, ed. Bieler, 4, trans. Watts, 6. Similar scenes appear in other medieval poems inspired by Boethius; in *De planctu naturae*, for example, Nature asks what 'alienatio mentis [disorientation of mind]' or 'debilitas sensum [defect of perception]' could have led the narrator to forget who she is, exclaiming 'tuae nutricis familiari cognitione tua intelligentia defraudetur [your understanding has been robbed of its intimate acquaintance with your nurse]'; Alan of Lille, *De planctu naturae*, 21–217 in *Literary Works*, ed. and trans. Winthrop Wetherbee (Cambridge, MA: Harvard University Press, 2013), 69 (6.3). See also Galloway, *Penn Commentary*, 1: 177.

[13] Zeeman, *Arts of Disruption*, 207–8, argues that Philosophy's response to Boethius in this scene manifests the 'agonistic dynamic' found in many later instructional dialogues, including Will's encounter with Holy Church in *Piers*. Zeeman writes that Philosophy takes 'a disciplinary and therapeutic stance ... using an artful combination of reprimand, proto-pastoralia, and moments of semi-flirtation'.

[14] Galloway, *Penn Commentary*, 1: 148–50; Rentz, *Imagining the Parish*, 8–9. Boethius was sometimes cited as an authority in parish preaching; see, for example, *A Late Fifteenth-Century Dominical Sermon Cycle*, ed. Stephen Morrison, 2 vols, EETS, os 337–8 (Oxford: Oxford University Press, 2012), 2:

In her reply to the dreamer, Holy Church returns him to the baptismal font where, she tells him, 'I vnderfeng þee first and þe feiþ tauȝte.' She also reminds him of the ethical commitments he made there: the ceremony of baptism involved a series of promises to renounce the devil and believe in God, made on a child's behalf by his godparents, acting as his 'borwes' or guarantors.[15] These are promises that last for a lifetime: in the B text, Holy Church tells Will that his baptismal vows will hold 'while þi lif dureþ', while in C she recalls his promise to 'Leue on [believe in] me and loue me al thy lyf-tyme' (C.1.75), referring still more explicitly to the 'lyf-tyme' as a single, interpreted unit of experience. Oaths and promises are often made for the term of an individual life in *Piers Plowman*. When Piers and the knight agree their reciprocal roles on the half-acre, for example, Piers promises to do 'labours... for þi loue al my lif tyme', and the knight agrees to maintain Piers for 'als longe as I lyue' (B.6.26, 36); at the end of this exchange, the knight reaffirms his commitments, using the same language that Holy Church applies to Will's baptismal vow: 'I assente, be Seint Iame... to werche bi þi wordes þe while my lif dureþ' (B.6.55–6). Piers himself shows how life-long promises can structure a biographical narrative, as I argued in Chapter 2: when he tells the people his life story in the second vision, he construes the different kinds of labour he performs as part of a plot that reveals his 'fourty wynter' of fidelity to Truth (B.5.539). In these examples, then, the poem reaffirms Ricoeur's conception of the promise as an expression of 'self-constancy', a commitment that both requires and sustains a narrative understanding of the self. When Holy Church recalls the dreamer's baptism, she also invites him to conceptualize his lived experience as a whole, to narrate the events of his life to himself as a plot.

Holy Church employs a strategy that was often found in late medieval sermons and pastoral texts, where preachers would invite their listeners to recall the promises they made at their baptism, and to use these to configure a narrative of their subsequent experiences. An Advent sermon from the dominical collection preserved in Bodleian Library, MS e Musaeo 180 and elsewhere, for example, encourages 'every man and woman that hathe resceyvyd þe blissed sacrament of baptym' to 'ransake his consciens well abowte and serche there whether he haue kept that counawnte [promise] þat he made to God at þe font-stone, or els broken it'.[16] Like Holy Church, the preacher invites his listeners to recall their first entry

---

245. On the early books of the *Consolatio* in medieval sermons, see Wenzel, 'Why the Monk?' 261–9 in *Words and Works: Studies in Medieval English Language and Literature in Honour of Fred C. Robinson*, ed. Peter S. Baker and Nicholas Howe (Toronto: University of Toronto Press, 1998).

[15] See Alford, *Glossary of Legal Diction*, 17–18, s.vv. 'borgh', 'borwen'. The Sarum rite of baptism is edited in *The Sarum Missal*, ed. J. Wickham Legg (Oxford: Clarendon Press, 1916), 123–57, and translated as 'The Rite of Baptism in the Sarum Manual', 158–79 in J. D. C. Fisher, *Christian Initiation: Baptism in the Medieval West: A Study in the Disintegration of the Primitive Rite of Initiation* (London: SPCK, 1965).

[16] *Dominical Sermon Cycle*, ed. Morrison, 1: 25. The injunction to 'ransake thi mynde', or 'ransake well all the corners of þi consciens' recurs on several occasions in this sermon collection, as the preacher

into the church: 'Firste, remember thiselfe when þu cammeste to the chirche dore.' He then rehearses the Sarum rite of baptism, presenting each question and answer in Latin and English, and asking his congregation to consider how they have 'broken or kepte' each part of 'this counawnt'.[17] The promises of baptism supply each listener with a framework to integrate and evaluate the events of their lives, to recognize themselves as coherent, 'self-constant' subjects. Parishioners were also encouraged to remember their baptismal vows as they received the last rites. The Middle English treatise 'How men that ben in hele sholde visite sike folk', which is copied after a B text of *Piers Plowman* in Cambridge University Library, MS Dd.1.17, provides a form of words for this purpose, which echoes the liturgy of baptism.[18] The treatise instructs the priest to skip forward to this section as death approaches, so that the dying man can restate his original promises 'or [before] hise mynde go fro hym', speaking them as his last rational words.[19] In his final moments, the dying parishioner looks back to his baptism and reflects on his life as an interpreted whole, affirming his 'self-constancy' through the mediation of a pastoral text. When Holy Church invites the dreamer to recall his baptismal promises in the middle of his life, then, she employs a recognizable pastoral strategy, recalling these first commitments as a way to conceptualize his lived experience as a *holos*.

In his collected sermons, many of which were addressed to an audience of clergy, Robert Rypon offers some more reflective and elaborate accounts of baptismal promises and the structure they provide for a Christian life.[20] In an Easter sermon on 1 Corinthians 5:7, Rypon reads the story of the Passover, its subsequent commemoration, and its typological fulfilment in the passion, to

---

encourages his listeners to recall their sins (1: 76; 2: 251; 2: 338). Morrison notes (2: 490) that these passages recall an injunction from Augustine's sermon 34: 'Bene, fratres mei, interrogate uos ipsos, cellas interiores discutite [Submit yourselves, my dear brothers, to a thorough interrogation, turn out your innermost closets and cupboards]'; Augustine, *Sermones de vetere testamento (1–50)*, ed. Cyril Lambot, CCSL 41 (Turnhout: Brepols, 1961), 426 (34.vii); translation from Augustine, *Sermons 20–50*, ed. John E. Rotelle, trans. Edmund Hill, WSA, 3.2 (New York: New City Press, 1990), 168.

[17] *Dominical Sermon Cycle*, ed. Morrison, 1: 25.

[18] On this treatise, which circulated in multiple versions, and later became a staple of fifteenth-century household books, see Amy Appleford, *Learning to Die in London, 1380–1540* (Philadelphia: University of Pennsylvania Press, 2015), 18–54. 'How men that ben in hele' is edited from Cambridge University Library, MS Dd.1.17 at 194–202 in *The World of Piers Plowman*, ed. Krochalis and Peters.

[19] 'How men that ben in hele', 200. Appleford, *Learning to Die*, 34–5, discusses the instruction to skip forwards to these questions as the moment of death approaches.

[20] On the audience for Rypon's sermons, see Wenzel, *Latin Sermon Collections*, 67. Johnson argues that the sermons in this collection were adapted for monastic readers, but derived from material that was actually preached; Johnson, 'Robert Rypon and the Creation of London, British Library, MS Harley 4894: A Master Preacher and His Sermon Collection', *Medieval Sermon Studies* 59 (2015): 38–56; and Johnson, 'Introduction', in Rypon, *Selected Sermons*, 1: 28–9. On Rypon's characteristic use of rich and multi-faceted figures, see Wenzel, *Latin Sermon Collections*, 68–71; Johnson, 'Introduction', in Rypon, *Selected Sermons*, 1: 23–6; Johnson, 'The Divine Dinner Party: Domestic Imagery and Easter Preaching in Late Medieval England', *Traditio* 67 (2012): 385–415; and Johnson, 'The Imaginative Landscape of an English Monk-Preacher: Robert Rypon and the Court of Memory', *Mediaeval Studies* 75 (2013): 177–204.

158 PREACHING AND NARRATIVE IN *PIERS PLOWMAN*

figure the beginning of a good life, its continuation, and its consummation at death. In the second principal part, he explains how catechetical instruction, beginning at baptism, provides a structure for the 'cursus et forma bone vite [the course and plan of a good life]'.[21] Noting that 'non sufficit per se inicium bone vite nisi eciam sequatur bonum opus cum continuacione [the beginning of the good life is not sufficient in itself unless good works also follow continuously]', he recommends the Ten Commandments as a 'dietam', or regimen, that the Christian should follow 'totam vitam suam [through his entire life]', that will enable him to keep his baptismal promises.[22] Rypon then offers another analogy, however, arguing that, during the sacrament of baptism, 'caracterem inuisibilem eciam indelibilem in anima impressam est [an invisible and indelible brand was imprinted on the soul]'.[23] The brand remains as a sign of baptism, even if the Christian forgets his original commitments and strays into sin, just as a farmer's brand remains on the skin of an animal even if the animal's hair grows over it.[24] These paired analogies offer contrasting ways to think about the sacrament of baptism and the structure it provides for the 'cursus et forma' of a good life: in the first, it sets a standard the Christian must continue to meet, while in the second it offers consolation for the Christian who falls short. Each requires different forms of narrative interpretation, moreover: in the first case, baptism forms an accessible framework to make sense of lived experience as it unfolds, but in the second it is a hidden sign, to be searched out and recovered at moments of spiritual lethargy or moral crisis.

Rypon returns to baptismal promises and to the narrative shape of a Christian life in an Advent sermon on John 1:22, where he imagines how a Christian might answer the question posed to John the Baptist, 'Tu quis es? [Who are you?]'. Rypon argues that a man who has broken his baptismal promises is not speaking truthfully when he calls himself a Christian: 'Si es Christianus de facto sicut et nomine, tunc facis in re quod dicis, et quod promisisti quando factus fueras Christianus.... Quando ergo non bene facis vel peccas mortaliter, responsio tua ad questionem falsa est [If you are a Christian in fact and name, then you do the thing that you say and what you promised when you were made a Christian.... So when you do not do good and sin mortally, your response to the question is false].'[25] Later in this part of the sermon, Rypon employs a musical metaphor to show how the successive phases of a human life can be integrated as part of a whole: if a man keeps his baptismal vows, he explains, then the middle and end of

---

[21] Rypon, *Selected Sermons*, ed. and trans. Johnson, 1: 120, 121.
[22] Rypon, *Selected Sermons*, ed. and trans. Johnson, 1: 120, 121.
[23] Rypon, *Selected Sermons*, ed. and trans. Johnson, 1: 120, 121.
[24] Rypon returns to this idea in his sermon for the feast of St John the Baptist, where he once more likens the grace of baptism to an impressed mark ('caracter') that remains on the soul even when the baptized Christian falls into sin. Rypon, *Selected Sermons*, ed. and trans. Johnson, 1: 208, 209.
[25] Rypon, *Selected Sermons*, ed. and trans. Johnson, 1: 72–4, 73–5.

his life will conform to the beginning, like three voices in harmony, 'Sic reuera si quis Christianus deuiet a promissis in baptismo, tempora sue vite nimis discrepant [But, indeed, if any Christian deviates from his baptismal promises, then the times of his life are exceedingly out of tune].'[26] Rypon imagines a narrative identity that is configured around ethical commitments: fidelity to baptismal promises serves to establish 'discordant concordance' between the disparate events of lived experience, while infidelity mitigates against ethical 'self-constancy' and the narrative coherence of an interpreted life.

When Holy Church recalls the dreamer's reception at the font, she also reminds him of the elementary education she provided for him there. The baptismal font was closely associated with the kinds of early instruction that formed the foundations of lay and clerical knowledge alike. Parents and godparents promised to teach the Pater Noster, Ave Maria, and Credo to the child as part of the baptism service, to supplement and reinforce the instruction that the parish priest delivered from the pulpit. Eamon Duffy describes an inscription on a fourteenth-century font in Bradley, Lincolnshire, that offers a reminder of this obligation: 'Pater Noster, Ave Maria, Criede,/ Leren the childe yt is nede'.[27] Children might also learn elementary Latin in the church building, as Christopher Cannon observes. Amongst other evidence, Cannon cites a deposition from 1496-7, where a witness recalls his schooling near the font in Kirkham, Lancashire.[28]

If the baptismal rite, recalled in later life, provides a simple framework to configure lived experience and to affirm 'self-constancy', this kind of instruction, both catechetical and grammatical, makes a much larger corpus of narrative texts available as resources to conceptualize the self as a *holos*. When Holy Church returns to her *thema*, commending faithful words and actions as an expression of 'treuþe', she continues to develop her claims about baptism, showing how many different kinds of Bible story might affirm the dreamer's perception of himself as a narrative subject. Holy Church tells the story of David, who 'dubbed kny3tes' in 1 Chronicles 12 and made them swear 'to seruen truþe euere' (B.1.99–100), before turning to Lucifer, who was 'kny3ted' by Christ, but who 'brak buxomnesse [obedience]' and fell from heaven, in violation of his oath (B.1.105, 113), inviting the dreamer to think about his baptismal vows by analogy with these knightly

---

[26] Rypon, *Selected Sermons*, ed. and trans. Johnson, 1: 76, 77.
[27] Eamon Duffy, *The Stripping of the Altars: Traditional Religion in England c.1400–c.1580*, 2nd edn (New Haven: Yale University Press, 2005), 32. The Longleat friar, who recalls this promise in a Rogation Day sermon, worries that some parents and godparents may lack the basic knowledge required to carry it out: 'þey byndin hem to techyn here godchyldryn here leuenesse & þe ten comaundementis or don hem be tau3t . . . But now neyþer þe child ne þe fader ne þe moder ne godfader ne godmoder connyn here leuenesse ne þe ten comaundementis & wol lytyl of onyþing þat ys nedful to here sauacioun'; Longleat MS 4, fol. 58v.
[28] Cannon, *From Literacy to Literature*, 45–6, and n. 20.

oaths, even as she continues to elaborate her account of Christian history.[29] The early instruction that Holy Church provides should allow him to recognize these connections, to develop a sense of himself as a subject in historical time, and to understand his own experiences in relation to scriptural texts.

Later in this sermon, the dreamer interrupts Holy Church once more, this time to protest that he has no 'kynde knowynge' of the lessons she is teaching him: when she affirms that 'Truþe is þe beste', he asks her to 'kenne me bettre/ By what craft in my cors it comseþ, and where' (B.1.135, 138–9). Holy Church rebukes him for his misunderstanding, in language that returns him once more to his early education at the font:

'Thow doted daffe!' quod she, 'dulle are þi wittes.	*silly fool*
To litel Latyn þow lernedest, leode, in þi youþe:	*man*
Heu michi quod sterilem duxi vitam iuuenilem!	
It is a kynde knowynge þat kenneþ in þyn herte	*instructs (you)*
For to louen þi Lord leuere þan þiselue,	*more dearly*
No dedly synne to do, deye þei3 þow sholdest—	*mortal, die*
This I trowe be truþe; who kan teche þee bettre,	*believe is; if anyone can*
Loke þow suffre hym to seye, and siþen lere it after;	*See; allow; then learn*
For þus witnesseþ his word; werche þow þerafter.'	*act accordingly*
	(1.140–6)

Holy Church responds to this request as though it is a further symptom of the dreamer's *lethargus*. Here again, she encourages Will to see his life as a whole, to understand his phenomenological present in relation to the remembered past. The Latin line 'Heu michi quod sterilem duxi vitam iuuenilem! [Alas, what a useless life I led in my youth]' is itself a schoolroom maxim: it also appears in Manchester, John Rylands Library, MS 394, in a list of proverbs that were probably used to teach elementary Latin.[30] Sloth will cite it later in *Piers Plowman*, when he describes his youth as an idle, disengaged student: 'I yarn aboute [ran around] in youþe, and yaf

---

[29] The ceremony for dubbing, as described for example in Raymond Lull's *Book of the Order of Chivalry*, contained deliberate echoes of baptism: before he was knighted, the aspirant would take a ceremonial bath to wash away his sins. Holy Church also draws out the association between a knight's oath and a religious vow, referring to a knight who breaks his oath as 'apostata in his ordre' (B.1.104), in language more commonly reserved for professed religious. On knighthood as a 'quasi-religious "order"', see Galloway, *Penn Commentary*, 1: 191. Catherine Nall, *Reading and War in Fifteenth-Century England: From Lydgate to Malory* (Cambridge: Brewer, 2012), 122–3, discusses this passage from *Piers* in the context of a larger late medieval discourse that emphasized the sacred purpose and function of knighthood.

[30] W. A. Pantin, 'A Medieval Collection of Latin and English Proverbs and Riddles, from the Rylands Latin MS 394', *Bulletin of the John Rylands Library* 14 (1930): 102. See also Cannon, *From Literacy to Literature*, 75–7. This collection also contains part of the Latin cited by Clergy at B.10.260a, and the rhyme 'Mesure ys tresur', which recalls Holy Church's 'Mesure is medecyne' (B.1.35), as well as the lines on St Maurus' wind, discussed in Chapter 2; see *Parallel Text*, ed. Schmidt, 2: 486, and Galloway, *Penn Commentary*, 1: 165–6.

me nau3t [did not commit myself] to lerne.../ *Heu michi quod sterilem vitam duxi iuuenilem*' (B.5.440–1a). This Latin line itself connects the moments of an individual life in a complex way, as an expression of adult regret first internalized in childhood and intended for recall in later life. Holy Church combines this Latin phrase with a reference to the most rudimentary catechetical instruction, 'No dedly synne to do'. Her rebuke, which is both stern and familiar, creates its own echoes of early instruction and the affective responses it produces. These, in Ricoeur's terms, are the 'traces' and 'vestiges' of a remembered past, which surface in the experiential present and demand a narrative explanation.

Holy Church's response to Will's request for 'kynde knowynge' in these lines seems counterintuitive: when he expresses his desire for natural, intuitive understanding, she answers with a reference to his early education and the Latin texts that it comprised. Yet, part of the point of this answer is to show how 'kynde knowynge' and clerical instruction inform and condition each other over the course of a lifetime. Latin lessons, internalized at the font, come to seem natural and intuitive, while lived experience, in its unfolding complexity, becomes comprehensible, even meaningful, through the mediation of clerical texts. Returning the dreamer to the scene of his earliest instruction, Holy Church invites him to see how the lessons he learned at the font have become a part of his 'kynde' experience and how they might serve to structure that experience in turn, providing the basis for narrative interpretation. Holy Church imagines that the dreamer might continue to learn in this way, understanding his future experience in relation to the lessons she has taught him. Truth himself will teach the dreamer to love God, if he will 'suffre hym to seye, and siþen lere it after' (B.1.145): lived experience will enrich and extend the lessons of her sermon, as the dreamer construes it as part of the narrative of his life, 'preueing' this early 'preching' and instruction, testing it, challenging it, and reaffirming it.[31]

In this important early scene in the poem, then, the dreamer's interjections prompt a first engagement with questions of narrative identity. Will has become unmoored from his own experience: a perceiving subject who exists exclusively in the phenomenological present, he is unable to recover the lessons of his past, or to see their implications for the future. Holy Church reminds him of their long relationship, and encourages him to use the teaching and instruction she has offered since his infancy as a narrative framework to organize and interpret his own experiences. These exchanges are framed as interruptions in a larger sermon, where Holy Church employs the discursive resources of biblical narrative to reconfigure the dreamer's perception of the contemporary world, locating the present time in eschatological history. They begin to suggest that these same

---

[31] Spencer, *English Preaching*, 41, argues that Holy Church imagines the dreamer learning by rote, like a grammar school student, in his future encounters with Truth. See also Spencer, *English Preaching*, 141, 198.

resources might serve to constitute an individual identity, as Will begins to recognize himself as a dynamic, 'self-constant' subject, confronting ethical choices in an interpreted present. As the poem addresses these questions, it also develops a theory of personal identity where clerical texts and lived experience are thoroughly integrated, as Holy Church makes clear when the dreamer complains that he lacks 'kynde knowynge'. For Holy Church, lived experience becomes meaningful when it is mediated by clerical texts, and clerical texts are best understood when they are assimilated into an interpreted life.

Fortune's Mirror, Scripture's Sermon

By the end of passus 10 in the B text, the dreamer's search for Do-wel has taken him far beyond the formative instruction that Holy Church provided at the font. Guided by Study, Clergy, and Scripture, Will has progressed through the academic curriculum to the point where he can read and interpret clerical texts for himself and engage in theological debate with his teachers. This advanced study produces a spiritual crisis at the point when he confronts the doctrine of predestination, however: in a fraught and angry outburst, he reflects that the fate of his soul might be predetermined, 'my name yentred/ In þe legende of lif [Book of Life, Rev. 20:12] longe er I were,/ Or ellis vnwriten for some wikkednesse' (B.10.374–6), so that his efforts to 'do wel' are irrelevant, and cites a long list of examples where the logic of salvation seems inscrutable or unfair. Here, as Nicolette Zeeman argues, the dreamer 'distorts and denigrates propositions and phenomena that are valued seriously elsewhere in the poem, turning Christian teaching about the gifts of grace and divine "acceptance" into a series of arguments for moral inaction'.[32] As passus 11 begins, Scripture rebukes the dreamer, criticizing him for his lack of self-knowledge and, in response, he falls into an inner dream, where he observes the events of his own life. In order to reconcile himself to the fearful implications of difficult doctrine, Langland suggests, the dreamer must first reflect on his own experiences and learn to configure those experiences into a narrative. In doing so, he will come to see how the most demanding and difficult doctrine can be held in productive tension with the elementary instruction of Holy Church, and 'preued' against the unfolding lessons of lived experience, as part of the 'discordant concordance' of an interpreted life.

As he remonstrates with Scripture, Will expresses a nostalgic desire for the kind of elementary instruction that he once received from Holy Church. Many learned people regret advancing beyond the basic catechetical curriculum, he declares:

---

[32] Zeeman, *Discourse of Desire*, 217. In *Arts of Disruption*, 107–8, Zeeman writes that Will succumbs to a form of 'paradiastolic self-deception' here, presenting degraded, distorted versions of 'real Christian teaching about moral effort, baptism, or divine foreknowledge'.

'men knowe clerkes þat han corsed þe tyme/ That euere þei kouþe [learnt] or knewe moore þan *Credo in Deum patrem* ["I believe in one God"]/And principally hir *Paternoster*—many a persone haþ wisshed' (B.10.466–8). Adapting the widely attested maxim 'brevis oratio penetrat celum [a short prayer pierces heaven]', which was often used to affirm the efficacy of the *Paternoster* in lay devotion, Will declares that agricultural labourers can 'Percen wiþ a *Paternoster* þe paleys of heuene', and be saved with this simple knowledge alone (B.10.463).[33] Citing Augustine's *Confessiones*, meanwhile, he contends that 'konnynge clerkes þat knowe manye bokes' are no closer to salvation: '*ipsi idiote rapiunt celum vbi nos sapientes in inferno mergimur* [the unlearned themselves take heaven by force while we wise ones are drowned in hell]' (B.10.458, 455). Will has not forgotten his early instruction in this scene, as he had in his encounter with Holy Church; instead, he seeks to return to it, and to forget all the knowledge he has accumulated since. The lack of self-knowledge that Scripture discerns in the dreamer arises from his failure to see how elementary catechesis and advanced, clerical 'konnynge' might inform and condition one another over the course of a lifetime. The opposition he perceives between these forms of knowledge reveals a lack of 'self-constancy', a confusion about the larger shape of his life.

Like Holy Church in passus 1, Scripture rebukes the dreamer with a line of Latin. She quotes the incipit to the pseudo-Bernardine *Meditationes piisimae de cognitione humanae condicionis*: '*Multi multa sciunt et seipsos nesciunt* [Many know many things, but do not know themselves]' (B.11.3).[34] In its original context, this line affirms that contemplative practice must begin with self-observation, a key premise of the *Meditationes* as a whole. As the pseudo-Bernard declares in his first chapter, 'ab exterioribus redeam ad interiora, et ab inferioribus ad superiora ascendam:... et ita per cognitionem mei valeam pervenire ad cognitionem Dei [I shall turn from outward things to inward things, and from inward things I shall ascend to higher things... and so by learning about myself I may arrive at the knowledge of God]'.[35] Other writers cite this incipit to show how self-knowledge could organize and regulate academic learning, rather than mystical ascent. As Rebecca Davis has noted, the incipit appears in chapter five of the *Floretus*, a versified manual of moral instruction that was widely

---

[33] On this maxim and its close identification with the *Paternoster*, see Alastair Bennett, '*Brevis Oratio Penetrat Celum*: Proverbs, Prayers, and Lay Understanding in Late Medieval England', *New Medieval Literatures* 14 (2012): 127–63.

[34] On the popularity of this text, and Langland's possible knowledge of it, see Wittig, 'Inward Journey', 211–13.

[35] *Meditationes piissimae de cognitione humanae conditionis*, 184: cols 485–508 in *PL*, ed. Migne, 184: col. 485. A fifteenth-century Middle English translation of this text survives in two closely related manuscripts: British Library, Royal MS 17 C XVIII and Oxford, Bodleian Library, MS Rawlinson C.894. See Alford, *Guide to the Quotations*, 71, and E. A. Jones, 'The Compilation(s) of Two Late Medieval Devotional Manuscripts', 79–97 in *Text and Controversy from Wyclif to Bale: Essays in Honour of Anne Hudson*, ed. Helen Barr and Ann M. Hutchison (Turnhout: Brepols, 2005).

studied in grammar schools.[36] Addressing students on the proper use of knowledge, the text declares that 'Multi multa sciunt et se bene scire relinquunt;/ Temet cognosce, Dominum cognoscere posce! [Many know many things, and they neglect to know themselves well; learn about yourself, and desire to learn about the lord].'[37] Humbert of Romans, meanwhile, quotes this incipit in a model sermon for educated listeners ('Ad omnes litteratos'), reminding them: 'Qui... plus scit, plus potest seipsum cognoscere, quod est summe utilitatis. Quo contra Bernardus, "Multi multa sciunt, et seipsos nesciunt" [The more a person knows, the more he is able to learn about himself, and this is extremely valuable. As Bernard writes, however, "Many know many things, but do not know themselves"].'[38] This, then, was an injunction that could be addressed to schoolboys or to learned scholars, a reminder that self-knowledge is a necessary precondition for assimilating knowledge of other kinds. Perhaps, like the maxim 'Heu michi quod sterilem duxi vitam iuuenilem', it was internalized in childhood for recall in adulthood, a piece of wisdom that might structure a larger reflection on the 'lyf tyme' as a narrative *holos*.

The inner dream that follows from Scripture's rebuke provides a new context to confront the fearful implications of divine foreknowledge, as Will considers this doctrine in relation to his own lived experience and to the texts and discourses that have helped him understand it. Before he tackles this question directly, however, Langland will use this part of the poem to explore the process of learning from experience itself, to insist that self-knowledge arises through acts of narrative interpretation, and to show how interpretation of this kind draws on the discourses that preaching supplies. Within the inner dream, Will is seduced by temptations that obscure the larger shape of his life and becomes absorbed in the pleasures of the phenomenological present. As he observes and interprets these experiences, however, he configures them into a *holos* and recuperates his own biography as a source of exemplary instruction. This part of the poem also returns to the dreamer's longstanding relationship with Holy Church: as he begins

---

[36] Davis, *Books of Nature*, 146, n. 42. The *Floretus* was part of the *Auctores Octo*, which superseded the 'Liber Catonianus' in grammar schools in continental Europe, and was also adopted, though partially and inconsistently, in England. See Nicholas Orme, *English Schools in the Middle Ages* (London: Methuen, 1973), 102–4; Orme, *Medieval Schools: From Roman Britain to Renaissance England* (New Haven: Yale University Press, 2006), 100–1; and Pascale Bourgain, 'The Circulation of Texts in Manuscript Culture', 140–59 in *The Medieval Manuscript Book: Cultural Approaches*, ed. Michael Johnston and Michael Van Dussen (Cambridge: Cambridge University Press, 2015), 154.

[37] *Liber Floretus*, ed. Árpád Orbán (Kastellaun: Henn, 1979), 31; translation from 'Floretus', 213–50 in *An English Translation of Auctores Octo, a Medieval Reader*, trans. by Ronald E. Pepin (Lewiston: Mellen, 1999), 235.

[38] Humbert of Romans, *De modo prompte cudendi sermones*, 25: 424–567 in *Maxima Bibliotheca Veterum Patrum et Antiquorum Scriptorum Ecclesiastiorum*, ed. Marguerin d la Bigne, 27 vols (Lyons: Anissonios, 1677), 25: 484 (lvi). As Alford notes (*Guide to the Quotations*, 71), the incipit was also cited in a Middle English sermon from the collection in MS Royal 18.B.XXIII. Here, the preacher uses it to introduce a summary of the *contemptus mundi* material from the early chapters of the *Meditationes*: 'In his Meditacions, que sic incipit *Multi multa sciunt*, capitulo iij°, he seyþ on þis wize: "Where ben all þese vorldely louers þat were here a litill before with vs? Now þer is no þinge lefte of hem but askes and vormes...".' *Middle English Sermons*, ed. Ross, 98.

to recognize the narrative shape of his own life, the dreamer also recalls the value of parochial instruction and the resources it provides for self-understanding. The inner dream presents an allegory for the emergence of a 'self-constant' subject, as Will reflects on the events of his life and then configures them into an integrated whole. It is only once the poem has considered this process of interpretation, where lived experience is mediated by clerical texts, and clerical texts are integrated into recollected life, that it turns again to confront the question of salvation.

In the early part of the inner dream, Will encounters Fortune, her daughters, *Concupiscencia Carnis* [Desire of the Flesh] and 'Coueitise of Ei3es', and their companion 'Pride of Parfit Lyuynge' (B.11.43, 46, 47); these personifications encourage him to experience his life as a simple succession of events and to ignore any intimations of its larger, narrative dimension. When the dream begins, Will is 'rauysshed' into the 'lond of longynge', where Fortune invites him to look 'in a mirour þat hi3te [was called] Middelerþe', promising to show him 'wondres' in an echo of the poem's opening lines (B.11.8–10). He abandons his search for Do-wel, and Fortune's daughters encourage him in worldly forms of pride and covetous desire. Life in the 'lond of longynge' is characterized by self-absorption rather than self-understanding, by what Davis has called 'a recklessly passive openness to natural experience'.[39] Sensory experience overwhelms the dreamer's attention in the present, and serves as a distraction from the past and the future. *Concupiscencia Carnis* encourages the dreamer to imagine his 'lif tyme' as a protracted experience of youth, where old age and death can be endlessly deferred:

'Thow art yong and yeep and hast yeres ynowe	*lusty*
For to lyue longe and ladies to louye;	
And in þis mirour þow my3te se myrþes ful manye	*delights*
That leden þee wole to likynge al þi lif tyme.'	*pleasure*
	(B.11.18–21)

Recklessness, who appears a little later in the vision, makes the same seductive argument. 'Folwe forþ þat Fortune wole', he tells the dreamer: 'þow hast wel fer to Elde./ A man may stoupe tyme yno3 whan he shal tyne þe crowne! [loose his hair]' (B.11.35–6). Imagined in these vague and limitless terms, as 'yeres ynowe' and 'tyme yno3', lived experience has no lessons to teach, and creates no imperatives for ethical action. Warnings do emerge as part of Will's unfolding experience. Elde appears while Will is still young, and predicts that Fortune will abandon him 'at þi mooste nede' (B.11.29). Yet, the experience of ageing, when it comes, does not encourage him to reflect on his lifetime as a whole: the dreamer says that 'I foryat youþe and yarn [ran] into elde [old age]' (B.11.60), as one experiential present

---

[39] Davis, *Books of Nature*, 152.

gives way to another. In due course, then, the warning of Elde comes true, as Fortune abandons the dreamer and he falls into poverty: 'And þanne was Fortune my foo, for al hir faire biheste [promises],/ And pouerte pursued me and putte me lowe [brought me down]' (B.11.61-2).

Through the device of the inner dream, however, Langland is also able to show how the dreamer interprets these events. Watching his own dissolute experience, he begins to configure his memories into a plot, 'grasping [them] together', as Ricoeur would have it, in a relationship of 'discordant concordance'. The poem draws attention to this creative, interpretative activity, as Will moves quickly through 'fourty wynter and a fifte moore' (B.11.47) to show how Fortune turns against him, discerning and articulating a pattern of narrative significance in the simple succession of events, and recognizing the narrative shape of his own life, which Fortune and her daughters had sought to obscure. From this interpreted perspective, it is possible to recognize the risks that Fortune and Recklessness create with their careless promises, and to see how the warnings of Elde foreshadow the turn of Fortune's wheel. His pursuit of Fortune and her daughters emerges as the negative image of his quest for Do-wel: during this period of his life, he reflects, 'Coueitise of Eiȝes com ofter [more often] in my mynde/ Than Dowel or Dobet among my dedes alle' (B.11.50-1).

These acts of interpretation are mediated by a range of clerical texts, drawn from scripture and patristic authors, whose influence can be seen in the way the dreamer tells the story of his life. In this part of the poem, as Zeeman writes, lived experience is overlaid with 'a tissue of revealed and natural textuality'.[40] Will figures his encounter with Fortune in terms that are drawn from James 1:22-4, which offers a narrative of self-deception and personal dissolution, organized around a glance into a mirror:

> Estote autem factores verbi, et non auditores tantum: fallentes vosmetipsos. Quia si quis auditor est verbi, et non factor, hic comparabitur viro consideranti vultum nativitatis suae in speculo: consideravit enim se, et abiit, et statim oblitus est qualis fuerit.[41]
>
> [But be ye doers of the word, and not hearers only, deceiving your own selves. For if a man be a hearer of the word, and not a doer, he shall be compared to a man beholding his own countenance in a glass. For he beheld himself, and went his way, and presently forgot what manner of man he was.]

---

[40] Zeeman, *Discourse of Desire*, 213. Zeeman argues that the inner dream shows how texts associated with Clergy and Scripture might reinforce and clarify the lessons of life in the created world; *Discourse of Desire*, 209; 'Condition of Kynde', 8. I contend that these clerical texts supply the narrative resources that the dreamer will use to represent his life as a plot, and so to recognize himself once more as a 'self-constant' subject.

[41] On this passage as a source for the inner dream, see Wittig, 'Inward Journey', 208, and Zeeman, *Discourse of Desire*, 210-11, citing Gerald Leo O'Grady, '*Piers Plowman* and the Medieval Tradition of Penance' (PhD thesis, University of Wisconsin, 1962), 382-3.

The first verse of this passage echoes the injunction to 'do wel' that motivates the dreamer's encounters with Study, Clergy, and Scripture in the earlier part of the third vision. As we have seen in previous chapters, Thomas Brinton preached on a later verse from this epistle, where James reiterates the injunction to do good works, in his convocation sermon for the Good Parliament in 1376; he exemplified it in the fable of the rodent parliament, and recast it as the proverb 'bene fac et bene habe', which also forms the text of Piers's pardon. In the inner dream, however, Langland draws on James's epistle to show how Fortune distracts the dreamer from these imperatives. It is through the mediation of this scriptural text, with its narrative of self-forgetting, that Will recovers the lessons of his own experience, reading the larger significance of his time in the 'lond of longynge'.

Augustine's *Confessiones*, which the dreamer cited in his earlier debate with Scripture, offers another important intertext for the inner dream. Middleton identified the poet's 'explicit anagrammatic signature' in his description of the 'lond of longynge', where the name 'longe-lond' appears in reverse, a gesture that implies his personal investment in this unfolding life story.[42] At the same time, as Joseph Wittig argues, the 'lond of longynge' also recalls the *regio dissimilitudinis* of Augustine's *Confessiones*, a 'region of unlikeness' where Augustine described himself before his conversion, alienated from God and unable to perceive the *imago Dei* in his own soul.[43] Augustine returned to the *regio dissimiltudinis* on many occasions in his writing, and it became a 'favourite metaphor' of Bernard of Clairvaux and other Cistercian authors in turn.[44] Here then, Langland alludes to his own biography in terms that also recall one of the most influential narrative accounts of lived experience to emerge from the patristic tradition.[45] As Wittig goes on to observe, moreover, Augustine's text supplies a model for the self-reflexive procedures of the inner dream itself: at this moment in the *Confessiones*, Augustine looks back at his earlier, dissolute life, and recognizes its instructive aspect, by rendering it in narrative terms.[46] As Curtis Gruenler has more recently put it, the inner dream 'mirrors the double perspective of Augustine's text, where a post-conversion narrator recounts his pre-conversion experience'.[47] *Piers Plowman* draws not only on Augustine's narrative but also on his self-conscious attention to the process of narration.

---

[42] Middleton, 'William Langland's "Kynde Name"', 44.

[43] Wittig, '*Piers Plowman* B, Passus IX–XII: Elements in the Design of the Inward Journey', *Traditio* 28 (1972): 232. See also Zeeman, *Discourse of Desire*, 211–12.

[44] Wittig, 'Inward Journey', 232. On the history of this topos, see Pierre Courcelle, *Les Confessions de saint Augustin dans la tradition littéraire*, 2nd edn (Paris: De Boccard, 1968), 278–88, 623–40. Life in the *regio dissimilitudinis* often involved encounters with the three temptations of 1 John 2:16 in this tradition, 'concupiscencia carnis..., concupiscentia oculorum, et superbia vitae', for whom Fortune's daughters are named in the inner dream. See Wittig, 'Inward Journey', 233.

[45] For Zeeman, the juxtaposition of this anagrammatic signature with a reference to Augustine's region of unlikeness serves to illustrate 'the ambiguous distinction between the textual and the "real" that is characteristic of the exemplary'; *Discourse of Desire*, 213.

[46] Wittig, 'Inward Journey', 247.   [47] Gruenler, *Poetics of Enigma*, 214.

Something similar can be said of the third key intertext for this part of the inner dream: the *Consolatio* of Boethius.[48] Will's life follows the pattern that Boethius describes in his opening *metrum*, as Fortune follows him in his youth, then turns against him with the approach of old age. Yet this text, too, supplies a paradigm for the way that Langland's dreamer recovers the lessons of his life in the process of narrating it. Fortune seems arbitrary and unpredictable to Boethius as he experiences his life, but, as Philosophy points out to him, he can recognize her true, consistent nature when he thinks about his lived experience as an interpreted whole: 'Deprehendisti caeci numinis ambiguos uultus [You have discovered the changing faces of the random goddess]'; 'Seruauit circa te propriam potius in ipsa sui mutabilitate constantiam [In the very act of changing she has preserved her own particular kind of constancy towards you].'[49] For Boethius, as for Augustine, the lessons of lived experience emerge through interpretation. The successive events of a human life become exemplary and instructive through the creative work of emplotment, when the subject configures them into a *holos*.

The mirror of Fortune comes to figure the way that clerical texts serve to clarify lived experience in this vision. Fortune presents the mirror to Will as a distraction, inviting him to see 'wondres' in it, but when Will interprets his life story, he associates this mirror with the 'speculum' of James 1:23 and, by extension, with the various texts and discourses that allow him to recognize himself.[50] For Davis, 'Fortune's mirror symbolizes and facilitates [the] reflexive quality of encyclopaedic study, which looks outside the self only to return to self-scrutiny'; it recalls patristic accounts of scripture as a 'mirror for self-appraisal', and the titles of various encyclopaedic works that sought to derive exemplary instruction from their observations of the world.[51] Texts serve as mirrors when they reveal the instructive dimension of lived experience, providing the discursive mediation that confers new significance on an examined life. This was a metaphor that also applied to preaching, which served to facilitate these forms of understanding. Medieval *artes* and sermons describe preaching as a mirror because it encouraged listeners to recognize the application of scriptural texts to their own lives. Humbert of Romans, for example, writes that 'Verbum enim praedicationis est

---

[48] On the relevance of Boethius to this part of the poem, see Wittig, 'Inward Journey', 235; Zeeman, *Discourse of Desire*, 213; Grady, 'Chaucer's Langland's Boethius', 279–80. Steven F. Kruger proposes that the transition from the vision of Fortune to the vision of kynde at the end of the inner dream can also be understood as a 'Boethian move' where, 'stepping away from the realm of Fortune within which events appear to be simply capricious, we gain a wider prospect and discover the order underlying even seemingly random events'; 'Mirrors and the Trajectory of Vision in *Piers Plowman*', *Speculum* 66, no. 1 (1991): 85.

[49] Boethius, *Philosophiae Consolatio*, 2 pr. 1, ed. Bieler, 18, trans. Watts, 23.

[50] Over the course of this episode, as Kruger writes, the distracting, 'narcissistic mirror' that Fortune presents is gradually recast as a 'reliable', instructive one; 'Mirrors and the Trajectory of Vision', 75. Zeeman argues that the mirror 'provides a dramatic visual version of various scriptural texts, in which the reader, and Wil himself, watch Wil seduced by the world'; *Discourse of Desire*, 211–12.

[51] Davis, *Books of Nature*, 149–51. Hugh of Saint-Cher reads the mirror of James 1:23 to refer to scripture as a text that facilitates self-knowledge in this way. See Wittig, 'Inward Journey', 236, n. 86.

sicut speculum, sicut dicitur Jacob. 1, in quo homo cognoscit seipsum [The word of preaching is a kind of mirror, as it says in James 1:23, and people recognize themselves in it]'; he adds that people who are deprived of sermons cannot fully understand their sinful condition and so do not know themselves ('Et ideo multi non cognoscunt se').[52] In this respect, perhaps, the image of the mirror anticipates Will's forthcoming encounter with Scripture, who will preach to him on the doctrine of predestination; it is in the form of a sermon that this most difficult doctrine will take its place as part of his lived experience.

The first part of the inner dream echoes the dreamer's encounter with Holy Church in passus 1 in several interrelated ways. When Scripture admonishes Will with a line of schoolroom Latin, she recalls the way that Holy Church rebuked him, as we have seen. As Frank Grady has argued, moreover, the appearance of Fortune in the 'lond of longynge' continues a series of allusions to Boethius that began in passus 1, where Holy Church, like lady Philosophy, discovered that the dreamer had forgotten her.[53] The inner dream casts this earlier encounter in a new light: it reveals how the dreamer fell into that state of lethargy where Holy Church discovered him, absorbed in the 'wondres' of the phenomenological present, with no conception of the larger, interpreted shape of his 'lif tyme', or of the imperatives it creates to 'do wel'. The teaching of Holy Church, meanwhile, enables Will to make sense of the inner dream: when he reads his life in the mirror of scripture, Will employs the knowledge and skills that he first began to cultivate at the font.

Will himself recalls his relationship to Holy Church when Elde appears and Fortune turns against him, a moment he will later identify as a turning point in his own life story. During his dissolute life in the 'lond of longynge', 'Coueitise of Ei3es' had advised him to confess to the friars and to become a member of a lay confraternity in order to benefit from their prayers, a way to ease his conscience without any real moral effort. After his encounter with Elde, however, the dreamer tells his friar confessor that he intends to be buried at his parish church and not at the fraternal house:

And þo fond I þe frere afered and flittynge boþe	*changeable*
Ayeins oure firste forward, for I seide I nolde	*agreement*
Be buried at hire hous but at my parisshe chirche	
(For I herde ones how Conscience it tolde	
That þere a man cristned were, by kynde he sholde be buryed).	

(B.11.63–7)

---

[52] Humbert of Romans, *Liber de eruditione praedicatorum*, 5.xxiv.295, ed. Berthier, 2: 437; trans Tugwell, 266 (adapted). Humbert returns to this analogy at 5.xxx.372, where he explains that a man who has seen his own sins in the mirror but does not repent is more detestable than a man who is ignorant of his sins; ed. Berthier, 2: 449; trans. Tugwell, 280–1.

[53] Grady 'Chaucer's Langland's Boethius', 282.

In these lines, Will recovers his original relationship to Holy Church, here specifically 'my parisshe chirche', by recollecting his baptismal promises. At the start of the inner dream, where Will is absorbed in the uninterpreted present, such life-long commitments can be made and abandoned, seemingly without consequence: Fortune and her daughters make many 'faire biheste[s]' that are soon forgotten (B.11.61). Now, however, as he begins to perceive his life as a *holos*, Will remembers his baptism and the obligations it entails, the ethical commitments that reveal his 'self-constancy' as a narrative subject. As he recalls his baptism, he also remembers the elementary instruction that followed from it, the parochial teaching and preaching that has given shape to his lived experience. Explaining his obligations to the friar, he cites texts that 'I herde ones', scripture expounded and applied in the pulpit. These forms of instruction are so fully assimilated into his personal memories that they seem to be spoken in the voice of Conscience, and affirmed by instinct and intuition, 'by kynde'.[54] The dreamer's recollections of Holy Church form an important supplement to the poem's exploration of self-knowledge. The inner dream has shown how lived experience becomes meaningful and comprehensible when it is mediated by texts, and how the human subject emerges through the application of narrative hermeneutics. When Will thinks back to his baptism, and to the teaching he heard at the font, however, he finds that these texts and discourses are part of his lived experience in turn.

It is at this point in the poem that Will returns to the question of God's foreknowledge, and considers its implications for his own salvation. Scripture appears suddenly in the inner dream, breaking into the action in a way that recalls the charismatic intervention of Piers Plowman in the second vision, and restates the doctrine of election in the form of a sermon: Will says that she 'skipte an heiȝ and preched' (B.11.108). Scripture's sermon, as Will reports it, concerns the parable of the feast from Matthew 22, and her *thema* comprises two words from Matthew 22:14, the *Multi* and *Pauci* of 'Multi enim sunt vocati, pauci vero electi [For many are called, but few are chosen]':

This was hir teme and hir text—I took ful good hede:	*paid close attention*
'*Multi* to a mangerie and to þe mete were sompned;	*Many; feast*
And what þe peple was plener comen, þe porter vnpynned þe yate	*unlocked*

---

[54] The layout of the building reinforces these lessons, as Rentz observes: when Will imagines the parish church, he refers to the font where Holy Church received him, and to the graveyard where he plans to be buried, mapping the contours of his life onto the surrounding architecture; *Imagining the Parish*, 29. Piers Plowman himself plans to be buried at his parish church when he makes his will in the second vision; in exchange for his tithes, which figure his lifelong commitment to the parish, he understands that the church will shelter his body while he awaits the final judgement: 'The kirke shal haue my caroyne, and kepe my bones, / For of my corn and my catel he craued þe tiþe' (B.6.91–2).

And plucked in *Pauci* pryueliche and leet þe remenaunt   *A few; wander off*
   go rome.'
                                                                         (B.11.111–14)

Will responds with fear and doubt as he considers the implications of Scripture's text, just as he did in their earlier confrontation. As he works to internalize this difficult doctrine, however, he also considers his relationship to Holy Church, and the promises he made to her at the font:

Al for tene of hir text trembled myn herte,	*distress at*
And in a weer gan I wexe, and wiþ myself to dispute	*state of perplexity*
Wheiþer I were chose or no3t chose; on Holy Chirche I þou3te,	
That vnderfonged me atte font for oon of Goddes chosene.	*received*
For Crist cleped vs alle, come if we wolde—	
Sar3ens and scismatikes, and so he dide þe Iewes:	*schismatics*
O vos omnes sicientes, venite...	
(B.11.115–20a)	

['All you that thirst, come to the waters', Isaiah 55:1]

In this scene, which James Simpson describes as 'the intellectual and emotional pivot of the whole poem', the dreamer reconciles himself to the doctrine that produced his earlier spiritual crisis by understanding it in relation to the lessons of his own, interpreted life.[55] Still trembling in response to the fearful summons that Scripture describes, Will also recalls the generous reception that Holy Church once offered him, a turning point in his own experience that has since been recalled and explicated in the discourse of parochial preaching.[56] In his earlier outburst, the dreamer drew a sharp distinction between the comforting consolations of parochial instruction and the fearful realizations that arise from advanced study, but now he recognizes that they counterbalance one another, not only in the context of a single, systematic theology but also in the context of his lived experience. Considering his 'lyf-tyme' as a whole, Will reconciles himself to the limits of what he can know—the question of 'Wheiþer I were chose or no3t chose' will only be answered after his death—and takes consolation from his baptism, which he construes as a reminder of God's mercy.

    The turn to preaching at this moment is highly significant, because preaching is the discourse that makes scriptural texts available in the context of lived

---

[55] Simpson, *Introduction*, 108.
[56] Schmidt argues that Scripture recalls the language of Holy Church's sermon in other terms here: 'Scripture's *sompned* correlates with [Holy Church's] *vnderfeng*, her *plihte* [in the C version of this passage] with *my biddyng to fulfille*'. Parallel Text, ed. Schmidt, 2: 603.

experience, and that holds them up as a mirror in which people might recognize themselves. In his earlier outburst against Scripture, Will cited a line from Augustine's *Confessiones* to prove that the learned are more likely to be damned, describing it as part of 'a sermon'; there, he revealed that he had encountered this text in the course of his academic study, rather than hearing it preached: 'I sei3 it writen ones' (B.10.454). The written sermon, abstracted from life, was emblematic of academic knowledge divorced from self-understanding in this context. When Scripture preaches in the inner dream, by contrast, her exegesis of Matthew unfolds as part of the dreamer's biography, and gives shape to his own, interpreted experience. Over the course of the inner dream, Will recovers a learning life that has been shaped and mediated by preaching; even in this moment of personal reflection, he refers to his baptism not as he remembers it, but as Holy Church described it to him in passus 1: 'Holi chirche I am... I vnderfeng þee first' (B.1.76). As he debates the implications of Scripture's sermon, he draws on that biography in turn, taking consolation and encouragement from the lessons it has to teach. Preached within the inner dream, this sermon forms part of an interpreted life, a life that has been mediated by other sermons, 'herde' and recollected in the parish church.

Still in dialogue with Scripture, the dreamer elaborates on the consolations of baptism, imagining the sacrament as a charter between a serf and his lord. A baptized Christian cannot renounce his Christianity, any more than a 'cherl' can make a charter and sell his lord's property without his lord's permission:

For þou3 a Cristen man coueited his Cristendom to reneye,	*abjure*
Ri3tfully to reneye no reson it wolde.	
For may no cherl chartre mak, ne his chattel selle	*property*
Wiþouten leue of his lord—no lawe wol it graunte.	*permission; allow*
	(B.11.125–8)

Even if the 'cherl' runs away, roaming 'recchelesly aboute' far 'fro home', Will goes on, this does not change his relationship to his lord under the law (B.11.129–30). When Reason and Conscience catch up with him 'at þe laste', the churl will face the penalty for his sins, but can also hope for mercy, precisely because this relationship persists (B.11.131).[57] Imagined as 'a contract of un-freedom', as Emily Steiner writes, baptism structures a life-long relationship between lord and servant, creating grounds for hope and reason to fear.[58]

---

[57] On the significance of the churl's charter, see Simpson, *Introduction*, 108–10; Steiner, *Documentary Culture*, 151. Elsewhere, Steiner reads the churl's charter as evidence for Langland's debts to Deguileville, and shows how this image from Langland informed later English versions of Deguileville in turn: Steiner, '*Piers Plowman* and Institutional Poetry', *Études Anglaises*, 66, no. 3 (2013): 297–310 (esp. 303–8).

[58] Steiner, 'Institutional Poetry', 307.

The language of reckless roaming links the servant's truancy to Will's own experience in the 'lond of longynge', the *regio dissimilitudinis*, where, encouraged by Recklessness, he abandoned the search for Do-wel in exchange for an uninterpreted life, experienced as a simple succession of events. The projected encounter with Reason and Conscience, however, will force the churl to consider his 'lyftyme' as a narrative *holos*, measured against the terms of the charter, which has always remained in force: 'Ac Reson shal rekene wiþ hym and rebuken hym at þe laste./ And Conscience acounte [settle accounts] wiþ hym and casten hym in arerage' (B.11.131–2). Imagined as a contract between lord and servant, the promises of baptism supply the basis to understand lived experience as a narrative, a model for self-constancy that is also grounded in ethical commitments.

In this first movement of the inner dream, then, *Piers Plowman* offers a richly imagined response to Scripture's call for self-knowledge. Life in the 'lond of longynge' demonstrates the spiritual risks that arise when Will becomes absorbed in the sights and sounds of the phenomenological present and no longer understands his experience as an interpreted whole. Through the device of the inner dream, however, the poem also shows the dreamer recovering the lessons of his own experience, presenting a narrative of his life that draws on a wide range of clerical texts, both scriptural and patristic. Finally, as the dreamer remembers his relationship to Holy Church, the poem turns its attention to preaching and parochial instruction, the contexts in which he has previously encountered these texts, and learned to see his own life reflected in them. Will's outburst at the end of passus B.10 reveals that he is thinking about difficult doctrine in isolation from the lessons of his own life: his experience of parochial instruction and his memory of the texts and discourses that it draws on. When he confronts this doctrine again, as Scripture appears in the inner dream, he encounters it as part of a sermon, delivered in the context of an interpreted life, where 'clergie' and 'kynde' are fully integrated and the lessons of each are mediated by the other.

Ymaginatif and the 'Self-constant' Subject

Piers Plowman consolidates and extends the lessons of the inner dream at the end of the third vision, when Will encounters Ymaginatif. Ymaginatif has long been understood to personify the *vis imaginativa*, the image-making power of the soul. This is the faculty that forms images from sense impressions, linking them together in provisional, hypothetical ways, and that makes them available as the basis for rational thought, as well as for retention in the memory.[59] Ralph Hanna,

---

[59] For definitions of Ymaginatif as a faculty of the mind, and on his role in organizing sense impressions see, amongst many others, Wittig, 'Inward Journey', 264–74; Minnis, 'Langland's Ymaginatyf and Late-Medieval Theories of Imagination', *Comparative Criticism* 3 (1981): 71–103;

who resists the use of scholastic terminology to describe Ymaginatif, identifies him even so with habits of associative thought: he is a figure of 'pragmatic learning', who perceives connections 'among specific, yet apparently dispersed, sense data, and groups these connected items together under abstract categories'.[60] Langland's Ymaginatif is responsible for 'making similitudes and likenesses', as Middleton notes, and his speech is unusually rich with analogies and illustrative examples, where observable phenomena are linked together in surprising and revealing ways.[61] He also makes connections across time, configuring the disparate events of lived experience into something like an interpreted narrative. In this aspect of his operations, as John Alford observes, he embodies 'the exercise of prudence', which enables Will to reflect on his past and to plan for his future.[62] More than any other figure in the poem, then, Ymaginatif personifies the mental faculty that performs the work of emplotment, the power of the soul that discerns significant relationships in the simple succession of events, and 'grasps [them] together' in a relation of 'discordant concordance'. As Middleton argues, Ymaginatif is 'the faculty that makes it possible to examine one's life as a comprehensive pattern, as the story one makes'.[63]

Ymaginatif begins the work of emplotment when he first appears, helping the dreamer to make sense of a recent confrontation with Reason, which has brought the inner dream to an abrupt conclusion. He refers to these activities still more explicitly at the beginning of the next passus, when he introduces himself to the dreamer and explains the function he performs. Ymaginatif reveals that he has followed Will throughout his life, referring to his forty-five years in the 'lond of longynge'. While the dreamer was absorbed in the mirror of Fortune, experiencing life as a simple succession of 'wondres' and 'myrþes', Ymaginatif was there, urging him to think about his lifetime as a whole:

'I am Ymaginatif', quod he; 'ydel was I neuere,	*idle*
Thouȝ I sitte by myself, in siknesse ne in helþe.	
I haue folwed þe, in feiþ, þise fyue and fourty wynter,	
And manye tymes haue meued þee to mynne on þyn ende,	*reflect*
And how fele fernyeres are faren, and so fewe to come;	*past years*
And of þi wilde wantownesse þo þow yong were,	*recklessness*

Carruthers, 'Imaginatif, Memoria, and "The Need for Critical Theory" in *Piers Plowman* Studies', *YLS* 9 (1995): 103–14; Zeeman, *Discourse of Desire*, 82–4, 245–6; Michelle Karnes, *Imagination, Meditation, and Cognition in the Middle Ages* (Chicago: University of Chicago Press, 2011), 179–206.

[60] Hanna, 'Langland's Ymaginatif: Images and the Limits of Poetry', 81–94 in *Images, Idolatry, and Iconoclasm in Late Medieval England: Textuality and the Visual Image*, ed. Jeremy Dimmick, Simpson, and Zeeman (Oxford: Oxford University Press, 2002), 82–3, 93.

[61] Middleton, 'Narration and the Invention of Experience', 113.

[62] Alford, 'The Design of the Poem', 29–65 in *A Companion to Piers Plowman*, ed. Alford, 48. As Middleton notes, 'Repentence...may arise from retrospection and Conscience, the making of choices, may be awakened in projected action'; 'Narration and the Invention of Experience', 113.

[63] Middleton, 'Narration and the Invention of Experience', 113.

To amende it in þi myddel age, lest my3t þe faille	*power (to do so)*
In þyn olde elde, þat yuele kan suffre	*poorly; endure*
Pouerte or penaunce, or preyeres bidde:	*say*
Si non in prima vigilia nec in secunda…'	

(B.12.1–9a)

['If not in the first watch or the second', Luke 12:38]

These lines return the dreamer to the moment when Fortune turned against him as 'youþe' turned into 'elde' (B.11.60) and he began to remember his relationship to Holy Church, recalling his baptism and imagining his burial. Ymaginatif reveals himself as the power of the soul that made this realization possible. He also shows how the interpretative labour of emplotment enables prudent action: considering his 'lif tyme' as a *holos*, the dreamer should recognize the imperatives to 'mynne on [his] ende' while he is still in his 'myddel age'.

Although he is continuously engaged with lived experience and the raw materials of sensory apprehension, Ymaginatif is also an outspoken advocate for clerical texts and pastoral instruction: Fiona Somerset calls him 'the poem's most committed spokesman for "clergie"'.[64] He refers to 'clergie' and 'kynde wit' as two complementary sources of knowledge, calling them 'kyn and nei3e cosynes boþe/ To Oure Lord', and urging the dreamer to value them equally (B.12.92–4). Kynde Wit derives from the senses, and especially from 'si3te', Ymaginatif explains, but the absence of 'clergie' would also constitute a form of blindness and sensory deprivation: 'For as a man may no3t see þat mysseþ [lacks] hise ei3en,/ Na moore kan no clerk but if he cau3te [obtained] it first þoru3 bokes' (B.12.99–100). Throughout this encounter, as Zeeman writes, Ymaginatif 'argues strongly for the indispensable good of clerical teaching, both revealed and natural, and, for much of the speech, he speaks of *clergie* and "kynde wit" together, as part of a joint pastoral and educational practice'.[65] As the faculty most concerned with emplotment, Ymaginatif is concerned to show how *clergie* and *kynde* become integrated over the course of an interpreted life. He describes them as mirrors that encourage self-knowledge and facilitate penitential action: 'For boþe as mirours ben to amenden oure defautes,/ And lederes [guides] for lewed men and for lettred boþe' (B.12.95–6). In these lines, Ymaginatif recalls the mirror of the inner dream, the dazzling instrument of Fortune, subsequently recast as a tool of self-knowledge; in doing so, he recalls the way that Will recovered the shape of his own life through the mediation of clerical texts.

---

[64] Somerset, *Clerical Discourse and Lay Audience*, 39.
[65] Zeeman, *Discourse of Desire*, 251. Both Karnes and Davis have described what Davis calls the 'integrative purpose' of this episode (*Books of Nature*, p. 164, n. 83), which 'enables Will to reconcile kynde knowynge and clergie'; Karnes, *Imagination, Meditation, and Cognition*, 181.

As he works with Will to recollect and interpret his lived experience, Ymaginatif invokes the memory of Holy Church, Will's earliest clerical instructor and the figure who first encouraged him to think about the narrative shape of his own life. When he first appears, Ymaginatif points out to Will that he might have learned more in the inner dream had he 'suffred' Reason to teach him, recalling Holy Church's aspiration that he might continue to 'suffre' the lessons of Treuþe: 'Loke þow suffre hym to seye, and siþen lere it after' (B.1.145). He goes on to paraphrase Boethius, as a warning against the combative 'entremetynge' that brought the dream to its early close: '*Philosophus esses, si tacuisses* [You would have been a philosopher if you had held your peace]' (B.11.414–14a); in doing so, he continues a series of Boethian allusions that leads back through the dream of Fortune to the dreamer's first encounter with Holy Church.[66] This Boethian paraphrase was used in elementary instruction and in parochial preaching: Bromyard cites Boethius in this form in his *Summa Praedicandium*, for example.[67] In the C text, Ymaginatif combines it with an aphorism paraphrased from the *Distichs of Cato*, as though to make these associations more explicit: '*Locutum me aliquando penituit, tacuisse nunquam* [I have sometimes regretted having spoken, but never having kept silent]' (C.13.225a).[68] The most compelling echo of the dreamer's first encounter with Holy Church, however, comes when he calls on Ymaginatif 'to kenne me his name', many lines after their dialogue begins (B.11.439). When Ymaginatif introduces himself, he reminds Will of their long relationship, like Holy Church before him: 'I haue folwed þe, in feiþ, þise fyue and fourty wynter' (B.12.3). Through these several allusions, Ymaginatif reminds the dreamer of the clerical instruction that has long been part of his kynde experience and that structures the acts of emplotment he now performs. As he awakes from the inner dream, Ymaginatif brings him to his senses in other ways, prompting a renewed recovery from his state of *lethargus*.

This dialogue with Ymaginatif does more than reiterate and reinforce the lessons of the inner dream, however. Ymaginatif also recalls other moments from earlier in the poem and invites the dreamer to construe them as part of the narrative of his own experience. Elaborating on the call for amendment that emerges from Will's interpreted life, for example, he looks back to the sermon that Reason delivered on the half-acre at the start of the second vision. Like Reason

---

[66] On this quotation from Boethius, see Alford, *Guide to the Quotations*, 78; Galloway, *Penn Commentary*, 1: 151, and Grady, 'Chaucer's Langland's Boethius', 273, n. 3.

[67] Bromyard, *Summa Praedicantium*, 1: 145–6 (L.5).

[68] Translation adapted from *C Text*, ed. Pearsall, 237. On the combination of these texts, and their association with elementary instruction, see Smith, 'The Silence of Langland's Study: Matter, Invisibility, Instruction', 263–83 in *Answerable Style: The Idea of the Literary in Medieval England*, ed. Grady and Galloway (Columbus: Ohio State University Press, 2013), 279; Cannon, *From Literacy to Literature*, 246. Hanna, who seeks to disassociate Ymaginatif from advanced, theological argumentation, argues instead that his characteristic methods of argument by analogy resemble the modes of instruction found in the grammar school; 'Langland's Ymaginatif', 87–8.

before him, Ymaginatif refers to the 'pestilences' of recent history, which he construes as a punishment for sin, and as a warning of the judgement still to come. Also like Reason, he compares these disasters to corporal punishment, calling them 'baleises' to discipline children, and contends that such punishments are also loving because they are instructive:

> Amende þee while þow my3t; þow hast ben warned ofte
> Wiþ poustees of pestilences, wiþ pouerte and with angres—   *outbreaks; tribulations*
> And wiþ þise bitter baleises God beteþ his deere children: *rods*
> *Quem diligo, castigo.*
> And Dauid in þe Sauter seiþ, of swiche þat loueþ Iesus,
> '*Virga tua et baculus tuus, ipsa me consolata sunt*:
> Alþou3 þow strike me wiþ þi staf, wiþ stikke or wiþ yerde,   *rod*
> It is but murþe as for me to amende my soule.'
>   (B.12.10–15)

[12a: 'Such as I love I... chastise', Apocalypse, 3:19; 13a: 'Thy rod and thy staff: they have comforted me', Psalm 22:4]

Hanna, who notes the echoes of Reason's sermon in these lines, draws a distinction between Reason's mode of argumentation, which operates by demonstration and proof, and Ymaginatif's approach, which identifies more generalized forms of correspondence, working by analogy and association.[69] Yet, the force of this allusion, looking back across hundreds of lines to the events of an earlier vision, is to show how the interpretative labour that Reason once performed, configuring a narrative from the disparate events of contemporary experience, enables the work that Ymaginatif does now, encouraging Will to conceptualize his lived experience as an integrated whole. When Ymaginatif alludes to Reason's sermon, he demonstrates how *clergie* and *kynde* become integrated as part of Will's experience, and also identifies preaching as the discourse that facilitates this kind of integration. The sermon, which provides the discursive resources for the dreamer to grasp his own life story, has become part of that story in turn.

Towards the end of this passus, Will asks Ymaginatif whether or not baptism is necessary for salvation, a question which recalls his earlier encounter with Scripture, where his own salvation had seemed to be in doubt, and the consolation he derived from his memory of Holy Church, who received him at baptism, even though the precise issue here, the fate of the unbaptized, is different. Will

---

[69] Hanna, 'Langland's Ymaginatif', 82–3.

associates arguments for the necessity of baptism with clergie and with preaching, claiming to have heard them in the 'sermons' of 'clerkes': '"Alle þese clerkes", quod I þo, "þat on Crist leuen [believe]/ Seyen in hir sermons þat neiþer Sarsens ne Iewes/ Ne no creature [human being] of Cristes liknesse withouten Cristendom worþ saued"' (B.12.274–6). Ymaginatif replies in the language of clerical disputation, '"*Contra!*" quod Ymaginatif þoo', as though hearing an echo of Will's earlier confusion in this question (B.12.177): the 'sermons' he alludes to recall the 'sermon' of Augustine that he once 'sei3...writen' (B.10.454), academic texts, abstracted from life.[70] In answer to these dogmatic statements, Ymaginatif recalls the example of Trajan, posthumously baptized through the intercession of Gregory, a figure who Will has encountered in the middle part of the inner dream, and reminds him of other exceptional circumstances where people have been baptized through martyrdom and tribulation, rather than at the font. Here as before, dogmatic doctrinal statements are tempered and qualified by the lessons of the dreamer's own life, where clerical teaching and experiential encounters are bound together.

Ymaginatif is also able to discern Will's earlier anxieties about salvation in the form of this question, and offers him a Latin text to address them: '"*Saluabitur vix iustus in die iudicii;/ Ergo saluabitur!*" quod he, and seide na moore Latyn ["The just man shall scarcely be saved" on the day of judgement; therefore—he *shall* be saved!]' (B.12.278–9). This text, based on 1 Peter 4:18, has its own associations with parochial instruction and the elementary schoolroom: as Alford notes, the verse from Peter was cited in school grammars 'to point a lesson regarding the word *vix*', and was glossed in a similar way in the *Prick of Conscience*: '"If þe ryghtwys man", yhit says he,/ "Sal unnethes [scarcely] þan saved be,/...Ryghtwys men, als þe buk tells,/ Sal be saf þan and nan ells".'[71] When Ymaginatif addresses these lines to Will, he recalls the fearful implications of Scripture's sermon alongside the forms of reassurance associated with the font and the parish church. Understood in the light of Will's foregoing experience, this familiar Latin argues once more for the proper balance of hope and fear, a balance that emerges when clerical teaching is construed in the context of an interpreted life. When Will returns to the waking world at the end of this scene, he begins to apply the techniques of association and configuration that Ymaginatif has taught him, looking back over the events of the inner dream and considering them as part of a narrative: 'First how Fortune me failed at my mooste [greatest] nede,/ And

---

[70] Zeeman reads Ymaginatif's '*Contra*' as a 'clerical-style rebuke' that recalls the language of Holy Church's admonishments in the first vision: both figures are 'using the language of the classroom, but doing pastoral and spiritual work'; *Arts of Disruption*, 246, 253.

[71] See Alford, *Guide to the Quotations*, 81, citing examples from David Thomson, *A Descriptive Catalogue of Middle English Grammatical Texts* (New York: Garland, 1979); *Richard Morris's Prick of Conscience*, ed. Hanna and Wood, EETS os 342 (Oxford: Oxford University Press, 2013), 149 (ll. 5398–403). See also Zeeman, *Discourse of Desire*, 256–7.

how þat Elde manaced [threatened] me, my3te we euere mete;/ And how þat freres folwede folk þat was riche' (B.13.5–7). At the end of this summary, he remembers the Latin line Ymaginatif offers him here, 'how Ymaginatif seide, "*Vix iustus saluabitur*"' (B.13.19). The dreamer's efforts at emplotment in this scene are tentative and provisional, offering only a partial account of his own experience, yet the line with which he concludes, a text that encapsulates the necessary counterposition of hope and 'drede', expresses an organizing principle that might serve to configure these disparate events as a *holos*.

In the midst of this encounter, as the dreamer learns to construe his own experience in narrative terms, the poem raises the question of whether or not his narrated life might constitute a legitimate basis for a new text, a work like *Piers Plowman* itself. Ymaginatif himself is sceptical about poetic composition, which he associates with the idle distractions of an uninterpreted life. Will's poetic 'makynge' suggests that he has forgotten the finite term of his own life, and the imperatives it creates for penitential action: 'And þow medlest þee wiþ makynge [dabble in verse-making]—and my3test go seye þi Sauter,/ And bidde [pray] for hem þat 3yueþ þee breed' (B.12.16–17). There is no need to supplement the corpus of texts that already exists, Ymaginatif claims, or the sermons that make them available as tools for self-knowledge: 'for þer are bokes ynowe/ To telle men what Dowel is, . . . / And prechours to preue what it is' (B.12.18–19). In his initial reply, Will seems to accept the terms of this critique, defending his 'makynge' only as a form of 'solace' that allows him to engage more effectively in penance and prayer (B.12.21), but he goes on to argue that writing poetry is a vital counterpart to clerical instruction: if books or sermons could tell him 'What were Dowel', he argues, then 'Wolde I neuere do werk, but wende to holi chirche/ And þere bidde [pray] my bedes but [except] whan Ich ete or slepe' (B.12.26–8). This imagined return to Holy Church and to the simplest forms of lay devotion recalls the nostalgia that Will expressed when he renounced his academic learning in his complaint to Scripture. With this reply, however, the dreamer also recalls the lessons of the inner dream, that elementary instruction 'atte font' is only the starting point for a life of learning, where the lessons of clergie and kynde are perceived and interpreted as part of an integrated *holos*. Cautiously and indirectly, the dreamer suggests that 'makynge' itself is an expression of this creative, interpretative activity, a new form in which the 'self-constancy' of a narrative subject might arise through the mediation of texts.

Last Things

In the final, apocalyptic passus of *Piers Plowman*, the dreamer has another encounter with Elde. This encounter prompts one last consideration of his 'lyf-time' as an interpreted, narrative *holos*, shaped by preaching and teaching and by his longstanding commitments to Holy Church. In this part of the poem, it is Kynde who encourages the dreamer to overcome his spiritual inertia, his absorption in the conditions of his present moment, and to think about his life as a larger *holos*; as he nears the end of his life, a personification of nature urges him to construe his experience in narrative terms, drawing on his long exposure to clerical texts. This final scene from the longer versions of the poem also served as part of the inspiration for a continuation of the A text by John But. But, too, imagines the dreamer approaching the end of his life, but pursues the story further than Langland, describing Will's death and its aftermath. As Sarah Wood has recently argued, But was one of many early readers who understood *Piers Plowman* as 'Will's life history', recognizing the story of the dreamer's 'lyf-time' as an organizing principle for the poem.[72] In his conclusion to the A text, I will argue, he draws on Langland's account of an interpreted life, organized around ongoing ethical commitments, as he reflects on the value of his poetic project.

Elde first appears in the final passus of the B text as a form of tribulation that afflicts the whole community. Conscience faces an attack from the forces of Antichrist and calls on Kynde for help; in response, Kynde attacks the followers of Antichrist with a litany of diseases, which the poem imagines personified as his 'forreyours', soldiers who collect provisions for an army in hostile territory (B.20.80–7).[73] 'Elde þe hoor [grey-haired]' appears as a herald in the vanguard of this army, carrying the banner of Death (B.20.95).[74] In this allegorical battle scene, the poem suggests that a large part of the Christian community has fallen into the self-indulgent spiritual lethargy that characterized the dreamer's life in the 'lond of longynge'. Fortune's daughters, *Concupiscencia Carnis* and 'Coueitise of Eiȝes', and their companion 'Pride of Parfit Lyuynge', appear reimagined as Pride and and 'a lord þat lyueþ after liking of body' (B.20.71), and Elde arrives again as a harbinger of death, encouraging people to reform their lives while they still can.[75] Many people on the field feel the lure of an uninterpreted life, experienced as a simple succession of events; the arrival of Elde, meanwhile, encourages them to perceive the limits of the 'lyf-tyme', and the ethical imperatives that they create.

Here, as in the first inner dream, the threat of Elde alone is insufficient to produce an effort at reform. After Kynde attacks with illness and disease, Conscience calls on him to 'cesse and suffre [stop and wait]', to see if the people will abandon their pride and reform their lives, but when Kynde suspends his assault 'to se þe peple amende', he finds that the survivors become still more

---

[72] Wood, *Manuscript Tradition*, 98.   [73] *MED*, 'foreour, n.', senses 1(a) and (c).

[74] On the role of Elde in this chivalric allegory, see Ad Putter, 'Personifications of Old Age in Medieval Poetry: Charles d'Orléans and William Langland', *Review of English* Studies 63, no. 260 (2011): 405–6.

[75] On the connections between these scenes, see Szittya, *Antifraternal Tradition*, 274, and Barney, *Penn Commentary*, 5: 211.

inclined to bodily indulgence after the sufferings they have experienced (B.20.106–9). Fortune flatters 'þo fewe þat were alyue', encouraging them in lechery and idleness (B.20.110), and Life, who becomes Fortune's lover, declares that there is no need to 'drede neiþer Deeþ ne Elde', and tells her to abandon any thoughts of penance: 'for3yte sorwe and 3yue no3t of [do not care about] synne' (B.20.154–5).

In the first inner dream, Will was able to perceive the events of his life as a narrative using discursive resources derived from his long experience of preaching, transforming the seductive mirror of Fortune into an instructive *speculum*. In the final vision, however, no preachers interpret these events for the people who live through them. Conscience, who had preached on the life of Christ at the start of the seventh vision, now simply watches to see if the people will derive moral lessons from their own experiences. Meanwhile, other, corrupt figures usurp the office of preaching: the dreamer describes how Covetousness 'giled þe peple' with 'glosynges and gabbynges', while Simony 'preched to þe peple', encouraging 'prelates.../ To holden wiþ Antecrist, hir temporaltees [temporalities] to saue' (B.20.125–9). In this part of the poem as a whole, moreover, the work of preaching and pastoral care is increasingly delegated to the friars, who Langland presents as allies of Antichrist, working to undermine the church.[76]

As the allegorical battle unfolds, the dreamer, who has so far been present as a witness to these events, is suddenly and unexpectedly involved in the action. As he chases after Life, Elde runs the dreamer over, rendering him bald: 'And Elde anoon [straight] after hym, and ouer my heed yede [ran],/ And made me balled bifore and bare on þe croune' (B.20.183–4). When the dreamer complains, Elde abuses and assaults him, punching his teeth out and leaving him deaf and impotent.[77] This violent encounter with Elde offers a new version of the meeting that was first depicted in the inner dream, fulfilling the warnings Elde offered there: '"Man", quod he, "if I mete wiþ þee, by Marie of heuene,/ Thow shalt fynde Fortune þee faille at þi mooste neede..."' (B.11.28–9).[78] This confrontation, which has also been the subject of repeated admonitions from Ymaginatif, now emerges once more in the dreamer's phenomenological experience, awaiting narrative interpretation.

It is Kynde who helps the dreamer to construe this experience as part of a plot. After the assault of Elde, Will asks Kynde to 'awreke [avenge]' him by bringing him 'out of care', declaring that 'I wolde ben hennes [far from here]' (B.20.201–3). The dreamer desires to abandon his life rather that to remain alive under these

---

[76] See Szittya, *Antifraternal Tradition*, 276–87; Barney, *Penn Commentary*, 5: 207–8, 226–38; Wood, *Conscience*, 87–106.

[77] On the parallels between physical violence and aggressive, insulting speech in this scene, see Zeeman, *Arts of Disruption*, 251.

[78] See, for example, Putter, 'Personifications of Old Age', 404. Hanna makes a related argument that the dreamer's baldness recalls Recklessness's comment in the inner dream that a man 'may stoupe tyme yno3 whan he shal tyne þe crowne! [loose his hair]' (B.11.36); 'Reading Prophecy / Reading Piers', *YLS* 12 (1998): 156, and see Barney, *Penn Commentary*, 5: 219.

circumstances, an 'abnegation of agency', as Zeeman writes, that is 'almost certainly the final temptation' he will face.[79] Kynde, however, replies with a new allegorical itinerary, telling the dreamer to make his way to the barn of Unity and take refuge there for the time that remains: 'hold þee [keep yourself] þere euere, til I sende for þee' (B.20.201–5). Even now, it seems, action and interpretation are possible and important. In this scene, as D. Vance Smith has observed, the poem recognizes a distinction between a passive experience of old age as the gradual loss of powers and abilities, and 'coming to a good end' as an active, ethical endeavour.[80]

The work of emplotment is central to this movement from passive experience to active interpretation. When Grace constructs the barn, 'þat hous Vnite', in the previous passus, he explains that Unity means 'Holy Chirche on Englissh' (B.19.329). Unity here recalls the 'parisshe chirche' of the first inner dream, the site of baptism and burial, which mark the limits of the Christian life, and of the preaching and pastoral care that render it meaningful (B.11.65). It also recalls the personification from passus 1, who first encouraged Will to perceive his life in narrative terms as she addressed her sermon to him. When Kynde directs the dreamer back to Unity after his encounter with Elde, he is directing him back towards 'Holy Chirche' in all these senses, inviting him to consider his present moment as part of a larger, interpreted 'lyf-time', and to recover from his own memories the forms of clerical instruction that are no longer available in the contemporary, apocalyptic scene. The dreamer trembles as he confronts his own death, just as he did when he listened to Scripture's sermon ('And Deeþ drogh nei3 [drew near] me; for drede gan I quake [I trembled]', B.20.200), but his relationship to Holy Church offers a source of consolation: once again, Will experiences the fear of death in the context of the lessons he has derived from his life.[81]

Kynde adds that Will should 'konne som craft' as the end of his life approaches, prompting further questions from the dreamer about what this might be:

'Counseilleþ me, Kynde', quod I, 'what craft be best to lerne?'	*Advise*
'Lerne to loue', quod Kynde, 'and leef alle oþere.'	*leave everything else*
'How shal I come to catel so, to cloþe me and to feede?'	*money*
'And þow loue lelly, lakke shal þee neuere	*If; loyally*
Weede ne worldly mete, while þi lif lasteþ.'	*Clothing*
	(B.20.207–11)

---

[79] Zeeman, *Arts of Disruption*, 294.   [80] Smith, *Arts of Dying*, 135.
[81] Aers, *Beyond Reformation?*, 112, argues that Will responds differently to the larger community when he encounters Elde and Death, because 'he has been on a pilgrimage of continual conversion, cultivating habits to resist the de-Christianization led by Antichrist'. Those habits, I suggest, include the capacity to understand his life in narrative terms, sustained by his relationship to Holy Church, and recalled for him now through this encounter with Kynde.

Davis reads this command to love as the surprising answer to Will's request to be avenged: 'Kynde's answer to Will's plea...to meet "lakke" with love, is its own form of restorative "vengeance"', restoring a kind of balance that has become obscured in Will's experience.[82] The discernment of love is also closely related to the making of narratives in *Piers Plowman*. The injunction 'Lerne to loue...while þi lif lasteþ' echoes Dame Study's instruction to 'louye as longe as þow durest', and her observation, later echoed by Patience and by Piers Plowman himself, that love is the 'science' most 'souereyn [beneficial] for þe soule' (B.10.207–8), as I noted in Chapter 3. This is the principle that guides and directs a virtuous life, and that enables the configurational work of emplotment, allowing the interpreter to distinguish the essential from the ephemeral. When Kynde addresses this injunction to the dreamer, directing him back to Unity, he also recalls the language of Will's baptismal promises: as Holy Church reminded him in passus 1, 'Thow brouȝtest me borwes [sponsors, guarantors] my biddyng to fulfille,/ And to louen me leelly [loyally] þe while þi lif dureþ [lasts]' (B.1.76–7). In the final passus, Kynde proposes love as the principle and the practice that will allow the dreamer to construe his life as a coherent narrative, conferring significance on his lived experience. Recalling his promise to 'loue...leelly' for the term of his life, he encourages him to perceive his 'self-constancy' in relation to his ethical commitments, even as the time of those obligations draws to an end.

The twelfth passus that survives partly or completely in three manuscripts of the A text of the poem provides another account of the dreamer's life as an interpreted *holos*, this time written from a perspective after his death.[83] This passus concludes with nineteen lines that refer to the dreamer in the third person and identify 'Iohan But' as the poet who 'made þis ende' to the poem (A.12.106–7).[84] Middleton argued that But was in fact responsible for the whole of passus 12, which reworks material from earlier in A and later in B and C, and includes elements that seem inconsistent with both the arguments and the

---

[82] Davis, *Books of Nature*, 131.
[83] The only complete text of A.12 survives in Oxford, Bodleian Library, MS Rawlinson Poetry 137; this is the only manuscript to preserve the final lines naming John But. The first 88 lines of A.12 appear in New York, Pierpont Morgan Library, MS M 818, and the first 11 lines in Oxford, University College, MS 45. Two A-text manuscripts that are now damaged at the end could once have contained A.12: Kane makes this case for Lincoln's Inn MS 150 (*A text*, ed. Kane, 11), and Míċeál Vaughan for Dublin, Trinity College, MS 213, D.4.12; Vaughan, 'Filling the Gap in *Piers Plowman* A: Trinity College, Dublin, MS 213', 87–106 in *'Yee? Baw for Bokes': Essays on Medieval Manuscripts and Poetics in Honor of Hoyt N. Duggan*, ed. Calabrese and Stephen H. A. Shepherd (Los Angeles: Marymount Institute Press, 2013). See also Wood, *Manuscript Tradition*, 105.
[84] Edith Rickert identified John But as a royal messenger who died in 1387: 'John But, Messenger and Maker', *Modern Philology* 11 (1913): 107–16. This identification was challenged by Scase, '"First Reckon to Richard": John But's *Piers Plowman* and the Politics of Allegiance', *YLS* 11 (1997): 49–66. Hanna (*William Langland*, 29–30) identifies a Norwich wool merchant called John Butt as another potential candidate, and Adams (*Langland and the Rokele Family*, 25–7) notes connections between the Norfolk Butts and the Rokele family, which raise the possibility that John But may have known Langland personally. Simon Horobin, however, has argued that But was most likely a scribe, with no personal knowledge of the poet: Horobin, 'John But and the Ending of the A Version of *Piers Plowman*', *YLS* 33 (2019): 127–42.

narrative of the preceding passūs.[85] Wood has recently endorsed this view of passus 12 as 'inauthentic scribal pastiche rather than authorial composition'.[86] Here, I follow Middleton and Wood in reading passus 12 as the work of John But, an attempt to conclude an unfinished A text that draws on his knowledge of the poem's later versions, and I argue that, in his account of the dreamer's death, But responds to and extends Langland's own strategies for interpreting the 'lyf-time'.

A.12 takes up the story of the third vision after Will complains to Scripture about the doctrine of predestination and expresses his desire to return to more elementary forms of instruction. In the B text, this is the outburst that provokes Scripture's rebuke, as she impugns the dreamer for his lack of self-knowledge, '*Multi multa sciunt et seipsos nesciunt* [Many know many things, but do not know themselves]' (B.11.3), and that leads into the inner dream, where Will reflects on the narrative shape of his own life, mediated by the discourses of preaching and instruction. In But's conclusion, both Clergy and Scripture rebuke the dreamer and refuse to continue his education, but when Will professes his continued loyalty to Scripture she relents and directs him to Kynde Wit, instructing a 'clerioun [schoolboy]' called *Omnia-probate* ['Test all things', 1 Thessalonians 5:21] to go with him (A.12.49–50). The narrative then moves forward suddenly: the dreamer remarks that 'Many ferlys [wonders] me byfel [happened to me] in a fewe ȝeris' (A.12.58) and, as he moves into the middle part of his life, he encounters Hunger and a personification of quartan fever, 'Feuere-on-þe-ferþe day' (A.12.82), who introduce themselves as associates of Death, and so resemble the heralds and 'forreyours' of B.20. The passus concludes in the voice of John But, who records that, once Will had composed *Piers Plowman*, 'Deþ delt him a dent [struck him a blow] and drof him to þe erþe,/ And is closed [buried] vnder clour [a mound of earth]—Crist haue his soule!' (A.12.104–5).[87]

Although it lacks the injunction to self-knowledge and the framing device of the inner dream, But's conclusion nevertheless responds to the dreamer's spiritual crisis by considering the shape of his life as a whole. Writing after the death of the dreamer, who he identifies as a representation of Langland himself, it is But who takes up the task of narrative interpretation, configuring the events of Will's experience into a meaningful *holos*. The sudden move forward through 'a fewe ȝeris' of time (A.12.58) recalls the transition through 'fourty wynter and a fifte moore' in the inner dream (B.11.47), which the dreamer experiences as a simple

---

[85] Middleton, 'Making a Good End: John But as a Reader of *Piers Plowman*', 243–66 in *Medieval English Studies Presented to George Kane*, ed. Edward Donald Kennedy, Ronald Waldron, and Joseph Wittig (Woodbridge: Brewer, 1988).

[86] Wood, *Manuscript Tradition*, 114. Schmidt, however, reads all but the final nineteen lines as Langland's own abandoned attempt to continue the poem, parts of which he later adapted for B and C (*Parallel Text*, ed. Schmidt, 2: 120–21, 600).

[87] *Parallel Text*, ed. Schmidt, 1: 449, has 'closed under clom'; for the emendation to 'clour' see Vaughan, 'Where is Wille Buried? *Piers Plowman*, A.12.105', *YLS* 25 (2011): 131–6, and *MED*, 'clour, n.', sense 1.

succession of events, but which he briskly elides when he configures his life experience as a narrative. For But, this prolepsis works in a similar way, bringing the 'lyf-time' into focus as a single unit of interpreted, narrative experience. Like Elde in the final passūs of B and C, Hunger and 'Feuere-on-þe-ferþe day' herald the arrival of death, but But is able to dramatize the end of the dreamer's life, an event that Will could only anticipate, mapping out the whole of his 'lyf-time' over the course of a single passus.

As she rebukes the dreamer at the start of passus A.12, Scripture calls for his baptism. Scripture tells Clergy that he should offer Will no further instruction unless he 'schriuen [confessed] were/ Of þe kynde cardinal Wit, and cristned in a fonte' (A.12.14–15). Middleton reads this moment as evidence for But's authorship of the whole passus, because it ignores 'the literal sense of the antecedent text', where Will has discussed his earlier baptism with Holy Church.[88] Wood suggests that this 'slip' in the literal sense is produced by But's desire to perform 'spiritually efficacious labour on Will's behalf', comparing this moment with the posthumous baptism of the pagan judge in *St Erkenwald*.[89] I propose, however, that these lines contain a deliberate allusion to the dreamer's earlier encounter with Holy Church, to his early education at the font, and to the baptismal promises that will endure for the term of his life. But refers to the dreamer's baptism in order to frame the final passus as a life story that runs from baptism to death, organized around lifelong commitments to 'louen ... leelly' (B.1.77). The 'clerioun' *Omnia-probate* who accompanies the dreamer on his journey to Kynde Wit provides another link to early education in this scene, and his name, 'Test all Things', recalls the *thema* of Holy Church's sermon, 'Whan alle tresors arn tried [tested] ... treuþe is þe beste' (B.1.85). The allusion to baptism here provides an alternate version of the scene where Will recalls his relationship to Holy Church in the B-text inner dream, except that there it was the dreamer who began the work of interpreting his own life, whereas here the trajectory from baptism to burial is visible only to But.

Confronting his death near the end of A.12, Will receives advice from 'Feuereon-þe-ferþe day' about the best way to spend his remaining time, a passage that echoes Kynde's advice to the dreamer in B.20, as Middleton notes.[90] In these lines, the dreamer is invited to consider his 'lyf-time' as a whole: Fever tells him to 'lyue as þis lyf is ordeyned for the', and 'do after Dowel whil þi dayes duren' (A.12.90, 94). Yet, it is But who explains how Will interpreted this advice, setting about the composition of the poem 'þat here is wryten and oþer werkes boþe/ Of Peres þe Plowman and mechel [many] puple also' (A.12.101–2).[91] For Middleton, these lines mark another departure from the logic of Langland's poem, where

---

[88] Middleton, 'Making a Good End', 259–60. [89] Wood, *Manuscript Tradition*, 114–15.
[90] Middleton, 'Making a Good End', 253.
[91] Warner has argued that But's reference to 'oþer werkes' implies his knowledge of other poems by Langland, distinct from the multiple versions of *Piers Plowman*: 'John But and the Other Works that Will Wrought (*Piers Plowman* A XII 101-2)', *Notes and Queries* 52, no. 1 (2005): 13–18. For a sceptical

poetic composition is imagined in opposition to useful, penitential activity.[92] As we have seen, this is the view of Ymaginatif, who criticizes Will for 'medl[ing] wiþ makynge' when he might instead 'go seye þ[e] Sauter' (B.11.16). Yet But, who is happy to echo Ymaginatif when he describes his own activities ('and for he medleþ of makyng, he made þis ende'), perhaps accepts the dreamer's self-defence in this encounter, that poetic composition, which draws on the narrative resources of existing texts, including sermons, can also supplement these instructive discourses in distinctive and valuable ways (A.12.109).

In the inner dream of B.11, the dreamer comes to understand the successive events of his life as part of an interpreted narrative, drawing on the preaching he has heard and the instruction he has received from Holy Church. Emplotment takes place within the allegorical action, as Will begins to reconcile himself to difficult doctrine by understanding it in the larger context of his own, interpreted experience. But performs a more straightforward act of emplotment in A.12, telling the story of the dreamer's life to supply a conclusion to the poem. Even so, But recalls the poem's own conception of the limits of the 'lyf-time' by framing this passus with references to baptism and burial and, in the encounter with Fever, he allows the narrator a moment of clarity, as Will perceives the narrative shape of his life and begins a new effort at amendment. But's last image of the poet, composing *Piers Plowman* as death approaches, suggests that the labour of poetic composition might supply opportunities for Will to 'loue...leelly', and to affirm his 'self-constancy' amidst the changing circumstances of his contemporary experience.

* * *

Over the course of successive encounters with Holy Church, Scripture, Ymaginatif, and Kynde, the dreamer comes to understand his own life as an integrated narrative, using resources that are drawn from a wide range of clerical texts, and techniques of interpretation that derive from his experience of preaching. These encounters take place at points in the poem when Will has become absorbed in his present circumstances, experiencing time as an undifferentiated succession of events, and they encourage him to think about the present time in relation to the other events of his life, configured and interpreted as a narrative. The dreamer recovers from his lethargy, from his unguarded absorption in the 'wondres' of direct experience, and from his sorrowful resignation in the face of old age, by recovering forms of instruction that invite him to conceptualize his life as a whole. For Langland, as for Ricoeur, narrative serves to structure a sense of 'self-

---

response, see *Parallel Text*, ed. Schmidt, 2: 600. Warner has more recently considered the possibility that Langland's 'oþer werkes' included the alliterative poem *William of Palerne: Myth of Piers Plowman*, 22–36.

[92] Middleton, 'Making a Good End', 253.

sameness' and 'self-constancy' that finds expression in ethical commitments: the dreamer recalls the promises he made at his baptism, and uses them to evaluate his later life, a strategy that was often encouraged in medieval preaching, and that found some complex elaboration in the sermons of Robert Rypon. In the 'lond of longynge', Will perceives that his baptismal promises create a bond with his parish church, the place where he should be buried, and finds that the early instruction he received at the font serves to counterbalance the difficult doctrine he has learned in later life: the ethical commitments that structure his narrated life create obligations for him, but they offer him consolation, too. After his violent encounter with Elde, this longstanding relationship with Holy Church allows the dreamer to reconcile himself with his new predicament, and to recognize the work that remains for him in the time he has left.

Two of the scenes I have considered in this chapter involve acts of preaching— both Holy Church and Scripture deliver sermons to Will—but all four encourage the dreamer to recall the preaching he has heard at other times and to think about the resources it provides to understand his life in narrative terms. Holy Church directs the dreamer to his earliest instruction: catechetical instruction at the font and sermons from the pulpit, where narratives from scripture were first made available to him. Scripture, meanwhile, recalls the sermons of Holy Church as a counterweight to her own demanding lessons about predestination. Ymaginatif looks back to both these earlier scenes, and to other scenes of preaching in the poem, recalling Reason's sermon on the half-acre for example, and Kynde invites the dreamer to recall his long relationship with Holy Church as he confronts his imminent death. Over the course of these interlinked episodes, I have argued, the poem draws attention to the way that clerical instruction becomes part of lived experience, a point that Holy Church first illustrates to Will when he laments his lack of 'kynde knowynge': sermons offer a narrative discourse that mediates their listeners' experience of the world, and provide resources to conceptualize the 'lyftyme' as a *holos*, but they also form part of that experience in turn, a 'tresor' to be 'tried' against the unfolding events of human life, preaching to be 'preued' in new circumstances. *Piers Plowman* explores the way that 'clergie' and 'kynde' condition one another over the course of a lifetime, as the dreamer recovers clerical instruction from his own experience and uses it to organize that experience in turn. In the final passus, it is a version of Kynde who recalls the preaching and teaching of Holy Church, who directs the dreamer to take refuge in the barn of Unity, and to learn the craft of love.

The encounter with Ymaginatif is also a moment of self-conscious reflection on the process of writing *Piers Plowman* itself. Looking back across the inner dream to the sermons of Reason and Holy Church, Ymaginatif suggests that the same acts of narrative interpretation that serve to constitute an individual identity might also reveal the underlying coherence of the poem *Piers Plowman*. Here, I have argued, Langland considers the extent to which the work of emplotment, dramatized and interrogated in the poem's many scenes of preaching, has given rise to the poem itself. John But's conclusion to the A text, meanwhile, shows an engaged, early reader thinking through the relationship between the shape of the poem as a whole and the shape of the dreamer's narrated life. But recovers strategies for narrating the 'lyf-time' that arise in the poem through engagement with preaching, and uses them to memorialize the poet, presenting the work of composing *Piers Plowman* as the activity that confers coherence on an interpreted life, a life-long commitment, and an expression of 'self-constancy'.

5
Histories of the Self, the World, and the Sermon
Anima and the Tree of Charity

In the fifth vision of *Piers Plowman*, the dreamer encounters Anima, a strange, disembodied personification of his own soul, and engages him in a conversation about charity. Will begins this conversation in a fragile state, alienated from himself and ostracized from his community, but Anima works to rehabilitate him, encouraging him first to articulate a narrative of his own experiences and then to understand this narrative in relation to the larger framework of eschatological history. In the B text of the poem, the meeting with Anima culminates in an inner dream where these narratives are integrated in surprising ways, as Will sees the Tree of Charity growing in the human heart, and his request to taste the fruit, apparently the climax of his search for Do-wel, produces instead a re-enactment of the Fall. Preaching is an important topic in Will's conversation with Anima and a major influence on Anima's techniques of argument and persuasion. Throughout this encounter, Anima acknowledges the way that sermons mediate lived experience and supply narrative structures to make sense of it. Early in their exchange, when Will unwittingly reveals his own *curiositas*, Anima criticizes the 'inparfit... prechours and techeris' who have encouraged this vice and spread confusion through the larger Christian community (B.15.95). As he prompts the dreamer to perceive himself as a 'self-constant' subject, and as an ethical actor in a larger, interpreted history, however, Anima draws on techniques of interpretation that have become strongly associated with preaching and pastoral care in the poem, encouraging Will to seek out manifestations of charity in the disparate events of his own experience, and to configure narratives from them.

A study of the dreamer's encounter with Anima forms a fitting final chapter for this book because this part of the poem returns to so many different aspects of Langland's thought about preaching and the forms of narrative understanding it enables and sustains. Anima shows how personal narratives, of the kind I considered in Chapter 4, can be integrated with the large-scale, political and eschatological narratives I considered in Chapter 1: the dreamer's life story unfolds in relation to the story of salvation, and a turning point in his quest for Do-wel coincides with an axial moment in the time of human history. Anima's critique of curious preaching and his promotion of charity as its antidote recall the

Preaching and Narrative in Piers Plowman. Alastair Bennett, Oxford University Press. © Alastair Bennett 2023.
DOI: 10.1093/oso/9780192886262.003.0006

arguments of Study's complaint and the allegorical drama of the feast of Conscience, which I discussed in Chapter 3. Anima also imagines preaching as an ongoing activity of narrative interpretation and pastoral care, echoing the hard-won lessons of Piers Plowman's experience on the half-acre, considered in Chapter 2. When the dreamer sees the Tree of Charity in the inner dream that follows from this encounter, Piers Plowman is there to explain it to him, taking up a new kind of pastoral-agricultural labour that combines the tasks of explication and cultivation. Before the final, historical movement of his poem begins, Langland here gathers together his thoughts about preaching, the conditions in which it takes place, and the forms of narrative understanding it makes available for its listeners.

On several occasions in his speech, Anima presents a series of *distinctiones* on a particular subject, itemizing different aspects of a topic for further discussion. Contemporary readers noted this technique: Wendy Scase draws attention to notes in three C-text manuscripts that mark the beginning of a 'distinctio caritatis' when Liberum Arbitrium, who replaces Anima in this version of the poem, describes Charity as a personification at C.16.296, or when he identifies Holy Church with charity at C.17.126 [Figure 5.1].[1] Preachers who used the 'modum modernum [modern method]' of preaching would structure their sermons in this way, generating *distinctiones* from their chosen *thema* and then developing them through exegesis, illustration, and the citation of confirmatory authorities.[2] We have already seen that preachers could use this exegetical procedure to structure a narrative, and that Langland represents this process in *Piers Plowman*: Conscience uses a set of exegetical *distinctiones* on the names and titles of Christ as the basis for an act of emplotment in the seventh vision, for example. In Will's encounter with Anima, however, the poem offers a reflective account of the way this process

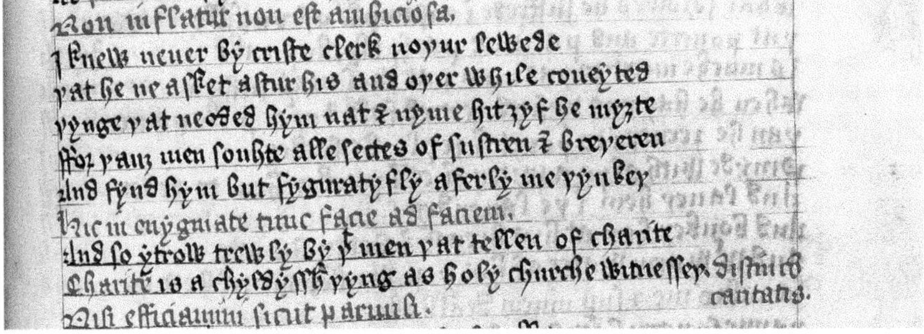

Figure 5.1 A passage from *Piers Plowman* C.16 with the marginal annotation that identifies a 'distinctio caritatis'. London, Senate House Library, MS SL V 17, fol. 69r.

---

[1] Scase, *New Anticlericalism*, 109, 207 note 104.
[2] Waleys, *De modo componendi sermones*, 1.vi, ed. Charland, 345.

works, as Anima elaborates *distinctiones* and then challenges the dreamer to construe them in narrative terms. Like many medieval preachers, Anima also employs visual metaphors to represent the relationship between a concept or a *thema* and the *distinctiones* that develop from it: perhaps the most commonplace of these, the tree with roots and branches, recurs at different moments in his dialogue with Will and in the concluding vision of the Tree of Charity itself. I argue that *figurae* like this represent multiple *distinctiones* as part of a tensive unity, analogous to the 'discordant concordance' of events in an interpreted plot. The poem makes its most intensive use of these figured *distinctiones* as it works to synthesize different kinds of narrative, rendering the universal and the personal as aspects of the same complex, integrated whole.

Anima draws on the discursive resources of preaching to position the dreamer's life in relation to eschatological history, imagining events from different orders of experience, and different scales of historical time, as part of a single narrative. In the later part of his discussion with Will, however, he also shows that preaching has a history of its own, and acknowledges that sermons have taken different forms in other times and places. As we will see in the final section of this chapter, Anima treats preaching itself as a manifestation of charity in this part of the poem, paying particular attention to evangelical preaching addressed to non-Christians. He considers the preaching of the apostles, the desert fathers, the early friars, and Augustine of Canterbury, all of whom offer examples for bishops in his own time who are appointed to sees in the Holy Land but are reluctant to take the risk of preaching there. This part of the poem also contains an account of the prophet Mohammed whose sermons have converted many people to Islam—the only extended depiction of non-Christian preaching in *Piers Plowman*. Anima looks to different examples from Christian history to imagine a form of preaching that might counteract the preaching of Mohammed, matching its persuasive power but promoting an alternative doctrine. Even as he positions the dreamer's lived experience in the narrative of salvation, then, Anima considers other people for whom this narrative is not available, in part because of the absence of effective Christian preaching. He deploys examples from his history of preaching in radical, experimental ways as he tries to imagine the kind of sermon that might convert non-Christians in the Holy Land in his own time.

'Whider I sholde and wherof I cam': Anima and the Narrated Self

Will encounters Anima at a moment of personal crisis. A long, fruitless search for Do-wel in the waking world has taken its toll on his mental faculties and his social relationships, to the point where his sense of himself is fragmented and confused: 'my wit weex and wanyed [waxed and waned] til I a fool weere;/ And some lakkede [criticized] my lif—allowed [approved] it fewe –/ And leten me for a lorel...' (B.15.3–4); 'folk helden me a fool; and in þat folie I rauede,/ Til Reson hadde ruþe [pity] on me and rokked me aslepe' (B.15.10–11). The crisis that the dreamer faces in these lines is more extreme than the spiritual lethargy that Holy Church discerns in the first passus, the product of an unexamined life, experienced as the simple succession of events; this waking episode finds him in a state of personal and social disassociation and intense distress. In the dream that follows, however, Anima helps the dreamer to recover his personal and social identity and to understand his place in the larger scheme of Christian history by configuring narratives from the disparate events of his own experience and from the texts and materials of religious instruction.[3] In lines that seem to summarize their conversation as a whole, Will says that Anima has helped him make sense of where he has come from and where he is going, to understand his life in narrative terms, and that this, in turn, has enabled him to discern some new knowledge about his own nature: 'I seiȝ, as it sorcerie were, a sotil [subtle] þing wiþalle—/ Oon wiþouten tonge and teeþ, tolde [who told] me whider I sholde/ And wherof I cam and of what kynde' (B.15.13–14).

Anima introduces himself to Will by listing his many names, which change according to what he is doing. These lines are based on a well-known passage from the *Etymologies* of Isidore of Seville that was cited in other authorities including the pseudo-Augustinian *De spiritu et anima*; Anima will later acknowledge these sources ('Austyn and Ysodorus,.../ Nempnede me þus to name,' B.15.37–8), and quote the Latin passage in its entirety.[4] As Anima presents the passage here, however, it resembles the *divisio thematis* of a scholastic sermon, the announcement of a multipart answer to the dreamer's single question, 'What are ye called...?' (B.15.22):

'The whiles I quykke þe cors', quod he, 'called am I *Anima*;	*animate; body; Soul*
And when I wilne and wold, *Animus* Ich hatte;	*desire; Intention*
And for þat I kan and knowe, called am I *Mens*, "Þouȝte";	*understand; Mind*
And whan I make mone to God, *Memoria* is my name;	*pray; Memory*
And whan I deme domes and do as truþe techeþ,	*make judgements*
Thanne is *Racio* my riȝt name, "Reson" on Englissh;	*Reason*

---

[3] Sarah Star has described this encounter with Anima as a 'prosthetic intervention', which address the dreamer's social and mental liminality at this moment in the poem; Star, 'Will's Prosthesis', *YLS* 35 (2021): 11–27. On the significance of the dreamer's folly in this moment, see also Julie C. Paulson, '*Piers Plowman* and the Wisdom of Folly', *YLS* 36 (2022): 11–43.

[4] On the quotation from Isidore's *Etymologies* and its citation in other texts, see Alford, *Guide to the Quotations*, 92, and Lawler, *Penn Commentary*, 4:149–50. For a detailed discussion of Langland's translation and a comparison with John Trevisa's translation of the same passage as cited in Bartholomeus Anglicus' *De proprietatibus rerum*, see Davis, *Books of Nature*, 172–5.

And whan I feele þat folk telleþ, my firste name is *Sensus*—	*perceive; Sense*
And þat is wit and wisdom, þe welle of alle craftes;	*source; skills*
And whan I chalange or chalange noȝt, chepe or refuse,	*claim; buy*
Thanne am I Conscience ycalled, Goddes clerk and his notarie;	*scribe*
And whan I loue leelly Oure Lord and alle oþere,	*faithfully*
Thanne is "Lele Loue" my name, and in Latyn *Amour*;	*Love*
And whan I flee fro þe flessh and forsake þe careyne,	*corpse*
Thanne am I spirit spechelees, and *Spiritus* þanne Ich hatte.	*Spirit*

(B.15.23–36)

Mary Carruthers has argued that while Anima appears at first to be an enigmatic figure in the tradition of *obscuritas*, a 'sotil þing' (B.15.12) inviting meditation and speculative thought, this subsequent account of his names and operations draws on a different allegorical topos, the *pictura*, offering a lucid, systematic overview of a complex subject.[5] Carruthers notes that the *pictura* was a familiar device in popular preaching where it could supply a visual image for the sermon's exegetical structure, an 'imagined form' for the 'scholastic *distinctio*'.[6] Introducing himself in this way, Anima announces a preoccupation of the passus to come, initiating the first of several attempts to think in schematic, figural ways about exegetical structures, and about the narrative logic that underpins them. The interplay of English and Latin here also recalls preacherly exegesis. Katharine Breen describes this passage as an innovative example of 'hybrid of macaronic thinking', where English and Latin terms supplement and qualify each other, providing new ways to conceptualize the soul. These hybrid forms were commonplace in vernacular sermons, where preachers would elaborate English *distinctiones* from a Latin *thema*, supporting them with proof texts in one or both languages.[7]

Anima's *distinctiones* have a latent narrative dimension. His composite identity emerges through a series of 'whan…thanne' constructions as the gradual accumulation of different actions under different circumstances. The activities he describes are loosely framed by the shape of a human life, beginning 'The whiles I quykke þe cors', and ending 'whan I flee fro þe flessh'. As a *pictura*, moreover, Anima's account of his operations supplies a guide for future actions: as

---

[5] Carruthers, 'Allegory Without the Teeth: Some Reflections on Figural Language in *Piers Plowman*', *YLS* 19 (2005): 35–7. Carruthers compares Langland's treatment of Anima with a passage from the sermon for the First Sunday in Lent from British Library, Royal MS 18 B XXIII; here, the preacher introduces the puzzling image of a sciopod, a creature with a single leg and one enormous foot, but then numbers and itemizes its features in a systematic way to map the concerns of his sermon; see *Middle English Sermons*, ed. Ross, 77.
[6] Carruthers, 'Allegory Without the Teeth', 41–2, and see also 34.
[7] Breen, *Machines of the Mind*, 308.

Carruthers notes, the *pictura* was often imagined as a map, like Piers Plowman's itinerary to Truth in the second vision of the poem, or Study's directions to Clergie in the third.[8] Elizabeth Robertson has argued that Anima's self-description already constitutes the 'dramatic biography of an agential soul' at this point in the poem.[9] I argue, however, that these lines present only the raw materials for narrative composition, the 'structures that call for narration' in ordinary experience in Ricoeur's account of *mimesis*[1]. Indeed, in his acts of recollection, perception, and anticipation, Anima himself displays the 'concordant discordance' of the Augustinian soul, stretching out to perceive time as it passes. He challenges the dreamer to construe his various operations as part of a plot, to establish them in a relation of 'discordant concordance', through the interpretative choices that Ricoeur identifies with *mimesis*[2]. Anima concludes his introduction by inviting the dreamer to choose from among his many names: 'now þow myȝt chese [choose]/ How þow coueitest to calle me, now þow knowest alle my names' (B.15.38–9). This is an invitation to distinguish and prioritize among the various operations of the soul, to discern the essential principle that might organize a narrative.

In response to this challenge, however, the dreamer inadvertently reveals his own *curiositas*, a disorderly and indiscriminate desire for knowledge that mitigates against the work of narrative composition, as I argued in Chapter 3.[10] Will replies with a flippant comparison between Anima's names and the many titles of a bishop, leading Anima to suspect his intentions: 'now I se þi wille!' Anima declares, 'Thow woldest knowe and konne þe cause of alle hire names,/ And of myne, if þow myȝtest...' (B.15.44–6). The dreamer, oblivious to his mistake, openly declares his desire to know 'Alle þe sciences vnder sonne and alle þe sotile craftes', and Anima rebukes him, calling him 'inparfit' and 'oon of Prides knyȝtes' (B.15.48, 50). Rebecca Davis argues that the poem negotiates the risks and rewards of encyclopaedic writing in this scene: adapting Isidore, Anima deploys the resources of the encyclopaedia to distinguish and organize his names and functions, but in doing so he stimulates the dreamer's desire for knowledge that exceeds his needs and capacities.[11] Stephanie Batkie makes a similar point about Anima's use of exegetical *distinctiones*: these present an organized catalogue of information, but they also show how knowledge can proliferate, creating temptations for the curious listener. Responding to Carruthers, Batkie argues that Anima is recast in the enigmatic tradition of *obscuritas* at this point, having exposed the dreamer's problematic 'delight in organized information' by offering himself as a *figura*.[12]

---

[8] Carruthers, 'Allegory Without the Teeth', 38–9, and see also Breen, *Machines of the Mind*, 311–12.
[9] Elizabeth Robertson, 'Soul-Making in *Piers Plowman*', *YLS* 34 (2020): 34.
[10] Middleton ('William Langland's "Kynde Name"', 45) describes the 'characteristic deflection of [Will's] desire for self-knowledge into curiosity for "science"' in this scene.
[11] Davis, *Books of Nature*, 172.
[12] Batkie, '"Thanne artow inparfit": Learning to Read in *Piers Plowman*', *Chaucer Review* 45, no. 2 (2010): 179.

Anima's rebuke to Will initiates a polemical attack on proud, acquisitive preachers that echoes the concerns of Study's complaint in the third vision.[13] Like Study, Anima attacks 'Freres and fele oþere maistres' who preach on difficult academic topics, appealing to the intellectual vanity of wealthy laymen while neglecting the spiritual needs of the *commune* as a whole: 'Ye moeuen [adduce] materes vnmesurables [unfathomable] to tellen of þe Trinite,/ That oftetymes þe lewed peple of hir bileue doute [doubt their faith]' (B.15.70–2). As we saw in Chapter 3, Anima accuses these preachers of the pride and profiteering that Bernard of Clairvaux associates with *curiositas*: they perform their 'heigh clergie . . . / Moore for pompe þan for pure charite' (B.15.79–80), and they cater to the rich in the hope of financial reward: 'That I lye no3t, loo!—for lordes ye plesen,/ And reuerencen þe riche þe raþer for his siluer' (B.15.80–1). Their ostentatious, academic discourse produces doubt and confusion among 'þe lewed peple' even as it indulges the *curiositas* of their patrons. Anima's critique of 'freres' and 'maistres' suggests that preaching like this has exacerbated the dreamer's *curiostias*, encouraging his indiscriminate desire for knowledge. In place of the sermons that might model and cultivate the discrimination required for emplotment, Will has been exposed to preaching that erodes and undermines the capacity to think in narrative terms.

This critique of 'freres' and 'maistres' gives rise to a new *figura*, where Anima compares the priesthood to the roots of a tree, whose condition affects the branches, flowers, and leaves of the church as a whole:

As holynesse and honeste out of Holy Chirche spredeþ	
Thoru3 lele libbynge men þat Goddes lawe techen,	*men who live righteously*
Right so out of Holi Chirche alle yueles spredeþ	
There inparfit preesthode is, prechours and techeris.	*imperfect*
And se it by ensaumple in somer tyme on trowes:	*trees*
Ther some bowes ben leued and some bereþ none,	*leafy*
Ther is a meschief in þe more of swiche manere bowes.	*disease; root*
Right so persons and preestes and prechours of Holi Chirche	
Is þe roote of þe right feiþ to rule þe peple;	
Ac þer þe roote is roten, reson woot þe soþe,	
Shal neuere flour ne fruyt, ne fair leef be grene.	

(B.15.92–102)

---

[13] On the echoes of Study's complaint in Anima's critique of proud, acquisitive preaching, see Fletcher, *Preaching, Politics, Poetry*, 206–7; Lawler, *Penn Commentary*, 4:155.

The tree was a commonplace figure for the divisions of a sermon in their relationship to the original scriptural *thema*, a familiar 'imagined form' for the 'scholastic *distinctio*' in Carruthers' terms. Many *artes* and sermons use the image of the tree to explain the way a sermon unfolds from its *thema*.[14] Siegfried Wenzel notes that in Bodleian Library, MS Bodley 649, the macaronic sermon collection attributed to Hugh Legat by Alan Fletcher, the division of the *thema* is frequently identified as 'radix sermonis [the root of the sermon]' in the margins (Figure 5.2).[15] Anima has already started to think about the schematic structure of sermons and pastoral texts in this way in his critique of curious preaching, urging 'doctors' to preach on 'þe seuene synnes,/ And... þe braunches þat burioneþ [spring, grow] of hem' rather than on 'materes vnmesurables' (B.15.72–5). Now, he deploys the metaphors that governed the exegetical practice of 'prechours and techeris' in order to examine the social and spiritual effects of preaching. Breen, who compares this tree of preaching with the trees of vice and virtue that proliferate in pastoral contexts, notes that Anima's tree is not a simple map of vices and virtues, but rather holds two alternative accounts of preaching and its effects in tension.[16] It shows how the 'þe right feiþ' flourishes when 'lele libbynge

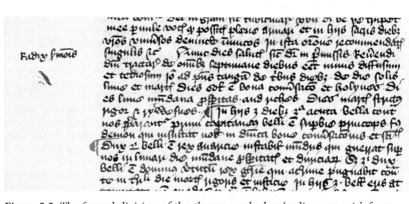

Figure 5.2 The formal division of the *thema*, marked as 'radix sermonis', from a sermon in Oxford, Bodleian Library, MS Bodley 649, fol. 2v.

---

[14] Otto A. Deiter, '*Arbor Picta*: The Medieval Tree of Preaching', *Quarterly Journal of Speech* 51, no. 2 (1965): 123–44. The *Tractatulus solemnis de arte et vero modo predicandi*, attributed to Thomas Aquinas, figures the elements of the 'sermo modernus' as the parts of a tree, and was accompanied by a diagram labelled 'arbor de arte sive modo predicandi'. For a discussion and translation, see Harry Caplan, 'A Late Medieval Tractate on Preaching', 40–79 in *Of Eloquence: Studies in Ancient and Mediaeval Rhetoric*, ed. Anne King and Helen North (Ithaca, NY: Cornell University Press, 1970). On the tree as a figure for the structure of medieval books more generally, see Sarah Kay, *The Place of Thought: The Complexity of One in Late Medieval French Didactic Poetry* (Philadelphia: University of Pennsylvania Press, 2007), 19–41.

[15] Wenzel, 'Arts of Preaching', 85. For details, see *Macaronic Sermon Collection*, ed. and trans. Horner, 33, 59, 265, 325, 467, 513.

[16] See Breen, 'Reading Step by Step', 124.

men' teach 'Goddes lawe', but produces no leaves or fruit when 'inparfit... prechours' poison it.

Like Anima's earlier account of his own names and operations, the figure of the tree provides a stimulus to narrative interpretation. Anima encourages the dreamer to understand this figure with reference to the natural world: the tree is not only an expository schema, he says, but also an 'ensaumple' that Will may 'se...in somer tyme'; its narrative logic draws on and supplements the dreamer's observations of growth and decay, the temporal changes that call for narration in the world around him. Where Anima invited the dreamer to choose, seemingly at random, between his many names, to prioritize one of his functions above the others, the tree encourages him to search for patterns of cause and effect, to discern the logic that explains its current condition. This interpretative technique is also enabling for Will because it provides him with a way to think in critical, evaluative terms about the preachers he encounters. Holy Church, who first encouraged Will to understand his present moment as part of an interpreted narrative, appears in these lines as an institution comprised of 'preestes and prechours' who are susceptible to pride and curiosity. As he learns to interpret the *figura* of the tree, however, Will discovers that it is possible to distinguish between 'lele libbynge' and 'inparfit' preachers by observing the effects of their preaching in the world and configuring a narrative from these observations.

Anima's complaint becomes increasingly digressive in its later stages, moving through a series of tangentially related topics: he alleges that corrupt clerics receive people's ill-gotten gains as alms and then spend the money on prostitutes, and that they leave their goods to underserving people when they die, or die intestate, so that bishops are free to spend their money frivolously; this last observation leads into a contrast between misers, whose money is dispersed after death, and people who are charitable in life, and who are remembered after they die 'In preieres and in penaunces and in parfit charite' (B.15.148). The oblique, associative connection between different topics suggests a discourse losing its focus; indeed, the passage is abbreviated in the C text, and revised to address what Traugott Lawler has called its 'sudden' and 'illogical' changes of focus in B.[17] At the end of this passage, however, Anima's mention of 'parfit charite' prompts a question from the dreamer that will lead in turn to a new act of emplotment, and that will provide a focal point for the rest of Anima's speech: '"What is charite?" quod I þo' (B.15.149). Some B-text manuscripts include a marginal note on this line, 'quid est caritas', that seems to recognize the structural significance of Will's question, marking it out as the beginning of a new, exegetical movement in the text, analogous to the sermon-like *distinctiones* on charity that are noted in

---

[17] Lawler, *Penn Commentary*, 4: 174.

some C-text manuscripts.[18] Nicolette Zeeman describes this question as an example of the poem's characteristic use of the non sequitur, a sudden intervention that 'changes the trajectory of the scene, but in a way that cannot be entirely explained by local circumstances'.[19] Yet, the dreamer's capacity to recognize and prioritize essential information, even as his interlocutor slips into digression, might also suggest that he has begun to cultivate the forms of discernment that are necessary for narrative understanding, as a belated response to Anima's earlier rebuke.

Reflecting on the question he has asked, the dreamer performs an act of emplotment, searching for charity in his own recollected experience:

'I haue lyued in londe', quod I, 'my name is Longe Wille—	
And fond I neuere ful charite, bifore ne bihynde.	*perfect*
Men beþ merciable to mendinaunt3 and to poore,	*compassionate*
And wollen lene þer þei leue lelly to ben paied.	*give; believe; loyally*
Ac charite þat Poul preiseþ best and moost plesaunt to Oure Saueour—	
As *Non inflator, non est ambiciosa, non querit que sua sunt*—	
I sei3 neuere swich a man, so me God helpe,	
That he ne wolde aske after his, and ouþerwhile coueite	*sometimes*
Thyng þat neded hym no3t—and nyme it, if he my3te!	*he needed*
'Clerkes kenne me þat Crist is in alle places;	*teach*
Ac I sei3 hym neuere sooþly but as myself in a mirour:	
Hic in enigmate, tunc facie ad faciem.'	

(B.15.152–62a)

[157: 'is not puffed up, is not ambitious, seeketh not her own', 1 Corinthians 13:4–5; 162a: '(We see) here (through a glass) in a dark manner; but then face to face', 1 Corinthians 13:12]

In these lines, Will configures his partial and elusive encounters with charity into a provisional narrative *holos*. The capacity to recognize and prioritize charity, which serves as the *res* or 'gist' of this life story, allows the dreamer to generate a coherent account of his own experience, to affirm his identity as a 'self-constant' subject, and to take instruction from the cumulative events of his own life. As he searches for charity 'bifore' and 'bihynde', Will experiences the 'concordant discordance' of

---

[18] John Burrow argues that this note formed part of a system of rubrication in the B-text archetype that originated with Langland himself: 'The Structure of *Piers Plowman* B XV–XX: Evidence from the Rubrics', *Medium Ævum* 77 (2008), 306–12, esp. 307–8. Wood has argued that the note originated instead 'with a very early scribe' who was 'particularly attentive to the poem's structure'; *Manuscript Tradition*, 52.

[19] Zeeman, *Arts of Disruption*, 375; for the dreamer's question to Anima, see 377–8.

the soul, stretching out in different directions to perceive time as it passes; as he figures his encounters with charity into a plot, however, he begins to perceive their 'discordant concordance', a discursive configuration that answers to the soul's perception of time. From his fragile, fragmented condition at the start of this passus, the dreamer has begun to recover a narrative understanding of himself, a sense of 'whider I sholde/ And wherof I cam' in relation to the span of his own life.

The dreamer begins this narrative by naming himself: '"I haue lyued in londe", quod I, "my name is Longe Wille"', in a line that also contains the poem's best-known authorial signature, an anagram of Wille Longe Londe. The narrator's strong statement of cohesive selfhood occasions an expression of what Kathryn Kerby-Fulton calls the 'bibliographical ego', as the poet identifies himself with his protagonist.[20] Some of the poem's early readers certainly construed the line as a reference to the poet, as Andrew Galloway has recently observed: an annotation to this line in British Library, Additional MS 10574 says '*Nomen auctoris huius libri est* Longe Wille', while a note in Oxford, Bodleian Library, MS Laud Misc. 581 says 'nota the name of thauctor'.[21] The same line also suggests that the dreamer's identity is the product of his cumulative experience, through a pun on *long-animitas*, long-suffering forbearance.[22] Anne Middleton has argued that this line both echoes and reinforces the earlier anagrammatic signature that appears in the first inner dream, where the dreamer observes his life in the 'lond of longynge'.[23] There, as I argued in Chapter 4, the dreamer recovers from his spiritual lethargy by learning to understand his life as a narrated *holos*, mediated by the texts and discourses of clerical instruction. Here, in the fifth vision, he names himself at a similar moment of lucid, narrative understanding, as he recovers the ability to think about his 'lyf-time' as an interpreted whole.

The B-text version of this narrative offers an oblique allusion to the preaching that has shaped the dreamer's self-understanding, as Will cites St Paul as an authority on charity: 'Ac charite þat Poul preiseþ best and moost plesaunt to Oure Saueour—/ As *Non inflator, non est ambiciosa, non querit que sua sunt*'. This description of charity, which 'is not puffed up, is not ambitious, [and] seeketh not her own' (1 Corinthians 13:4-5), offers a clear contrast with the pride, ambition, and desire for material rewards that motivate curious preaching, and recalls the satirical juxtaposition between preaching at St Paul's and the preaching of St Paul that emerges in Study's complaint and again at the feast of Conscience, as we saw in Chapter 3. In the C-text version of this passage, however, the dreamer's biography is framed explicitly by his recollected experiences of preaching in London:

---

[20] Kerby-Fulton, 'Bibliographic Ego', esp. 72-8, 85-6.
[21] Galloway, 'Long Will and the Scandal of 1385', 47.
[22] Middleton, 'William Langland's "Kynde Name"', 43.
[23] Middleton, 'William Langland's "Kynde Name"', 44.

'Charite!' quod Y tho, 'þat is a thyng, forsothe,	*then*
That maistres commenden moche; where may hit be yfounde?	*learned men*
Ich haue yleued in Londone monye longe ʒeres	*lived*
And fonde I neuere, in faith, as freres hit precheth,	*found*
Charite, þat chargeth naught, ne chyt, thow me greue him…'	*get upset or angry*
	(C.16.284–8)

In this version of the poem, Will construes 'monye longe ʒeres' as a narrative organized around the search for charity, and uses it to critique the 'freres and faitours' whose sermons had previously undermined his capacity to think in these terms. Anima's earlier *figura* of the tree with rotten roots, reassigned to Liberum Arbitrium in C, supplies the logic for this critique: the absence of charity in Will's contemporary world is itself revealing about the 'inparfit… prechours and techeris' who direct the 'folk' through their teaching and example.

At the end of this narrative in the B text, the dreamer glimpses a vision of Christ in the 'mirour' of his own person: 'Clerkes kenne me þat Crist is in alle places;/ Ac I seiʒ hym neuere sooþly but as myself in a mirour:/ *Hic in enigmate, tunc facie ad faciem*' (B.15.161–2a). This insight is part of the new understanding he described in his earlier overview of the encounter with Anima: here, an interpreted account of 'whider I sholde/ And wherof I cam' affords the dreamer new insights about his 'kynde' (B.15.13–14). Yet, the poem also suggests that the dreamer's self-understanding is not yet complete, that his connection to Christ, and so to charity, is only perceptible *in enigmate*.[24] Will's exegesis of his own life resolves into a new enigma or *obscuritas*, in an inversion of the process Carruthers described in her reading of Anima; as Curtis Gruenler writes, Will now perceives himself as 'a riddle to which Christ is the answer'.[25] Here, the poem points to the next step in the dreamer's recovery of his narrated identity. To understand his 'kynde' association with Christ, the dreamer will need to understand himself not only in terms of his own 'lyf-time' but also in relation to the central events of eschatological history: the creation, the Fall, and the atonement.

The Tree of Charity and the Shape of History

Piers Plowman returns to these questions at the beginning of passus 16 in the B text, when Will encounters the Tree of Charity. This encounter unfolds in two stages, first as Anima describes and explicates the tree, and then as the dreamer

---

[24] On the significance of the dreamer's partial perception in this scene, see Davis, *Books of Nature*, 150–1.
[25] Gruenler, *Poetics of Enigma*, 2. See also Simpson, *Introduction*, 163.

falls into an inner dream where he sees the tree for himself, tended by Liberum Arbitrium under the direction of Piers Plowman. It culminates in Will's request to taste the fruit of the Tree of Charity, which leads in turn to a re-enactment of the Fall as the fruit falls from the tree and the devil carries it away. In this scene, as Robertson writes, the 'temporal scheme of Will's own biography as he comes to desire the apple is mapped on to the larger temporal scheme of salvation history as the drama evokes the temptation of Adam and Eve'.[26] The questions 'whider I sholde/ And wherof I cam and of what kynde' take on new dimensions in this context, as Will perceives himself as a 'self-constant subject' with a role in the larger story of salvation.

The dreamer begins this passus 'in a weer [quandary] what charite is to mene' (B.16.3), and Anima responds with a new expository schema, describing charity as 'a ful trie [choice] tree' (B.16.4):

Mercy is þe more þerof; þe myddul stok is ruþe;	*root; trunk*
The leues ben lele wordes, þe lawe of Holy Chirche;	*faithful*
The blosmes beþ buxom speche and benigne lokynge;	*kind*
Pacience hatte þe pure tree, and pore symple of herte,	*tree itself*
And so þoru3 God and goode men groweþ þe fruyt Charite.	

(B.16.5–9)

Anima presents a new set of *distinctiones* in these lines, announcing an ongoing concern with preacherly exegetical forms in this new section of the poem.[27] The tree provides a *figura* for the relationship between different virtues: pity grows from mercy, and produces faithful speech, ecclesiastical law, and kind words in turn; through patience, the whole tree produces charity. The passage recalls the terms in which Anima first introduced himself to Will as it elaborates different aspects of a single idea. It also echoes his earlier account of 'prechours and techeris' as the hidden root of a tree, whose moral condition can be seen in the visible evidence of its leaves and branches. By this point in his dialogue with Anima, the dreamer is well-equipped to engage with exegetical schemata of this kind, and to recognize the opportunities they present for narrative interpretation.

---

[26] Robertson, 'Soul-Making', 39.

[27] Several readers have identified precedents for Anima's account of the tree in late medieval exegetical writing. Both Conor McKee and Denise Baker have identified Peter of Lombard's account of the will assisted by grace as an important source for the logic of Langland's image. See McKee, 'Langland's "Tree of Patience"', *YLS* 36 (2022): 101–22, and Baker, '*Liberum Arbitrium* and the Tree of Charity in *Piers Plowman*', *YLS* 36 (2022): 77–99. Baker also reads the Lombard as a source for the later development of the tree in the inner dream. Hanna, meanwhile, identifies the *Glossa Ordinaria* on the Song of Songs as an important source for Anima's account of the tree, and for the tree in the inner dream that follows; Hanna, 'The Tree of Charity—Again', 125–39 in *Medieval Alliterative Poetry: Essays in Honour of Thorlac Turville-Petre*, ed. John A. Burrow and Hoyt N. Duggan (Dublin: Four Courts Press, 2010).

Will replies that 'I wolde trauaille [travel]...twenty hundred myle' to see the tree, and give up all other food 'to haue my fulle of þat fruyt' that grows on it (B.16.10–11), a response that underscores his capacity to distinguish the central issue in a complex, explicated discourse, but that also reveals his appetite to understand charity in a new way. As many readers have noted, his ambition to 'taste' the fruit figures his desire for a 'sapiential' understanding of charity, at once 'cognitive...affective, and experiential', through a pun on *sapientia*, 'wisdom', and *sapor*, 'to taste'.[28] Will describes this new form of knowledge as the goal of a projected journey, perhaps expecting that Anima will offer him an allegorical itinerary of the kind that Piers Plowman presented to the pilgrims in the second vision, or that Study mapped out for him in the third. This, as we have seen, was a well-established use of the *figura*, and one that offered a framework for the narrative interpretation of future events, bounded by the limits of the 'lyf-time'. Anima, however, directs his attention inwards, explaining that charity grows 'Amyddes mannes body' in a 'gardyn' or 'herber' called the 'Herte', where it is tended by Liberum Arbitrium and by Piers Plowman (B.16.13–17).[29] Perhaps paradoxically, this movement into the self will allow the dreamer to see how the condition of his own heart is related to the larger narrative of salvation history.

Anima's mention of Piers provokes 'pure ioye' in the dreamer and initiates the second inner dream: 'I swowned after,/ And lay longe in a loue-dreem' (B.16.18–20); here, as with the earlier mention of charity, the dreamer discerns the larger significance of a passing detail in Anima's speech, and makes it central to the next part of their encounter. When the dreamer reacts in this way, he also responds to Anima's claim in the previous passus that Piers is the pre-eminent exegete of charity. Anima describes Charity as a personification, but warns that the dreamer will never meet him without the ploughman's help: '"Wiþouten help of Piers þe Plowman", quod he, "his persone sestow neuere"' (B.15.196). Piers, he explains, knows charity in a more immediate way than clerical preachers and teachers:

'Where clerkes knowen him', quod I, 'þat kepen Holi   *Do*
   Kirke?'
'Clerkes haue no knowynge', quod he, 'but by werkes and
   by wordes.
Ac Piers þe Plowman parceyueþ moore depper   *perceives; deeply*

---

[28] Zeeman, *Discourse of Desire*, 2. See also, Simpson, *Introduction*, 168; Hanna, 'Tree of Charity', 134; Robertson, 'Soul-Making', 39.

[29] The C text resolves the apparent tension between these alternatives, as Liberum Arbitrium leads Will on a long journey into the heart, regaling him with stories as they go: 'Thenne louh *Liberum Arbitrium* and ladde me forth with tales,/ Til we cam into a contre, *Cor-hominis* hit heihte' (C.18.3–4). In B, however, Anima's response marks the transition into the poem's second inner dream, suggesting that a 'sapiential' knowledge of charity becomes available at some deeper level of experience.

>   That is þe wille, and wherfore þat many wight suffreþ:
>   Et vidit Deus cogitaciones eorum.'
>
>   (B.15.197-200a)
>
> ['And God saw their thoughts', cf. Luke 11:17]

Anima's own account of the Tree of Charity reveals the limitations of a clerical understanding: this was an image of charity as manifest in 'werkes' and 'wordes', in 'lele wordes', 'buxom speche', and 'benigne lokynge'. A meeting with Piers, however, promises a 'depper' encounter with charity, located in the 'wille', a form of exegesis that produces 'sapiential' knowledge.

As the inner dream begins, Piers himself will show the dreamer the tree and explain its significance, inviting him to 'toten...on top and on roote' (B.16.22). At first, his exegesis reiterates and supplements Anima's account of the tree. The dreamer's attention is drawn to the three props that support the tree, and to the different kinds of fruit that hang on it, none of which Anima had mentioned explicitly. Piers enumerates these features like a preacher, explicating the props as figures of the Trinity and the different fruits as three grades of perfection: marriage, widowhood, and chastity, respectively. Yet, he also approaches the tree as a living thing, requiring cultivation and protection in order to flourish: the props, for example, are designed to protect the tree against the winds that assault it 'in blowing tyme': covetousness, which comes from the 'wikked wynd' of the world 'and crepeþ among þe leues', and the flesh, 'a fel [fierce] wynd' that strips away the blossoms in 'flouryng tyme' (B.16.26-8, 31). The tree supplies a schema to conceptualize different aspects of charity in their relationship to one another, an 'imagined form' for a set of *distictiones* in Carruthers' terms, but it also exists in historical time, persisting through the changing seasons. Piers relates to the tree as an agricultural labourer as well as an exegete: it is the ploughman's job to cultivate the tree of charity as well as to explain its significance. In this sense, his role in the inner dream recalls the labour he performed on the half-acre, a form of preacherly exegesis that is also an ongoing project of pastoral care.[30]

At the dramatic climax of this scene, the dreamer's request to taste the fruit produces a re-enactment of the Fall. Will asks Piers 'to pulle adoun an appul, and [if] he wolde,/ And suffre [allow] me to assaien [find out] what sauour it hadde' (B.16.73-4), but as Piers reaches out to fulfil this request, the fruit begins to cry out and weep, and, as it drops from the tree, the devil gathers it up and carries it away. The fruit that once figured charity now represents Adam and his descendants,

---

[30] Andrew Cole reads the ploughman's labour at the tree in relation to the project of preaching and pastoral care: 'Trifunctionality and the Tree of Charity: Literary and Social Practice in *Piers Plowman*', *ELH* 62 (1995): 1-27. Drawing parallels between the props of the tree and the 'forkid trees' that bear up the vine in sermons on the parable of the vineyard, Cole argues that this aspect of Langland's allegory comments on the role of different estates in supporting the work of the church, and draws attention to the tensions between them. See also Lawler, *Penn Commentary*, 4: 299, 305, 308.

'Adam and Abraham and Ysaye þe prophete', who are consigned to hell, '*in Limbo Inferni*' (B.15.81), where they await the coming of Christ. The ramifications of this event will be felt through the remaining passūs of the poem, which trace the broad outlines of salvation history from the Fall to the atonement and on towards the apocalypse. Will's desire for 'sapiential' knowledge, recalled in his request to 'assaien' the 'sauour' of the fruit, is answered in an unexpected way: the fullest apprehension of charity, the poem suggests, is available not through a tactile encounter with some desired object like the fruit, but rather in the interpreted experience of eschatological history, which now encloses and informs the dreamer's perception of his own life. At this moment, as James Simpson writes, the poem affirms that 'the self... is in its most profound realisation a historical entity, and to know the springs of the self, one must know one's history'.[31] As the Fall plays out at the Tree of Charity, the dreamer comes to a new understanding of himself as a 'self-constant' subject in the context of a history that predates and outlasts him.[32]

The scene that unfolds at the Tree of Charity finds an analogue in Robert of Gretham's Anglo-Norman sermon cycle the *Mirour des Évangiles*, as Margaret Connolly has observed.[33] Robert composed the *Mirour* c.1250 for an aristocratic laywoman, 'dame Aline', perhaps Elena de Quincy, countess of Winchester, but it also circulated among clerical readers who may have preached from it, including the Benedictines of St Mary's Abbey in York and a 'chapeleyn' called Thomas.[34] The Anglo-Norman text was translated into Middle English in the late fourteenth-century in a version that survives in six manuscripts, four of them produced in London as Ralph Hanna points out.[35] In his Prologue, as Nicholas Watson writes, Robert explains the 'pastoral and pedagogical imperatives' that animate his work, and many other vernacular sermon collections from this period.[36] Here, he likens scripture to a tree with fruit concealed among its verdant leaves, and compares the exegesis he will offer in his sermons to the act of shaking the tree so that the fruit falls down for people to eat:

---

[31] Simpson, *Introduction*, 166.

[32] Danielle Allor has argued that the figure of the tree makes it possible to perceive the individual lifetime and universal history as entangled in this way, producing vertiginous changes of 'spatial and temporal scale': Allor, 'Propping the Tree of Charity: Allegory and Salvation History in *Piers Plowman*', *YLS* 35 (2021): 30.

[33] Margaret Connolly, 'Shaking the Language Tree: Translating the Word in the Vernacular in the Anglo-Norman *Miroir* and the Middle English *Mirror*', 17–28 in *The Theory and Practice of Translation in the Middle Ages*, ed. Rosalynn Voaden, René Tixier, Teresa Sanchez Roura, and Jenny Rebecca Rytting, The Medieval Translator, 8 (Turnhout: Brepols, 2003), 28.

[34] On the identity of 'dame Aline' see K. V. Sinclair, 'The Anglo-Norman Patrons of Robert the Chaplain and Robert of Greatham', *Forum for Modern Language Studies* 27 (1992): 193–208. For manuscripts of the *Mirour* and their owners, see *The Middle English Mirror: Sermons from Advent to Sexagesima*, ed. Thomas G. Duncan and Margaret Connolly (Heidelberg: Winter, 2003), xii–xxviii.

[35] Hanna, *London Literature*, 154.

[36] Nicholas Watson, *Balaam's Ass: Vernacular Theology Before the English Reformation, vol. 1: Frameworks, Arguments, English to 1250* (Philadelphia: University of Pennsylvania Press, 2022), 109.

> Saint escripture ad la custume
> Del arbre qui port noyz u pume;
> Quant est fuillie esspessement
> Del fruit i pert petit u nient,
> Mai si l'em escust l'arbrecel
> Li fruit enchet espes e bel,
> El la ducur ke fu celee,
> Quant l'em en guste, mult li agree.
> Alsi est de sainte escripture:
> La lettre pert obscure e dure,
> Mais qui i mettrat sun purpens
> Pur ueer l'espirital sens,
> E si l'escut cum par espundre
> Le bien ke Deus i uolt respundre
> Mult i uerrat pumettes cheres,
> Ço sunt sentences de maneres;
> E mult li sauura bien
> La dulcur dunt ainz ne sout rien.
>
> (ll. 197–214)

As the Middle English translator has it:

> Holy writ haþ a liknesse vnto tre þat bereþ note [nuts] oþer appel. Whan it is þicke leued, of þe frout it lest [loses] litel oþer nouȝt; ac ȝif men schake þe tre, þe frout falleþ doun þicke & fair: þan þe swettnesse þat was hidde aforn [before], whan man eteþ it, it likeþ him wel. So it fareþ [goes] bi holi writ. Þe letter semeþ derk & hard, ac he þat setteþ his entent to se þe gostlich writ [spiritual meaning], & ȝif he schake it as þurȝth vndoinge [expounding] þe gode þat God wold don vs, michel [much] gode frout he schal finde þerinne & derworþ [valuable], þat ben sentens of mani maners, & michel þat swettnesse schal turnen him to gode whiche þat aforn [previously] he ne vnderstode nouȝt.[37]

Robert himself employed a version of the 'antiquus modus [ancient method]' of preaching in his sermons, explicating the whole gospel pericope for a given occasion, rather than elaborating *distinctiones* from a short, scriptural *thema*.[38]

---

[37] Anglo Norman and Middle English texts from *Middle English Mirror*, ed. Duncan and Connolly, 6, 7; for further extracts in Anglo Norman, see Marion Aitken, *Étude sur Miroir ou les Évangiles des Domnées de Robert de Gretham suivie d'extraits inédits* (Paris: Champion, 1922); and for a complete edition of the Middle English text, see *The Middle English 'Mirror': An Edition Based on Bodleian Library MS Holkham misc. 40*, ed. Kathleen Marie Blumreich, Medieval and Renaissance Texts and Studies, 182 (Tempe: Arizona Center for Medieval and Renaissance Studies, 2002).

[38] On the form of these sermons, see Aitken, *Étude sur Miroir*, 24–6; Connolly, 'Shaking the Language Tree', 17–18; Hanna, *London Literature*, 177.

Even so, this imagery of falling fruit offers a *figura*, an 'imagined form', for the proliferation of commentary and for the distinction and enumeration of clarificatory categories that recalls the exegetical activities of Anima and of Piers Plowman. Robert describes the 'gostlich... swettnesse' of the fruit, drawing on the same association of *sapor* and *sapientia* that informs the dreamer's request to 'assaien' the 'sauour' of the apples in Langland's poem. In Robert's image, however, the act of interpretation makes the fruit available to eat: he describes the preacher 'vndoinge' the enigmatic text of scripture, the 'letter [that] semeþ derk & hard', and argues that listeners will perceive its 'gostlich... swettnesse' as its meanings become clear to them.

An adapted version of this passage appears in the lollard tract 'A comendacioun of holy writ in oure owne langage', which borrows extensively from Robert's *Mirour*.[39] As Fiona Somerset has recently argued, the author's use of material from Robert reveals the close affinities between lollard exegesis and the mainstream pastoral tradition, even as his careful revisions serve to differentiate a distinctively lollard approach to scripture.[40] 'A comendacioun of holy writ' draws attention to the intellectual and spiritual condition of the exegete himself, who must first 'sette his herte to see þe gostly witt [spiritual significance]' contained in scripture, and then shake the tree 'þorou3 studyynge þerof and by good lyuynge'.[41] Elsewhere in the Prologue, Robert acknowledges that 'vndoinge' scripture necessarily involves translating it for different audiences, since 'it is ful gret foli to spek Latyn to lewed folke'; the author of 'A comendacioun of holy writ', however, adds new references to translation in his passage on shaking the tree: 'and þe swetnesse þerof schal turne him to gret goodnesse, whiche þat a man vnderstondeþ not tyl it be drawen and schaken into his owne langage'.[42] While, for Robert, translation is a matter of pastoral pragmatism, for the author of 'A comendacioun of holy writ' it is a crucial step towards sapiential understanding: 'whanne by þe voys of his owne langage' scripture 'entreþ into' the listener's 'soule, it moysteþ [nourishes] alle his wittis'.[43]

In *Piers Plowman*, by contrast, the activities of exegesis and translation, undertaken first by Anima and then by Piers himself, produce an apprehension of history that both experienced and narrated, where sapiential understanding is finally available. Will comes to know charity as an experience of sweetness and satisfaction in the phenomenological present, only when his present time is

---

[39] Connolly, 'Shaking the Language Tree', 26–7; Watson, 'Lollardy: The Anglo-Norman Heresy?', 334–46, *Language and Culture in Medieval Britain: The French of England, c.1100–c.1500*, ed. Jocelyn Wogan-Browne with Carolyn Colette, Maryanne Kowaleski, Linne Mooney, Ad Putter, and David Trotter (Woodbridge: York Medieval Press, 2009), 339.

[40] Somerset, *Feeling Like Saints: Lollard Writings after Wyclif* (Ithaca, NY: Cornell University Press, 2014), 205–15.

[41] 'A comendacioun of holy writ in oure owne langage', 126–9 in *The Earliest Advocates of the English Bible*, ed. Dove, 126.

[42] *Middle English Mirror*, ed. Duncan and Connolly, 5; 'A comendacioun of holy writ', 126.

[43] 'A comendacioun of holy writ', 126.

configured as part of a larger plot. Many readers have argued that the Tree of Charity marks a transition from schematic exegesis into narrative allegory. Elizabeth Salter, in a highly influential reading, charted the poem's '[changing] idiom' as 'plain expository allegory' gives rise to the 'allegory of dramatic action', and the ploughman's interpretation of the tree in 'the "continuous present" of the dream' produces a movement 'into the "historical past" of the Biblical narrative'.[44] For David Aers, this moment marks a decisive turn away from preacherly exegesis, as the poem transcends and repudiates the 'picture models' found in contemporary sermons and adopts instead a form of allegory that can accommodate 'dramatic activity, change and mutability'.[45] For Breen, by contrast, the dreamer's experience at the tree shows how figurative schemata can develop their own forms of dynamism and sophistication as readers put them to work: Will 'does not pass out of the realm of pictorial allegory', she argues, 'but rather begins to understand it more deeply, and use it more effectively, as an instrument for the care of souls'.[46] I argue that the dreamer's exposure to exegetical schemata in the preceding passūs has prepared him for this fruitful encounter with history, because it has cultivated the forms of discernment that allow for narrative interpretation. The dreamer draws on the discursive resources of preaching to make sense of history as it unfolds, to perceive it not as a simple succession of events, but rather as an interpreted *holos* that discloses the operations of charity and that encompasses and informs his own narrated life.

For Robert of Gretham, the act of exegesis begins a larger process of dissemination that is both social and historical. Clerics who are 'proude, oþer coueitouse, oþer licherouse' often lead the laity into error, sustained by the patronage of lay lords: 'And who þat maintaineþ swiche men, hii [they] schal gon to helle wiþ hem, bot ȝif hii amenden hem' he warns.[47] Yet, both clergy and laity can take part in the dissemination of God's word, either through virtuous preaching or through the circulation of books like the *Mirror* itself: 'Now I beseche wiþ gode hert to alle þat þis writ han [have this writing], þat hii lene [give, loan] it wiþ gode wille to al þat it wil writen [copy]. For þe custome is of Goddes word, þe more þat it spredeþ obrode, þe better it is, & more hii quemen [please] God þat it owen.'[48] Here, as Claire Waters writes, the *Mirror* imagines a broad and collaborative 'effort at education performed jointly by clergy and laity'; Hanna adds that lay readers in particular are 'enjoined to... acts of learned dissemination' that involve significant risk and expense, releasing their copy of the book 'into alien hands'.[49] *Piers Plowman* often explores these relationships, as we have seen, imagining the

---

[44] Salter, *Introduction*, 74, 76. [45] Aers, *Christian Allegory*, 89, 94.
[46] Breen, 'Reading Step by Step', 125. [47] *Middle English Mirror*, ed. Duncan and Connolly, 9.
[48] *Middle English Mirror*, ed. Duncan and Connolly, 21.
[49] Waters, *Translating 'Clergie': Status, Education, and Salvation in Thirteenth-Century Vernacular Texts* (Philadelphia: University of Pennsylvania Press, 2016), 45. Hanna, *London Literature*, 187. See also Watson, *Balaam's Ass*, 109–10.

different ways in which preachers and their lay patrons might subvert or reinforce one another in a shared spiritual project.

As the devil runs off with the fallen fruit, Piers Plowman takes one of the three props that support the tree and throws it after him 'for pure tene' (B.15.86). This is the prop that represents God the Son, the second person of the Trinity, and, in the act of throwing it, the ploughman seems to set in motion the incarnation and the atonement. With this enigmatic action, moreover, he also reaffirms his commitment to preacherly exegesis, taking part of the schematic *figura* of the tree and hurling it into unfolding, historical time. The ploughman's 'pure tene' in this moment echoes his earlier reaction to the wasters on the half-acre and the attitude in which he tears the pardon after the challenge from the priest. Here as there, it responds to a moment where the pastoral labour of narrative interpretation must begin again in some newly re-imagined form. As the Fall recurs in the dreamer's soul, the poem acknowledges that exegesis, too, will take place in historical time, unfolding alongside the events of eschatological history and articulating their significance. With an echo of Gretham's Prologue, *Piers Plowman* imagines that the ongoing labour of emplotment will be a collaborative project, as Will discerns patterns of narrative significance in the simple succession of events, drawing on the instruction he has received from Anima and from Piers.

'Ite in vniuersum mundum et predicate': Christian Evangelism and the Preaching of Mohammed

In the later parts of B.16, which are marked off as a separate passus in the C text, Anima traces a history of charity from the time of the apostles to the poem's contemporary moment. Emily Steiner, who reads this part of the poem alongside Higden's *Polychronicon*, argues that Langland is here engaged with the kinds of emplotment that are required to navigate the 'compendious form' of a universal history: like Higden, she argues, Langland articulates a history of the world that retains a particular focus on English kings, saints, and martyrs.[50] These examples proliferate in a similar way to the *distinctiones* that Anima presents elsewhere on his own names and on the nature of charity; here, too, he challenges the dreamer to discern the essential principles they have in common, and to 'grasp [them] together' as part of an interpreted *holos*. Lawler notes that Anima's history is characterized by 'golden age thinking'.[51] When Anima identifies charity among the friars, for example, he observes that this was 'fern [a long time] ago, in Seint

---

[50] Steiner, *John Trevisa's Information Age: Knowledge and the Pursuit of Literature, c.1400* (Oxford: Oxford University Press, 2021), 66–105 (quotation at 68). In *Reading Piers Plowman*, Steiner argues that sermon cycles could be similarly compendious, offering an 'omnibus version' of the biblical narrative (177); Steiner considers the possibility that sermon compendia themselves 'gave rise' to sprawling vernacular histories like the *Cursor mundi* (176).

[51] Lawler, *Penn Commentary*, 4: 201.

Fraunceis tyme' (B.15.230) and, while he says that charity can still be found in the 'kynges court' (B.15.235), his examples of charitable kings are also from the distant past: 'Edmond and Edward, eiþer were kynges/ And seintes yset [considered]—stille charite hem folwede' (B.15.223-4).[52] In the present time, by contrast, charity is undermined by clerical covetousness: Anima warns 'lordes and ladies' against clerics who seek donations of land and money for themselves rather than offering charity to others (B.15.320), and ultimately calls on them to bring about the disendowment of the church: 'Takeþ hire landes, ye lordes, and let hem lyue by dymes [tithes]' (B.15.563). At these moments in Anima's speech, as Steiner suggests, Langland recognizes the radical potential of universal histories like Higden's, which offer examples from the past as a model for future reform.[53]

In the last part of the discussion, Anima thinks about evangelism to non-Christians as an important expression of charity, 'analogous', as Davis writes, 'to almsgiving'.[54] Anima compares the apostles, 'Elleuene holy men' who converted 'al þe world.../ Into lele [faithful] bileue' (B.15.437-8), with contemporary bishops who are appointed to 'preche þe passioun of Iesus' in Nazareth, Damascus and elsewhere, but who prefer to 'huppe [hop] aboute in Engelond' as suffragans, consecrating altars and interfering in the work of parish priests rather than pursuing this evangelical mission (B.15.528).[55] As Davis has shown, Anima's calls for evangelism supplement and qualify the claims about universal salvation that appear elsewhere in the poem. For Anima, the 'kynde kinship' that connects all human beings with Christ does not itself guarantee the salvation of non-Christians, but rather places obligations on Christians to convert people of other faiths, reframing their intuitive grasp of natural law in the context of the gospel story.[56] Here, Anima considers preaching itself as part of his radical, experimental history of charity in the church, invoking heroic examples from the past for contemporary preachers to emulate. Citing Mark 16:15, he reminds contemporary clerics of their original calling to evangelism, asking 'What pope or prelat now parfourneþ [performs] þat Crist hiȝte [commanded]—/ Ite in vniuersum mundum et predicate... [Go ye into the whole world and preach]?' (B.15.490- 90a).

As I have argued in the previous sections of this chapter, the fifth vision of *Piers Plowman* describes the dreamer's gradual recovery from a point of personal dissolution as, guided and encouraged by Anima, he learns first to perceive the narrative shape of his own life, and then to understand himself in the larger context of Christian salvation history, drawing on the expository techniques of

---

[52] Scase (*Anticlericalism*, 91-3) argues that Anima echoes late-fourteenth-century anticlerical polemic, both in his choice of examples and in his argument that contemporary monks, friars, and priests should emulate the apostles as the founders of their orders had done.
[53] Steiner, *Information Age*, 90-1, 96-8.   [54] Davis, *Books of Nature*, 232.
[55] On the appointment of suffragan bishops to notional sees in the Holy Land, see Lawler, *Penn Commentary*, 4: 265-6.
[56] Davis, *Books of Nature*, 230.

contemporary preaching. In this part of his conversation with Anima, however, the poem considers the situation of Jews and Muslims who do not perceive themselves with reference to this Christian narrative because, as Anima reasons, no Christian preachers will articulate it for them. As it moves towards the inner dream and Will's encounter with the Tree of Charity, the poem shows how different narratives can be synthesized and integrated, as the dreamer perceives his own biography in relation to the larger movement of salvation history. As he calls for Christian preaching in the Holy Land, however, Anima deploys historical narrative in a more experimental way, testing competing models of preaching from the past against the demands of evangelism in the present.

Anima's prescriptions for Christian evangelism emerge in response to his account of the preaching of Mohammed, which has spread 'mysbileue' among the people of 'Surrie', broadly and vaguely defined to encompass the Muslim territories of the Levant.[57] Langland depicts Mohammed as a heresiarch, a frustrated candidate for the papacy who installed himself as the head of his own, corrupted version of Christianity, and as a skilful trickster and illusionist, characterizations which had a long history in Western writing about the Prophet.[58] He also recognizes him as a compelling preacher whose sermons had a transformative effect on the people who heard them. Anima explains how the Prophet Mohammed trained a dove to eat seeds from his ear as he preached, and then convinced his listeners that the bird brought messages from God:

> This Makometh was Cristene man, and for he moste noȝt ben a pope,   *might*
> Into Surrie he souȝte, and þoruȝ his sotile wittes   *went*
> Daunted a dowue, and day and nyȝt hire fedde.   *Tamed; dove*
> The corn þat she croppede, he caste it in his ere;   *ate; ear*
> And if he among þe peple preched, or in places come,
> Thanne wolde þe coluere come to þe clerkes ere   *dove*
> Menynge as after mete—þus Makometh hire enchauntede,   *Seeking food*
> And dide folk þanne falle on knees, for he swoor in his prechyng
> That þe coluere þat com so com from God of heuene
> As messager to Makometh, men for to teche.
>
> (B.15.398–407)

---

[57] Lawler, *Penn Commentary*, 4: 251–2, and see *MED*, 'Sirie (n)', 1(a).

[58] On the traditions of Western writing about Mohammed, see Norman Daniel, *Islam and the West: The Making of an Image* (Edinburgh: Edinburgh University Press, 1960); John V. Tolan, *Saracens: Islam in the European Imagination* (New York: Columbia University Press, 2002); Geraldine Heng, *The Invention of Race in the European Middle Ages* (Cambridge: Cambridge University Press, 2018), 116–18. Stories from this tradition appeared in preaching contexts: Robert Rypon presents an extended account of Mohammed that he found 'in quodam tractatu compilato de vita sua [in a certain tract compiled about his life]' in his first sermon for the feast of St Oswald; Rypon, *Selected Sermons*, 1: 282, 283.

The story of Mohammed and the dove circulated widely in the Middle Ages.[59] An early version appears in the *Speculum historiale* of Vincent of Beauvais, who claimed to have read it in an unnamed 'libellus...de Machometi fallaciis [little book...about Mohammed's deceptions]'.[60] It found its way into later chronicles including Higden's *Polychronicon*, and into several late medieval preachers' anthologies including the *Alphabetum narrationum*, a Latin compendium of exemplary narratives that was translated into Middle English around the turn of the fifteenth century.[61] Laurent de Premierfait added it to his translation of Boccaccio's *De casibus virorum illustrium*, the text that formed the basis for John Lydgate's *Fall of Princes*, and manuscripts of both works include some striking illustrations of the scene.[62]

Langland may have known more than one version of this story, but his most immediate source is almost certainly the *The Golden Legend* by James of Voragine which includes an account of Mohammed as part of the life of St Pelagius: Anima cites this text by its alternate title, the *Legenda Sanctorum* as the source for his earlier discussion of the lives of 'holy seintes' (B.15.269), and in the C text Liberum Arbitrium names it again before this account of Mohammed as an authority on the beliefs of 'Sarresynes and Iewes' (C.17.156-7).[63] The *Golden Legend* was also the pre-eminent authority for late medieval sermons on the saints and the major source for the forty-five *sacerdotale* sermons in John Mirk's *Festial*.[64] Some later versions of the *Golden Legend* treat the story of Mohammed and the dove with scepticism, distinguishing it from subsequent material on the life and teachings of the prophet, which James derived from Peter Alfonsi's *Dialogi contra Iudaeos* among other sources: 'Hoc quidem uulgariter dicitur', James writes at the conclusion of this narrative, 'sed uerius est quod inferius habetur [This at least is the

---

[59] On the transmission of this story see Daniel, *Islam and the West*, 32; Dorothee Metliztski, *The Matter of Araby in Medieval England* (New Haven: Yale University Press, 1977), 205-7; Stefano Mula, 'Muhammad and the Saints: The History of the Prophet in the *Golden Legend*', *Modern Philology* 101.2 (2003): 175-88; Lawler, *Penn Commentary*, 4: 252-3; Tolan, *Faces of Muhammad: Western Perceptions of the Prophet of Islam from the Middle Ages to Today* (Princeton, NJ: Princeton University Press, 2019), 44-6, 66-72.

[60] Vincent of Beauvais, *Speculum quadruplex, sive Speculum maius, vol 4: Speculum Historiale* (Douai: Bellerus, 1624; repr. Graz: Akademische Druck- und Verlagsanstalt, 1965), 913 (xxiii:40); cited and translated in Lawler, *Penn Commentary*, 4: 252.

[61] Higden, see *Polychronicon*, 6: 18-21 (v.14). The story is no. 1762 in Frederic C. Tubach, *Index Exemplorum: A Handbook of Medieval Religious Tales* (Helsinki: Finnish Academy of Science and Letters, 1969). For the story of Mohammed and the dove in the Middle English translation of the *Alphabetum narrationum*, see *An Alphabet of Tales: An English 15th Century Translation of the Alphabetum Narrationum*, ed. Mary Macleod Banks, 2 of 3 vols, EETS, os 126-7 (London: Paul, Trench, Trübner, 1904-5), 1: 165.

[62] On Laurent de Premierfait and Lydgate, see Tolan, *Faces of Muhammad*, 66-72.

[63] Metliztski, *Matter of Araby*, 205-6; Lawler, *Penn Commentary*, 4: 249-50. Wood has recently drawn attention to Cambridge University Library MS Dd.1.17, where the story of Mohammed and the dove from *The Golden Legend* appears with a B text of *Piers Plowman* and a range of other, more scholarly Christian writing about Islam; *Manuscript Tradition*, 121-32.

[64] On the *Legenda Sanctorum*, also called the *Legenda Aurea*, as a source for the *Festial*, see Mirk, *Festial*, ed Powell, 1: xxxii-v.

popular story, but the following account is closer to the truth]'; then later, as a comment on the subsequent material, 'Et istud est uerius quam illud quod supra de columba est dictum et sic est tenendum [This account is more true than what was said about the dove, and is therefore to be accepted].'[65] Even if he knew these caveats, however, Langland chose to place this story about the dove at the centre of his engagement with Mohammed, in part, I suggest, because it attributes the success of Islam to the power of Mohammed's preaching.[66]

Anima's description of Mohammed recalls some of the most charismatic preaching imagined in other parts of the poem, but in distorted, ambivalent forms. The dove brings messages directly from God, 'preuing' Mohammed's sermons in the moment when he preaches them, and Mohammed relays these messages to his listeners in clear, compelling language. The complex forms of linguistic and physical 'hybridity' that Waters identifies when the *artes* imagine Christian preachers as messengers from God, and that were manifest in the Prologue to *Piers Plowman* where the preaching angel speaks Latin before the *commune*, are simply absent here.[67] Anima describes Mohammed's hold over the dove as a kind of enchantment, which extends in turn to his listeners. The people fall to their knees in response to this sermon, a detail that may be unique to Langland's version of the story as Lawler notes.[68] This is a gesture that marks out receptive listeners throughout the poem, sometimes in response to beneficial instruction, as when the dreamer kneels to Holy Church or Dame Study (B.1.79, 10.144), and sometimes in response to corrupt but seductive preaching, as when 'Lewed men.../ Comen vp knelynge' to the Pardoner who promises them absolution in the Prologue (B.Prol.72–3).[69]

In the subsequent parts of his speech, as he calls on Christian preachers to travel to 'Surrie' and convert the people who live there, Anima turns to different historical examples of Christian evangelism, in search of a model that might rival the preaching of Mohammed. In the B text, he introduces Augustine of Canterbury, who converted the people of England and Wales:

---

[65] James of Voragine, *Legenda Aurea*, ed. Giovanni Paolo Maggioni, 2 vols (Florence: SISMEL Edizioni del Galluzzo, 2007), 2: 1262, 1264; translation from James of Voragine, *The Golden Legend: Readings on the Saints*, trans. William Granger Ryan, 2nd edn (Princeton, NJ: Princeton University Press, 2012), 756, 758. For discussion, see Mula, 'Muhammad and the Saints', 180–3.

[66] In the C text, Liberum Arbitrium considers the affinities between Christians and Muslims and the forms of charity that Muslims recognize before he relates this story, as though to frame the popular exemplum with some more substantive material on Islamic beliefs and practices.

[67] Waters, *Angels and Earthly Creatures*, and see Chapter 1.

[68] Lawler, Penn Commentary, 4: 252–3.

[69] On the significance of kneeling in the poem, see James F. G. Weldon, 'Gesture of Perception: The Pattern of Kneeling in *Piers Plowman* B.18–19', YLS 3 (1989): 49–66; Burrow, *Gestures and Looks in Medieval Narrative* (Cambridge: Cambridge University Press, 2002), 22; Davlin, 'Devotional Postures in *Piers Plowman* B, with an Appendix on Divine Postures', *Chaucer Review* 42 (2007): 163–4; Davis, 'Calling', 78–88. None of these studies considers kneeling in response to Mohammed's preaching.

Al was heþynesse som tyme Engelond and Walis,	*entirely pagan*
Til Gregory garte clerkes to go here and preche.	*caused*
Austyn at Canterbury cristnede þe kyng þere,	
And þoruȝ miracles, as men mow rede, al þat marche he tornede	*may; district*
To Crist and to Cristendom, and cros to honoure,	
And follede folk faste, and þe feiþ tauȝte	*baptized*
Moore þoruȝ miracles þan þoruȝ much prechyng,	
As wel þoruȝ hise werkes as wiþ his holy wordes,	
And fourmed hem what fullynge and feiþ was to mene.	*taught; baptism*
(B.15.442–50)[70]	

For Anima, Augustine of Canterbury offers an example of a Christian preacher who engages his audience with miracles, just as Mohammed appears to do with his dove. Gregory issues a simple command to Augustine at the start of his evangelical mission, telling him to 'go...and preche', in language that echoes Mark 16:15, and when Augustine arrives in England, he teaches people about baptism and explains the tenets of the faith, both through his words and through his example. Yet, Anima gives special emphasis to the role of Augustine's miracles: 'þoruȝ miracles, as men mow rede, al þat marche he tornede/ To Crist'. Indeed, he stresses the primacy of miracles over sermons, saying that Augustine 'follede folk faste, and þe feiþ tauȝte/ Moore þoruȝ miracles þan þoruȝ much prechyng'.

Anima's account of Augustine reflects a selective and eccentric reading of the historical and hagiographical sources.[71] Bede, in his *Ecclesiastical History*, records that Augustine and his companions converted the English primarily through their preaching: 'uerbum uitae quibus poterant praedicando [they preached the word of life to as many as they could]'.[72] Bede describes only one miracle, where Augustine

---

[70] Peter the Venerable anticipated this connection between Augustine's mission to England and contemporary preaching to Muslims in his *Contra sectam Saracenorum*, where he urges Muslim princes to listen patiently to Christian missionaries, just as Ethelbert of Kent received Augustine; given the limited circulation of Peter's text, however, it seems highly unlikely that Langland knew it. *Contra sectam Saracenorum*, 189: cols 659–720 in *PL*, ed. J. P. Migne, 217 vols (Paris: Migne, 1844–55), cols 684–5 (1.52–4); for a translation see *Peter the Venerable: Writings Against the Saracens*, trans. Irven M. Resnick (Washington DC: Catholic University of America Press, 2016), 96–9.

[71] The *Legenda sanctorum* contains only a very brief account of Augustine of Canterbury, embedded in the life of Saint Gregory the Great, and it seems likely that Langland drew on other sources for these lines in Anima's speech. Wood suggests that he may have drawn on the account of Augustine in the *South English Legendary*; *Manuscript Tradition*, 90. On the medieval traditions of writing about Augustine of Canterbury, see Richard Gameson and Fiona Gameson, 'From Augustine to Parker: The Changing Face of the First Archbishop of Canterbury', 13–38 in *Anglo-Saxons: Studies Presented to Cyril Roy Hart*, ed. Simon Keynes and Alfred P. Smyth (Dublin: Four Courts Press, 2006), and Lawler, *Penn Commentary*, 4: 260–1.

[72] Bede, *Historia ecclesiastica gentis Anglorum*, ed. and trans. Bertram Colgrave and R. A. B. Mynors (Oxford: Clarendon, 1969), 1.xxvi (pp. 76, 77).

heals a blind man to establish his authority in a dispute with other clerics.[73] Later historical and hagiographical accounts introduced new miracles, drawing on the early-eleventh-century *vita* by the Benedictine writer Goscelin of Canterbury, but here too writers acknowledged the important role of Augustine's preaching. The supplementary life in the *Gilte Legende*, for example, records that Augustine 'prechid the feiþ of Crist to þe peple and...confermyd them stedfastly in þe same', and converted king Ethelbert with a sermon that 'enflawmed hym so wiþin his soule'.[74] The special priority given to Augustine's miracles in Anima's version is distinctive, then, and seems designed in part as a response to the account of Mohammed; Anima challenges contemporary bishops to emulate Augustine's mission, answering the Prophet's counterfeit miracles with genuine miracles of their own.

Anima's call for a return to the age of miracles is also at odds with patristic and medieval commentary on Mark 16:15, 'euntes in mundum universum predicate [Go ye into the whole world and preach]', the verse that he addresses to suffragan bishops earlier in this passus (B.15.490a). In the subsequent verses, Christ predicts that the apostles will perform miracles when they preach (Mark 16:17–18). Far from calling on preachers to perform these miracles, however, patristic commentators sought to explain why they were no longer necessary in the church of their own time. Gregory the Great explains that miracles were necessary to affirm that faith of the early church, but have since been supplanted by preaching, which brings about spiritual transformation.[75] Isidore of Seville argues that miracles have been superseded by good works: 'Quod nunc Ecclesia non ea miracula faciat quae sub apostolis faciebat, ea causa est, quia tunc oportebat mundum miraculis credere, nunc vero iam credentem oportet bonis operibus coruscare [The reason why the church does not now perform miracles, as it did under the apostles, is that then it was necessary to make the world believe through miracles, whereas now belief should shine forth through good works].'[76] Medieval preachers cited these authorities and reaffirmed their arguments. A sermon from the collection preserved in British Library, Additional MS 41321 assembles 'diuerse doctoures' including Gregory and Isidore to explain why contemporary preachers no longer 'conferme...her wordes wiþ bodily miracles' as 'holi seintes in þe begynnynge of þe cherche' once did.[77] The Longleat friar, similarly, remarks that miracles 'wern

---

[73] Bede, *Historia ecclesiastica*, ed. and trans. Colgrave and Mynors, 2.ii. Bede also records a letter from Pope Gregory, who has heard of Augustine performing miracles, and cautions him to guard against the excessive pride that can arise from such displays; 1.xxxi.

[74] *Supplementary Lives in Some Manuscripts of the 'Gilte Legende'*, ed. Richard Hamer and Vida Russell, EETS, os 315 (Oxford: Oxford University Press, 2000), 372.

[75] Gregory, *Homiliae in Evangelia*, ed. Étaix, 248, trans. Hurst, 229 (xxix.4). This passage was later cited by Bede, *In Marci Evangelium Expositio*, 427–648 in *Opera Exegetica II, 3*, ed. David Hurst, CCSL 120 (Turnhout: Brepols, 1960), 645–6 (4, on Mark 16:17–18).

[76] Isidore of Seville, *Sententarium*, 83: cols 537–738 in *PL*, ed. J. P. Migne, 217 vols (Paris: Migne, 1844–55), cols 591B–592A, 1.xxiv. Translation from Cigman's notes to *Lollard Sermons*, 246–8.

[77] *Lollard Sermons*, ed. Cigman, 33–4.

nedful in þe begynnynge of holy chyrche as seyth Seynt Gregory, but now þe feyth is stabelyd and rotid and þerfore yt ben nout nedful now...'.[78] When Anima calls on contemporary clerics to go to 'Surrie' and emulate the example of Augustine, he challenges the assumptions of this commentary tradition, by pointing to a context where the church is not yet established. Yet, he also ignores the historical distinctions that this tradition seeks to recognize, its claim that spiritual forms of transformation have supplanted physical miracles in the present time.

In a sermon to the bishops of the province of Canterbury, assembled in convocation in 1373, Thomas Brinton also called on contemporary clerics to emulate Augustine, but interprets Augustine's example in a very different way. Brinton reminds his audience that they inherit Augustine's legacy as English pastors and preachers: 'Et certe nos prelati Anglie debemus esse valde solliciti circa curam animarum si attenderemus sollicitudines et labores precedencium nos prelatorum, et maxime Sancti Augustini et eius sociorum, qui Angliam conuertebant [And certainly we, the prelates of England, ought to be very concerned about the cure of souls, if we consider the care and effort of our predecessors, and especially Saint Augustine and his companions who converted England].'[79] He encourages his audience to continue the labour Augustine performed, not by travelling abroad to convert non-Christians, but by confirming the faith of the English through a new commitment to preaching and pastoral care, 'et precipue post curam nostram Londoniis predicando, quia est ciuitas Anglie principalis [and especially by preaching in London, as appropriate to our office, because it is the principal city of England]'.[80] This pragmatic use of Augustine's example throws Anima's radicalism into sharp relief. Brinton, who elsewhere identifies Bede as his source on the life of Augustine, makes no reference to miracles at all, noting instead that Augustine converted the English through fasting, prayer, and preaching ('ieiuniis et oracionibus ac predicacionibus').[81]

Augustine of Canterbury disappears from the C text; this, it seems, is a model of evangelism that the poem sets to one side. In this version of the poem, Langland turns to different examples from his history of preaching to develop an alternative

---

[78] Longleat House, MS 4, fol. 60v.
[79] Brinton, *Sermons*, ed. Devlin, 1: 110. For discussion of this passage from Brinton as an analogue for Anima's account of Augustine of Canterbury, see Gallemore, 'The Sermons of Bishop Brinton and the B Text of *Piers the Plowman*', 174-6.
[80] Brinton, *Sermons*, ed. Devlin, 1: 110.
[81] Brinton, *Sermons*, ed. Devlin, 1: 110. Brinton identifies Bede as his source on Augustine of Canterbury in a Good Friday sermon, also delivered in 1373; see Brinton, *Sermones*, ed. Davlin, 1: 89-90. Pearsall compares Anima's injunction to evangelism with a sermon by Brinton that calls for the conversion of 'Jews and infidels' as 'a challenge to a decayed priesthood'; *C Text*, ed. Pearsall, 292. This sermon, on St Louis of Toulouse, was probably delivered at the papal curia in Rome or in Avignon, as Margaret Harvey has suggested; it calls for the conversion of Jews 'in hac ciuitate gloriosa in qua deberet florere forcius fides firma [in this glorious city in which firm faith should flourish strongly]', rather than for evangelism to the Holy Land. See Brinton, *Sermons*, ed. Devlin, 2: 383, and Margaret Harvey, 'Preaching in the Curia: Some Sermons by Thomas Brinton', *Archivum Historiae Pontificiae* 33 (1995): 300.

response to the preaching of Mohammed. Already in the B text, Anima reminds bishops with sees in Syria that that every bishop who carries a cross is obliged to travel through his diocese, teaching people about the faith, and providing for the needy: 'Euery bisshop þat bereþ cros, by þat he is holden [obliged]/ Thoruȝ his prouince to passe, and to his peple to shewe hym,/ Tellen hem and techen hem on þe Trinite to bileue...' (B.15.569–71). Lawler discerns a reference to the cross as military standard earlier in this passus, where Anima declares that virtuous clerics should 'go bifore' the people as 'a good banyer' (B.15.435).[82] This allusion might associate the bishop's progress around his diocese with the project of crusading and evangelism in the Holy Land.[83] In other parts of the poem, however, the cross is a sign of the pastoral responsibilities that fall on all Christian bishops, with no particular reference to the conversion of non-Christians in 'Surrie': Reason appears 'wiþ a cros afore þe Kyng' when he delivers his sermon in the second vision (B.5.12), for example, performing his duty to the Christian *commune*, and Thought in the third vision reads the bishop's crosier as a reminder of his obligation to 'halie [draw] men fro helle' and 'to pulte [push] adown þe wikked' (B.8.95–7). When Anima addresses the bishops of Nazareth and Damascus in these lines, he does not require them to perform miracles like the saints of another age, but simply to fulfil the pastoral duties of their office.

Anima acknowledges the risk of martyrdom that comes with preaching in Syria, but presents this as a risk for all bishops, pointing to the example of Thomas Becket, who was martyred by 'vnkynde Cristene' in his cathedral in England (B.15.522). As Lawrence Warner has noted, Becket was associated with crusading and evangelism through the hagiographical tradition that identified his mother as a 'Saracen' princess, and in miracle stories where he rescued Richard I from a shipwreck on crusade; he was also the patron of an order of hospitallers, whose London headquarters, the house of St Thomas of Acre, retained an important place in civic life in Langland's time.[84] In these lines, however, Anima cites his example to suggest that every bishop must accept the possibility of martyrdom, not to associate the risk of martyrdom with Syria in particular, or

---

[82] Lawler, *Penn Commentary*, 4: 259–60.

[83] In the *South English Legendary*, Augustine of Canterbury and his companions process behind a cross when they arrive in England, in a back-formation from crusading practice: 'A crois of seluer wiþ þe forme of God hi lete rere/ And in a stude of baner touore hom alle bere/ And ȝeode forþ wel baldeliche as hardi kniȝtes and gode'; *South English Legendary*, ed. Charlotte D'Evelyn and Anna J Mill, 3 vols, EETS, os, 235, 236, 244 (London: Oxford University Press, 1956–59), 1: 215. My thanks to Nicholas Watson for this reference.

[84] Warner, 'Becket and the Hopping Bishops', *YLS* 17 (2003): 107–34; see also Steiner, *John Trevisa's Information Age*, pp. 102–3, and Bennett, 'Thomas of Acre'. As Lawler points out, however, this reference to Thomas Becket was sufficiently surprising that Langland sought to clarify it in the C text: here, Liberum Arbitrium refers to 'Seynte Thomas of Canterbury', to avoid confusion with Thomas of India (C.274); see Lawler, *Penn Commentary*, 4: 280.

to call for martyrdom as a tool of conversion in its own right.[85] In this part of the poem, Anima offers a model of evangelism that emphasizes the patient, persistent work of preaching and pastoral care, rather than the singular drama of martyrdom. Muslims, like, Jews, already accept the first clause of the Creed, '*Credo in Deum patrem omnipotentem* [I believe in God the Father Almighty]' Anima argues, and preachers can build on this understanding to convert them, by increments, to Christianity: 'Lere [teach] hem litlum and litlum *Et in Iesum Christum filium* [And in Jesus Christ his son],/ Til þei kouþe speke and spelle [declare] *Et in Spiritum sanctum*... [And in the Holy Ghost]' (B.15.607, 609–10).

In the C text, Langland introduces new material that frames this account of patient, incremental evangelism as another response to the preaching of Mohammed. Urging the clergy to abandon the exercise of political power, Liberum Arbitrium tells them they can instead achieve a peaceful settlement between 'Alle londes' through 'preyeres' and 'pacience' (C.17.236–7). To illustrate this claim, he recalls the story of Mohammed and the dove from earlier in the discussion:

And take hede how Macometh throw a mylde dowue	*dove*
Hadde al Surie as hymsulue wolde and Sarrasines in quyete.	*peace*
Naught thorw manslaght and mannes strenghe Macometh hadde þe maistrie,	
Bote thorw pacience and priué gyle he was prince ouer hem alle.	*secret trickery*
In such manere, me thynketh, moste þe Pope,	*must*
Prelates and prestis preye and biseche	
Deuouteliche day and nyhte and withdrawe hem fro synne,	
And crie to Crist a wolde his coluer sende,	*that he would; dove*
The whiche is þe hy Holy Gost þat out of heuene descendet	*high*
To make a perpetuel pees bitwene þe prince of heuene	
And alle maner men þat on this molde libbeth.	*earth; live*
	(C.17.239–49)

---

[85] In his *Summa de arte praedicandi*, Thomas of Chobham questions the value of preaching to 'Saracens' when martyrdom is the inevitable consequence. The Saracens have decreed that any preacher who names Christ will be put to death, 'Et ideo dicunt quod ire ad tales non esset ire ad predicandum, sed ire ad moriendum sine predicatione, nec sunt certi quod Dominus in morte eorum faceret pro eis miracula; et ideo hoc modo ire potius esset ad temptandum Deum quam ad predicandum [And so they say that to go to such people is not to go to preaching, but rather to go to death without preaching. Nor are they certain that God will produce miracles through them when they die; and they go rather to tempt God than to preach].' On the other hand, Thomas reflects, many *legenda* report that God performed miracles when martyrs died, and that those who saw them converted to Christianity. Chobham, *Summa de arte praedicandi*, ed. Morenzoni, 85–6; translation from Tolan, *Saracens*, 230–1.

'In this final reprise of the dove image', as Lawler observes, 'Mohammed has become a model of patience, and the Saracens he subdued to his will a model of "equitee"'.[86] Clerics should apply the same persistence in their prayers that Mohammed displayed in training his dove, asking 'day and nyhte' for Christ to reform and inspire them. This kind of patient, persistent endeavour will produce a more 'parfyt' priesthood, Liberum Arbitrium reasons, and will encourage all those who 'contraryen now Cristes lawes and Cristendoem dispisen' to 'amende' and convert (C.17.250–1).

This new passage leads into the poem's call for 'prelates… / That bereth name of Neptalym, of Niniue and of Damaske' to perform their obligations as bishops and preach in their diocese (C.17.260–1), positioning these new efforts at evangelism as a manifestation, and a consequence, of reform in the church. In this version of the poem, Mohammed's 'pacience and priué gyle' serves as an example for Christian preachers, even as they work to counteract the effect of his sermons (C.17.260–1). Preachers working 'litlum and litlum' to convert non-Christians to Christianity can take inspiration from the patient persistence of the Prophet training his dove. Langland revises the material on the duties of bishops to include echoes of the earlier discussions of Mohammed: while Anima says that every bishop 'is holden/ Throuȝ his prouince to passe', Liberum Arbitrium says that he should 'walke / … pacientliche throw his prouynce', in language that recalls the patience of Mohammed (B.15.569–70, C.17.283–4); when Anima calls on bishops to teach people about the Trinity, Liberum Arbitrium adds that they should 'enchaunten hem to charite', an echo of the scene where Mohammed 'enchauntede' the dove with the hidden grains, and the people with his preaching and his miracles (B.15.571, C.17.286). In this version of the poem, Christian evangelists to Muslim countries counter the preaching of Mohammed by performing their pastoral duties with an equivalent commitment, rather than by adducing miracles of their own on the model of earlier missionary saints.

As he searches for a model of preaching and evangelism that might counter the sermons of Mohammed, Anima reveals a capacity to think in radical, experimental ways with examples from different times and places. Reading figures like Augustine of Canterbury and Thomas Becket against the grain of conventional interpretations, he offers them as examples for preachers to emulate in his own time, reframing expectations for what the pastoral office entails. As Steiner writes, the call to perform miracles and face death seems to set 'a high bar for the average preacher', beyond the demands articulated in other parts of the poem.[87] In the B text, this process produces unexpected and problematic conclusions: calling for contemporary preachers to work miracles, Anima uses historical examples in a way that elides some important and widely acknowledged distinctions between

---

[86] Lawler, *Penn Commentary*, 4: 277–8.   [87] Steiner, *Information Age*, 98.

different eras in ecclesiastical history, and his emphasis on the miraculous seems to prioritize the expression of charity through 'werkes and...wordes', above the 'depper' manifestations of charity that Piers Plowman discerns in the will (B.15.198–9). In B and C, the example of Thomas Becket suggests that the risks to preachers are the same in all times and places, while in C the recuperated example of Mohammed himself proves that persistent preaching and pastoral care can establish universal peace, arguments with their own problematic elisions and silences.

These provisional, inconclusive responses to the preaching of Mohammed have an important role to play in the larger context of the fifth vision, even so. As it charts the dreamer's progress from personal dissolution to self-understanding, the poem deploys the exegetical forms of preaching to structure and integrate personal and universal narratives: Will comes to perceive himself as an individual subject in search of charity, and as a created person encountering charity in the framework of Christian eschatology. Anima's account of evangelism at different moments in history creates further opportunities for the dreamer to sharpen his skills of narrative interpretation, recognizing new examples of charity in a complex, unfolding discourse, and configuring them as part of a larger plot. Yet, this part of Anima's speech also complicates the larger trajectory of the fifth vision in important ways. It shows that the large-scale, universal history that supplies the dreamer with his fullest answer to the question of 'whider I sholde/ And wherof I cam and of what kynde' is not universally available or universally accepted. It also argues that the exegetical structures that mediate and facilitate his self-understanding might be disseminated to non-Christians or withheld from them, depending on the courage and imagination of contemporary preachers. In a part of the poem that tends towards synthesis, as an interpreted life is gradually absorbed into an interpreted history, this passage also points to other, more experimental approaches to narrative, generating alternate possibilities from the future from the story of the past. The dreamer's perception of the shape of his life and of the larger shape of Christian history, and Anima's experiments with different models of evangelism, both introduce what Ricoeur would call 'the shock of the possible' as narrative reconfigures lived experience in the present time, but they do so in strikingly different ways.[88]

* * *

In this book, I have read the preaching scenes in *Piers Plowman*, and the many scenes where preaching and preachers are the subject of discussion, as evidence for Langland's sustained, critical, and imaginative engagement with sermons and with the forms they provide for making sense of lived experience. Langland, I have argued, recognized that narrative was essential to the preacher's task: the best preachers in his poem encourage new forms of spiritual effort by locating the

---

[88] Ricoeur, *Time and Narrative*, 1: 79.

present moment in a larger, interpreted plot that reveals the opportunities and imperatives for reform. Preachers encounter listeners who are absorbed in their present concerns, experiencing life as a simple succession of events, and invite them instead to understand their experience configured in narrative terms, as part of a life story, or the story of their larger community, or of salvation history on its broadest scale. The poem understands the work of narrative interpretation as a central part of the preacher's responsibility to his listeners, a pastoral obligation that sits alongside his duty to offer elementary instruction in the catechism and the tenets of the faith. Langland's preachers offer narratives like this on grand, public occasions, delivering sermons before the king and the assembled *commune*, but also in parochial contexts, where they constitute a form of ongoing pastoral labour. The poem shows how sermons provided a framework for their listeners to re-examine their own experiences, newly conscious of their ethical obligations, of the baptismal promises that endure for the term of a human life, and of the proper balance of hope and fear in the face of God's impending judgement. It also argues that, as preachers engaged their audiences in the work of narrative interpretation, they encouraged them to discern patterns of significance and forms of value amid the complexities of unmediated experience, to recognize truth as the best treasure, love as the sovereign science.

The work of Paul Ricoeur has provided a framework to think about the composition of narrative as a dynamic process, configuring disparate events into meaningful plots, and as a process that shapes and informs the lives of readers and listeners, reconfiguring their perception of the world; in both respects, I have argued, Ricoeur describes the aspects of narrative discourse that matter most to Langland, both in his reflections on preaching and in his approach to poetry. Ricoeur shows how the composition of narratives constitutes an intervention in individual and social life, how the interpretative labour of emplotment mediates self-understanding and locates individual subjects in a shared, social history that predates and outlasts them, illuminating many different aspects of the preacher's task as Langland understood it. At the same time, however, the account of emplotment in *Piers Plowman* can also be seen to supplement and extend aspects of Ricoeur's thought. As we have seen, Langland's preachers often perform acts of emplotment in difficult, contested circumstances, negotiating different languages and registers, confronting hostile or indifferent audiences, competing for attention with corrupt and covetous practitioners, and persisting with listeners who forget what they have been taught. *Piers Plowman* acknowledges that the co-production of meaning requires co-operation between speakers and listeners, and that this co-operation is not always easy to achieve. Langland also argues that the most foundational activities of narrative configuration have an ethical dimension: for Ricoeur, as for Aristotle, the capacity to discern the most important events in a sequence and construe them as a plot is a kind of practical wisdom, but for Langland it is closely identified with the capacity to recognize and prioritize examples of charity, a capacity that can be cultivated through patience and study.

Reading scenes from Langland's poem alongside contemporary sermons by Thomas Brinton, Henry Harclay, Robert Rypon, and their named and anonymous contemporaries, I have sought not only to reaffirm that Langland was immersed in the preaching culture of his own time, as critics since G. R. Owst have been aware, but also to argue that his account of preacherly emplotment offers an insight into the way that real medieval sermons engaged their audiences. *Piers Plowman* contains, in its allegorical drama, a theory of preaching, rooted in observation and also perhaps in practice, with different emphases and priorities to contemporary *artes praedicandi*. Surviving sermon texts preserve a record of the preaching that Langland represents, sometimes in compressed and elliptical forms as part of the action of his poem, and *Piers Plowman* represents the contexts in which sermons were delivered, and the effects they achieved, both in the moment of their performance and subsequently, in the individual and social lives of their listeners. As we have seen, however, Langland's poem also articulates distinctive, sceptical positions that depart from the common assumptions of contemporary sermons. Langland is less certain than contemporary preachers that sermons can influence royal policy, for example, or that debate at the preaching cross can supply a resolution to contentious issues. *Piers Plowman* contains its own, radical prescriptions for the reform of preaching, too, imagining a return to an earlier age of heroic evangelism, a version of preaching that looks like stoic agricultural labour, and a version that resembles the performances of virtuous minstrels.

Preaching is one of many topics in Langland's poem, and one of many influences on his poetic practice. As readers since Owst have sought to acknowledge, however, it seems to have a special place among the many discourses that Langland engaged and explored. The forms and languages of preaching pervade the poem, as we have seen, and sermons proliferate at important moments in the allegorical action, offering an impetus for social and spiritual reform, and sometimes a subject for heated debate. I hope that the account of preaching and narrative in this book provides a new way to estimate and understand the importance of sermons for Langland's project, as a literary form that mediates lived experience at the intersection of 'clergie' and 'kynde', that reveals the operations of God's justice and mercy in the complex realities of the contemporary world, and that establishes new possibilities for social and spiritual endeavour in the context of an interpreted present.

Coda

Atonement and Emplotment at the Harrowing of Hell

As a Coda to the main part of this book, I turn to the sixth vision of *Piers Plowman*, where the dreamer witnesses the crucifixion and the harrowing of hell, and to the speech of Christ, addressed to the devil as the harrowing takes place, that forms the climax of the allegorical action. This part of *Piers Plowman* employs images and ideas that were widely instantiated in medieval preaching in order to imagine a moment in time when the central events of the Christian story were still unfolding. Langland figures the crucifixion as a joust, where Christ, dressed as a knight in the armour of his incarnate body, will fight with the devil for the souls of Adam and Eve and their descendants, the 'fruyt' that fell from the Tree of Charity in the second inner dream (B.18.20); he supplements this reimagining of the biblical story with an allegorical debate between the four daughters of God: Righteousness and Truth, who argue that human beings are condemned forever, citing God's first judgement on Adam and Eve, and Mercy and Peace, who argue that God will eventually redeem the souls of human beings from hell, citing the prophecies of Old Testament patriarchs. As Mary Raschko has recently shown, the four daughters are themselves engaged in successive acts of emplotment, as they seek to discern the principles of God's justice, or of his mercy, at work in the history of the world.[1] It is not until the arrival of Christ at the end of the passus, however, that these disparate acts of narrative interpretation are synthesized into a single plot. As part of the atonement, I argue, Christ makes available the narrative that later preachers would elaborate in their sermons, and models the kind of interpretation they would use to reconfigure their listeners' understanding of their present moment.

The sixth vision of *Piers Plowman* takes up and combines elements from many different genres and traditions, reimagining biblical narrative in terms drawn from romance and debate poetry, for example. As a result, this part of the poem offers a compact demonstration of Nicolette Zeeman's claim that allegory emerges from the juxtaposition of multiple discourses.[2] Many of the elements in this vision

---

[1] Raschko, 'Storytelling at the Gates of Hell'.
[2] Zeeman, *Arts of Disruption*, 2. Elizabeth Kirk writes that one 'dominant feature' of this vision is its 'juxtaposition of so many short segments in totally different kinds of discourse, throwing each other

are found in works of commentary and exegesis, notably in Robert Grosseteste's *Château d'Amour*, an allegory of salvation history that includes a debate between the four daughters and a parliament of devils and that served as a direct source for this part of *Piers Plowman*.[3] They also appear, individually and in combination, in medieval sermons and resources for preachers. Representations of Christ as a knight who goes into battle for the soul were a 'homiletic commonplace', as Siegfried Wenzel writes, and sometimes the occasion for lyrical, vernacular poetry in Latin preaching.[4] One popular exemplum, found in sermons by Thomas Brinton and John Dygon as well as in several anonymous collections, imagines the persons of the Trinity as Knights of the Round Table attending a tournament where Christ is chosen to joust with the devil.[5] In another, found in Bromyard's *Summa praedicantium*, the sermons of John Felton, and the *Gesta Romanorum*—a story collection that often served as a resource for preachers, a lady (or in Bromyard, a male friend) venerates the bloody armour of a knight who has died fighting on her behalf. Here, as in *Piers Plowman*, the knight's armour figures Christ's incarnate body.[6] The debate between the four daughters appears in sermons, too.[7] An early and influential account appears in a sermon for the Annunciation by Bernard of Clairvaux, and other versions are found in a sermon by Peter of St Victor that was sometimes attributed to Bede, and in the *Gesta Romanorum*.[8] G. R. Owst describes an account of the debate between the four daughters in a late medieval sermon for the third Sunday in Advent from British

---

and their implied genres and contexts into relief'; 'Langland's Narrative Christology', 17–35 in *Art and Context in Late Medieval English Narrative: Essays in Honor of Robert Worth Frank, Jr.*, ed. Robert R. Edwards (Cambridge: Brewer, 1994), 22.

[3] On Grosseteste's *Château* as a source for *Piers Plowman*, see Barney, *Penn Commentary*, 5: 2–3. Barney argues that it is impossible to say whether Langland knew the Anglo-Norman version or one of the Middle English translations; *Penn Commentary*, 5: 3; Davis, who proposes Grosseteste's *Château* as an influence on Langland's conception of Kynde as *natura naturans*, argues for Langland's knowledge of the Anglo-Norman version; *Books of Nature*, 113–19.

[4] Wenzel, *Preachers, Poets, and the Early English Lyric* (Princeton, NJ: Princeton University Press, 1986), 233.

[5] Wenzel, *Preachers, Poets*, 233 n. 68. Warner notes that Dygon, like Langland, employs a chivalric metaphor to synthesize two competing theories of the atonement; Warner, 'Jesus the Jouster: The Christ-Knight and Medieval Theories of Atonement in *Piers Plowman* and the "Round Table" Sermons", *YLS* 10 (1996): 129–43.

[6] See Tubach, *Index Exemplorum*, no. 4020; Bromyard, *Summa Praedicantium*, 2: 176r–v ('Passio Christi', ii.25); *Gesta Romanorum*, ed. Hermann Oesterley (Berlin: Weidmann, 1872), 376–7; *The Anglo-Latin 'Gesta Romanorum' from Oxford, Bodleian Library, MS Douce 310*, ed. and trans. Philippa Bright with Diane Speed and Juanita Ruys (Oxford: Oxford University Press, 2019), 76–81. For Felton, and for other uses of this story in literary and devotional texts, see Bright, *Anglo-Latin 'Gesta'*, 76 n. 15.

[7] On the history of the debate between the four daughters, see Hope Traver, *The Four Daughters of God: A Study in the Versions of this Allegory with Special Reference to those in Latin, French, and English* (Bryn Mawr: Bryn Mawr College, 1907).

[8] Bernard of Clairvaux, *In annuntiatione Dominica sermo prius*, 5: 13–29 in *Sancti Bernardi opera*, ed. Leclercq, Talbot, and Rochais; Pseudo-Bede, *Homiliae*, in Bede, *Opera Omnia*, vol. 5, 94: cols 267–516 in *PL*, ed. J. P. Migne, 217 vols (Paris: Migne, 1844–55), 94: cols 505–7 (54); *Gesta Romanorum*, ed. Oesterley, 350–4; *Anglo-Latin 'Gesta'*, ed. and trans. Bright, 256–63. See also Tubach, *Index Exemplorum*, no. 4427. For Peter of St Victor, see Mary Immaculate, 'The Four Daughters of God in the *Gesta Romanorum* and the *Court of Sapience*', *PMLA* 57, no. 4 (1942):

Library, Royal MS 8 F VII, a fifteenth-century manuscript that also contains twenty-seven chapters of the *Gesta*.[9]

Some of these elements appear combined in a sermon for the Annunciation from British Library, Harley MS 2268, one of four sermons in this manuscript that Veronica O'Mara has attributed to Thomas Spofford, Abbot of St Mary's in York from 1405 to 1421.[10] In the second division, Spofford describes the debate between the four daughters, naming Bernard of Clairvaux as his source.[11] Spofford's sermon then continues with the story of the lady who venerates the knight's bloody armour ('scho [she] toke hys armor þat he was slayn in, and als blody als yt was, scho set it in hyr chambyr opynly þat scho myth thynk vpon him') and a moralization that names the knight as Christ.[12] Then, after a reference to a 'law and ordinaunce emang þe knythys of þe Rounde Tabyll of kyng Arthurow' that is left undeveloped, Spofford imagines Christ's incarnate body as a knight's armour, explaining that his 'habirion [mail coat]' was 'owre manhede'.[13] In another sermon from this manuscript, Spofford repeats the story of the lady who keeps the knight's armour and the account of Christ's body as a 'habyrione of owre manhede', and makes still more explicit that the allegorical reading applies to the armour in the exemplum.[14] Even in the Annunciation sermon, where the relationship between these materials has to be inferred from their sequential arrangement, it is clear that the debate between the daughters and the *exempla* imagining the incarnate Christ as a knightly champion reveal different aspects of the same story. Spofford's Annunciation sermon, then, shows a late medieval preacher with no necessary knowledge of *Piers Plowman* combining elements from the exegetical tradition in a way that resembles Langland's poem.

If the sixth vision of *Piers Plowman* draws on exegetical materials that were often found in preaching, however, it also imagines the texts and authorities that later preachers would cite at a moment when their claims were provisional and open to question. Book, a personification of the Bible who appears at the end of the debate between the four daughters, speaks not only as a textual record of the life of Christ but also as a living witness to events that are happening around him in the world ('"By Goddes body!", quod þis Book, "I wol bere witnesse..."',

---

951–65. Another exemplum, found in the *Alphabetum narrationum* and in the Middle English sermon cycle *Jacob's Well*, imagines the four daughters appearing to a sinful scholar in Bologna and Mercy urging him to join the Dominicans. See Tubach, *Index Exemplorum*, no. 4193.

[9] Owst, *Literature and Pulpit*, 91.

[10] *Four Middle English Sermons, edited from British Library MS Harley 2268*, ed. O'Mara (Heidelberg: Winter, 2002), 37–40. O'Mara (*Four Middle English Sermons*, 27) argues that Spofford delivered this sermon on Sunday 25 March 1414.

[11] *Four Middle English Sermons*, ed. O'Mara, 94.

[12] *Four Middle English Sermons*, ed. O'Mara, 95.

[13] *Four Middle English Sermons*, ed. O'Mara, 95, 96.

[14] *Four Middle English Sermons*, ed. O'Mara, 140.

B.18.231).[15] At the conclusion of his speech, he openly declares the provisional nature of his own authority at this point in history, when his assertions about the atonement remain unproven, declaring that 'I, Book, wole be brent [burned], but Iesus rise to lyue' (B.18.254). Speakers in this passus often cite the 'patriarkes and prophetes' of the Old Testament in support of their competing arguments. During the debate between the four daughters, Mercy recalls that the 'patriarkes and prophetes' often 'preched' about the coming atonement while they were alive (B.18.138) and, in the parliament of devils, Satan declares that they continue to preach in hell: 'Patriarkes and prophetes han parled [spoken] herof longe—/ That swich a lord and a light shal lede hem alle hennes' (B.18.270–1).[16] In this historical moment, however, the prophecies of these patriarchs have not yet been fulfilled, and the status of their preaching is open to challenge. Mercy cites their prophecies to support her argument that God will redeem the souls of human beings from hell: 'For patriarkes and prophetes han preched herof often' (B.18.138). Truth, however, points to their present situation as evidence that God's first judgement still holds: 'Adam and Eue and Abraham wiþ oþere/ Patriarkes and prophetes... in peyne liggen' (B.18.143–4).

The patriarchs and prophets are 'indispensable' to the overall design of this passus, as Emily Steiner writes, 'because they enfold Christ's life into the long history of belief, a history...[that] rolls backwards to Eden and forward to the saints, consuming everything in its wake'.[17] They supply what Sarah Elliot Novacich has described as an 'infernal archive' of legitimizing authorities.[18] Yet, for much of the passus, the authority of their preaching appears uncertain. It is only at the moment of the harrowing that Christ appropriates and recuperates the preaching of these Old Testament figures, making it available for later Christian exegesis, an 'interpretative process', as Novacich writes, that 'fuses typology to a supersessionary schema'.[19] As I will argue, the work of emplotment is central to this process of reinterpretation: Christ will 'preue' what the patriarchs have 'preched' by atoning for Adam's sin, but he will also provide a new narrative

---

[15] Book tells the story of Christ's life through a succession of scenes where the elements recognize him as their creator. In this respect, as Davis notes, he recalls the trope of the 'book of nature', as well as the written Bible; *Books of Nature*, 11. This part of Book's speech derives from a passage in the homilies of Gregory the Great that was later translated as part of the *Northern Homily Cycle*, as R. E. Kaske was the first to observe: Gregory, *Homiliae in Evangelia*, ed. Étaix, 66–7, trans. Hurst, 55 (X.2); see Kaske, 'The Speech of "Book" in *Piers Plowman*', *Anglia* 77 (1959): 119–21, and Barney, *Penn Commentary*, 5: 55. It offers another example of Langland drawing on the homiletic tradition to describe this formative, transitional moment in Christian history.

[16] Sarah Elliott Novacich, writing on dramatic representations of the harrowing, notes that 'the scriptural recitations' of the Old Testament patriarchs could often be heard as part of the 'cacophony' that issued from hell on the medieval stage. Novacich, *Shaping the Archive in Late Medieval England: History, Poetry, and Performance* (Cambridge: Cambridge University Press, 2017), 145.

[17] Steiner, *Reading Piers Plowman*, 179.   [18] Novacich, *Shaping the Archive*, 143, 152, 159.

[19] Novacich, *Shaping the Archive*, 148.

context to understand these authorities, as he explains the justice of the atonement with reference to the larger shape of eschatological history.

The debates that precede the harrowing of hell in this passus are characterized by successive, competing acts of emplotment, as different speakers seek to understand the events of the crucifixion in narrative terms. Mishtooni Bose has described the debate between the four daughters as a kind of 'narrative... simulation' where the daughters 'generate arguments grounded in their respective natures'.[20] As Raschko has argued, moreover, the debate itself plays out as a scene of 'collective, reiterative storytelling', as each of the participants offers their own, partial account of 'the same story in which they participate'.[21] When she first appears in this vision, Truth has heard the 'din' of the crucifixion, seen the 'derknesse' that follows from the eclipse of the sun, and noted 'a light and a leme [glow]' at the borders of hell, and is travelling to find out what they mean (B.18.123–4).[22] Mercy responds with a 'tale', relating the narrative of Christ's life, his conception and birth, his 'þritti [thirty] wynter' in the world, and his death on the cross (B.18.132, 133). This narrative offers a new discursive context to understand the phenomena that Truth has observed in the present moment ('þat is cause of þis clips [eclipse] þat closeþ now þe sonne', B.18.138), and forms the basis for Mercy's confident prediction that Christ will save the souls of Adam and Eve and their descendants from hell. Truth replies by dismissing her narrative as a 'tale of waltrot [absurdity]' (B.18.142) and asserting that God's original judgement is absolute and cannot be changed; this argument too has a narrative dimension, as Truth looks back to the story of Adam and Eve, marking the Fall as the axial moment that determines the conditions of subsequent history.

Righteousness and Peace, who join the debate, offer their own acts of emplotment as they work to make sense of the events that are happening around them. Peace recalls the prophecies of the patriarchs and predicts that Christ will redeem the souls of 'Adam and Eue and oþere mo [many others] in helle' (B.18.177), while Righteousness recalls God's judgement at the Fall, supplying the narrative context for Truth's earlier pronouncement: 'At þe bigynnyng God gaf þe doom hymselue—/ That Adam and Eue and alle þat hem suwede [followed] / Sholden deye downrighte [absolutely], and dwelle in peyne after...' (B.18.190–2). These speakers frame their acts of emplotment with reference to contemporary legal practice. Peace carries letters from Love, containing promises of salvation. Holding one out for her sisters to read, she describes it as a legal document— 'Lo, here þe patente!' (B.18.185)—and explains that it allows for her and Mercy to

---

[20] Mishtooni Bose, 'Piers Plowman and God's Thought Experiment', 71–97 in *Medieval Thought Experiments: Poetry, Hypothesis, and Experience in the European Middle Ages*, ed. Philip Knox, Jonathan Morton, and Daniel Reeve, Disuptatio 31 (Turnhout: Brepols, 2018), 77.

[21] Raschko, 'Storytelling at the Gates of Hell', 166, 167.

[22] Zeeman (*Arts of Disruption*, 162) likens this scene to other moments in the poem when 'speakers and seekers walk across the landscape in search of spiritual "news"'.

act as 'mannes meynpernour', standing surety for human beings at the last judgement (B.18.184).[23] Righteousness, meanwhile, imagines herself and Truth as *recordeurs*, rehearsing the events of the Fall in court: 'I, Rightwisnesse, recorde þus wiþ Truþe,/ That hir peyne be perpetual and no preiere hem helpe' (B.18.198-9).[24] Peace and Righteousness raise the stakes of the argument with these allusions to the law: the 'tales' that Righteousness will tell have the force of testimony at a trial, while the letters that Peace displays transform Love's promises into a legal contract. Both sisters offer narratives that cohere around a binding commitment made by God, offering competing accounts of divine 'self-constancy'.

Raschko writes that narrative provides the four daughters with 'a tool for exploration and discovery' in this scene, a way to make sense of history as it unfolds. Citing Ricoeur on the selection and configuration of events that constitutes an act of emplotment, she argues that 'when the daughters tell stories, they engage in acts of discernment, integrating select aspects of biblical history in unique configurations and then using those narrative memories to predict, and possibly shape the future'.[25] As Raschko goes on to note, however, the debate between the sisters also serves to illustrate 'the insufficiency of single stories', as the sisters construe the same events in different ways.[26] The four daughters have competing, conflicting understandings of the logic that animates the story of God's relationship to human beings, the *res* or 'gist' to which it gives expression. Mercy and Peace configure the events of Christ's life in the world to express the hope of salvation, whereas Truth and Righteousness offer an interpretation of history that continually reaffirms God's first judgement on Adam and Eve.

The speakers at the devils' parliament offer their own versions of these competing narratives. Lucifer restates God's original judgement, made 'longe ago' on Adam and Eve (B.18.273): this judgement has lasted for 'seuenty hundred wynter [seven thousand years]', establishing the unchanging conditions of subsequent history (B.18.283). Like Righteousness and Peace, Lucifer understands this judgement as a legal commitment, as well as the organizing principle for an act of emplotment: as we saw in Chapter 1, Lucifer refers to Christ as a king who must act according to the law rather than enforcing his will like a tyrant. Satan, meanwhile, offers another narrative of Christ's life, reminding his companions that Christ has already raised Lazarus from the dead, a miracle that foreshadows the harrowing. He also offers a new perspective on the Fall, reminding Lucifer of

---

[23] For the legal terminology in this speech, see Alford, *Glossary of Legal Diction*, 87-8, s.v. 'lettre'; 65, s.v. 'given and graunten'; 93-4, s.v. 'mainpernour'; 111, s.v. 'patente'; 43, s.v. 'dede'. Steiner reads Peace's 'patente' in relation to Truth's pardon and a series of other documents in the poem that imagine salvation in legal terms: *Documentary Culture*, 115-20. Davis, *Books of Nature*, 105-7, reads Peace's 'patente' in relation to the 'Charters of Christ'.
[24] On the legal significance of 'recording' in these lines, see Alford, *Glossary of Legal Diction*, 127-8, s.v. 'recorden'.
[25] Raschko, 'Storytelling at the Gates of Hell', 172, citing Ricoeur, *Time and Narrative*, 1: x.
[26] Raschko, 'Storytelling at the Gates of Hell', 173.

his own role in the temptation of Adam and Eve: 'For þow gete hem [obtained them] wiþ gile, and his gardyn breke,/ And in semblaunce of a serpent sete on þe appultree,/ And eggedest [urged] hem to ete' (B.18.286–8). Integrating these events into his narrative account, Satan casts doubt on the devil's claim to human souls. 'We haue no trewe title to them', exclaims Goblin, 'for þoruȝ treson were þei dampned!' (B.18.293).

In his triumphant speech at the gates of hell, Christ performs an extended act of emplotment that incorporates the partial, fragmentary narratives of the foregoing debates into a single, cohesive *holos*. The speech unfolds simultaneously with the action of the harrowing: Christ addresses the devil as he saves the souls of the righteous from hell ('And þo þat Oure Lord louede, into his light he laughte [caught],/ And seide to Sathan...', B.18.327–8) and he binds the devil as he speaks the final words: '["]Thow shalt abeyen [pay for] it bitter!"—and bond hym wiþ cheynes' (B.18.404). Stephen Barney argues that this speech was most likely inspired by the tradition of allegorical debates between Christ and the devil, and principally by the scene in Grosseteste's *Château* where Christ answers each of the devil's arguments against the atonement in turn, but he also notes an interpretation of 1 Peter 3:19, found in Origen and elsewhere, that imagines Jesus preaching in hell during the harrowing.[27] Shortly before Christ appears, one of the devils refers to his evangelical ministry in the world, raising the possibility that this speech, too, might be considered as a sermon: 'Thise þritty wynter, as I wene, he wente aboute and preched' (B.18.295). Whether or not the speech can be considered a sermon in its own right, however, it stands in an important relation to preaching in other parts of the poem because it establishes, as though for the first time, the story that later preachers would echo and elaborate. The act of emplotment that Christ performs reveals the narrative shape of eschatological history in a way that both reaffirms and supersedes the preaching of the patriarchs, and establishes the possibility of salvation for people living under the New Law.

At the beginning of his speech, Christ presents an account of the Fall that confirms his original judgement on Adam and Eve as just and reasonable but that also allows for an end to their punishment and acknowledges the role of the devil's temptation:

Alþouȝ reson recorde, and riȝt of myselue,	*declare; my own justice*
That if þei ete þe appul, alle sholde deye,	
I bihiȝte hem noȝt here helle for euere.	*decreed, promised*
For þe dede þat þei dide, þi deceite it made;	*caused it*
Wiþ gile þow hem gete, ageyn alle reson.	*got; against*

(B.18.331–5)

---

[27] Barney, *Penn Commentary*, 5: 73.

He describes his death on the cross as recompense for Adam's fall and his appearance as a knight at the joust as a trick on the devil that repays him for deceiving Adam and Eve. Understood in this narrative context, the act of mercy that inaugurates the New Law can be seen to express, rather than to contravene, the strict justice of the Old:

Thus ylik a lusard wiþ a lady visage,	*serpent; woman's face*
Thefliche þow me robbedest. Þe Olde Lawe grauntep	*Like a theif*
That gilours be bigiled—and þat is good reson:	
Dentem pro dente et oculum pro oculo.	
Ergo soule shal soule quyte and synne to synne wende,	*pay for*
And al þat man haþ misdo, I, man, wole amende it.	*done wrong*
Membre for membre was amendes by þe Olde Lawe,	*satisfaction*
And lif for lif also—and by þat lawe I clayme	
Adam and al his issue at my wille herafter.	
	(B.18.338–45)

['Tooth for tooth and eye for eye', cf. Ex 21:24]

At this point in the poem, the competing narratives that emerge in the foregoing debates are integrated into a single plot, one that acknowledges the ramifications of God's first judgement on Adam and Eve, but that also vindicates the prophets and patriarchs, and fulfils the promises made by Love. Rather than suppress one side of the argument in favour of the other, this act of emplotment construes elements from all the previous narratives as part of a single *holos*. Novacich, writing on representations of the harrowing in medieval drama, and Steiner, writing on this scene in *Piers Plowman*, have both emphasized Christ's appeal to ideas of 'fittingness' at this moment.[28] For Steiner, Christ's speech at the harrowing exemplifies 'a poetics of fittingness' that draws on 'different legal and ethical systems' to show how his actions have restored a proper balance to history.[29] This essential fittingness, I suggest, finds expression in narrative, as Christ configures disparate events into an interpreted whole, giving expression to their 'discordant concordance'.

Christ extends this narrative of salvation history in the second part of his speech, where he looks ahead to the last judgement:

For I þat am lord of lif, loue is my drynke,	
And for þat drynke today, I deide vpon erþe.	
I fauȝt so, me þursteþ yet, for mannes soule sake;	*fought; thirst*
May no drynke me moiste, ne my þurst slake,	

---

[28] Novacich, *Shaping the Archive*, 143; Steiner, *Reading Piers Plowman*, 203.
[29] Steiner, *Reading Piers Plowman*, 202–3.

> Til þe vendage falle in þe vale of Iosaphat,   *vintage take place*
> That I drynke riȝt ripe must, *resureccio mortuorum.*   *the resurrection of the dead*
> And þanne shal I come as a kyng, crouned, wiþ aungeles,
> And haue out of helle alle mennes soules.
>
> (B.18.366–73)

In the first part of this speech, Christ revealed his 'self-constancy' through a narrative that demonstrated how his interventions in human history are consistent with both justice and mercy, but here, in the second part, he expresses that 'self-constancy' in a different way, as a form of persistent and insatiable desire. Christ's exclamation from the cross, 'sicio [I thirst]' (John 19:28), is reimagined to express a desire for human souls that will persist until the end of time; at the apocalypse, the grapes will ripen in the valley of Jehoshaphat, imagined as the scene of the resurrection in Joel 3:2, 12–13, and Christ will drink the wine of the resurrection of the dead. In this passage, as Jill Mann observes, 'God is driven by a need which is as concrete, as impossible to paraphrase, as the need of hunger or thirst.'[30] The passionate commitments that were codified in his letters to Peace are now reimagined as an expression of the most fundamental, physical need for food and drink, and this essential need in turn forms the 'single thought' that confers coherence on a large-scale narrative of human history.

The physical experience of hunger forms part of the new knowledge that Christ acquires as a result of his incarnation in *Piers Plowman*. In the debate between the four daughters, Peace explains that the suffering that Adam and Eve have experienced since the Fall will allow them a fuller apprehension of joy after the atonement. She draws an analogy with hunger, which can only be known through experience: 'For hadde þei wist of no wo', she argues, 'wele hadde þei noȝt knowen;/ For no wight woot what wele is, þat neuere wo suffrede,/ Ne what is hoot [called] hunger, þat hadde neuere defaute' (B.18.206). Here, Peace invokes what Derek Pearsall has called the 'doctrine of contraries' to argue that each experience is most fully and profoundly understood in the light of its opposite.[31] In a radical development of this idea, Peace declares that Christ himself became incarnate as a human being so that he could understand sorrow and joy in the same way:

> Forþi God, of his goodnesse, þe firste gome Adam,   *man*
> Sette hym in solace and in souereyn murþe;   *supreme joy*
> And siþþe he suffred hym synne, sorwe to feele –   *afterwards; allowed*

---

[30] Mann, 'Eating and Drinking', 43. See also *C-text*, ed. Pearsall, 339; Barney, *Penn Commentary*, 5: 83; Burrow, 'God and the Fullness of Time', 303.

[31] Pearsall, 'The Necessity of Difference: The Speech of Peace and the Doctrine of Contraries in Langland's *Piers Plowman*', 125–65 in *Medieval Latin and Middle English Literature: Essays in Honour of Jill Mann*, ed. Christopher Cannon and Maura Nolan (Cambridge: Brewer, 2011).

To wite what wele was, kyndeliche to knowe it.	*know; suffering*
And after, God auntrede hymself and took Adames kynde	*ventured*
To wite what he haþ suffred in þre sondry places,	
Boþe in heuene and in erþe—and now til helle he þenkeþ,	*to (go to)*
To wite what alle wo is, þat woot of alle ioye.	

(B.18.217-24)

In these lines, as Bose has observed, 'the soteriological purpose of the Incarnation is temporarily sidelined in favour of its experiential dividends', as if God became man primarily to experience joy and sorrow, hunger and thirst, as human beings do.[32] As Pearsall notes, Langland places a higher value on these experiential contrasts than other writers who invoke the 'doctrine of contraries', imagining the acquisition of such knowledge as an important benefit of the Fall, and as part of the rationale for the incarnation.[33]

As she makes these claims for experiential knowledge, Peace also makes a powerful case for narrative as a tool of understanding. 'Wo' and 'wele', like 'hunger' and 'defaute', are experienced in the phenomenological present, but their significance emerges through the mediation of narrative, which contrasts them with one another as part of an interpreted plot. The knowledge that the Fall makes available, and that Christ seeks himself at the incarnation, is available not through direct, unmediated experience, but through a narrative understanding that places that experience in relation to others.

Both Pearsall and Bose read this part of *Piers Plowman* in the light of a passage from the *Tractatus de gradibus humilitatis et superbiae* of Bernard of Clairvaux that reflects on the temporal aspect of Christ's incarnate experience.[34] Bernard asks in what sense Christ could be said to have acquired new knowledge at the incarnation, and concludes that while God's knowledge is always complete and eternal, the incarnation afforded an opportunity to experience the acquisition of knowledge over time: 'Non ergo debet absurdum videri, si dicitur Christum non quidem aliquid scire coepisse, quod aliquando nescierit, scire tamen alio modo misericordiam ab aeterno per divinitatem, et aliter in tempore didicisse per carnem [Therefore it ought not seem absurd if it is said not that Christ began to know for the first time something which he did not know before, but that there is no contradiction in saying that something he knew from all eternity by his divine

---

[32] Bose, 'Thought Experiment', 83-4.

[33] Pearsall writes that other texts that invoke the doctrine of contraries argue for a 'sharpening of sensation' rather than a 'deepening of moral or intellectual awareness'; 'Necessity of Difference', 158-9. Steiner (*Reading Piers Plowman*, 208) observes that knowledge by contraries becomes both 'the ground of experience' and 'the foundation of divine Reason' in *Piers Plowman*.

[34] Pearsall, 'Necessity of Difference', 160; Bose, 'Thought Experiment', 84-5; and see also Barney, *Penn Commentary*, 5: 52.

knowledge he now began in time to learn by human experience].'[35] 'In his human condition', as Bose writes, summarizing this argument, 'Christ had to submit to the gradual process of learning enforced by temporality.'[36] This experiential kinship with human beings, established through the incarnation, also means that Christ is able to perceive the need for narrative interpretation in a new way. Christ experiences what Ricoeur describes as the 'concordant discordance' of the distended soul, stretching out in three directions to apprehend time as it passes. The act of emplotment he performs in his speech responds to the human perception of time by gathering disparate events into a cohesive, interpreted *holos*, answering the 'concordant discordance' of the soul with the 'discordant concordance' of narrative.

In the sixth vision of *Piers Plowman*, then, Langland draws on a range of tropes and discourses that were familiar from the pulpit in order to imagine a moment in time when the texts, the interpretative premises, and the underlying narrative of later Christian preaching were under formation. The preaching of the prophets and patriarchs, which anticipates the coming atonement, has yet to be 'preued' by the events of the crucifixion and the harrowing. This part of the poem stages debates between successive speakers who attempt to construe the unfolding events in narrative terms, performing partial, conflicting acts of emplotment, each of which illustrates different aspects of God's mercy and justice at work in historical time. The speech of Christ, which marks the culmination of this passus, presents a new narrative of salvation history that integrates the stories these speakers tell and reconciles the apparent contradictions they reveal; in doing so, it offers a template for the preaching scenes that proliferate in other parts of the poem, establishing the 'narrative frame' that Wenzel describes as 'ever present' in late medieval preaching *ad populum*.[37] Langland's distinctive account of the incarnation also implies that Christ perceives the need for narrative interpretation in a new way, as a means to construe experiences in the light of their contraries. If the incarnation establishes Christ in a new, 'kynde' relation to human beings that argues retroactively for the justice of the atonement, it also establishes him in a unique position as a maker of narratives, answering to the human perception of time with a new interpretation of history.

---

[35] Bernard of Clairvaux, *Liber de gradibus humilitatis et superbiae*, 3: 1–59, in *Sancti Bernardi opera*, ed. J. Leclercq, C. H. Talbot, and H. M. Rochais, 8 vols (Rome: Editiones Cistercienses, 1957–8), 23 (3.10); translation from Bernard of Clairvaux, *The Steps of Humility and Pride*, 1–82, in *Treatises II*, trans. M. Ambrose Conway (Washington DC: Cistercian Publications, 1974), 38.

[36] Bose, 'Thought Experiment', 85.   [37] Wenzel, *Latin Sermon Collections*, 245.

Works Cited

Manuscripts

London, British Library, Harley MS 5398.
London, British Library, Royal MS 15 A XXX.
London, Lambeth Palace Library, MS 61.
Warminster, Longleat House, MS 4.

Primary Sources

Alan of Lille, *De arte praedicatoria*, 210: cols 111-98 in *PL*, ed. J. P. Migne, 217 vols, Paris: Migne, 1844-55.
Alan of Lille, *The Art of Preaching*, trans. Gillian R. Evans, Kalamazoo: Western Michigan University Press, 1981.
Alan of Lille, *De planctu naturae*, 21-217 in *Literary Works*, ed. and trans. Winthrop Wetherbee, Cambridge, MA: Harvard University Press, 2013.
Alkerton, Richard, 'Easter Week Sermon', 21-80 in *A Study and Edition of Selected Middle English Sermons*, ed. Veronica O'Mara, Leeds Texts and Monographs, new series 13, Leeds: School of English, University of Leeds, 1994.
An Alphabet of Tales: An English 15th Century Translation of the Alphabetum Narrationum, ed. Mary Macleod Banks, 2 of 3 vols, EETS, os 126-7, London: Paul, Trench, Trübner, 1904-5.
The Anglo-Latin 'Gesta Romanorum' from Oxford, Bodleian Library, MS Douce 310, ed. and trans. Philippa Bright with Diane Speed and Juanita Ruys, Oxford: Oxford University Press, 2019.
The Anonimalle Chronicle, 1333-1381, ed. V. H. Galbraith, Manchester: Manchester University Press, 1927, repr. 1970.
Augustine, *Contra Faustum Manichaeum*, 249-797 in *De Utilitate credendi* [...], ed. Joseph Zycha, CSEL 25, no. 1, Vienna: Tempsky, 1891.
Augustine, *In Iohannis Evangelium tractatus CXXIV*, ed. Radbodus Willems, CCSL 36, Turnhout: Brepols, 1954.
Augustine, *De civitate Dei*, ed. Bernard Domart and Alfons Kalb, 2 vols, CCSL 47-8, Turnhout: Brepols, 1955.
Augustine, *Enarrationes in Psalmos*, ed. Eligius Dekkers and Johannes Fraipont, 3 vols, CCSL 38-40, Turnhout: Brepols, 1956.
Augustine, *Sermones de vetere testamento (1-50)*, ed. Cyril Lambot, CCSL 41, Turnhout: Brepols, 1961.
Augustine, *De doctrina Christiana*, ed. Joseph Martin, CCSL 32, Turnhout: Brepols, 1962.
Augustine, *Confessionum libri XII*, ed. Martin Skutella, rev. Luca Verheijen, CCSL 27, Turnhout: Brepols, 1981.
Augustine, *Sermons 20-50*, ed. John E. Rotelle, trans. Edmund Hill, WSA, 3.2, New York: New City Press, 1990.

WORKS CITED

Augustine, *Teaching Christianity*, trans. Edmund Hill, OP, WSA 1.11, Hyde Park, NY: New City Press, 1996.

Augustine, *Expositions of the Psalms, 33–50*, ed. John E. Rotelle, trans. Maria Boulding, WSA 3, no. 16, Hyde Park, NY: New City Press, 2000.

Bede, *In Marci Evangelium Expositio*, 427–648 in *Opera Exegetica II, 3*, ed. David Hurst, CCSL 120, Turnhout: Brepols, 1960.

Bede, *Historia ecclesiastica gentis Anglorum*, ed. and trans. Bertram Colgrave and R. A. B. Mynors, Oxford: Clarendon, 1969.

Bernard of Clairvaux, *In annuntiatione Dominica sermo prius*, 5: 13–29 in *Sancti Bernardi opera*, ed. J. Leclercq, C. H. Talbot, and H. M. Rochais, 8 vols, Rome: Editiones Cistercienses, 1957–8.

Bernard of Clairvaux, *Liber de gradibus humilitatis et superbiae*, 3: 1–59, in *Sancti Bernardi opera*, ed. J. Leclercq, C. H. Talbot, and H. M. Rochais, 8 vols, Rome: Editiones Cistercienses, 1957–8.

Bernard of Clairvaux, *Sermones super Canticum Canticorum*, vols. 1–2 in *Sancti Bernardi opera*, ed. J. Leclercq, C. H. Talbot, and H. M. Rochais, 8 vols, Rome: Editiones Cistercienses, 1957–8.

Bernard of Clairvaux, *Sermons on the Song of Songs*, trans. Killian Walsh, 4 vols, Kalamazoo: Cistercian Publications, 1971–80.

Bernard of Clairvaux, *The Steps of Humility and Pride*, 1–82, in *Treatises II*, trans. M. Ambrose Conway, Washington DC: Cistercian Publications, 1974.

Boethius, *Philosophiae Consolatio*, ed. Ludwig Bieler, CCSL 94, Turnhout: Brepols, 1957; rev edn, 1984.

Boethius, *The Consolation of Philosophy*, trans. Victor Watts, London: Penguin, 1969; rev edn, 1999.

Bracton, Henry, *De Legibus et consuetudinibus Angliæ (On the Laws and Customs of England)*, ed. George E. Woodbine, trans. Samuel E Thorne, 2 vols, Cambridge, MA: Belknap Press of Harvard University Press, 1968.

Brinton, Thomas, *The Sermons of Thomas Brinton, Bishop of Rochester (1373–1389)*, ed. Mary Aquinas Devlin, OP, 2 vols, Camden Third Series 85–6, London: Royal Historical Society, 1954.

Brinton, Thomas, 'Sermon 44', 115–24 in *The World of Piers Plowman*, ed. and trans. Jeanne Krochalis and Edward Peters, Philadelphia: University of Pennsylvania Press, 1982.

Brinton, Thomas, 'Sermon 69', 241–54 in *Preaching in the Age of Chaucer: Selected Sermons in Translation*, trans. Siegfried Wenzel, Washington, DC: Catholic University of America Press, 2008.

Bromyard, John, *Summa praedicantium*, 2 vols, Venice: Nicolini, 1586.

Chaucer, Geoffrey, *The Riverside Chaucer*, gen. ed. Larry D. Benson, 3rd edn, Boston: Houghton Mifflin, 1987.

Cicero, *On the Republic; On the Laws*, trans. Clinton W. Keyes, LCL 213, Harvard: Harvard University Press, 1928.

Chronicon Anonymi Cantuariensis: The Chronicle of Anonymous of Canterbury, 1346–1365, ed. and trans. Charity Scott-Stokes and Chris Given-Wilson, Oxford: Oxford University Press, 2008.

Disciplinary Decrees of the General Councils, ed. and trans. H. J. Schroeder, OP, St Louis: Herder, 1937.

The Earliest Advocates of the English Bible: The Texts of the Medieval Debate, ed. Mary Dove, Exeter: University of Exeter Press, 2010.

'An Edition of a Fifteenth Century Middle English Temporale Sermon Cycle in MSS Lambeth Palace 392 and Cambridge University Library Additional 5338', ed. Ruth Evans, 2 vols, PhD thesis, University of Leeds, 1986.

English Coronation Records, ed. and trans. Leopold G. Wickham Legg, Westminster: Constable, 1901.

English Wycliffite Sermons, ed. Anne Hudson and Pamela Gradon, 5 vols, Oxford: Clarendon, 1983-96.

Fasciculus morum: A Fourteenth-century Preacher's Handbook, ed. and trans. Siegfried Wenzel, University Park: Pennsylvania State University Press, 1989.

Fleta, ed. and trans. H. G. Richardson and G. O. Sayles, 3 of 4 vols, London: Quaritch, 1955-84.

'Floretus', 213-50 in *An English Translation of Auctores Octo, a Medieval Reader*, trans. Ronald E. Pepin, Lewiston: Mellen, 1999.

Four Middle English Sermons, edited from British Library MS Harley 2268, ed. Veronica O'Mara, Heidelberg: Winter, 2002.

Gesta Romanorum, ed. Hermann Oesterley, BerlIN: Weidmann, 1872.

Gerald of Wales, *Instruction for a Ruler (De Principis Instructione)*, ed. and trans. Robert Bartlett, Oxford: Clarendon, 2018.

Gregory the Great, *Pastoral Care*, trans. Henry Davis, SJ, Ancient Christian Writers 11, New York, Newman Press, 1950.

Gregory the Great, *Moralia in Iob*, ed. Marc Adriaen, 3 vols, CCSL 143-143B, Turnhout: Brepols, 1979-85.

Gregory the Great, *Forty Gospel Homilies*, trans. David Hurst, Kalamazoo: Cistercian Publications, 1990.

Gregory the Great, *Regula Pastoralis*, ed. Floribert Rommel, trans. Charles Morel, 2 vols, Sources chrétiennes, Paris: Editions du Cerf, 1992.

Gregory the Great, *Homiliae in Evangelia*, ed. Raymond Étaix, CCSL 141, Turnhout: Brepols, 1999.

Gregory the Great, *Moral Reflections on the Book of Job*, trans. Brian Kerns, 6 vols, Collegeville, MN: Cistercian Publications, 2014-22.

The Complete Harley 2253 Manuscript, ed. Susanna Greer Fein, 3 vols, Kalamazoo, MI: Medieval Institute Publications, 2014-15.

Henry, Archdeacon of Huntingdon, *Historia Anglorum (History of the English People)*, ed. and trans. Diana Greenway, Oxford: Clarendon, 1996.

Henry of Harclay, *Ordinary Questions*, ed. Mark G. Henninger, SJ, trans. Raymond Edwards and Mark G. Henninger, SJ, 2 vols, Oxford: Oxford University Press, 2008.

Higden, Ranulph, *Ars componendi sermones*, ed. Margaret Jennings, Leiden: Brill, 1991.

Higden, Ranulph, *Ars componendi sermones*, trans. Margaret Jennings and Sally A. Wilson, Leuven: Peeters, 2003.

The Holy Bible...by John Wycliffe and his Followers, ed. Josiah Forshall and Sir Frederic Madden, 4 vols, Oxford: Oxford University Press, 1850.

Honorius of Autun, *Speculum ecclesiae*, 172: cols 813-1108 in *PL*, ed. J. P. Migne, 217 vols, Paris: Migne, 1844-55.

'How men that ben in hele sholde visite sike folk', 194-202 in *The World of Piers Plowman*, ed. and trans. Jeanne Krochalis and Edward Peters, Philadelphia: University of Pennsylvania Press, 1982.

Hugh of St Victor, 'De institutione novitiorum', 58-74 in *L'œuvre de Hugues de Saint-Victor, 1: De institutione novitiorum, De virtute orandi, De laude caritatis, De arrha animae*, ed. H. B. Feiss and P. Sicard, trans. D. Poirel, H. Rochais and P. Sicard, Turnhout: Brepols, 1997.

Humbert of Romans, *De modo prompte cudendi sermones*, 25: 424–567 in *Maxima Bibliotheca Veterum Patrum et Antiquorum Scriptorum Ecclesiastiorum*, ed. Marguerin de la Bigne, 27 vols, Lyons: Anissonios, 1677.

Humbert of Romans, *Liber de eruditione praedicatorum*, 2: 373–484 in *Opera de vita regulari*, ed. Joachim Joseph Berthier, 2 vols, Rome: Befani, 1888–89; repr. Rome: Marietti, 1956.

Humbert of Romans, *Treatise on the Formation of Preachers*, 179–384 in *Early Domnicans: Selected Writings*, trans. Simon Tugwell, London: SPCK, 1982.

Isidore of Seville, *Sententarium*, 83: cols 537–738 in *PL*, ed. J. P. Migne, 217 vols, Paris: Migne, 1844–55.

Isidore of Seville, *Etymologiarum*, ed. W. M. Lindsay, 2 vols, Oxford: Clarendon Press, 1911.

James of Voragine, *Legenda Aurea*, ed. Giovanni Paolo Maggioni, 2 vols, Florence: SISMEL Edizioni del Galluzzo, 2007.

James of Voragine, *The Golden Legend: Readings on the Saints*, trans. William Granger Ryan, 2nd edn, Princeton, NJ: Princeton University Press, 2012.

Jerome, *Epistulae 1–70*, ed. Isidorus Hilderg and Johannes Divjak, rev. Margit Kamptner, CSEL 54, Vienna: Tempsky, 1996.

Jerome, 'Letter 52', 31–57 in Andrew Cain, *Jerome and the Monastic Clergy: A Commentary on Letter 52 to Nepotian, with an Introduction, Text, and Translation*, Leiden: Brill, 2013.

John of Salisbury, *Policraticus: Of the Frivolities of Courtiers and the Footprints of Philosophers*, trans. Cary J. Nederman, Cambridge: Cambridge University Press, 1990.

Knighton, Henry, *Knighton's Chronicle, 1337–1396*, ed. and trans. G. H. Martin, Oxford: Oxford University Press, 1995.

Langland, William, *The Vision of William Concerning Piers the Plowman in Three Parallel Texts*, ed. W. W. Skeat, 2 vols, Oxford: Oxford University Press, 1886.

Langland, William, *Piers Plowman: The Prologue and Passus I–VII of the B text as found in Bodleian MS Laud 581*, ed. J. A. W. Bennett, Oxford: Clarendon Press, 1972.

Langland, William, *Piers Plowman: The B Version*, ed. George Kane and E. Talbot Donaldson, rev. edn, London: Athlone, 1988.

Langland, William, *The Vision of Piers Plowman: A Critical Edition of the B-Text Based on Trinity College Cambridge MS B.15.17*, ed. A.V. C. Schmidt, 2nd edn, London: J. M. Dent, 1995.

Langland, William, *Piers Plowman: The C Version*, ed. George Russell and George Kane, London: Athlone, 1997.

Langland, William, *Piers Plowman: A New Annotated Edition of the C Text*, ed. Derek Pearsall, Exeter: Exeter University Press, 2008.

Langland, William, *Piers Plowman: A Parallel-Text Edition of the A, B, C, and Z Versions*, ed. A. V. C. Schmidt, 2nd edn, 2 vols, Kalamazoo, MI: Medieval Institute Publications, 2011.

Langland, William, *Piers Plowman: The A Version*, ed. Mí·eál F. Vaughan, Baltimore: Johns Hopkins University Press, 2011.

A Late Fifteenth-Century Dominical Sermon Cycle, ed. Stephen Morrison, 2 vols, EETS, os 337–8, Oxford: Oxford University Press, 2012.

Liber Floretus, ed. Árpád Orbán, Kastellaun: Henn, 1979.

Lollard Sermons, ed. Gloria Cigman, EETS, os 294, Oxford: Oxford University Press, 1989.

A Macaronic Sermon Collection from Late Medieval England: Oxford, MS Bodley 649, ed. and trans. Patrick J. Horner, Studies and Texts 153, Toronto: Pontifical Institute of Mediaeval Studies, 2006.

Maidstone, Richard, *Concordia (The Reconciliation of Richard II with London)*, ed. David R. Carlson, trans. A. G. Rigg. Kalamazoo, MI: Medieval Institute Publications, 2003.

Martin of Cordoba, 'Ars praedicandi de Fray Martin de Cordoba', ed. Fernando Rubio, *La Ciudad de Dios* 172 (1959): 327–48.

Middle English Dictionary, ed. Hans Kurath et al., Ann Arbor, MI: University of Michigan, 1954–2001.

The Middle English 'Mirror': An Edition Based on Bodleian Library MS Holkham misc. 40, ed. Kathleen Marie Blumreich, Medieval and Renaissance Texts and Studies, 182, Tempe: Arizona Center for Medieval and Renaissance Studies, 2002.

The Middle English Mirror: Sermons from Advent to Sexagesima, ed. Thomas G. Duncan and Margaret Connolly, Heidelberg: Winter, 2003.

Middle English Sermons, ed. Woodburn O. Ross, EETS, os 209, London: Oxford University Press, 1940.

Mirk, John, *Festial*, ed. Susan Powell, 2 vols, EETS, os 334–5, Oxford: Oxford University Press, 2009–11.

'A Mirror of the Perfection of the Status of a Lesser Brother (The Sabatier Edition, 1928)', 3: 253–372 in *Francis of Assisi: Early Documents*, ed. Regis J. Armstrong, J. A. Wayne Hellmann, and William J. Short, 3 vols, Hyde Park, NY: New City Press, 1999–2001.

Munimenta Gildhallae Londoniensis, vol. 2: *Liber Custumarum, with Extracts from the Cottonian MS. Claudius D.II*, ed. Henry Thomas Riley, London: Longman, 1860; repr. Cambridge: Cambridge University Press, 2012.

Nicholas of Aquavilla, *Sermones dominicales reverendi patris Nicolai ab Aquevilla*, Paris: Badium Ascensium and de Marnef, 1519.

Paris, Matthew, *Chronica Majora*, ed. Henry Richards Luard, 7 vols, London: Longman, 1872–80; repr. Cambridge: Cambridge University Press, 2012.

Peter the Chanter, *Summa de sacrament's et animae consiliis*, ed. Jean-Albert Dugauquier, 3 vols in 5 fas., Louvain: Éditions Nauwelaert, 1954–7.

Peter the Venerable, *Contra sectam Saracenorum*, 189: cols 659–720 in *PL*, ed. J. P. Migne, 217 vols, Paris: Migne, 1844–55.

Peter the Venerable, *Writings Against the Saracens*, trans. Irven M. Resnick, Washington DC: Catholic University of America Press, 2016.

Prick of Conscience [*Richard Morris's Prick of Conscience*], ed. Ralph Hanna and Sarah Wood, EETS, os 342, Oxford: Oxford University Press, 2013.

Pseudo-Aquinas, *Tractatulus solemnis de arte et vero modo predicandi*, trans. Harry Caplan as 'A Late Medieval Tractate on Preaching', 61–90 in *Studies in Rhetoric and Public Speaking in Honor of James A. Winans*, ed. A. M. Drummond, New York: Century, 1925; repr. at 40–79 in Caplan, *Of Eloquence: Studies in Ancient and Mediaeval Rhetoric*, ed. Anne King and Helen North, Ithaca, NY: Cornell University Press, 1970.

Pseudo-Bede, *Homiliae*, in Bede, *Opera Omnia*, vol. 5, 94: cols 267–516 in *PL*, ed. J. P. Migne, 217 vols, Paris: Migne, 1844–55.

Pseudo-Bernard, *Meditationes piissimae de cognitione humanae conditionis*, 184: cols 485–508 in *PL* 184, ed. J. P. Migne, 217 vols, Paris: Migne, 1844–55.

Pseudo-Jerome, *Regula monachorum*, 30: cols 391–426 in *PL*, ed. J. P. Migne, 217 vols, Paris: Migne, 1844–55.

Puttenham, George, *The Art of English Poetry*, ed. Frank Whigham and Wayne A. Rebhorn, Ithaca, NY: Cornell University Press, 2007.

'The Rite of Baptism in the Sarum Manual', 158–79 in J. D. C. Fisher, *Christian Initiation: Baptism in the Medieval West: A Study in the Disintegration of the Primitive Rite of Initiation*, London: SPCK, 1965.

Robert of Basevorn, *Forma praedicandi*, 233-323 in *Artes Praedicandi: Contribution à l'histoire de la rhétorique au moyen âge*, ed. Thomas Marie Charland, Paris: De Vrin, 1936.

Robert of Basevorn, *The Form of Preaching*, trans. Leopold Krul, 109-215 in *Three Medieval Rhetorical Arts*, ed. James J. Murphy, Berkeley and Los Angeles: University of California Press, 1971.

Rolle, Richard, *Two Revisions of Rolle's English Psalter Commentary and the Related Canticles*, ed. Anne Hudson, EETS, os 340, 341, 343, 3 vols, Oxford: Oxford University Press, 2012-14.

Rypon, Robert, *Selected Sermons*, ed. and trans. Holly Johnson, 1 of 2 vols, Leuven: Peeters, 2019.

The Sarum Missal, ed. J. Wickham Legg, Oxford: Clarendon Press, 1916.

Sedulius, *The Paschal Song and Hymns*, ed. and trans. Carl P. E. Springer, Atlanta: Society of Biblical Literature, 2013.

Segbrok, Richard, *Liber Sententiarum*, 1:420-34, in *Yorkshire Writers: Richard Rolle of Hampole and his Followers*, ed. Carl Horstmann, 2 vols, London: Sonnenschein, 1895-6, repr. Cambridge: Brewer, 1976.

South English Legendary, ed. Charlotte D'Evelyn and Anna J Mill, 3 vols, EETS, os, 235, 236, 244, London: Oxford University Press, 1956-59.

Speculum perfectionis, ed. Charles Sabatier, Paris: Fischbacher, 1898.

Stow, John, *A Survey of London*, ed. C. L. Kingsford, 2 vols, Oxford: Clarendon, 1908, repr. Cambridge: Cambridge University Press, 2015.

Supplementary Lives in Some Manuscripts of the 'Gilte Legende', ed. Richard Hamer and Vida Russell, EETS, os 315, Oxford: Oxford University Press, 2000.

Taylor, William, 'The Sermon of William Taylor', 3-23 in *Two Wycliffite Texts*, ed. Anne Hudson, EETS, os 301, Oxford: Oxford University Press, 1993.

Testamenta Eboracensia: A Selection of Wills from the Registry of York (1300-1551), ed. James Raine Sr, James Raine Jr, and John Clay, 6 vols, London: Nichols & Son, 1836-1902.

Thomas of Chobham, *Summa Confessorum*, ed. F. Broomfield, Analceta Mediaevalia Namurcensia 25, Louvain: Éditions Nauwelaert, 1968.

Thomas of Chobham, *Summa de arte praedicandi*, ed. Franco Morenzoni, CCCM 83, Turnhout: Brepols, 1987.

Thomas of Chobham, *Summa de arte praedicandi*, 614-38 in *Medieval Grammar and Rhetoric: Language arts and Literary Theory, AD 300-1475*, ed. and trans. Rita Copeland and Ineke Sluiter, Oxford: Oxford University Press, 2009.

Thorpe, William, *The Testimony of William Thorpe*, 24-93 in *Two Wycliffite Texts*, ed. Anne Hudson, EETS, os 301, Oxford: Oxford University Press, 1993.

Three Middle English Sermons from the Worcester Chapter Manuscript F.10, ed. D. M. Grisdale, Kendal: Wilson, 1939.

Vincent of Beauvais, *Speculum quadruplex, sive Speculum maius, vol 4: Speculum Historiale*, Douai: Bellerus, 1624; repr. Graz: Akademische Druck- und Verlagsanstalt, 1965.

Vita Edwardi Secundi: The Life of Edward II, ed. and trans. Wendy R. Childs, Oxford: Clarendon Press, 2005.

de Vitry, Jacques, *Sermones vulgares vel ad status 1*, ed. Jean Longère, CCCM 225, Turnhout: Brepols, 2013.

Waleys, Thomas, *De modo componendi sermones*, 328-423 in *Artes Praedicandi: Contribution à l'histoire de la rhétorique au moyen âge*, ed. Thomas Marie Charland, Paris: De Vrin, 1936.

Waleys, Thomas, 'On the Quality of the Preacher: Chapter 1 of *On the Method for Composing Sermons*', trans. by Martin Camargo as an appendix to 'How (Not) to Preach: Thomas Waleys and Chaucer's Pardoner', 146–78 in *Sacred and Profane in Chaucer and Late Medieval Literature: Essays in Honour of John V. Fleming*, Toronto: University of Toronto Press, 2010.

Walsingham, Thomas, *The St Albans Chronicle: The Chronica Maiora of Thomas Walsingham*, ed. and trans. John Taylor, Wendy R. Childs, and Leslie Watkiss, 2 vols, Oxford: Oxford University Press, 2003–11.

Walsingham, Thomas, *The Chronica Maiora of Thomas Walsingham, 1376–1422*, trans. David Preest, Introd. and notes James G. Clark, Woodbridge: Boydell, 2005.

The Wars of Alexander, ed. Hoyt N. Duggan and Thorlac Turville-Petre, EETS, ss 10, Oxford: Oxford University Press, 1989.

Wharton, Henry, *Anglia sacra, sive Collectio historiarum* [...], 2 vols, London: Chiswell, 1691.

Wimbledon, Thomas, *Wimbledon's Sermon 'Redde rationem villicationis tue': A Middle English Sermon of the Fourteenth Century*, ed. Ione Kemp Knight, Pittsburgh, PA: Duquesne University Press, 1967.

Secondary Sources

Adams, Robert, 'Editing and the Limitations of *Durior Lectio*', YLS 5 (1991): 7–15.

Adams, Robert, *Langland and the Rokele Family: The Gentry Background to 'Piers Plowman'*, Dublin: Four Courts, 2013.

Adams, Robert, 'The Rokeles: An Index for a "Langland" Family History', 85–96 in *The Cambridge Companion to 'Piers Plowman'*, ed. Andrew Cole and Andrew Galloway, Cambridge: Cambridge University Press, 2014.

Adler, Gillian, *Chaucer and the Ethics of Time*, Cardiff: University of Wales Press, 2022.

Aers, David, *'Piers Plowman' and Christian Allegory*, London: Arnold, 1975.

Aers, David, *Community, Gender, and Individual Identity: English Writing 1360–1430*, London: Routledge, 1988.

Aers, David, *Beyond Reformation? An Essay on William Langland's 'Piers Plowman' and the End of Constantinian Christianity*, Notre Dame, IN: University of Notre Dame Press, 2015.

Aitken, Marion, *Étude sur Miroir ou les Évangiles des Domnées de Robert de Gretham suivie d'extraits inédits*, Paris: Champion, 1922.

Alford, John A., 'The Role of the Quotations in *Piers Plowman*', *Speculum* 52, no. 1 (1977): 80–99.

Alford, John A., 'More Unidentified Quotations in *Piers Plowman*', *Modern Philology* 81, no. 3 (1984): 278–85.

Alford, John A., 'The Design of the Poem', 29–65 in *A Companion to Piers Plowman*, ed. John A. Alford, Berkeley: University of California Press, 1988.

Alford, John A., 'The Idea of Reason in *Piers Plowman*', 199–215 in *Medieval Studies Presented to George Kane*, ed. Edward Donald Kennedy, Ronald Waldron, and Joseph S. Wittig, Cambridge: Brewer, 1988.

Alford, John A., *Piers Plowman: A Glossary of Legal Diction*, Cambridge: Brewer, 1988.

Alford, John A., *Piers Plowman: A Guide to the Quotations*, Medieval and Renaissance Texts and Studies, 77, Binghamton, NY: Medieval and Renaissance Texts and Studies, 1992.

Allen, Elizabeth, *False Fables and Exemplary Truth in Later Middle English Literature*, New York: Palgrave Macmillan, 2005.

Allor, Danielle, 'Propping the Tree of Charity: Allegory and Salvation History in *Piers Plowman*', *YLS* 35 (2021): 29–59.

Appleford, Amy, *Learning to Die in London, 1380–1540*, Philadelphia: University of Pennsylvania Press, 2015.

Baker, Denise N., '*Liberum Arbitrium* and the Tree of Charity in *Piers Plowman*', *YLS* 36 (2022): 77–99.

Baldwin, Anna, 'The Historical Context', 67–86 in *A Companion to Piers Plowman*, ed. John A. Alford, Berkeley: University of California Press, 1988.

Barney, Stephen A., 'The Plowshare of the Tongue: The Progress of a Symbol from the Bible to *Piers Plowman*', *Mediaeval Studies* 35 (1973): 261–93.

Barney, Stephen A., *The Penn Commentary on Piers Plowman, vol. 5: C Passūs 20–22; B Passūs 18–20*, Philadelphia: University of Pennsylvania Press, 2006.

Barron, Caroline M., 'London and St Paul's Cathedral in the Later Middle Ages', 126–49 in *The Medieval English Cathedral: Papers in Honour of Pamela Tudor-Craig*, ed. Janet Backhouse, Donington: Shaun Tyas, 2003.

Barron, Caroline M., and Marie-Hélène Rousseau, 'Cathedral, City, and State, 1300–1540', 33–44 in *Saint Paul's: The Cathedral Church of London 604–2004*, ed. Derek Keene, Arthur Burns, and Andrew Saint, New Haven: Yale University Press, 2004.

Batkie, Stephanie L., '"Thanne artow inparfit": Learning to Read in *Piers Plowman*', *Chaucer Review* 45, no. 2 (2010): 169–93.

Batkie, Stephanie L., 'Of Poets and Prologues', *YLS* 32 (2018): 245–70.

Bennett, Alastair, '*Brevis Oratio Penetrat Celum*: Proverbs, Prayers, and Lay Understanding in Late Medieval England', *New Medieval Literatures* 14 (2012): 127–63.

Bennett, Alastair, 'Covetousness, "Unkyndenesse", and the "Blered Eye" in *Piers Plowman* and *The Canon's Yeoman's Tale*', *YLS* 28 (2014): 29–64.

Bennett, Alastair, 'Carding with Covetousness in *Piers Plowman*', *Notes and Queries* 65, no. 1 (2018): 5–8.

Bennett, Alastair, 'A Middle English Sermon Based on Gregory the Great's Homily for the Second Sunday in Advent', *Mediaeval Studies* 83 (2021): 27–57.

Bennett, Alastair, 'An Excerpt from *Piers Plowman* in the Hospital of St Thomas of Acre', *Medium Ævum* 92, no. 1 (2023): 104–20.

Bennett, J. A. W., 'The Date of the B-text of *Piers Plowman*', *Medium Ævum* 12 (1943): 55–64.

Bennett, J. A. W., '"Sum Rex, Sum Princeps, etc.": *Piers Plowman* B, Prologue 132–8', *Notes and Queries* 205 (1960): 364.

Bennett, Michael, 'William Called Long Will', *YLS* 26 (2012): 1–25.

Berrouard, M.-F., 'Saint Augustin et le ministère de la predication', *Recherches Augustiniennes* 2 (1962): 447–501.

Bland, Cynthia Renée, 'Langland's Use of the Term *Ex vi Transicionis*', *YLS* 2 (1988): 125–35.

Bloomfield, Morton W., *Piers Plowman as a Fourteenth-Century Apocalypse*, New Brunswick: Rutgers University Press, 1962.

Bourgain, Pascale, 'The Circulation of Texts in Manuscript Culture', 140–59 in *The Medieval Manuscript Book: Cultural Approaches*, ed. Michael Johnston and Michael Van Dussen, Cambridge: Cambridge University Press, 2015.

Bose, Mishtooni, '*Piers Plowman* and God's Thought Experiment', 71–97 in *Medieval Thought Experiments: Poetry, Hypothesis, and Experience in the European Middle Ages*, ed. Philip Knox, Jonathan Morton, and Daniel Reeve, Disuptatio 31, Turnhout: Brepols, 2018.

Bradley, Henry, 'Some Cruces in *Piers Plowman*', MLR 5 (1910): 340-1.
Breen, Katharine, 'Reading Step by Step: Pictorial Allegory and Pastoral Care in *Piers Plowman*', 90-135 in *Taxonomies of Knowledge: Information and Order in Medieval Manuscripts*, ed. Emily Steiner and Lynn Ransom, Philadelphia: University of Pennsylvania Press, 2015.
Breen, Katharine, *Machines of the Mind: Personification in Medieval Literature*, Chicago: University of Chicago Press, 2021.
Brett, Cyril, 'Notes on Old and Middle English', *Modern Language Review* 22, no. 3 (1927): 257-64.
Brooks, E. St John, 'The *Piers Plowman* Manuscripts in Trinity College, Dublin', *The Library*, 5th ser., 6 (1951): 141-53.
Burnley, David, 'Langland's Clergial Lunatic', 31-8 in *Langland, the Mystics and the Medieval English Religious Tradition: Essays in Honour of S. S. Hussey*, ed. Helen Phillips, Cambridge: Brewer, 1990.
Burrow, John A., 'The Action of Langland's Second Vision', *Essays in Criticism* 15 (1965): 247-68, repr. as 79-101 in Burrow, *Essays on Medieval Literature*, Oxford: Clarendon, 1984.
Burrow, John A., *Gestures and Looks in Medieval Narrative*, Cambridge: Cambridge University Press, 2002.
Burrow, John A., 'The Structure of *Piers Plowman* B XV-XX: Evidence from the Rubrics', *Medium Ævum* 77 (2008), 306-12.
Burrow, John A., 'Conscience on Knights, Kings, and Conquerors: *Piers Plowman* B.19.26-198', YLS 23 (2009): 85-95.
Burrow, John A., 'God and the Fullness of Time in *Piers Plowman*', *Medium Ævum* 79 (2010): 300-5.
Burrow, John A., '"Quod" and "Seide" in *Piers Plowman*', *Notes and Queries* 64, no. 2 (2015): 521-4.
Bynum, Caroline Walker, 'The Spirituality of Regular Canons in the Twelfth Century: A New Approach', *Medievalia et Humanistica*, new series 4 (1973): 3-24.
Bynum, Caroline Walker, *Docere Verbo et Exemplo: An Aspect of Twelfth-century Spirituality*, Missoula, MT: Scholars Press, 1979.
Bynum, Caroline Walker, *Jesus as Mother: Studies in the Spirituality of the High Middle Ages*, Berkeley: University of California Press, 1982.
Calabrese, Michael, 'Posthuman Piers?', YLS 32 (2018): 3-36.
Cannon, Christopher, *From Literacy to Literature: England, 1300-1400*, Oxford: Oxford University Press, 2016.
Capellanus, Georg, *Sprechen Sie Lateinisch? Moderne Konversation in lateinischer Sprache*. Leipzig: Koch, 1892. 10th edn, ed. Hans Lamer, BerlIN: Dümmler, 1929.
Caplan, Harry, 'A Late Medieval Tractate on Preaching', 40-79 in *Of Eloquence: Studies in Ancient and Mediaeval Rhetoric*, ed. Anne King and Helen North, Ithaca, NY: Cornell University Press, 1970.
Carruthers, Mary, *The Book of Memory: A Study of Memory in Medieval Culture*, Cambridge: Cambridge University Press, 1990.
Carruthers, Mary, 'Imaginatif, Memoria, and "The Need for Critical Theory" in *Piers Plowman* Studies', YLS 9 (1995): 103-14.
Carruthers, Mary, *The Craft of Thought: Meditation, Rhetoric, and the Making of Images, 400-1200*, Cambridge: Cambridge University Press, 2000.
Carruthers, Mary, 'Allegory Without the Teeth: Some Reflections on Figural Language in *Piers Plowman*', YLS 19 (2005): 27-43.

Carruthers, Mary, 'Terror, Horror, and the Fear of God, or, Why There Is No Medieval Sublime', 17-36 in *'Truthe is the beste': A Festschrift in Honour of A. V. C. Schmidt*, ed. Nicholas Jacobs and Gerald Morgan, Oxford: Peter Lang, 2014.

Cigman, Gloria, '*Luceat Lux Vestra*: The Lollard Preacher as Truth and Light', *Review of English Studies*, new series 40, no. 160 (1989): 479-96.

Cervone, Cristina Maria, 'Langland and the Truelove Tradition', *YLS* 22 (2008): 27-55.

Cervone, Cristina Maria, *Poetics of the Incarnation: Middle English Writing and the Leap of Love*, Philadelphia: University of Pennsylvania Press, 2012.

Chambers, E. K., *The Medieval Stage*, 2 vols, London: Oxford University Press, 1903.

Clifton, Linda J., 'Struggling with Will: Jangling, Sloth, and Thinking in *Piers Plowman* B', 29-52 in *'Suche Werkis to Werche': Essays on Piers Plowman in Honor of David C. Fowler*, ed. Mí·eál F. Vaughan, East Lansing: Colleagues Press, 1993.

Clopper, Lawrence M., *'Songes of Rechelesnesse': Langland and the Franciscans*, Ann Arbor: University of Michigan Press, 1997.

Cole, Andrew, 'Trifunctionality and the Tree of Charity: Literary and Social Practice in *Piers Plowman*', *ELH* 62 (1995): 1-27.

Cole, Andrew, 'Commentaries on Unknown Texts: On Morton Bloomfield and Friedrich Nietzsche', *YLS* 25 (2011): 25-35.

Connolly, Margaret, 'Shaking the Language Tree: Translating the Word in the Vernacular in the Anglo-Norman *Miroir* and the Middle English *Mirror*', 17-28 in *The Theory and Practice of Translation in the Middle Ages*, ed. Rosalynn Voaden, René Tixier, Teresa Sanchez Roura, and Jenny Rebecca Rytting, The Medieval Translator, 8, Turnhout: Brepols, 2003.

Copeland, Rita, '*Pathos* and Pastoralism: Aristotle's *Rhetoric* in Medieval England', *Speculum* 89, no. 1 (2014): 96-127.

Copeland, Rita, *Emotion and the History of Rhetoric in the Middle Ages*, Oxford: Oxford University Press, 2021.

Copeland, Rita, 'The Porous Genres of Persuasion: A London Preacher and a Royal Advisor in the Fifteenth Century', 210-23 in *'Of latine and of othire lare': Essays in Honour of David R. Carlson*, ed. Richard Firth Green and R. F. Yeager, Toronto: Pontifical Institute of Mediaeval Studies, 2022.

Cornelius, Roberta, '*Piers Plowman* and the *Roman de Fauvel*', *PMLA* 47 (1932): 363-7.

Courcelle, Pierre, *Les Confessions de saint Augustin dans la tradition littéraire*, 2nd edn, Paris: De Boccard, 1968.

Crassons, Kate, *The Claims of Poverty: Literature, Culture, and Ideology in Late Medieval England*, Notre Dame, IN: University of Notre Dame Press, 2010.

Craun, Edwin D., *Lies, Slander, and Obscenity in Medieval English Literature: Pastoral Rhetoric and the Deviant Speaker*, Cambridge: Cambridge University Press, 1997.

Craun, Edwin D., *Ethics and Power in Medieval English Reformist Writing*, Cambridge: Cambridge University Press, 2010.

Crawford, Jason, *Allegory and Enchantment: An Early Modern Poetics*, Oxford: Oxford University Press, 2017.

Daniel, Norman, *Islam and the West: The Making of an Image*, Edinburgh: Edinburgh University Press, 1960.

Davies, Rees, 'The Life, Travels, and Library of an Early Reader of *Piers Plowman*', *YLS* 13 (1999): 49-64.

Davis, Isabel, 'Calling: Langland, Gower, and Chaucer on Saint Paul', *Studies in the Age of Chaucer* 34 (2012): 53-97.

Davis, Rebecca, *Piers Plowman and the Books of Nature*, Oxford: Oxford University Press, 2016.

Davlin, Mary Clemente, '*Kynde Knowyng* as a Major Theme in *Piers Plowman* B', *Review of English Studies* 22 (1971): 1–19.
Davlin, Mary Clemente, '*Piers Plowman* and the Gospel and First Epistle of John', *YLS* 10 (1996): 89–127.
Davlin, Mary Clemente, 'Devotional Postures in *Piers Plowman* B, with an Appendix on Divine Postures', *Chaucer Review* 42 (2007): 163–4.
D'Avray, D. L., *Death and the Prince: Memorial Preaching before 1350*, Oxford: Clarendon, 1994.
Deiter, Otto A., '*Arbor Picta*: The Medieval Tree of Preaching', *Quarterly Journal of Speech* 51, no. 2 (1965): 123–44.
Dinshaw, Carolyn, *How Soon is Now? Medieval Texts, Amateur Readers, and the Queerness of Time*, Durham, NC: Duke University Press, 2012.
Donaldson, E. Talbot, *Piers Plowman: The C-text and its Poet*, New Haven: Yale University Press, 1949, repr. London: Cass, 1966.
Dowling, William C., *Ricoeur on Time and Narrative: An Introduction to Temps et Récit*, Notre Dame, IN: University of Notre Dame Press, 2011.
Duffy, Eamon, *The Stripping of the Altars: Traditional Religion in England c.1400–c.1580*, 2nd edn, New Haven: Yale University Press, 2005.
Emden, A. B., *A Biographical Register of the University of Oxford to AD 1500*, 3 vols, Oxford: Clarendon Press, 1957–9.
Emmerson, Richard K., '"Coveitise to Konne", "Goddes Pryvetee", and Ambiguous Dream Experience in *Piers Plowman*', 89–121 in '*Suche Werkis to Werche*': *Essays on Piers Plowman in Honor of David C. Fowler*, ed. Mí·eál F. Vaughan, East Lansing: Colleagues Press, 1993.
Felski, Rita, *The Limits of Critique*, Chicago: University of Chicago Press, 2015.
Figal, Günter, 'Hermeneutical Phenomenology', 525–42, in *The Oxford Handbook of Contemporary Phenomenology*, ed. Dan Zahavi, Oxford: Oxford University Press, 2012.
Fletcher, Alan J., 'John Mirk and the Lollards', *Medium Ævum* 56 (1987): 217–24.
Fletcher, Alan J., *Preaching, Politics and Poetry in Late-Medieval England*, Dublin: Four Courts Press, 1998.
Fletcher, Alan J., 'The Essential (Ephemeral) William Langland', *YLS* 15 (2002): 61–84.
Fletcher, Alan J., *Late Medieval Popular Preaching in Britain and Ireland: Texts, Studies, and Interpretations*, Turnhout: Brepols, 2009.
Fletcher, Alan J., '*Piers Plowman* and the Benedictines', 43–62 in *Chaucer in Context: A Golden Age of English Poetry*, ed. Gerald Morgan, Oxford: Peter Lang, 2012.
Frank Jr, Robert Worth, '"The Hungry Gap", Crop Failure, and Famine: The Fourteenth-Century Agricultural Crisis and *Piers Plowman*', *YLS* 4 (1990): 87–104.
Gallemore, Melvin, 'The Sermons of Thomas Brinton and the B Text of *Piers the Plowman*', PhD thesis, University of Washington, 1966.
Galloway, Andrew, 'The Rhetoric of Riddling in Late-Medieval England: The "Oxford" Riddles, the *Secretum philosophorum*, and the Riddles in *Piers Plowman*', *Speculum* 70, no. 1 (1995): 86–93.
Galloway, Andrew, 'Latin England', 41–95 in *Imagining a Medieval English Nation*, ed. Kathy Lavezzo, Minneapolis: University of Minnesota Press, 2004.
Galloway, Andrew, *The Penn Commentary on Piers Plowman, vol. 1: C Prologue–Passus 4; B Prologue–Passus 4; A Prologue–Passus 4*, Philadelphia: University of Pennsylvania Press, 2006.
Galloway, Andrew, 'Long Will and the Scandal of 1385', *YLS* 36 (2012): 45–76.

Galloway, Andrew, 'The Common Voice in Theory and Practice in Late Fourteenth Century England', 243–86 in *Law, Governance, and Justice: New Views on Medieval Constitutionalism*, ed. Richard W. Kaeuper with Paul Dingman and Peter Sposato, Leiden: Brill, 2013.

Galloway, Andrew, 'Madame Meed: *Fauvel*, Isabella, and the French Circumstances of *Piers Plowman*', *YLS* 30 (2016): 227–52.

Galloway, Andrew, 'Parallel Lives: William Rokele and the Satirical Literacies of *Piers Plowman*', *Studies in the Age of Chaucer* 40 (2018): 43–111.

Galloway, Andrew, 'Langland and the Reinvention of Array in Late Medieval England', *Review of English Studies*, new series 71, no. 301 (2020): 607–29.

Gameson, Richard, and Fiona Gameson, 'From Augustine to Parker: The Changing Face of the First Archbishop of Canterbury', 13–38 in *Anglo-Saxons: Studies Presented to Cyril Roy Hart*, ed. Simon Keynes and Alfred P. Smyth, Dublin: Four Courts Press, 2006.

Gayk, Shannon, '"As Plouȝmen Han Preued": The Alliterative Work of a Set of Lollard Sermons', *YLS* 20 (2006): 43–65.

Gayk, Shannon, 'Apocalyptic Ecologies: Eschatology, the Ethics of Care, and the Fifteen Signs of Doom in Early England', *Speculum* 96, no. 1 (2021): 1–37.

Giancarlo, Matthew, *Parliament and Literature in Late Medieval England*, Cambridge: Cambridge University Press, 2007.

Gilchrist, Roberta, 'Norwich Cathedral Tower and Spire: Recording and Analysis of a Cathedral's *Longue Durée*', *Archaeological Journal* 158, no. 1 (2001): 291–324.

Girouard, Mark, *Life in the English Country House: A Social and Architectural History*, New Haven: Yale University Press, 1978.

Goering, Joseph, *William de Montibus (c.1140–1213): The Schools and the Literature of Pastoral Care*, Toronto: Pontifical Institute of Mediaeval Studies, 1992.

Grady, Frank, 'Chaucer's Langland's Boethius', *YLS* 32 (2018): 271–87.

Grant, W. Leonard, 'The *Liber Sententiarum* of Richard of Segbrok', *Phoenix* 3, no. 3 (1949): 94–101.

Gray, Nick, 'Langland's Quotations from the Penitential Tradition', *Modern Philology* 84 (1986): 55–6.

Gruenler, Curtis A., *Piers Plowman and the Poetics of Enigma: Riddles, Rhetoric, and Theology*, Notre Dame, IN: University of Notre Dame Press, 2017.

Gwynn, A., 'The Date of the B-Text of *Piers Plowman*', *Review of English Studies* 19 (1943): 1–24.

Hanna, Ralph, *William Langland*, Aldershot: Variorum, 1993.

Hanna, Ralph, *Pursuing History: Middle English Manuscripts and their Texts*, Stanford, CA: Stanford University Press, 1996.

Hanna, Ralph, 'Reading Prophecy / Reading Piers', *YLS* 12 (1998): 153–7.

Hanna, Ralph, 'Alliterative Poetry', 488–512 in *The Cambridge History of Medieval English Literature*, ed. David Wallace, Cambridge: Cambridge University Press, 1999.

Hanna, Ralph, 'Langland's Ymaginatif: Images and the Limits of Poetry', 81–94 in *Images, Idolatry, and Iconoclasm in Late Medieval England: Textuality and the Visual Image*, ed. Jeremy Dimmick, James Simpson, and Nicolette Zeeman, Oxford: Oxford University Press, 2002.

Hanna, Ralph, *London Literature, 1300–1380*, Cambridge: Cambridge University Press, 2005.

Hanna, Ralph, 'The Tree of Charity—Again', 125–39 in *Medieval Alliterative Poetry: Essays in Honour of Thorlac Turville-Petre*, ed. John A. Burrow and Hoyt N. Duggan, Dublin: Four Courts Press, 2010.

Hanna, Ralph, *Patient Reading / Reading Patience: Oxford Essays on Medieval English Literature*, Liverpool: Liverpool University Press, 2017.
Hanna, Ralph, *The Penn Commentary on Piers Plowman, vol. 2: C Passūs 5–9; B Passūs 5–7; A Passūs 5–8*, Philadelphia: University of Pennsylvania Press, 2017.
Hanna, Ralph, '"Put the Load Right on Me": Langland on The Incarnation (With Apologies to the Band)', *Notes and Queries* 66, no. 2 (2019): 197–201.
Harvey, Margaret, 'Preaching in the Curia: Some Sermons by Thomas Brinton', *Archivum Historiae Pontificiae* 33 (1995): 299–301.
Haye, Thomas, *Päpste und Poeten: Die mittelalterliche Kurie als Objekt und Förderer panegyrischer Dichtung*, Berlin: de Gruyter, 2009.
Heng, Geraldine, *The Invention of Race in the European Middle Ages*, Cambridge: Cambridge University Press, 2018.
Holland, Alexander William, 'John Bromyard's *Summa Praedicantium*: An Exploration of Late-Medieval Falsity Through a Fourteenth-Century Preaching Handbook', PhD thesis, University of Kent, 2018.
Horner, Patrick J., 'Preachers at Paul's Cross: Religion, Society, and Politics in Late Medieval England', 261–82 in *Medieval Sermons and Society: Cloister, City, University*, ed. Jacqueline Hamesse, Beverly Mayne Kienzle, Debra L. Stoudt, and Anne T. Thayer, Louvain-La-Neuve: Fédération Internationale des Instituts d'études médiévales, 1998.
Horobin, Simon, 'The Scribe of Rawlinson Poetry 137 and the Copying and Circulation of *Piers Plowman*', *YLS* 19 (2005): 3–26.
Horobin, Simon, 'Manuscripts and Readers of *Piers Plowman*', 179–97 in *The Cambridge Companion to Piers Plowman*, ed. Andrew Cole and Andrew Galloway, Cambridge: Cambridge University Press, 2014.
Horobin, Simon, 'John But and the Ending of the A Version of *Piers Plowman*', *YLS* 33 (2019): 127–42.
Hudson, Anne, 'Aspects of the "Publication" of Wyclif's Latin Sermons', 121–9 in *Late Medieval Religious Texts and their Transmission: Essays in Honour of A. I. Doyle*, ed. A. J. Minnis, Cambridge: Brewer, 1994.
Hudson, Anne, and H. Leith Spencer, 'Old Author, New Work: The Sermons of MS Longleat 4', *Medium Ævum* 53, no. 2 (1984): 221–38.
Immaculate, Mary, 'The Four Daughters of God in the *Gesta Romanorum* and the *Court of Sapience*', *PMLA* 57, no. 4 (1942): 951–65.
James, M. R., and Claude Jenkins, *A Descriptive Catalogue of the Manuscripts in the Library of Lambeth Palace*, 2 vols, Cambridge: Cambridge University Press, 1930–32, repr. 2011.
Jennings, Margaret, '"Non ex virgine": The Rise of the Thematic Sermon Manual', *Collegium Medievale* 1–2 (1992): 27–44.
Johnson, Holly, 'The Divine Dinner Party: Domestic Imagery and Easter Preaching in Late Medieval England', *Traditio* 67 (2012): 385–415.
Johnson, Holly, 'The Imaginative Landscape of an English Monk-Preacher: Robert Rypon and the Court of Memory', *Mediaeval Studies* 75 (2013): 177–204.
Johnson, Holly, 'Robert Rypon and the Creation of London, British Library, MS Harley 4894: A Master Preacher and His Sermon Collection', *Medieval Sermon Studies* 59 (2015):38–56.
Johnston, Michael, 'William Langland and John Ball', *YLS* 30 (2016): 29–74.
Johnston, Michael, 'The Clerical Career of William Rokele', *YLS* 33 (2019): 111–25.
Jones, E. A., 'The Compilation(s) of Two Late Medieval Devotional Manuscripts', 79–97 in *Text and Controversy from Wyclif to Bale: Essays in Honour of Anne Hudson*, ed. Helen Barr and Ann M. Hutchison, Turnhout: Brepols, 2005.

Jurkowski, Maureen, 'The Arrest of William Thorpe in Shrewsbury and the Anti-Lollard Statute of 1406', *Historical Research* 75, no. 189 (2002): 273-95.
Justice, Steven, 'The Genres of *Piers Plowman*', *Viator* 19 (1988): 291-306.
Kane, George, 'Langland, William (*c*.1325-*c*.1390)', *ODNB*, <https://doi.org/10.1093/ref:odnb/16021>
Karnes, Michelle, *Imagination, Meditation, and Cognition in the Middle Ages*, Chicago: University of Chicago Press, 2011.
Kaske, R. E., 'The Speech of "Book" in *Piers Plowman*', *Anglia* 77 (1959): 117-44.
Kaske, R. E., '"*Ex vi Transicionis*" and its Passage in *Piers Plowman*', *JEGP* 62 (1963): 32-60, rev. and repr. 228-63 in *Style and Symbolism in Piers Plowman*, ed. Robert J. Blanch, Knoxville: University of Tennessee Press, 1969.
Kay, Sarah, *The Place of Thought: The Complexity of One in Late Medieval French Didactic Poetry*, Philadelphia: University of Pennsylvania Press, 2007.
Keene, Derek, 'From Conquest to Capital: St Paul's *c*.1100-1300', 17-32 in *Saint Paul's: The Cathedral Church of London 604-2004*, ed. Derek Keene, Arthur Burns, and Andrew Saint, New Haven: Yale University Press, 2004.
Kemp, E. W., 'History and Action in the Sermons of a Medieval Archbishop', 349-65 in *The Writing of History in the Middle Ages: Essays Presented to Richard William Southern*, ed. R. H. C. Davis and J. M. Wallace-Hadrill with R. J. A. I. Catto and M. H. Keen, Oxford: Clarendon, 1981.
Kennedy, Ruth, '"A Bird in Bishopswood": Some Newly-Discovered Lines of Alliterative Verse from the Late Fourteenth Century', 71-87 in *Medieval Literature and Antiquities: Studies in Honour of Basil Cottle*, ed. Myra Stokes and T. L. Burton, Cambridge: Brewer, 1987.
Kerby Fulton, Kathryn, 'Langland and the Bibliographic Ego', 67-143 in *Written Work: Langland, Labor, and Authorship*, ed. Steven Justice and Kathryn Kerby-Fulton, Philadelphia: University of Pennsylvania Press, 1997.
Kerby-Fulton, Kathryn, *Books Under Suspicion: Censorship and Tolerance of Revelatory Writing in Late Medieval England*, Notre Dame, IN: University of Notre Dame Press, 2006.
Kerby-Fulton, Kathryn, 'Confronting the Scribe-Poet Binary: The Z-Text, Writing Office Redaction, and the Oxford Reading Circles', 489-515 in *New Directions in Medieval Manuscript Studies and Reading Practices: Essays in Honor of Derek Pearsall*, ed. Kathryn Kerby-Fulton, John Thompson, and Sarah Baechle, Notre Dame, IN: University of Notre Dame Press, 2014.
Kerby-Fulton, Kathryn, *The Clerical Proletariat and the Resurgence of Medieval English Poetry*, Philadelphia: University of Pennsylvania Press, 2021.
Killian, Anne, 'Menacing Books: *The Prick of Conscience* and the Rhetoric of Reproof', *YLS* 31 (2017): 5-41.
King'oo, Clare Costley, *Misereri Mei: The Penitential Psalms in Late Medieval and Early Modern England*, Notre Dame, IN: University of Notre Dame Press, 2012.
Kipling, Gordon, *Enter the King: Theatre, Liturgy, and Ritual in the Medieval Civic Triumph*, Oxford: Clarendon, 1998.
Kirk, Elizabeth D., 'Langland's Narrative Christology', 17-35 in *Art and Context in Late Medieval English Narrative: Essays in Honor of Robert Worth Frank, Jr.*, ed. Robert R. Edwards, Cambridge: Brewer, 1994.
Kruger, Steven F., 'Mirrors and the Trajectory of Vision in *Piers Plowman*', *Speculum* 66, no. 1 (1991): 74-95.
Lawler, Traugott, 'Harlot's Holiness: The System of Absolution for Miswinning in the C Version of *Piers Plowman*', *YLS* 20 (2006): 141-89.

Lawler, Traugott, 'Langland Versificator', *YLS* 25 (2011): 37–76.
Lawler, Traugott, *The Penn Commentary on Piers Plowman, vol 4: C Passūs 15–19; B Passūs 13–17*, Philadelphia: University of Pennsylvania Press, 2018.
Lawton, David, 'The Subject of *Piers Plowman*', *YLS* 1 (1987): 1–30.
Lawton, David, *Voice in Later Medieval English Literature: Public Interiorities*, Oxford: Oxford University Press, 2017.
Leclercq, Jean, *The Love of Learning and the Desire for God: A Study of Monastic Culture*, trans. Catharine Misrahi, 3rd edn, New York: Fordham University Press, 1982.
Lightsey, Scott, *Manmade Marvels in Medieval Culture and Literature*, Basingstoke: Palgrave Macmillan, 2007.
Macray, W. D., 'Sermons for the Festivals of St. Thomas Becket, etc., Probably by Archbishop Stratford', *English Historical Review* 8, no. 29 (1893): 85–91.
Mallard, William, 'Dating the *Sermones Quadraginta* of John Wyclif', *Medievalia et Humanistica* 17 (1966): 86–105.
Mann, Jill, 'Eating and Drinking in *Piers Plowman*', *Essays and Studies* 32 (1979): 26–43.
Mann, Jill, 'Some Observations on Structural Annotation', *YLS* 25 (2011): 1–8.
Mann, Jill, 'Allegory and *Piers Plowman*', 65–82 in *The Cambridge Companion to Piers Plowman*, ed. Andrew Cole and Andrew Galloway, Cambridge: Cambridge University Press, 2014.
Marcett, Mildred, *Uthred de Boldon, Friar William Jordan and Piers Plowman*, New York: by the author, 1938.
McDermott, Ryan, *Tropologies: Ethics and Invention in England, c.1350–1600*, Notre Dame, IN: University of Notre Dame Press, 2016.
McKee, Conor, 'Langland's "Tree of Patience"', *YLS* 36 (2022): 101–22.
Megna, Paul, 'Dread, Love, and the Bodies of *Piers Plowman* A.10, B.9 and C.10', *YLS* 29 (2015): 61–88.
Metliztski, Dorothee, *The Matter of Araby in Medieval England*, New Haven: Yale University Press, 1977.
Middleton, Anne, 'Two Infinites: Grammatical Metaphor in *Piers Plowman*', *ELH* 39, no. 2 (1972): 169–88.
Middleton, Anne, 'The Idea of Public Poetry in the Reign of Richard II', *Speculum* 53, no. 1 (1978): 94–114.
Middleton, Anne, 'The Audience and Public of *Piers Plowman*', 101–23 in *Middle English Alliterative Poetry and its Literary Background*, ed. David Lawton, Cambridge: Brewer, 1982.
Middleton, Anne, 'Narration and the Invention of Experience: Episodic Form in *Piers Plowman*', 91–122 in *The Wisdom of Poetry: Essays in Early English Literature in Honor of Morton W. Bloomfield*, edited by Larry D. Benson and Siegfried Wenzel, Kalamazoo, MI: Medieval Institute Publications, 1982.
Middleton, Anne, 'The Passion of Seint Averoys (B.13.91): "Deuynyng" and Divinity in the Banquet Scene', *YLS* 1 (1987): 31–40.
Middleton, Anne, 'Making a Good End: John But as a Reader of *Piers Plowman*', 243–66 in *Medieval English Studies Presented to George Kane*, ed. Edward Donald Kennedy, Ronald Waldron, and Joseph Wittig, Woodbridge: Brewer, 1988.
Middleton, Anne, 'William Langland's "Kynde Name": Authorial Signature and Social Identity in Late Fourteenth-Century England', 15–82 in *Literary Practice and Social Change in Britain, 1380–1530*, ed. Lee Patterson, Berkeley: University of California Press, 1990.

Middleton, Anne, 'Acts of Vagrancy: the C Version "Autobiography" and the Statute of 1388', 208–317 in *Written Work: Langland, Labor, and Authorship*, ed. Justice and Kerby-Fulton, Philadelphia: University of Pennsylvania Press, 1997.

Middleton, Anne, 'Commentary on an Unacknowledged Text: Chaucer's Debt to Langland', *YLS* 24 (2010): 113–37.

Middleton, Anne, 'Do-wel, the Proverbial, and the Vernacular: Some Versions of Pastoralia', 143–69 and 231–8 in *Medieval Poetics and Social Practice: Responding to the Work of Penn Szittya*, ed. Seeta Chaganti, New York: Fordham University Press, 2012.

Middleton, Anne, 'Playing the Plowman', 113–42 in *Chaucer, Langland, and Fourteenth-Century Literary History*, ed. Steven Justice, Farnham: Ashgate, 2013.

Miller, Mark, 'Displaced Souls, Idle Talk, Spectacular Scenes: *Handlyng Synne* and the Perspective of Agency', *Speculum* 71 (1996): 606–32.

Minnis, Alastair, 'Langland's Ymaginatyf and Late-Medieval Theories of Imagination', *Comparative Criticism* 3 (1981): 71–103.

Minnis, Alastair, *Fallible Authors: Chaucer's Pardoner and Wife of Bath*, Philadelphia: University of Pennsylvania Press, 2008.

Mitchell, J. Allan, *Ethics and Exemplary Narrative in Chaucer and Gower*, Cambridge: Brewer, 2004.

Muessig, Carolyn, 'Audience and Preacher: *Ad status* Sermons and Social Classification', 255–76 in *Preacher, Sermon and Audience in the Middle Ages*, ed. Carolyn Muessig, Leiden: Brill, 2002.

Mula, Stefano, 'Muhammad and the Saints: The History of the Prophet in the *Golden Legend*', *Modern Philology* 10, no. 2 (2003): 175–88.

Nall, Catherine, *Reading and War in Fifteenth-Century England: From Lydgate to Malory*, Cambridge: Brewer, 2012.

Newhauser, Richard, 'The Sin of Curiosity and the Cistercians', 71–95 in *Erudition at God's Service: Studies in Medieval Cistercian History*, ed. John R. Sommerfeldt, Kalamazoo, MI: Cistercian Publications, 1985; repr. in Newhauser, *Sin: Essays on the Moral Tradition*, Aldershot: Ashgate, 2007.

Newhauser, Richard, 'Augustinian *Vitium curiositas* and its Reception', 99–104 in *Saint Augustine and his Influence in the Middle Ages*, ed. Edward B. King and Jacqueline T. Schaefer, Sewanee, TN: Press of the University of the South, 1988; repr. in Newhauser, *Sin: Essays on the Moral Tradition*, Aldershot: Ashgate, 2007.

Newhauser, Richard, 'Curiosity', 849–52 in *The Oxford Guide to the Historical Reception of Augustine*, ed. Karla Pollmann and Willemien Otten, Oxford: Oxford University Press, 2013.

Nolan, Maura, 'The Fortunes of *Piers Plowman* and its Readers', *YLS* 20 (2006): 1–41.

Novacich, Sarah Elliott, *Shaping the Archive in Late Medieval England: History, Poetry, and Performance*, Cambridge: Cambridge University Press, 2017.

O'Grady, Gerald Leo, '*Piers Plowman* and the Medieval Tradition of Penance', PhD thesis, University of Wisconsin, 1962.

O'Mara, Veronica, 'Thinking Afresh about Thomas Wimbledon's Paul's Cross Sermon of *c*.1387', *Leeds Studies in English*, ns. 41 (2010): 155–71.

O'Mara, Veronica, and Suzanne Paul, *A Repertorium of Middle English Prose Sermons*, 4 vols, Turnhout: Brepols, 2007.

Orlemanski, Julie, 'Langland's Poetics of Animation: Body, Soul, Personification', *YLS* 33 (2019): 159–83.

Orme, Nicholas, *English Schools in the Middle Ages* (London: Methuen, 1973), 102–4.

Orme, Nicholas, *Medieval Schools: From Roman Britain to Renaissance England*, New Haven: Yale University Press, 2006.
Owen, Dorothy L., *Piers Plowman: A Comparison with Some Earlier and Contemporary French Allegories*, London: Hodder & Stoughton, 1912.
Owst, G. R., 'The "Angel" and the "Goliardeys" of Langland's Prologue', *Modern Language Review* 20 (1925): 270-9.
Owst, G. R., *Preaching in Medieval England: An Introduction to Sermon Manuscripts of the Period, c.1350-1450*, Cambridge: Cambridge University Press, 1926, repr. 2010.
Owst, G. R., *Literature and Pulpit: A Neglected Chapter in the History of English Letters and of the English People*, Cambridge: Cambridge University Press. 1933; 2nd rev. edn Oxford: Blackwell, 1961.
Page, Christopher, *The Owl and the Nightingale: Musical Life and Ideas in France, 1100-1300*, London: Dent, 1989.
Pantin, W. A., 'A Medieval Collection of Latin and English Proverbs and Riddles, from the Rylands Latin MS 394', *Bulletin of the John Rylands Library* 14 (1930): 81-113.
Parsons, Ben, 'Beaten for a Book: Domestic and Pedagogic Violence in *The Wife of Bath's Prologue*', *Studies in the Age of Chaucer* 37 (2015): 163-94.
Paulson, Julie C., '*Piers Plowman* and the Wisdom of Folly', *YLS* 36 (2022): 11-43.
Pearsall, Derek, 'The Necessity of Difference: The Speech of Peace and the Doctrine of Contraries in Langland's *Piers Plowman*', 125-65 in *Medieval Latin and Middle English Literature: Essays in Honour of Jill Mann*, ed. Christopher Cannon and Maura Nolan, Cambridge: Brewer, 2011.
Pearsall, Derek, 'G. R. Owst and the Politics of Sermon Studies', 11-30 in *Preaching the Word in Manuscript and Print in Late Medieval England: Essays in Honour of Susan Powell*, ed. Martha W. Driver and Veronica O'Mara, Turnhout: Brepols, 2013.
Powell, Susan, 'A New Dating of John Mirk's *Festial*', *Notes and Queries*, ns 29 (1982): 487-9.
Putter, Ad, 'Personifications of Old Age in Medieval Poetry: Charles d'Orléans and William Langland', *Review of English Studies* 63, no. 260 (2011): 388-409.
Raschko, Mary, *The Politics of Middle English Parables: Fiction, Theology, and Social Practice*, Manchester: Manchester University Press, 2019.
Raschko, Mary, 'Storytelling at the Gates of Hell: Narrative Epistemology in *Piers Plowman*', *Studies in the Age of Chaucer* 44 (2022): 165-92.
Reeves, Marjorie, *The Influence of Prophecy in the Later Middle Ages: A Study in Joachimism*, Oxford: Oxford University Press, 1969.
Rentz, Ellen, 'Half-Acre Bylaws: Harvest-Sharing in *Piers Plowman*', *YLS* 25 (2011): 95-115.
Rentz, Ellen, *Imagining the Parish in Late Medieval England*, Columbus: Ohio State University Press, 2015.
Ricoeur, Paul, 'Narrative Time', 165-86 in *On Narrative*, ed. W. J. T. Michell, Chicago: University of Chicago Press, 1981.
Ricoeur, Paul, *Time and Narrative*, trans. Kathleen McLaughlin and David Pellauer, 3 vols, Chicago: University of Chicago Press, 1990.
Ricoeur, Paul, 'Narrated Time', 338-54 in *A Ricoeur Reader: Reflection and Imagination*, ed. Mario J. Valdés, New York: Harvester Wheatsheaf, 1991.
Ricoeur, Paul, 'Narrative Identity', 188-99 in *On Paul Ricoeur: Narrative and Interpretation*, ed. David Wood, London: Routledge, 1991.
Ricoeur, Paul, *Oneself as Another*, trans. Kathleen Blamey, Chicago: University of Chicago Press, 1992.

Ricoeur, Paul, 'Interpretive Narrative', 181–99 in *Figuring the Sacred: Religion, Narrative, and Imagination*, ed. Mark I. Wallace, trans. David Pellauer, Minneapolis: Fortress Press, 1995.

Ricoeur, Paul, 'Philosophical Hermeneutics and Biblical Hermeneutics', 89–101 in *From Text to Action: Essays in Hermeneutics II*, trans. Kathleen Blamey and John B. Thompson, Evanston: Northwestern University Press, 2007.

Rickert, Edith, 'John But, Messenger and Maker', *Modern Philology* 11 (1913): 107–16.

Roberts, Phyllis B., 'University Masters and Thomas Becket: Sermons Preached on St Thomas of Canterbury at Paris and Oxford in the Thirteenth and Fourteenth Centuries', *History of Universities* 6 (1986): 65–79.

Roberts, Phyllis B., *Thomas Becket in the Medieval Latin Preaching Tradition: An Inventory of Sermons about St Thomas Becket c.1170–c.1400*, Instrumenta Patristica 25, The Hague: Nijhoff, 1992.

Roberts, Phyllis B., 'Thomas Becket: The Construction and Deconstruction of a Saint from the Middle Ages to the Reformation', 1–22, in *Models of Holiness in Medieval Sermons: Proceedings of the International Symposium (Kalamazoo, 4–7 May 1995)*, ed. Beverly Mayne Kienzle and others, Louvain-la-Neuve: Fédération Internationale des Instituts d'Études Médiévales, 1996.

Roberts, Phyllis B., 'The *Artes praedicandi* and the Medieval Sermon', 41–62 in *Preacher, Sermon and Audience in the Middle Ages*, ed. Carolyn Muessig, Leiden: Brill, 2002.

Robertson, Elizabeth, 'Soul-Making in *Piers Plowman*', *YLS* 34 (2020): 11–56.

Royer-Hemet, Catherine, *Prédication et Propagande au Temps D'Édouard III Plantagenêt*, Paris: University of the Sorbonne Press, 2014.

Rudd, Gillian, 'The State of the Ark: A Metaphor in Bromyard and *Piers Plowman* B. X.396–401', *Notes and Queries*, n.s. 37 (1990): 6–10.

Salter, Elizabeth, *Piers Plowman: An Introduction*, Oxford: Blackwell, 1962, 2nd edn 1969.

Scanlon, Larry, *Narrative, Authority, and Power: The Medieval Exemplum and the Chaucerian Tradition*, Cambridge: Cambridge University Press, 1994.

Scase, Wendy, *Piers Plowman and the New Anticlericalism*, Cambridge: Cambridge University Press, 1989.

Scase, Wendy, '"First Reckon to Richard": John But's *Piers Plowman* and the Politics of Allegiance', *YLS* 11 (1997): 49–66.

Schirmer, Elizabeth, 'William Thorpe's Narrative Theology', *Studies in the Age of Chaucer* 31 (2009): 267–99.

Schott, Christine, 'The Intimate Reader at Work: Medieval Annotators of *Piers Plowman* B', *YLS* 26 (2012): 163–85.

Simpson, James, 'The Transformation of Meaning: A Figure of Thought in *Piers Plowman*', *Review of English Studies*, n.s, 37, no. 146 (1986): 161–83.

Simpson, James, 'Spirituality and Economics in Passus 1–7 of the B Text', *YLS* 1 (1987): 83–103.

Simpson, James, '"After Craftes Conseil clotheth yow and fede": Langland and London City Politics', 109–27 in *England in the Fourteenth Century: Proceedings of the 1991 Harlaxton Symposium*, ed. Nicholas Rogers, Stamford: Paul Watkins, 1993.

Simpson, James, 'Desire and the Scriptural Text: Will as Reader in *Piers Plowman*', 215–43 in *Criticism and Dissent in the Middle Ages*, ed. Rita Copeland, Cambridge: Cambridge University Press, 1996.

Simpson, James, 'The Power of Impropriety: Authorial Naming in *Piers Plowman*', 145–65 in *William Langland's Piers Plowman: A Book of Essays*, ed. Kathleen M. Hewett-Smith, New York: Routledge, 2001.

Simpson, James, *Piers Plowman: An Introduction*, 2nd edn, Exeter: Exeter University Press, 2007.
Sinclair, K. V., 'The Anglo-Norman Patrons of Robert the Chaplain and Robert of Greatham', *Forum for Modern Language Studies* 27 (1992): 193–208.
Smith, Jr., Ben H., 'Patience's Riddle, *Piers Plowman* B, XIII', *MLN* 76 (1961): 675–82.
Smith, D. Vance, *The Book of the Incipit: Beginnings in the Fourteenth Century*, Minneapolis: University of Minnesota Press, 2001.
Smith, D. Vance, 'The Silence of Langland's Study: Matter, Invisibility, Instruction', 263–83 in *Answerable Style: The Idea of the Literary in Medieval England*, ed. Frank Grady and Andrew Galloway, Columbus: Ohio State University Press, 2013.
Smith, D. Vance, *Arts of Dying: Literature and Finitude in Medieval England*, Chicago: University of Chicago Press, 2020.
Somerset, Fiona, *Clerical Discourse and Lay Audience in Late Medieval England*, Cambridge: Cambridge University Press, 1998.
Somerset, Fiona, '"Al þe comonys with o voys atonys": Multilingual Latin and Vernacular Voice in *Piers Plowman*', *YLS* 19 (2005): 107–36.
Somerset, Fiona, *Feeling Like Saints: Lollard Writings after Wyclif*, Ithaca, NY: Cornell University Press, 2014.
Spearing, A. C., 'The Art of Preaching and *Piers Plowman*', 107–34 in *Criticism and Medieval Poetry*, London: Arnold, 1964, 2nd edn 1972.
Spencer, H. Leith, *English Preaching in the Late Middle Ages*, Oxford: Clarendon, 1993.
Star, Sarah, 'Will's Prosthesis', *YLS* 35 (2021): 11–27.
Steiner, Emily, 'Commonality and Literary Form in the 1370s and 1380s', *New Medieval Literatures* 6 (2003): 199–221.
Steiner, Emily, *Documentary Culture and the Making of Medieval English Literature*, Cambridge: Cambridge University Press, 2003.
Steiner, Emily, '*Piers Plowman* and Institutional Poetry', *Études Anglaises*, 66, no. 3 (2013): 297–310.
Steiner, Emily, *Reading Piers Plowman*, Cambridge: Cambridge University Press, 2013.
Steiner, Emily, 'William Langland', 121–34 in *The Cambridge Companion to Medieval English Law and Literature*, ed. Candace Barrington and Sebastian Sobecki, Cambridge: Cambridge University Press, 2019.
Steiner, Emily, *John Trevisa's Information Age: Knowledge and the Pursuit of Literature, c.1400*, Oxford: Oxford University Press, 2021.
Steiner, Emily, 'Neck Verse', *New Literary History* 53 (2022): 333–62.
Strakhov, Elizaveta, '"But Who Will Bell the Cat?": Deschamps, Brinton, Langland, and the Hundred Years' War', *YLS* 30 (2016): 253–76.
Strakhov, Elizaveta, 'Political Animals: Form and the Animal Fable in Langland's Rodent Parliament and Chaucer's *Nun's Priest's Tale*', *YLS* 32 (2018): 289–313.
Strong, David, 'Illumination of the Intellect: Franciscan Sermons and *Piers Plowman*', 197–220 in *Speculum Sermonis: Interdisciplinary Reflections on the Medieval Sermon*, ed. Georgiana Donavin, Cary J. Nederman, and Richard Utz, Turnhout: Brepols, 2004.
Sutherland, Annie, 'Performing the Penitential Psalms in the Middle Ages', 15–37 in *Aspects of the Performative in Medieval Culture*, ed. Manuele Gragnolati and Almut Suerbaum, Berlin: De Gruyter, 2010.
Sutherland, Annie, *English Psalms in the Middle Ages, 1300–1450*, Oxford: Oxford University Press, 2015.
Szittya, Penn R., *The Antifraternal Tradition in Medieval Literature*, Princeton, NJ: Princeton University Press, 1986.

Thomas, Arvind, *Piers Plowman and the Reinvention of Church Law in the Late Middle Ages*, Toronto: University of Toronto Press, 2019.

Thomson, David, *A Descriptive Catalogue of Middle English Grammatical Texts*, New York: Garland, 1979.

Thomson, John A. F., 'Taylor, William (d.1423)', *ODNB*, <https://doi.org/10.1093/ref:odnb/27091>

Tolan, John V., *Saracens: Islam in the European Imagination*, New York: Columbia University Press, 2002.

Tolan, John V., *Faces of Muhammad: Western Perceptions of the Prophet of Islam from the Middle Ages to Today*, Princeton, NJ: Princeton University Press, 2019.

Traver, Hope, *The Four Daughters of God: A Study in the Versions of this Allegory with Special Reference to those in Latin, French, and English*, Bryn Mawr: Bryn Mawr College, 1907.

Truitt, E. R., *Medieval Robots: Mechanism, Magic, Nature, and Art*, Philadelphia: University of Pennsylvania Press, 2015.

Tubach, Frederic C., *Index Exemplorum: A Handbook of Medieval Religious Tales*, Helsinki: Finnish Academy of Science and Letters, 1969.

Vaughan, Mí·eál F., 'Where is Wille Buried? *Piers Plowman*, A.12.105', *YLS* 25 (2011): 131–6.

Vaughan, Mí·eál F., 'Filling the Gap in *Piers Plowman* A: Trinity College, Dublin, MS 213', 87–106 in '*Yee? Baw for Bokes*': *Essays on Medieval Manuscripts and Poetics in Honor of Hoyt N Duggan*, ed. Calabrese and Stephen H. A. Shepherd, Los Angeles: Marymont Institute Press, 2013.

von Nolcken, Christina, 'Some Alphabetical Compendia and How Preachers Used Them in Fourteenth-Century England', *Viator* 12 (1981): 271–88.

Walling, Amanda, 'Friar Flatterer: Glossing and the Hermeneutics of Flattery in *Piers Plowman*', *YLS* 21 (2007): 57–76.

Walls, Keith, *John Bromyard on Church and State: The Summa Predicantium and Early Fourteenth-Century England*, Market Weighton: Clayton-Thorpe, 2007.

Walther, Hans, *Initia carminum ac versuum medii aevi posterioris latinorum*, Göttingen: Vandenhoeck & Ruprecht, 1959.

Warner, Lawrence, 'Jesus the Jouster: The Christ-Knight and Medieval Theories of Atonement in *Piers Plowman* and the "Round Table" Sermons', *YLS* 10 (1996): 129–43.

Warner, Lawrence, 'The Ur-B *Piers Plowman* and the Earliest Production of C and B', *YLS* 16 (2002): 3–39.

Warner, Lawrence, 'Becket and the Hopping Bishops', *YLS* 17 (2003): 107–34.

Warner, Lawrence, 'John But and the Other Works that Will Wrought (*Piers Plowman* A XII 101–2)', *Notes and Queries* 52, no. 1 (2005): 13–18.

Warner, Lawrence, 'The Ending, and End, of *Piers Plowman* B: The C-Version Origins of the Final Two Passus', *Medium Ævum* 76, no. 2 (2007): 225–50.

Warner, Lawrence, *The Lost History of Piers Plowman: The Earliest Transmission of Langland's Work*, Philadelphia: University of Pennsylvania Press, 2011.

Warner, Lawrence, *The Myth of Piers Plowman: Constructing a Medieval Literary Archive*, Cambridge: Cambridge University Press, 2014.

Waters, Claire M., *Angels and Earthly Creatures: Preaching, Performance, and Gender in the Later Middle Ages*, Philadelphia: University of Pennsylvania Press, 2004.

Waters, Claire M., *Translating 'Clergie': Status, Education, and Salvation in Thirteenth-Century Vernacular Texts*, Philadelphia: University of Pennsylvania Press, 2016.

Watson, Nicholas, 'Lollardy: The Anglo-Norman Heresy?' 334–46, *Language and Culture in Medieval Britain: The French of England, c.1100–c.1500*, ed. Jocelyn Wogan-Browne with Carolyn Colette, Maryanne Kowaleski, Linne Mooney, Ad Putter, and David Trotter, Woodbridge: York Medieval Press, 2009.

Watson, Nicholas, *Balaam's Ass: Vernacular Theology Before the English Reformation, vol. 1: Frameworks, Arguments, English to 1250*, Philadelphia: University of Pennsylvania Press, 2022.

Weldon, James F. G., 'Gesture of Perception: The Pattern of Kneeling in *Piers Plowman* B.18–19', *YLS* 3 (1989): 49–66.

Wenzel, Siegfried, *Preachers, Poets, and the Early English Lyric*, Princeton, NJ: Princeton University Press, 1986.

Wenzel, Siegfried, 'Medieval Sermons', 155–72 in *A Companion to Piers Plowman*, ed. John A. Alford, Berkeley: University of California Press, 1988.

Wenzel, Siegfried, *Macaronic Sermons: Bilingualism and Preaching in Late-Medieval England*, Ann Arbor: University of Michigan Press, 1994.

Wenzel, Siegfried, 'A New Version of Wyclif's *Sermones Quadraginta*', *Journal of Theological Studies* 49, no. 1 (1998): 155–61.

Wenzel, Siegfried, 'Why the Monk?' 261–9 in *Words and Works: Studies in Medieval English Language and Literature in Honour of Fred C. Robinson*, ed. Peter S. Baker and Nicholas Howe, Toronto: University of Toronto Press, 1998.

Wenzel, Siegfried, 'Eli and His Sons', *YLS* 13 (1999): 137–52.

Wenzel, Siegfried, 'The Arts of Preaching', 84–96 in *The Cambridge History of Literary Criticism, vol. 2: The Middle Ages*, ed. Alastair Minnis and Ian Johnson, Cambridge: Cambridge University Press, 2005.

Wenzel, Siegfried, *Latin Sermon Collections from Later Medieval England: Orthodox Preaching in the Age of Wyclif*, Cambridge: University of Cambridge Press, 2005.

Wenzel, Siegfried, *Medieval Artes Praedicandi: A Synthesis of Scholastic Sermon Structure*, Toronto: University of Toronto Press, 2015.

Wenzel, Siegfried, 'Richard Alkerton's Sermon on "Amice, Ascende Superius"', *Mediaeval Studies* 83 (2021): 1–25.

White, Hugh, *Nature and Salvation in Piers Plowman*, Cambridge: Brewer, 1988.

Whitehead, J. R., 'Waterton, Robert (d.1425)', *ODNB*, <https://doi.org/10.1093/ref:odnb/54421>

Williams, Arnold, 'Some Documents on English Pardoners, 1350–1400', 197–207 in *Medieval Studies in Honor of Urban Tigner Homles, Jr.* ed. John Mahoney and John Esten Keller, Chapel Hill: University of North Carolina Press, 1965.

Wittig, Joseph, '*Piers Plowman* B, Passus IX–XII: Elements in the Design of the Inward Journey', *Traditio* 28 (1972): 211–80.

Wittig, Joseph, *Piers Plowman: Concordance*. London: Athlone, 2001.

Wood, Robert A., 'A Fourteenth-Century Owner of *Piers Plowman*', *Medium Ævum* 74 (2005): 248–69.

Wood, Sarah, '"Ecce Rex": *Piers Plowman* B.19.1–212 and its Contexts', *YLS* 21 (2007): 31–56.

Wood, Sarah, *Conscience and the Composition of Piers Plowman*, Oxford: Oxford University Press, 2012.

Wood, Sarah, *Piers Plowman and its Manuscript Tradition*, Woodbridge: York Medieval Press, 2022.

Woodman, Francis, 'The Gothic Campaigns', 185–96 in *Norwich Cathedral: Church, City and Diocese, 1096–1996*, ed. Ian Atherton, Eric Fernie, Christopher Harper-Bill, and Hassell Smith, London: Hambledon, 1996.

Yunck, John A., *The Lineage of Lady Meed: The Development of Mediaeval Venality Satire*, Notre Dame, IN: University of Notre Dame Press, 1963.

Zeeman, Nicolette, 'The Condition of *Kynde*', 1–30 in *Medieval Literature and Historical Inquiry: Essays in Honor of Derek Pearsall*, ed. David Aers, Cambridge: Brewer, 2000.

Zeeman, Nicolette, *Piers Plowman and the Medieval Discourse of Desire*, Cambridge: Cambridge University Press, 2006.

Zeeman, Nicolette, *The Arts of Disruption: Allegory and Piers Plowman*, Oxford: Oxford University Press, 2020.

Index

For the benefit of digital users, indexed terms that span two pages (e.g., 52–53) may, on occasion, appear on only one of those pages.

'A Bird in Bishopswood' 128–9
'A comendacioun of holy writ in oure owne langage' 206
Adams, Robert 14–15, 21–2
Adler, Gillian 28–9
Aers, David 12–13, 35–6, 62–3, 70–1, 206–7
Alan of Lille, *De arte praedicatoria* 50–1, 124–5
Alfonsi, Peter, *Dialogi contra Iudaeos* 211–12
Alford, John 10–12, 78–9, 106, 173–4, 178–9
Alkerton, Richard 31–2, 113, 132–7
Alphabetum narrationum 211
Ambrose 99–100, 141–2
angels 49–51
Anonimalle Chronicle 39–40
Aristotle
  Poetics 2–3, 25, 75–6, 112–13, 220–1
  Physics 23–4, 26–7
  Rhetoric 96–7
artes praedicandi 4–7, 11–12, 15–18, 49–50, 116–17, 123–5, 152–3, 168–9, 196–7, 212, 221
  See also, Alan of Lille, *De arte praedicatoria*; Higden, Ranulph, *Liber de eruditione praedicatorum*; Humbert of Romans, *Liber de eruditione praedicatorum*; Robert of Basevorn, *Forma praedicandi*; Thomas of Chobham, *Summa de arte praedicandi*; Waleys, Thomas, *De modo componendi sermones*
Arundel, Thomas 135–6
Augustine of Hippo 99–100, 142
  Confessiones 24–7, 167–8, cited in *Piers Plowman* 162–3, 171–2
  Contra Faustum Manichaeum 50–1
  De Civitate Dei 45–6, 49–50, 67–8
  De doctrina Christiana 139–40
  De spiritu et anima (pseudo-Augustine) 192
  Enarrationes in Psalmos 45–6, 49–50, 67–8
  In Iohannis Evangelium tractatus CXXIV 50–1
Augustine of Canterbury 191, 212–16, 218–19
Averroes 137–8

Ball, John 14–15
baptism 32, 97–8, 150–1, 153–7, 170–3, 175, 177–8, 182–3, 185–7, 213, 219–20
  See also, preaching on baptism; parish church
Barney, Stephen 36–7, 62, 69–70, 99–100, 228
Batkie, Stephanie 194
Becket, Thomas 30, 37, 53–7, 60–1, 73, 90–1, 216–19
Bede
  In Lucam 88
  Historia ecclesiastica gentis Anglorum 213–14, cited by Thomas Brinton 215
  Homiliae (pseudo-Bede) 222–4
Bennett, J. A. W. 39–40
Bernard of Clairvaux
  In annunciatione Dominica sermo prius 222–4, cited by Thomas Spofford 224
  Meditationes piisimae de cognitione humanae condicionis (pseudo-Bernard) 163–4, 184, cited in the *Floretus* 163–4, cited by Humbert of Romans 163–4, cited in *Piers Plowman* 163–4, 184
  Sermones super Canticum Canticorum 115–17, 119–20, 127, 129, 195, cited by William Taylor 134
  Tractatus de gradibus humilitatis et superbiae 231–2
Bloomfield, Morton 8–9, 11–12
Boccaccio, Giovanni, *De casibus virorum illustrium* 211
Boethius, *De consolatione Philosophiae* 155, 168–9, 176
Bose, Mishtooni 226, 231–2
Breen, Katharine 97–8, 193, 196–7, 206–7
Brett, Cyril 38–9
Brinton, Thomas 8, 10–11, 30–1, 38–42, 47–9, 51–2, 72–3, 85–9, 91–2, 107–8, 110, 115, 167, 215, 221–4
Bromyard, John, *Summa praedicantium* 10–11, 176, 222–4
Brynstan, John 15–16
Bude, Tekla 151–2

Burrow, John 21–2, 75–6, 92–3, 104, 110
But, John 152–3, 179–80, 183–6

Calabrese, Michael 151–2
Cannon, Christopher 145–6, 159
Carruthers, Mary 25, 79–80, 86, 193–4, 196–7, 200, 203
Cervone, Cristina Maria 21–2
Chronicon Anonymi Cantuariensis 77–8
Cole, Andrew 8–9
Connolly, Margaret 204
Copeland, Rita 3–4, 96–7
coronation of Richard II 34–5, 39–46, 52, 67–70
Crawford, Jason 151–2
curiositas 111–13, 115–21, 123–4, 127, 130–1, 134–8, 142–3, 145–8, 189, 194–5
  See also, preaching on curiosities

Davlin, Mary Clemente 18–19
Davis, Isabel 62–3
Davis, Rebecca 163–5, 168–9, 183, 194, 209
Dinshaw, Carolyn 28–9
Distichs of Cato, cited in *Piers Plowman* 176
distinctiones 11–12, 17–21, 47–8, 55, 62, 64–7, 73, 81, 107–8, 153, 190–8, 201, 203, 205–6, 208–9, 224
Dives and Pauper 49–50
divisiones, see *distinctiones*
Donaldson, E. Talbot 38–40, 145
Duffy, Eamon 159
Durham Cathedral 15–16
Dygon, John 222–4

Edward II 57–8
Edward III 47–8
Eggesfeld, Agnes 15–16
English Wycliffite Sermons 13–14, 88
etymology 44–50, 65–8, 71, 192–3

Fasciculus morum 21–2, 82–3, 145–6
Felski, Rita 28–9
Felton, John 65–6, 222–4
fifteen signs before doomsday 77–8
FitzRalph, Richard 115, 140–1
Fletcher, Alan 3, 12–16, 66–7, 74–5, 81, 196–7
Floretus 163–4
Fortune 46, 169
  See also, *Piers Plowman*: Fortune
Frank, Robert Worth 102–3
friars as preachers 1, 15–16, 18, 111, 115, 130–1, 140–1
  See also, *Fasciculus morum*, Humbert of Romans; Longleat sermons, Waleys, Thomas, *De modo componendi sermones*
  See also, *Piers Plowman*: friars preaching

Gadamer, Hans-Georg 25–6, 77
Galloway, Andrew 14–15, 17–18, 39–40, 46, 52, 80, 95–6, 145–8, 155, 199
Gascoigne, Thomas 58
Gaveston, Piers 53–5
Gesta Romanorum 222–4
Giancarlo, Matthew 35
Gilte Legende 213–14
Gloucester College, Oxford 15–16
Goscelin of Canterbury 213–14
Gradon, Pamela 88
Grady, Frank 169
Gregory the Great 99–100, 177–8, 213
  Homiliae in Evangelia 49–50, 85–92, 110, 214–15, cited by Henry Harclay 90–1
  Moralia in Iob 48–9
  Regula pastoralis 50–1, 98
Grosseteste, Robert 48–9
  Château d'Amour 222–4, 228
Gruenler, Curtis 12–13, 108–9, 143, 147–8, 167, 200
Gwynn, Aubrey 36–7

Hanna, Ralph 12–13, 21–2, 36–7, 39–40, 81, 125–6, 128–9, 147, 173–4, 177, 204, 207–8
Harclay, Henry 221
  Sermon on Thomas Becket 30, 37, 53–61, 73
  Quaestiones Ordinariae 90–1
Henry II 56
Henry of Huntingdon, *Historia Anglorum* 56
Higden, Ranulph
  Ars componendi sermones 116–17
  Polychronicon 53–5, 208–9, 211
'How men that ben in hele sholde visiet sike folk,' 156–7
Hudson, Anne 88
Humbert of Romans
  Liber de eruditione praedicatorum 49–50, 127, 130–1, 141–2, 168–9
  De modo prompte cudendi sermones 163–4

Isidore of Seville
  Etymologiarum 67–8, cited in *Piers Plowman* 192, 194
  Sententarium 214–15

James, M. R. 53–5
James of Vitry 81, 139–40
James of Voragine, *Legenda Sanctorum* 211–12
Jerome 89–90, 99–100
  Epistles 139–40
Joachim of Fiore 56, 90–1
John I 56–8
Johnston, Michael 14–15

INDEX 257

Jordan, William 140–1
Jurkowski, Maureen 135–6

Kane, George 145
Kaske, R. E. 145–6
Kendall, John 15–16
Kennedy, Ruth 128–9
Kerby-Fulton, Kathryn 15–16, 90–1, 128–9, 199
Kipling, Gordon 41–2, 67

Langland, William
  authorial signatures 151–2, 167, 199
  as William Rokele 14–15, 135n.68
  See also, *Piers Plowman*
Langton, Stephen 57–8
Laurent de Premierfait, *De Cas des nobles hommes et femmes* 211
'Laus tua, non tua fraus' 58–61, 73
Lawler, Traugott 53–5, 142, 197–8, 208–9, 212, 215–16, 218
Lawton, David 151–2
Legat, Hugh 15–16, 66–7, 97–8, 196–7
Liber custumarum 67–8
Liber regalis 39–40
Longleat sermons 49–50, 95, 117–18, 121, 214–15
Lydgate, John, *Fall of Princes* 211

Mann, Jill 4–5, 230
Manuscripts
  Cambridge, Cambridge University Library, Additional MS 5338 88
  Cambridge, Cambridge University Library, MS Dd.1.17 156–7
  Cambridge, Peterhouse, MS 57 96–7
  Cambridge, St John's College, MS G.22 88
  Dublin, Trinity College, MS 212 14–15
  Dublin, Trinity College, MS 213 15–16
  Dublin, Trinity College, MS 241 88–90
  London, British Library, Additional MS 10574 199
  London, British Library, Additional MS 37677 132–3
  London, British Library, Additional MS 41321 214–15
  London, British Library, Cotton MS Faustina A V 82–3
  London, British Library, Harley MS 2268 224
  London, British Library, Royal MS 8 F VII 222–4
  London, British Library, Royal MS 14 C XII 53–5
  London, British Library, Royal MS 18 B XXIII 10
  London, Lambeth Palace, MS 61 37, 53–61
  Manchester, John Rylands Library, MS 394 160–1
  Oxford, Bodleian Library, MS Bodley 649 66–7, 97–8
  Oxford, Bodleian Library, MS Bodley 851 15–16
  Oxford, Bodleian Library, MS Douce 53 133–4
  Oxford, Bodleian Library, MS e Musaeo 180 156–7
  Oxford, Bodleian Library, MS Laud Misc. 581 199
  Oxford, Bodleian Library, MS Rawlinson Poetry 137 15–16
  Oxford, Trinity College, MS 42 132–3
  Warminster, Longleat House, MS 4 49–50
  Worcester Cathedral Library MS F.10 10
  Worcester Cathedral Library MS F.126 10
Martin of Cordoba 95–6
McDermott, Ryan 12–13
Mercers' Guild 53–5
Middle English 'Mirror' 204–8
  See also, Robert of Gretham, *Mirour des Évangiles*
Middleton, Anne 5–6, 15–16, 38, 104–7, 137–8, 143–4, 151–2, 167, 173–4, 183–6, 199
minstrels 126, 128n.47
  distinguished from preachers in the *artes praedicandi* 124–5
  friars as *ioculatores Domini* 128–9
  see also, *Piers Plowman*: minstrels
Mirk, John, *Festial* 10, 211–12
mirrors for princes 3–4, 45–6, 51–2
  See also, preaching and royal counsel
Mohammed 32–3, 191, 210–19

Newhauser, Richard 115–16
Nicholas of Aquavilla, *Sermones dominicales* 65–6
Nicholas of Tusculum 56–7
Norwich Cathedral 87–8
Novacich, Sarah Elliot 225–6, 229

Odo of Cheriton 139–40
O'Mara, Veronica 9, 89, 224
Origen 228
Owen, Dorothy L. 38–9
Owst, G. R. 8–13, 38–41, 222–4

Palmere, William 15–16
parish church 159; see also, *Piers Plowman*: parish church, site of preaching and instruction
parish priests as preachers 1, 10, 14–16, 83–4, 93, 96–7, 113, 156–7, 159, 176, 178–9; see also, *Piers Plowman*: parish priests preaching

258 INDEX

Paul, Suzanne 9, 89
Pearsall, Derek 8–9, 230–2
pestilence 76, 80, 85–9
   See also, *Piers Plowman*: pestilence; preaching on natural disasters
Peter of Blois 145–6
Peter the Chanter, *Summa de sacramentis* 130–1
Peter de la Mare 38–9
Peter of St Victor 222–4
Piers Plowman
   angel 8, 30, 34, 37–44, 46, 49–55, 59–61, 64–5, 67–73, 212
   Anima 6–7, 32–3, 93, 114, 118, 124–5, 189–219
   Antichrist 70–1, 77–8, 180–1
   apostles preaching 191, 209; see also, *Piers Plowman*: St Paul
   bishops preaching 1, 83–4, 93, 104, 191, 209–10, 213–18
   Book 224–5
   Christ 20–2, 30, 33–4, 41–2, 61–5, 67–73, 92, 129, 142, 145–7, 153, 190–1, 200, 222, 228–32
   clergie and *kynde*, distinguished and related 6–7, 32, 151, 160–1, 168–72, 175, 177, 179, 187, 221
   Clergy 120–1, 137, 143–5, 147–8, 162, 167, 184
   Concupiscencia Carnis 165–6, 180
   confessions of the sins 92; see also, *Piers Plowman*: Covetousness, Sloth, and Wrath
   Conscience 30–2, 34–7, 52–3, 61–5, 67–73, 93–4, 97–8, 111–13, 137, 141–9, 170, 172–3, 180–1, 189–91, 199
   Covetousness 181
   Covetise of Eyes 165–6, 169, 180
   desert fathers preaching 191
   devils' parliament 63–4, 224–5, 227–8
   Do-wel triad 7, 23, 62, 65, 67, 79–80, 82, 109–12, 143–8, 162, 165–6, 173, 179, 185–6, 189–92
   Elde 32, 165–6, 169, 178–82
   Fever-on-the-Fourth-Day 184–5
   Fortune 165–70, 174–5, 178–81
   friars preaching 1, 6n.21, 7, 17–18, 113–16, 118–19, 123–4, 130–1, 137–40, 142–3, 147–9, 181, 191, 195, 200, 208–9
   gluttonous doctor 31–2, 111–12, 137–45, 147–9
   goliard 30, 34, 38–42, 44–6, 49, 52–3, 63, 65–7, 70–2
   Grace 70–1, 182
   harrowing of hell 33, 61, 63–5, 67–8, 222–32
   Haukyn 95
   Holy Church 1–2, 7, 17–23, 32, 123, 150–1, 153–6, 159–65, 169–72, 175–80, 182–3, 185–8, 191–2, 197, 212
   Hophni and Phineas 10–11, 52–3
   Hunger 102–3, 184–5
   Kynde 32, 149–51, 179–83, 185–7
   Kynde Wit 37–8, 52, 68–9, 93–4, 97–8, 175, 184–5
   the knight (second vision) 99–100, 102–3, 127–8, 156
   Knighthood 37–8
   Liberum Arbitrium 190–1, 200–2, 211–12, 217–18
   Life 180–1
   lunatic 30, 34, 38–44, 46, 63, 67–73
   minstrels
      iaperis and *iangleris* 31–2, 111–13, 124–9, 140–1, 145, 148–9
      virtuous minstrels 31–2, 111–13, 124, 128–31, 137, 141–3, 146–9, 221
   Mercy 63–4, 222, 224–7
   Omnia-probate 184–5
   pardoners preaching 1, 17–18, 104–5, 212
   parish church, site of preaching and instruction 155, 160–1, 164–5, 169–73, 176, 178–9, 186–7, 219–20
   parish priests preaching 1, 18, 83–4, 93, 105–6, 155, 171–3, 176, 178–9, 209, 219–20
   patriarchs and prophets preaching 222, 224–6, 228
   Patience 31–2, 95, 111–12, 137–42, 144–9, 183
   Peace 95–6
   Peace (seventh vision) 63–4, 222, 226–8, 230–1
   Pestilence 6–7, 30–1, 74, 76–7, 80, 84, 103, 118–20, 176–7
   Piers Plowman 30–1, 65, 70, 74–6, 93–109, 112–13, 118–21, 123–4, 127–8, 143–4, 147–8, 156, 170, 189–90, 193–4, 200–8, 218–19
   plante of pees 21–2
   preching and *preueing* 6–7, 18–19, 51–2, 63, 67–8, 78–9, 83–4, 95–6, 98, 103–4, 106, 124–5, 138–40, 144, 147–8, 161–2, 187, 218, 225–6, 232
   Pride 70–1, 180, 194
   Pride of Parfit Lyuynge 165, 180
readers and owners 15–16
Reason 1–2, 6–7, 23, 30–1, 74–88, 90–9, 101–4, 106, 109–10, 118–19, 123–4, 142, 144, 172–4, 176–7, 187–8, 215–16
Recklessness 165–6, 173

Repentance 92
Righteousness 63–4, 222, 226–7
rodent parliament 38–9, 51–2, 70
Scripture 32, 141–2, 150–1, 162–4, 167–73, 177–9, 182, 184–7
Sloth 160–1
St Maur's wind 6–7, 30–1, 74, 76–7, 80–1, 84, 103
St Paul 121, 123–4, 129, 131, 138–41, 144, 147–9, 199
St Paul's Cross 60–1, 111–16, 118–21, 123–6, 128–9, 137–9, 142–3, 147–9, 199
Study 31–2, 82, 111–45, 147–9, 162, 167, 183, 189–90, 193–5, 199, 202, 212
Thought 93, 215–16
Trajan 177–8
Tree of Charity 32–3, 61, 189–91, 200–4, 206–10, 222
Truth 18–20, 74–5, 84–5, 92–9, 101–2, 104–5, 109–10, 120–1, 156, 161, 193–4
Truth's pardon 43, 104–9, 167, 208
Truth (seventh vision) 63–4, 222, 224–7
Unity 181–2
wastours 100–1
Will, the dreamer 1–7, 17–18, 20–3, 32–3, 37–40, 49, 51–2, 61–5, 69–71, 78–9, 83–4, 92, 104–5, 109–12, 120–3, 137–42, 148–56, 159–66, 169–95, 197–204, 206–10, 212, 219, 222
Wit 79–80, 82
Wrath 114, 124–5
Wrong 18–20
Ymaginatif 7, 32, 150–3, 173–9, 181, 185–7
See also, Langland, William
preaching
  ad status 81
  and evangelism 213–17
  and miracles 214–15
  and poetry 7, 12–13, 179
  and royal counsel 47–9, 51–2, 107–8
  as a mirror 168–9, 181
  for Advent 34, 41–2, 48–50, 65–7, 85, 156–7
  for the coronation of Richard II 34, 40–2
  on baptism 152–3, 156–9, 186–7, 213; *see also*, baptism
  on the Christ-knight 222–4
  on curiosities 116–18
  on domestic discipline 82–3
  on exegesis 204–6
  on the four daughters of God 222–4
  on the last judgement 76, 81, 85–91, 95
  on natural disasters 76, 85–92
  on preaching and preachers 47–51, 116–18, 133–4

on riddles 145–6
on the Ten Commandments 97–8
See also, sermons; *sermo antiquus*; *sermo modernus*
Prick of Conscience 178–9
proverbs and axioms 18–20, 23, 76, 82–3, 105–8, 147–8, 153, 160–1, 167, 176

Ralph de Baldock 126
Ramsey Abbey 15–16
Raschko, Mary 3–4, 28–9, 62–3, 222, 226–7
Rentz, Ellen 155
reportatio 78–9, 104–5
Richard I 57–8, 216–17
Richard II, *see* coronation of Richard II
Richard of Segbrok, *Liber sententiarum* 59
Ricoeur, Paul 2–3, 7, 23–9, 220–1
  axial moment 26–7, 30, 34–5, 72, 80, 146–7
  biblical narrative 27–8
  emplotment 2–3, 25–8, 30–2, 42, 62, 74–7, 100–1, 112–13, 166, 218–21, 227, 231–2
  'Interpretative Narrative' 27–8, 107
  Oneself as Another 150
  'Philosophical Hermeneutics and Biblical Hermeneutics' 27–8
  on preaching 27–8, 107
  threefold *mimesis* 25–6, 42, 74–7, 218–19
  référence croisée of history and fiction 26
  single thought, the *res* or 'gist' of narrative 25, 78–9, 107, 147–8
  self-constancy 27, 32, 150–2, 156, 166, 186–7
  Time and Narrative 23–7
  traces and vestiges 26–7, 80–1, 160–1
riddles 31–2, 103, 111–12, 143–8, 200
Royer-Hemet, Catherine 47–8
Robert of Basevorn, *Forma praedicandi* 116–17, 122–3
Robert of Gretham, *Miour des Évangiles* 204–8
  See also, *Middle English 'Mirror'*
Robertson, Elizabeth 193–4, 200–1
Rolle, Richard 125–6
Rudd, Gillian 10–11
Rypon, Robert 10, 15–16, 48–9, 65–6, 72–3, 157–9, 186–7, 221

Salter, Elizabeth 11–12, 206–7
Scase, Wendy 190–1
Schmidt, A. V. C. 103, 145
Schott, Christine 15–16
Sedulius, *Paschale carmen*, cited by Thomas Brinton 86

sermo antiquus or 'homiletic sermon' 11–12, 205–6
sermo modernus or 'scholastic sermon' 11–12, 17–19, 95–6, 190–3, 196–7, 205–6
See also, *distinctiones*; *thema*
sermons
   manuscript collections 8–10, 13–14
   See also, preaching; *sermo antiquus*; *sermo modernus*
'Sermon of Dead Men' 99–100
Simpson, James 65, 69–70, 171, 203–4
Smith, D. Vance 5–6, 181–2
Somerset, Fiona 35–6, 44–5, 49, 175, 206
Spearing, A. C. 11–12
Speculum perfectionis 128–9
Spencer, H. Leith 9, 88, 139–40
Spofford, Thomas 224
Steiner, Emily 35, 49, 74–5, 92, 102–3, 108–9, 172, 208–9, 218–19, 225–6, 229
St Erkenwald 128–9, 185
St Francis of Assisi 128–9, 208–9
St Mary, Bishopsgate 115, 132–3
St Mary's Abbey, York 204
St Maur's Wind (storm of 1362) 76–8, 85–9
   See also, *Piers Plowman*: St Maur's Wind (storm of 1362); preaching on natural disasters
St Paul 108–9, 121–3
   See also, *Piers Plowman*: St Paul
St Paul's Cathedral 47–8, 69–70, 128–9
St Paul's Cross 13–14, 31–2, 81, 113, 115, 132–7, 139–41; See also, *Piers Plowman*: St Paul's Cross
St Thomas of Acre, Cheapside 53–5, 59–60, 216–17
Stow, John, *Survey of London* 115, 132–3
Strakhov, Elizaveta 51–2
studiositas 119–21, 123, 129, 131, 137, 141–6, 149
Sudbury, Simon 40–1, 45–6, 67–8

Taylor, William 113, 132–7, 139–42
thema 11–12, 17–20, 47–8, 55–6, 64–7, 69, 85, 92, 95–6, 99–102, 107–8, 153, 159–60, 170, 185, 190–3, 196–7, 205–6
Thomas, Arvind 125–6
Thomas of Chobham, *Summa de arte praedicandi* 95–6
Thorpe, William, *Testimony* 113, 132, 135–7
Tickhill, John 128–9
Tobit 129–31, 142

'Veni Creator Spiritus' antiphon 41–2, 46–7, 69–70
Vincent of Beauvais, *Speculum historiale* 211

Waldeby, John 21–2
Waleys, Thomas, *De modo componendi sermones* 11–12, 49–50, 116–17
Walsingham, Thomas, *St Albans Chronicle* 39–41, 43–6, 113, 115, 134–5
Walter de Brugge 15–16
Warner, Lawrence 15–16, 36–7, 53–5, 216–17
Waterton, Robert 132, 134–7
Waters, Claire 50–1, 207–8, 212
Watson, Nicholas 204
Wenzel, Siegfried 1, 3, 9–11, 17–18, 23, 196–7, 222–4, 232
William of Moerbeke 96–7
William de Montibus, *Similitudinarium* 106–8
William of Newburgh 55
Wimbledon, Thomas 13–14, 81, 90–1, 95, 98–9, 115
Wittig, Joseph 167
Wood, Sarah 15–16, 36–7, 61, 65–6, 179–80, 183–5
Wormynton, John 15–16
Wyclif, John 13–14, 132
   Sermones Quadraginta 13–14
Wyndill, John 15–16

Zeeman, Nicolette 4–6, 10–11, 119–20, 140–1, 162, 166, 175, 181–2, 197–8, 202, 222–4